Writing and Community Action

A Service-Learning Rhetoric and Reader

THOMAS DEANS

Haverford College

Longman

New York • San Francisco • Boston
London • Toronto • Sydney • Tokyo • Singapore • Madrid
Mexico City • Munich • Paris • Cape Town • Hong Kong • Montreal

Senior Vice President and Publisher: Joseph Opiela
Acquisitions Editor: Susan Kunchandy
Development Manager: Janet Lanphier
Development Editor: Michael Greer
Senior Supplements Editor: Donna Campion
Executive Marketing Manager: Ann Stypuloski
Production Manager: Eric Jorgensen
Project Coordination, Text Design, and Electronic Page Makeup:
    UG / GGS Information Services, Inc.
Cover Designer and Cover Design Manager: Wendy Ann Fredericks
Cover Art: A Pieced and Quilted Cotton Coverlet, Western Pennsylvania, Early 20th
    Century/Christie's Images
Publishing Services Manager: Al Dorsey

For permission to use copyrighted material, grateful acknowledgment is made to the copyright holders on pp. 439–441, which are hereby made part of this copyright page.

Library of Congress Cataloging-in-Publication Data

Deans, Thomas, 1967–
    Writing and community action : a service-learning rhetoric and reader / Thomas Deans.
        p. cm.
    Includes index.
    ISBN: 0-321-09480-8 (pbk.)
    1. English language—Rhetoric. 2. Community life—Problems, exercises, etc. 3.
Readers—Community life. 4. College readers. 5. Report writing. I. Title.

PE1127.S6 D43 2002
808'.0427—dc21

                                                                    2002016141

Please visit our Web site, at http://www.ablongman.com

ISBN 0-321-09480-8

Dedication

With gratitude to my many teachers and colleagues at
Georgetown University,
Link Community School,
University of Massachusetts Amherst,
and
Kansas State University

Detailed Contents

4 Writing in Academic Communities   134

Preface

During my college years I would catch a bus on the edge of campus and take a twenty-minute ride across the city to a public housing project. There I tutored a ten-year-old boy, Brian. We'd sit together and talk, read, and joke around. A few hours later I'd close the books, say goodbye, get back on the bus, and return to campus to get ready for the next day's classes.

As I shuttled between these worlds, my social consciousness deepened in tandem with my investment in academic inquiry. I knew that my studies and my emerging commitment to community action were connected, and I could articulate the link in the language of liberal education: I was becoming a more critical reader of both texts and culture. But this explanation, while true, was only partly gratifying, as it didn't seem to account for the visceral experience of my time with Brian and the questions I would ponder on the bus rides back and forth. It was, I thought, a loss that while I could explore social issues in my academic courses, I was never invited to integrate my intellectual study with my community work.

Jump ahead six years when, as a novice writing teacher, I overhear a colleague talking about his composition students working with local organizations on writing and research projects. I was intrigued, but also a bit skeptical. After all, could our first-year students, most struggling mightily to learn the codes and conventions of academic writing, really handle such community writing projects? I wasn't sure; but I also wanted to see. And so I introduced one small, optional service-learning project to my class. And I quickly learned that students not only could do it, but wanted to do it, and learned through it.

Since then, I've moved community themes and community-based assignments from the periphery to the center of my courses. I want my writing classroom to be an optimistic, action-oriented space—to be inflected with what philosopher Richard Rorty calls *social hope*. Even as I encourage students to adopt a healthy skepticism about the world around them, I want them to see themselves as participants *in* that world, not just spectators of it. I also want students to understand writing as a versatile tool for engaging in not only academic inquiry but also community life.

As my students write about, for, and with the community, I see them grappling with complex rhetorical situations, exploring pressing social issues, contributing to local organizations, and growing as writers. And nearly every time I include a community project in a course, end-of-term evaluations rank it as the most meaningful part of the class. Students remark not only on how their writing abilities have improved but also on how their motives for writing have changed. Consider one student's self-assessment: "Rather than try to impress my professor with my work (that was a goal nonetheless), I was motivated to produce quality documents for my cooperating organization. Because of my group and issue (violence against women), I was very excited to be part of my community project. I wanted to produce quality work for the sake of the organization, not just to garner a high grade." This kind of testimony, combined with my understanding of writing as a deeply social activity, are what led me to write this book.

In the pages that follow, writing is viewed—and practiced—as a versatile tool for *action*—action in academic, workplace, and civic communities. But each assignment in *Writing and Community Action* also accounts for the fact that most college students are still emerging as thinkers and writers, that they are in the initial stages of becoming full-fledged readers and writers in academic and civic contexts. To develop, they need sustained practice in generating ideas, doing research, and crafting arguments; they need pragmatic strategies for interpreting texts and stretching their intellects; they need provocative reading selections by both professional writers and fellow students; and they need plain-spoken instruction in composing essays, reports, and community-based projects.

By combining academic inquiry with community outreach, *Writing and Community Action* builds on recent advances in service-learning, an emerging movement in higher education. Teachers across the disciplines—myself among them—have testified to the ways that introducing service-learning has reinvigorated their courses. And now a growing body of research suggests that service-learning, when done well, does indeed help students to learn subject matter, to see issues from multiple perspectives, to solve complex problems, and to develop personally and ethically.

This book also has its roots in rhetoric, the ancient art of persuasion. Rhetoric, originally focused on the theory and practice of public oratory, emerged from the community life of Greek and Roman citizens arguing over governance and justice, working to solve public problems, figuring out ways to avoid hazards and advance the common good. The assignments in each chapter recall this tradition by structuring opportunities for citizen-writers not only to step back and reflect on public matters but also to step up and participate in them.

Key Features of this Book

This book is about engagement—engagement with learning, with texts, with local communities. It is also about writing—writing as a student, as a citizen, as a participant in local community organizations. Even better, *Writing and Community Action* seamlessly integrates community engagement with writing instruction as it delivers the tools for making this powerful amalgam successful.

Several features make this textbook distinctive. Even as it includes innovative community-based research and service-learning assignments, *Writing and Community Action* retains the kinds of instruction in academic reading and writing that have proven effective in the past.

The readings and assignments are challenging, but ample instructional support is supplied. The book includes a diverse range of resources to help students develop as critical readers and versatile writers. These resources include:

- **Balance of provocative readings and pragmatic support for writing.** Reading selections are deeply integrated with corresponding writing activities. Each chapter includes both advice on critical reading and instruction in specific rhetorical strategies.
- **Diversity of discourses and genres.** A wide range of discourses— academic, expressive, literary, workplace, and public—are valued and supported. This means that a range of genres—personal essays, critical essays, research reports, and community projects—are likewise represented. Students learn to write for varied audiences and purposes.
- **Support for several kinds of service-learning projects.** Community writing can take many forms and this book values several approaches to service-learning. Moreover, it provides step-by-step guidance in building community partnerships and completing successful projects.
- **Accent on writing as action, writing as relevant.** Assignments and readings underscore how writing is a collaborative, contextual activity and how it functions as social action in academic, workplace, and community-based contexts. The purposes for writing—beyond simply for a grade— are explained and, more importantly, discovered by students through experience.
- **Emphasis on the writing process.** A range of activities in each chapter support invention, discussion, drafting, peer workshops, collaboration, revision, and editing.

- **Focus on ethics and reflection.** Because all writing involves ethical decisions, and because service-learning raises particularly complicated questions of reciprocity and social justice, many readings, activities, and assignments spur reflection on ethical concerns.
- **Instruction in fieldwork, interviewing, and community-based research.** Several chapters offer practical advice for doing original research in campus and local communities. Such fieldwork and interviewing encourage original thinking, discourage plagiarism, and breathe new life into research projects that might otherwise include only library and Web sources.
- **Abundant student samples.** Nearly every chapter includes student writing, and several chapters include more than one student sample.

All of these features, along with traditional textbook staples such as reading response questions and explanations of key concepts, work in concert to help diverse learners navigate even difficult readings and assignments.

Futhermore, *Writing and Community Action* comes with an integrated instructor's manual that delivers pragmatic advice for teachers, particularly those trying service-learning for the first time or exploring new ways to support writing as social action. The manual lays out several options for planning courses that incorporate instuctor priorities, local community circumstances, and common English department or writing program requirements. The manual also includes an extensive section on how to discern which kinds of service-learning projects to pursue, how to set up projects with local community organizations, and how to assess student writing done in community settings. Finally, chapter-by-chapter sections recommend experience-tested classroom practices.

Academic Writing, Community-Based Research, and Service-Learning

Not all assignments in this book involve service-learning; but all of them are connected to the idea of *community*, and most ask students to do some kind of fieldwork or community-based research beyond the classroom. However, adopting a community-based orientation does not mean leaving academic writing behind. Quite the opposite. Throughout this book community engagement is explicitly linked to academic and writing goals, and this combination propels students into deeper and more sustained academic inquiry.

A core mandate of most college writing courses is to teach academic discourse, especially such genres as the essay and the research paper, and this book takes that mandate seriously. Academic genres and scholarly habits of mind—particularly critical analysis and research—are deeply valued and amply supported in *Writing and Community Action*. Moreover, in addition to treating local communities as sites for writing, several chapters emphasize that the university is itself and particular academic disciplines within it are themselves dynamic communities in which participants use writing to perform social action.

As for its community-based components, this book offers experience-tested assignments and activities. However, a textbook can't do it all. Both instructors and students should recognize that—to adapt Tip O'Neil's dictum about politics—all service-learning is local. In other words, no book can substitute for building thoughtful and reciprocal relationships with local community partners. Such relationships, in combination with the resources here, set the stage for powerfully engaged writing.

Acknowledgments

Every book is a collaborative act, and many people deserve credit for making this one possible. As developmental editor, Michael Greer helped enormously by recognizing my many mistakes, suggesting wise alternatives, and reminding me to stay student-centered. Without his sharp eye and encouraging manner, this text would have been both less effective and longer in coming.

Susan Kunchandy at Longman convinced me of the merits of this project. Then Longman reviewers offered excellent advice at every stage of the writing process. Those reviewers include Harold Ackerman, Bloomsburg University; David Crowe, Augustana College; Kirk Combe, Denison University; Roger Graves, DePaul University; Jane Hammons, University of California at Berkeley; Andrea Ivanov-Craig, Azusa Pacific University; Laura Julier, Michigan State University; Janice M. Kelly, Arizona State University; Lisa Langstraat, University of Southern Mississippi; Michael Martin, San Francisco State University; Marcia McDonald, Belmont College; Libby Miles, University of Rhode Island; Joddy Murray, Syracuse University; Stacia Neeley, Texas Christian University; Frank Pisano, Central Methodist College; and Lynn O. Scott, Michigan State University.

In recent years a growing number of service-learning supporters have emerged in rhetoric and composition studies and they have nurtured and enriched my own work. Special appreciation goes to Nora Bacon, Barbara Roswell, Bruce Herzberg, Linda Flower, Linda Adler-Kassner, Edward Zlotkowski, and Susie Lan Cassell.

Much of the material in this book is drawn from my own teaching, which was deeply influenced by friends and mentors at the University of Massachusetts

Amherst, where I first taught college writing. I am particularly indebted to Zan Goncalves, Nick Carbone, Anne Herrington, Charlie Moran, and Peter Elbow.

I have also long learned from John Hirsh of Georgetown University, a scholar-teacher committed to both intellectual inquiry and community work.

I wrote this text while on the faculty at Kansas State University, where I had the pleasure of outstanding colleagues. I'm particularly grateful to those who run the writing program—Dave Smit, Irene Ward, Deborah Murray, and Robin Mosher—all reflective teachers who helped me grow personally and professionally.

My appreciation extends to my students at Kansas State University, several of whom contributed their essays and projects for publication, and to my community partners in Kansas, many of whom also contributed to this text.

I am also grateful to my mother, Barbara Kelling, and my in-laws, Richard and Lois Roberts, for hosting and feeding me during the summer when I wrote the core of this book.

Final thanks go to my wife Jill, who graciously endured all my little frustrations and grumblings as I worked. She provided the sustained support that made the book possible.

Thomas Deans

1

Writing as Social Action

Why do we write? How do successful writers approach the composing process? Chapter 1 explores some of the many reasons for writing and describes key elements of the writing process that are common to many successful writers. The central theme of this chapter, an idea that runs throughout this book, is that writing is a kind of social action—a way of doing things in the world. Chapter 1 also looks at how academic writing, particularly the essay genre, functions as action. Service-learning, which combines community service and academic learning, is introduced here as well, providing the foundation for later chapters.

For me, writing is a form of action, capable of influencing change.
—Ingrid Bengis, writer

According to one common view, learning to write means learning a set of rules—rules for grammar, rules for structure, rules for research, and so on. Teachers and experienced writers know the rules. And once *you* know the rules, the thinking goes, you can write effectively.

To some extent, this is true. Most readers expect that writers will follow certain rules, and therefore knowing them is certainly important. But to think only of rules leaves the writer in a lurch when the rules change over time (as they inevitably do) or when the rules for one kind of writing (a research paper, for example) do not apply to another kind (such as a job application letter).

More importantly, a larger question gets overlooked: Why write at all?

Students usually write because instructors require them to; and teachers usually assign writing because they hope to prompt learning or discover what students know. Yet school writing constitutes but a small faction of the writing in

1

the world. Consider all the kinds of texts that circulate in your life and in our culture. For example:

- Friends exchange email messages. *Why?* Perhaps to coordinate plans for the coming weekend, but more fundamentally to maintain or deepen the relationship.
- An attorney writes up a contract to close a business deal. *Why?* To record the transaction and sanction it with the power of established laws.
- A novelist composes a novel. *Why?* To share a story, render art, entertain, and perhaps even make a living.
- A mechanical engineer writes a proposal to her supervisor. *Why?* To demonstrate the solution to a technical problem (and thereby prove her worth to the company and keep her job).
- A citizen writes a letter to the editor of a newspaper. *Why?* To respond to a previous article, assert an opinion, or influence a local policy.
- The director of the local Boys and Girls Club writes a grant proposal. *Why?* To acquire money from a funding agency to support community projects.

The list could go on and on. Even private writing like that in a diary or a journal usually has a discernable purpose, such as to help sort through complicated emotions or to record events for recall years later. When looking at things this way, it becomes clear that writing is not simply a collection of rules but rather a tool for *action*, a means by which to pursue a variety of personal and social goals.

WRITING TO DISCOVER

Jot down the different ways that you have used writing in the past few months. Consider both school writing and out-of-school writing. Include

- Personal writing (journal entries, reminder notes to yourself, etc.)
- Correspondence (email messages, letters, cards, etc.)
- Creative writing (stories, poems, comics, music lyrics, etc.)
- Writing as part of a job
- Writing for school (reports, essays, notes, marginal comments in books, etc.)
- Public writing (a letter to the campus newspaper, a publicity flyer for an event, a speech or song for a performance, etc.)
- Writing that might seem trivial (shopping lists, phone messages, etc.)

Pick four items and consider the *purposes* for those occasions of writing—the *why* behind the writing. Share your findings.

If we think of writing as a practical and versatile tool, we move away from the misconception that writing well requires inborn talent or a special calling. As sociolinguist Frank Smith asserts, "It is unproductive to think of writing as a special kind of activity that requires unusual talents or lengthy training and can only be used for a few specialized ends, which perhaps do not concern many people. It is wrong to regard writing ability as a particularly esoteric skill that only a few can achieve, and then usually only with a great deal of effort."[1] Given the right motivation and support—plus some hard work and a commitment to revision—everyone can craft effective prose. Moreover, such writing can be put to a wide range of pragmatic uses, only some of which are traditionally valued in school. The inventory below may not be complete, but it certainly affirms writing as a technology fundamental to the personal, professional and civic lives of most people.

Personal and Social Uses for Writing

Use/Action	Examples
Meet material needs (get job, money, credit, food, shelter, etc.)	Job applications, academic assignments to earn grades, grocery lists, grant proposals
Communicate information	Newspaper articles, lab/technical reports, brochures, web pages
Express ideas, emotions, identity	Essays, editorials, personal journals, graffiti, oral histories, literature
Explore new knowledge	Academic scholarship, government and corporate research, empirical reports
Explain all manner of things	Expository essays, magazine features, instructions, software documentation
Persuade others to adopt beliefs or take action	Political speeches, persuasive essays, proposals, advertising, marketing
Establish and maintain personal relationships	Letters, cards, email messages
Assert authority and regulate behavior	Laws, policies, contracts, employee manuals
Demonstrate knowledge, competence, or subject mastery	School assignments and tests, professional certification and licensure (e.g., bar exam, medical boards)
Exercise the imagination and have fun	Stories, poems, scripts, screenplays, songs, cartoons, jokes
Record the past	Records, databases, histories, diaries, memoirs, notes
Help organizations (businesses, nonprofits, governments) do their work	Reports, memos, internal and external communications
Solve problems	Feasibility reports, proposals, community organizing materials, agreements
Reflect, analyze, interpret, and critique	Cultural criticism, essays, reviews, satire, academic scholarship

---

[1]Smith, Frank. *Writing and the Writer.* NY: Holt, Reinhart and Winston, 1982, pp. 16–17.

Some contend that emerging technologies are taking the place of writing. But in fact, quite the opposite trend is afoot. Because each new scientific discovery or technological advance requires writing to explain and implement it, new technologies usually produce *more* rather than less text. Just consider how much new writing the World Wide Web has generated. Likewise, writing is, more than ever, vital to most workplaces. A 1997 survey of the 1,000 largest employers in the U.S. reported that 96% say employees must have good communication skills to get ahead. Another study discovered that among college graduates, those in the highest quintile in writing earn, on average, three times more than those with the worst writing skills.[2] Given our information-driven world, writing isn't going away.

In this chapter and throughout this book you will be asked to think about how writing functions as action. Just as importantly, you will find pragmatic advice on how to craft successful writing in academic, workplace, and community settings. What distinguishes this book from most others on writing instruction is the unifying theme of *community* and the emphasis on combining academic learning and community action through the practice of *service-learning*. The nature of community and the process of service-learning will become more and more clear as you progress through the chapters that follow.

ASSIGNMENT
Reflections on Your Writing Process

Describe the process you used the last time you wrote an essay or a paper for a class. What steps did you use to move from initial ideas to finished draft? How much time did you spend on each task or stage? What problems or obstacles did you encounter? How did you overcome them? How would you do it differently if you had a second chance?

Consider when and why you write, as well as how you move from initial ideas to a finished text. Although you could draw on the readings in this chapter, keep the focus on your own experience.

The Writing Process

Writing doesn't just happen. It takes a writer and a context—and it involves a *process*. Sometimes the process is rather simple and brief, as when a writer sits at a keyboard and taps out an email message to a friend, clicks send, and off the

---

[2]Fisher, Anne. "The High Cost of Living and Not Writing Well." *Fortune* (December 7, 1998), p. 244.

message goes. Sometimes the process is longer and more complicated, as when a college student writes an essay in three or four drafts, or when several dissenting employees at an insurance company take 51 days and nearly as many drafts before they arrive at a final one-page executive letter for an annual report (which, by the way, really happened).[3]

No two people share exactly the same writing process. But most successful writers, whether first-year students in college or long-time professionals, follow a process that involves the following activities:

- Planning
- Drafting
- Gathering feedback
- Revising
- Editing

These activities are listed here in their most logical order, but in fact, most writers engage in a *recursive* composing process, which means that they repeatedly loop through several of the activities, often in a haphazard order. Sometimes this complex writing process is evident in the moment of composing (as when you write a phrase and then a second later replace it with one you like better); other times it is stretched out over longer periods of time (as when you share a draft of an essay with a peer workshop group and then revisit the feedback later as you revise the draft).

WRITING TO DISCOVER

Reflect on your own writing process, taking notes in response to each of the following questions:

- When you write, how do you usually generate ideas?
- How do you move from the initial ideas to the final text? Identify any discernable steps.
- Do you think or plan first? How? Is it all in your head, or do you take notes, make sketches, do outlines, etc.?
- Do you compose on paper or at a keyboard?
- Is there a special place where you write? Are certain conditions more or less conducive to writing?

---

[3]Cross, Geoffrey A. "The Interrelation of Genre, Context, and Process in the Collaborative Writing of Two Corporate Documents." *Writing in the Workplace: New Research Perspectives.* Ed. Rachel Spilka. Carbondale: Southern Illinois University Press, 1993, pp. 141–157.

- Do you ever revise documents? If so, do you revise as you go along, or do you generate multiple drafts? Do you revise some kinds of documents but not others?
- Do you procrastinate? If so, when and how? What are the typical consequences?
- Do you have any special writing rituals or idiosyncrasies?
- Does your process differ depending on the kind of writing, the audience, or the timing?
- Has your writing process changed since you arrived at college? Explain.

Compare your findings to someone else's.

The following readings render three perspectives on the composing process. Maxine Hairston lists the habits common to experienced writers and describes two important kinds of academic writing. Anne Lamott renders a lively (and often funny) first-person account of her struggles with writing and her strategies for success. Donald Murray explores how revision is, in his words, "a condition of the writer's life."

Excerpt: Maxine Hairston, *What Happens When People Write?*

Maxine Hairston is a former professor at the University of Texas at Austin and a scholar who researches writing, particularly the teaching of college writing. The following selection is taken from her textbook Successful Writing.

Many people who have trouble writing believe that writing is a mysterious process that the average person cannot master. They assume that anyone who writes well does so because of a magic mixture of talent and inspiration, and that people who are not lucky enough to have those gifts can never become writers. Thus they take an "either you have it or you don't" attitude that discourages them before they even start to write.

Like most myths, this one has a grain of truth in it, but only a grain. Admittedly the best writers are people with talent just as the best musicians or athletes or chemists are people with talent. But that qualification does not mean that only talented people can write well any more than it means that only a few gifted people can become good tennis players. Tennis coaches know differently. From experience, they know any reasonably well-coordinated and healthy person can learn to play a fairly good game of tennis if he or she will learn the principles of the game and work at putting them into practice. They help people become tennis players by showing them the strategies that experts use and by giving them criticism and reinforcement as they practice those strategies. In recent years, as we have learned more about the processes of working writers, many teachers have begun to work with their writing students in the same way.

AN OVERVIEW OF THE WRITING PROCESS

How Professional Writers Work

- Most writers don't wait for inspiration. They write whether they feel like it or not. Usually they write on a schedule, putting in regular hours just as they would on a job.
- Professional writers consistently work in the same places with the same tools—pencil, typewriter, or word processor. The physical details of writing are important to them so they take trouble to create a good writing environment for themselves.
- Successful writers work constantly at observing what goes on around them and have a system for gathering and storing material. They collect clippings, keep notebooks, or write in journals.
- Even successful writers need deadlines to make them work, just like everyone else.
- Successful writers make plans before they start to write, but they keep their plans flexible, subject to revision.
- Successful writers usually have some audience in mind and stay aware of that audience as they write and revise.
- Most successful writers work rather slowly; four to six double-spaced pages is considered a good day's work.
- Even successful writers often have trouble getting started; they expect it and don't panic.
- Successful writers seldom know precisely what they are going to write before they start, and they plan on discovering at least part of their content as they work. (See section below on explanatory and exploratory writing.)
- Successful writers stop frequently to reread what they've written and consider such rereading an important part of the writing process.
- Successful writers revise as they write and expect to do two or more drafts of anything they write.
- Like ordinary mortals, successful writers often procrastinate and feel guilty about it; unlike less experienced writers, however, most of them have a good sense of how long they can procrastinate and still avoid disaster.

Explanatory and Exploratory Writing

Several variables affect the method and speed with which writers work—how much time they have, how important their task is, how skilled they are, and so on. The most important variable, however, is the kind of writing they are doing. I am going to focus on two major kinds here: *explanatory* and *exploratory*. To put it briefly, although much too simply, explanatory writing *tends* to be about information; exploratory writing *tends* to be about ideas.

Explanatory writing can take many forms: a movie review, an explanation of new software, an analysis of historical causes, a report on a recent political development, a biographical sketch. These are just a few possibilities. The distinguishing feature of all these examples and other kinds of explanatory writing is that the writer either knows most of what he or she is going to say before starting to write or knows where to find the material needed to get started. A typical explanatory essay might be on some aspect of global warming for an environmental studies course. The material for such a paper already exists—you're not going to create it or discover it within your subconscious. Your job as a writer is to dig out the material, organize it, and shape it into a clearly written, carefully supported essay. Usually you would know who your readers are for an explanatory essay and, from the beginning, shape it for that audience.

Writers usually make plans when they are doing explanatory writing, plans that can range from a page of notes to a full outline. Such plans help them to keep track of their material, put it in some kind of order, and find a pattern for presenting it. For explanatory writing, many writers find that the traditional methods work well; assertion/support, cause and effect, process, compare/contrast, and so on. Much of the writing that students do in college is explanatory, as is much business writing. Many magazine articles and nonfiction books are primarily explanatory writing. It's a crucially important kind of writing, one that we depend on for information and education, one that keeps the machinery of business and government going.

Explanatory writing is not necessarily easy to do nor is it usually formulaic. It takes skill and care to write an accurate, interesting story about the physician who won a Nobel Prize for initiating kidney transplants or an entertaining and informative report on how the movie *Dick Tracy* was made. But the process for explanatory writing is manageable. You identify the task, decide what the purpose and who the audience are, map out a plan for finding and organizing information, then divide the writing itself into doable chunks and start working. Progress may be painful, and you may have to draft and revise several times to clarify points or get the tone just right, but with persistence, you can do it.

Exploratory writing may also take many forms: a reflective personal essay, a profile of a homeless family, an argument in support of funding for multimillion dollar science projects, or a speculative essay about the future of the women's movement. These are only a few possibilities. What distinguishes these examples and exploratory writing in general is that the writer has only a partially formed idea of what he or she is going to write before starting. A typical piece of exploratory writing might be a speculative essay on why movies about the Mafia appeal so much to the American public. You might hit on the idea of writing such a piece after you have seen several mob movies—*Goodfellas, Miller's Crossing,* and *Godfather III*—but not really know what you would say or who your audience would be. The material for such a paper doesn't exist; you would have to begin by reading, talking to people, and by drawing on the ideas and insights you've gleaned from different sources to reach your own point of view. And you would certainly expect some of your most important ideas—your own conclusions—to come to you as you wrote.

Because you don't know ahead of time exactly what you're going to say in exploratory writing, it's hard to make a detailed plan or outline; however, you can and should take copious notes as you prepare to write. You might be able to put down a tentative thesis sentence, for example, "American moviegoers are drawn to movies about the Mafia and mob violence because they appeal to a streak of lawlessness that has always been strong in American character." Such a sentence could be an anchor to get you started writing, but as a main idea, it could change or even disappear as the paper developed.

Many papers you write in college will be exploratory papers, for example, an interpretive paper in a literature course, an essay on the future of an ethnic community for a cultural anthropology course, or an argumentative paper for a government course proposing changes in our election laws. Many magazine articles and books are also exploratory, for example, an article on the roots of violence in American cities or an autobiographical account of being tagged a "slow learner" early in one's school career. Both in and out of college, exploratory writing is as important as explanatory writing because it is the springboard and testing ground for new ideas.

Exploratory writing isn't necessarily harder to do than explanatory writing, but it is harder to plan because it resists any systematic approach. That makes it appeal to some writers, particularly those who have a reflective or speculative turn of mind. They like the freedom of being able just to write to see what is going to develop. But although exploratory writers start out with more freedom, eventually they too have to discipline themselves to organize their writing into clear, readable form. They also have to realize that exploratory writing usually takes longer and requires more drafts.

When you're doing exploratory writing, anticipate that your process will be messy. You have to tolerate uncertainty longer because ideas keep coming as you write and it's not always clear what you're going to do with them and how—or if—you can fit them into your paper. Exploratory writing is also hard to organize—sometimes you'll have to outline *after* you've written your first draft in order to get the paper under control. Finally, you also have to have confidence in your own instincts; now that you are focusing on ideas and reflections more than on facts, you have to believe that you have something worth writing about and that other people are interested in reading it.

Of course, not all writing can be easily classified as either explanatory or exploratory; sometimes you'll be working with information and ideas in the same paper and move from presenting facts to reflecting about their implications. For example, in an economics course you might report on how much Japan has invested in the United States economy over the last decade and where those investments have been made; then you could speculate about the long-range impact on American business. If you were writing a case study of a teenage mother for a social work class, you would use mostly explanatory writing to document the young woman's background, schooling, and important facts about her present situation; then you could go to exploratory writing to suggest how her options for the future can be improved.

In general, readers respond best to writing that thoughtfully connects facts to reflections, explanations to explorations. So don't hesitate to mix the two kinds of writing if it makes your paper stronger and more interesting. At this point, you might ask "Why do these distinctions matter to me?" I think there are several reasons.

First, it helps to realize that there isn't *a* writing process—there are writing *processes,* and some work better than others in specific situations. Although by temperament and habit you may be the "just give me the facts, ma'am," kind of person who prefers to do explanatory writing, you also need to become proficient at exploratory writing in order to write the speculative, reflective papers that are necessary when you have to write about long-range goals or speculate about philosophical issues. If, on the other hand, by temperament you'd rather ignore outlines and prefer to spin theories instead of report on facts, you also need to become proficient at explanatory writing. In almost any profession, you're going to have to write reports, summarize data, or present results of research.

Second, you'll become a more proficient and relaxed writer if you develop the habit of analyzing before you start, whether you are going to be doing primarily explanatory or exploratory writing. Once you decide, you can consciously switch into certain writing patterns and write more efficiently. For instance, when you're writing reports, case studies, research papers, or analyses, take the time to rough out an outline and make a careful list of the main points you need to make. Schedule time for research and checking facts; details are going to be important. Review some of the routine but useful patterns you could use to develop your paper: cause and effect, definition, process, narration, and so forth. They can work well when you have a fairly clear idea of your purpose and what you're going to say.

If you're starting on a less clearly defined, more open-ended paper—for example, a reflective essay about Picasso's portrayal of women for an art history course—allow yourself to be less organized for a while. Be willing to start without knowing where you're going. Look at some paintings to get your ideas flowing, talk to some other students, and then just start writing, confident that you'll find your content and your direction. Don't worry if you can't get the first paragraph right—it will come later. Your first goal with exploratory writing should be to generate a fairly complete first draft in order to give yourself something to work with. Remember to give yourself plenty of time to revise. You'll need it.

Finally, resist the idea that one kind of writing is better than another. It's not. Sometimes there's a tendency, particularly in liberal arts classes, to believe that people who do theoretical or reflective writing are superior; that exploratory writing is loftier and more admirable than writing in which people present facts and argue for concrete causes. That's not really the case. Imaginative, thoughtful writing about theories and opinions is important and interesting, but informative, factual writing is also critically important, and people who can do it well are invaluable. Anyone who hopes to be an effective, confident writer should cultivate the habits that enable him or her to do both kinds of writing well. ∎

Because Maxine Hairston has done research on writing, she can offer a helpful reality check, especially for student writers who might not have much contact with the day-to-day lives of professional writers. She provides something of a map to help us better understand academic and professional territories. The following questions can help explore and extend Hairston's thinking.

Responding to Reading

1. Review the bulleted items in the "How Professional Writers Work" section. Did any of these findings surprise you? Which ones resonate with your own writing process? Which ones seem odd to you?

2. Explain the major differences between explanatory writing and exploratory writing. Draw on your own past experiences to provide a few specific examples of each.

Excerpt: Anne Lamott, *Shitty First Drafts*

Born in San Francisco, Anne Lamott is the author of five novels and three works of nonfiction. She has been a book reviewer for Mademoiselle, *a restaurant critic for* California *magazine, and a columnist for the* San Francisco Chronicle. *She also writes a popular column for the online magazine* Salon. *What follows is a chapter from her book* Bird by Bird: Some Instructions on Writing and Life.

Now, practically even better news than that of short assignments is the idea of shitty first drafts. All good writers write them. This is how they end up with good second drafts and terrific third drafts. People tend to look at successful writers, writers who are getting their books published and maybe even doing well financially, and think that they sit down at their desks every morning feeling like a million dollars, feeling great about who they are and how much talent they have and what a great story they have to tell; that they take in a few deep breaths, push back their sleeves, roll their necks a few times to get all the cricks out, and dive in, typing fully formed passages as fast as a court reporter. But this is just the fantasy of the uninitiated. I know some very great writers, writers you love who write beautifully and have made a great deal of money, and not *one* of them sits down routinely feeling wildly enthusiastic and confident. Not one of them writes elegant first drafts. All right, one of them does, but we do not like her very much. We do not think that she has a rich inner life or that God likes her or can even stand her. (Although when I mentioned this to my priest friend Tom, he said you can safely assume you've created God in your own image when it turns out that God hates all the same people you do.)

Very few writers really know what they are doing until they've done it. Nor do they go about their business feeling dewy and thrilled. They do not type a few stiff warm-up sentences and then find themselves bounding along like huskies across the snow. One writer I know tells me that he sits down every morning and says to himself nicely, "It's not like you don't have a choice, because you do—you can either type or kill yourself." We all often feel like we are pulling teeth, even those writers whose prose ends up being the most natural and fluid. The right words and sentences just do not come pouring out like ticker tape most of the time. Now, Muriel Spark is said to have felt that she was taking dictation from God every morning—sitting there, one supposes, plugged into a Dictaphone, typing away, humming. But this is a very hostile and aggressive position. One might hope for bad things to rain down on a person like this.

For me and most of the other writers I know, writing is not rapturous. In fact, the only way I can get anything written at all is to write really, really shitty first drafts.

The first draft is the child's draft, where you let it all pour out and then let it romp all over the place, knowing that no one is going to see it and that you can shape it later. You just let this childlike part of you channel whatever voices and visions come through and onto the page. If one of the characters wants to say, "Well, so what, Mr. Poopy Pants?," you let her. No one is going to see it. If the kid wants to get into really sentimental, weepy, emotional territory, you let him. Just get it all down on paper, because there may be something great in those six crazy pages that you would never have gotten to by more rational, grown-up means. There may be something in the very last line of the very last paragraph on page six that you just love, that is so beautiful or wild that you now know what you're supposed to be writing about, more or less, or in what direction you might go—but there was no way to get to this without first getting through the first five and a half pages.

I used to write food reviews for *California* magazine before it folded. (My writing food reviews had nothing to do with the magazine folding, although every single review did cause a couple of canceled subscriptions. Some readers took umbrage at my comparing mounds of vegetable puree with various ex-presidents' brains.) These reviews always took two days to write. First I'd go to a restaurant several times with a few opinionated, articulate friends in tow. I'd sit there writing down everything anyone said that was at all interesting or funny. Then on the following Monday I'd sit down at my desk with my notes, and try to write the review. Even after I'd been doing this for years, panic would set in. I'd try to write a lead, but instead I'd write a couple of dreadful sentences, xx them out, try again, xx everything out, and then feel despair and worry settle on my chest like an x-ray apron. It's over, I'd think, calmly. I'm not going to be able to get the magic to work this time. I'm ruined. I'm through. I'm toast. Maybe, I'd think, I can get my old job back as a clerk-typist. But probably not. I'd get up and study my teeth in the mirror for a while. Then I'd stop, remember to breathe, make a few phone calls, hit the kitchen and chow down. Eventually I'd go back and sit down at my desk, and sigh for the next ten minutes. Finally I would pick up my one-inch picture frame, stare into it as if for the answer, and every time the answer would come: all I had to do was to write a really shitty first draft of, say, the opening paragraph. And no one was going to see it.

So I'd start writing without reining myself in. It was almost just typing, just making my fingers move. And the writing would be *terrible*. I'd write a lead paragraph that was a whole page, even though the entire review could only be three pages long, and then I'd start writing up descriptions of the food, one dish at a time, bird by bird, and the critics would be sitting on my shoulders, commenting like cartoon characters. They'd be pretending to snore, or rolling their eyes at my overwrought descriptions, no matter how hard I tried to tone those descriptions down, no matter how conscious I was of what a friend said to me gently in my early days of restaurant reviewing. "Annie," she said, "it is just a piece of *chick*en. It is just a bit of *cake*."

But because by then I had been writing for so long, I would eventually let myself trust the process—sort of, more or less. I'd write a first draft that was maybe twice as long as it should be, with a self-indulgent and boring beginning, stupefying descriptions of the meal, lots of quotes from my black-humored friends that made them sound more like the Manson girls than food lovers, and no ending to speak of. The whole thing would be so long and incoherent and hideous that for the rest of the day I'd obsess about getting creamed by a car before I could write a decent second draft. I'd worry that people would read what I'd written and believe that the accident had really been a suicide, that I had panicked because my talent was waning and my mind was shot.

The next day, though, I'd sit down, go through it all with a colored pen, take out everything I possibly could, find a new lead somewhere on the second page, figure out a kicky place to end it, and then write a second draft. It always turned out fine, sometimes even funny and weird and helpful. I'd go over it one more time and mail it in.

Then, a month later, when it was time for another review, the whole process would start again, complete with the fears that people would find my first draft before I could rewrite it.

Almost all good writing begins with terrible first efforts. You need to start somewhere. Start by getting something—anything—down on paper. A friend of mine says that the first draft is the down draft—you just get it down. The second draft is the up draft—you fix it up. You try to say what you have to say more accurately. And the third draft is the dental draft, where you check every tooth, to see if it's loose or cramped or decayed, or even, God help us, healthy.

What I've learned to do when I sit down to work on a shitty first draft is to quiet the voices in my head. First there's the vinegar-lipped Reader Lady, who says primly, "Well, *that's* not very interesting, is it?" And there's the emaciated German male who writes these Orwellian memos detailing your thought crimes. And there are your parents, agonizing over your lack of loyalty and discretion; and there's William Burroughs, dozing off or shooting up because he finds you as bold and articulate as a houseplant; and so on. And there are also the dogs: let's not forget the dogs, the dogs in their pen who will surely hurtle and snarl their way out if you ever *stop* writing, because writing is, for some of us, the latch that keeps the door of the pen closed, keeps those crazy ravenous dogs contained.

Quieting these voices is at least half the battle I fight daily. But this is better than it used to be. It used to be 87 percent. Left to its own devices, my mind spends much of its time having conversations with people who aren't there. I walk along defending myself to people, or exchanging repartee with them, or rationalizing my behavior, or seducing them with gossip, or pretending I'm on their TV talk show or whatever. I speed or run an aging yellow light or don't come to a full stop, and one nanosecond later am explaining to imaginary cops exactly why I had to do what I did, or insisting that I did not in fact do it.

I happened to mention this to a hypnotist I saw many years ago, and he looked at me very nicely. At first I thought he was feeling around on the floor for the silent alarm button, but then he gave me the following exercise, which I still use to this day.

Close your eyes and get quiet for a minute, until the chatter starts up. Then isolate one of the voices and imagine the person speaking as a mouse. Pick it up by the tail and drop it into a mason jar. Then isolate another voice, pick it up by the tail, drop it in the jar. And so on. Drop in any high-maintenance parental units, drop in any contractors, lawyers, colleagues, children, anyone who is whining in your head. Then put the lid on, and watch all these mouse people clawing at the glass, jabbering away, trying to make you feel like shit because you won't do what they want—won't give them more money, won't be more successful, won't see them more often. Then imagine that there is a volume-control button on the bottle. Turn it all the way up for a minute, and listen to the stream of angry, neglected, guilt-mongering voices. Then turn it all the way down and watch the frantic mice lunge at the glass, trying to get to you. Leave it down, and get back to your shitty first draft.

A writer friend of mine suggests opening the jar and shooting them all in the head. But I think he's a little angry, and I'm sure nothing like this would ever occur to you.   ■

Anne Lamott is an astute observer who has a refreshing sense of humor and a sharp wit. She might remind you of a friend who has good advice to share but who spices it with sarcasm. The following questions can help you explore and extend Lamott's thinking.

Responding to Reading

1. Lamott questions the myth that good writing comes easily. Her title and much of her text are devoted to emphasizing the struggles that often come with writing. Did what she expressed seem at all familiar to you? Describe how you struggle with writing. (It may be helpful to start by focusing on one particular experience.)

2. Revisit the place in paragraph 10 where Lamott writes of the first draft as the "down draft," the second as the "up draft," and the third as the "dental draft." Why does Lamott recommend this process? How does this compare to your own writing process? And how does it compare with the successful writing habits described by Maxine Hairston?

3. Consider Lamott's use of irony, wit, and humor. How do these work to create her own voice? Where do you find her humor effective (or ineffective)?

4. Go to www.amazon.com and look up *Bird by Bird: Some Instructions on Writing and Life* (the book from which this chapter is culled). Find the place where readers post reviews and read through at least four of them. How does your opinion of Lamott's writing compare with those of the online reviewers?

Essay: Donald M. Murray, *The Maker's Eye: Revising Your Own Manuscripts*

Donald Murray was born in Boston and was for many years a professor at the University of New Hampshire. He has published novels, short stories, poetry, and several books on teaching writing. In 1954 he won the Pulitzer Prize for editorials in the Boston Globe.

When students complete a first draft, they consider the job of writing done—and their teachers too often agree. When professional writers complete a first draft, they usually feel that they are at the start of the writing process. When a draft is completed, the job of writing can begin.

That difference in attitude is the difference between amateur and professional, inexperience and experience, journeyman and craftsman. Peter F. Drucker, the prolific business writer, calls his first draft "the zero draft"—after that he can start counting. Most writers share the feeling that the first draft, and all of those which follow, are opportunities to discover what they have to say and how best they can say it.

To produce a progression of drafts, each of which says more and says it more clearly, the writer has to develop a special kind of reading skill. In school we are taught to decode what appears on the page as finished writing. Writers, however, face a different category of possibility and responsibility when they read their own drafts. To them the words on the page are never finished. Each can be changed and rearranged, can set off a chain reaction of confusion or clarified meaning. This is a different kind of reading which is possibly more difficult and certainly more exciting.

Writers must learn to be their own best enemy. They must accept the criticism of others and be suspicious of it; they must accept the praise of others and be even more suspicious of it. Writers cannot depend on others. They must detach themselves from their own pages so that they can apply both their caring and their craft to their own work.

Such detachment is not easy. Science-fiction writer Ray Bradbury supposedly puts each manuscript away for a year to the day and then rereads it as a stranger. Not many writers have the discipline or the time to do this. We must read when our judgment may be at its worst, when we are close to the euphoric moment of creation.

Then the writer, counsels novelist Nancy Hale, "should be critical of everything that seems to him most delightful in his style. He should excise what he most admires, because he wouldn't thus admire it if he weren't . . . in a sense protecting it from criticism." John Ciardi, the poet, adds, "The last act of the writing must be to become one's own reader. It is, I suppose, a schizophrenic process, to begin passionately and to end critically, to begin hot and to end cold; and, more important, to be passion-hot and critic-cold at the same time."

Most people think that the principal problem is that writers are too proud of what they have written. Actually, a greater problem for most professional writers is one shared by the majority of students. They are overly critical, think everything is dreadful, tear up page after page, never complete a draft, see the task as hopeless.

The writer must learn to read critically but constructively, to cut what is bad, to reveal what is good. Eleanor Estes, the children's book author, explains: "The writer must survey his work critically, coolly, as though he were a stranger to it. He must be willing to prune, expertly and hard-heartedly. At the end of each revision, a manuscript may look . . . worked over, torn apart, pinned together, added to, deleted from, words changed and words changed back. Yet the book must maintain its original freshness and spontaneity."

Most readers underestimate the amount of rewriting it usually takes to produce spontaneous reading. This is a great disadvantage to the student writer, who sees only a finished product and never watches the craftsman who takes the necessary step back, studies the work carefully, returns to the task, steps back, returns, steps back, again and again. Anthony Burgess, one of the most prolific writers in the English-speaking world, admits, "I might revise a page twenty times." Roald Dahl, the popular children's writer, states, "By the time I'm nearing the end of a story, the first part will have been reread and altered and corrected at least 150 times. . . . Good writing is essentially rewriting. I am positive of this."

Rewriting isn't virtuous. It isn't something that ought to be done. It is simply something that most writers find they have to do to discover what they have to say and how to say it. It is a condition of the writer's life.

There are, however, a few writers who do little formal rewriting, primarily because they have the capacity and experience to create and review a large number of invisible drafts in their minds before they approach the page. And some writers slowly produce finished pages, performing all the tasks of revision simultaneously, page by page, rather then draft by draft. But it is still possible to see the sequence followed by most writers most of the time in rereading their own work.

Most writers scan their drafts first, reading as quickly as possible to catch the larger problems of subject and form, and then move in closer and closer as they read and write, reread and rewrite.

The first thing writers look for in their drafts is *information*. They know that a good piece of writing is built from specific, accurate, and interesting information. The writer must have an abundance of information from which to construct a readable piece of writing.

Next writers look for *meaning* in the information. The specifics must build to a pattern of significance. Each piece of specific information must carry the reader toward meaning.

Writers reading their own drafts are aware of *audience*. They put themselves in the reader's situation and make sure that they deliver information which a reader wants to know or needs to know in a manner which is easily digested. Writers try to be sure that they anticipate and answer the questions a critical reader will ask when reading the piece of writing.

Writers make sure that the *form* is appropriate to the subject and the audience. Form, or genre, is the vehicle which carries meaning to the reader, but form cannot be selected until the writer has adequate information to discover its significance and an audience which needs or wants that meaning.

Once writers are sure the form is appropriate, they must then look at the *structure,* the order of what they have written. Good writing is built on a solid framework of logic, argument, narrative, or motivation which runs through the entire piece of writing and holds it together. This is the time when many writers find it most effective to outline as a way of visualizing the hidden spine by which the piece of writing is supported.

The element on which writers may spend a majority of their time is *development.* Each section of a piece of writing must be adequately developed. It must give readers enough information so that they are satisfied. How much information is enough? That's as difficult as asking how much garlic belongs in a salad. It must be done to taste, but most beginning writers underdevelop, underestimating the reader's hunger for information.

As writers solve development problems, they often have to consider questions of *dimension*. There must be a pleasing and effective proportion among all the parts of the piece of writing. There is a continual process of subtracting and adding to keep the piece of writing in balance.

Finally, writers have to listen to their own voices. *Voice* is the force which drives a piece of writing forward. It is an expression of the writer's authority and concern. It is what is between the words on the page, what glues the piece of writing together. A good piece of writing is always marked by a consistent, individual voice.

As writers read and reread, write and rewrite, they move closer and closer to the page until they are doing line-by-line editing. Writers read their own pages with infinite care. Each sentence, each line, each clause, each phrase, each word, each mark of punctuation, each section of white space between the type has to contribute to the clarification of meaning.

Slowly the writer moves from word to word, looking through language to see the subject. As a word is changed, cut, or added, as a construction is rearranged, all the words used before that moment and all those that follow that moment must be considered and reconsidered.

Writers often read aloud at this stage of the editing process, muttering or whispering to themselves, calling on the ear's experience with language. Does this sound right—or that? Writers edit, shifting back and forth from eye to page to ear to page. I find I must do this careful editing in short runs, no more than fifteen or twenty minutes at a stretch, or I become too kind with myself. I begin to see what I hope is on the page, not what actually is on the page.

This sounds tedious if you haven't done it, but actually it is fun. Making something right is immensely satisfying, for writers begin to learn what they are writing about by writing. Language leads them to meaning, and there is the joy of discovery, of understanding, of making meaning clear as the writer employs the technical skills of language.

Words have double meanings, even triple and quadruple meanings. Each word has its own potential of connotation and denotation. And when writers rub one word against the other, they are often rewarded with a sudden insight, an unexpected clarification.

The maker's eye moves back and forth from word to phrase to sentence to paragraph to sentence to phrase to word. The maker's eye sees the need for variety and balance, for a firmer structure, for a more appropriate form. It peers into the interior of the paragraph, looking for coherence, unity, and emphasis, which make meaning clear.

I learned something about this process when my first bifocals were prescribed. I had ordered a larger section of the reading portion of the glass because of my work, but even so, I could not contain my eyes within this new limit of vision. And I still find myself taking off my glasses and bending my nose toward the page, for my eyes unconsciously flick back and forth across the page, back to another page, forward to still another, as I try to see each evolving line in relation to every other line.

When does this process end? Most writers agree with the great Russian writer Tolstoy, who said, "I scarcely ever reread my published writing, if by chance I come across a page, it always strikes me: all this must be rewritten; this is how I should have written it."

The maker's eye is never satisfied, for each word has the potential to ignite new meaning. This article has been twice written all the way through the writing process [. . .]. Now it is to be republished in a book. The editors made a few small suggestions, and then I read it with my maker's eye. Now it has been re-edited, re-revised, re-read, and re-re-edited, for each piece of writing to the writer is full of potential and alternatives.

A piece of writing is never finished. It is delivered to a deadline, torn out of the typewriter on demand, sent off with a sense of accomplishment and shame and pride and frustration. If only there were a couple more days, time for just another run at it, perhaps then. . .   ■

It is worth listening to experienced writers. As someone who writes for both academic and popular audiences, Donald Murray knows both worlds and offers sage advice for success in each. The following questions can help you reflect on Murray's approach.

Responding to Reading

1. How does the process of revision described by Murray compare to that of Lamott? Which ideas do they share? Where do they differ?

2. Was there anything in the Murray piece that surprised you? Note the sentence or paragraph and share it with a classmate.

3. In paragraph 14 Murray writes that "Each piece of specific information must carry the reader toward meaning." What does he mean by this?

4. According to Murray, what is the relationship between reading and writing?

This book emphasizes the process of planning, drafting, gathering feedback, revising, and editing that is practiced—even if in different ways—by successful writers such as Hairston, Lamott, and Murray. Breaking down composing into stages helps to take some of the mystery out of writing and affords a degree of control over the process. After all, nearly anyone who commits time and effort to each of the stages can improve his or her writing. No one promises that writing will suddenly be quick and easy; but engaging in a process that has time and again proven successful for others makes good sense.

Writing in School

It is often easier to see the social purpose of workplace writing than it is to see the purpose of school writing. After all, most writing in the workplace is done in response to an immediate, concrete need to solve a concrete problem or get something done. A staff person at a nonprofit community agency, for example, may write a grant proposal in order to get money that will fund an after-school tutoring program. If the writing is effective, the money is secured, and the agency can do its work.

When asked why we write in school, some might respond, "Because it is required to pass the course" or "To get good grades." And indeed this, in part, is true. But the reasons for school writing run deeper than that, especially when we consider not just the immediate motivations for students to write but the institution's reasons for assigning it in the first place.

If we think of writing as action, then what action does student writing perform? Consider the following purposes for school writing:

- Writing serves as a way to demonstrate, document, or communicate that learning has happened.
- Writing plays a role in evaluating, sorting, and ranking students (usually through grading).
- Writing can propel new learning, new insights, and new connections.
- Writing can encourage and deepen personal and critical reflection.
- Writing opens a way to express oneself, one's ideas, and one's view of the world.

Sometimes a single piece of writing serves just one of these purposes; but more often it serves several at once. You might be assigned an essay in your composition class because your instructor needs to assess how effectively you express or analyze a particular idea. But the essay is intended not just to show what you know but also to help you spark new thinking and reflection. Ultimately, the essay will also be graded, because grading is the way schools rank, reward, and certify students.

What Is an Essay?

In English and other humanistic disciplines, the essay is the most common genre, or form, for writing. Nearly everyone has taken English classes and written essays before, but there is still some value in revisiting a very basic question: What exactly is an essay?

WRITING TO DISCOVER

Jot down all the rules about writing essays that you have been taught. Include rules about planning, purpose, structure research methods, style, etc.—just get down all the rules and advice that echo in your head as you write an essay for school.

For example, have you been taught that an essay must have a certain number of paragraphs? that the thesis must go in a particular place? that you should or shouldn't use the personal pronoun *I*?

Which advice has served you especially well? Which hasn't been helpful?

The etymology of the word *essay* is instructive. It derives from the Latin *exagire*, which means "to weigh," and the old French *essaier*, which means "to try." So, at their most basic, essays can be thought of as opportunities to weigh ideas and to try out new lines of thinking. The 18th-century English writer Samuel Johnson defined the essay as "a loose sally of the mind." Johnson reminds us that essays should adopt an energetic demeanor and reflect speculative thinking. English professor Paul Heilker drives this point home, asserting that "the essay is less a thing than it is an action, less an artifact than an activity, less a noun than a verb."[4]

There are many different kinds of essays, and much of what an essay writer does depends on the particular kind. Yet most essays share a few basic features. They generally

- Center on one main topic
- Develop a claim or a tension or an idea, supporting it with particulars
- Move the reader from the *known* to the *new*

The major kinds of essays emphasized in this book are:

- *Personal essays.* These are usually grounded in narrative, in stories of personal experience. Personal essays often explore a key tension, and when they assert a claim or thesis (not all do), it is often delayed or implied rather than directly stated. They rely on description and reflection, and they generally render experience, bringing it closer to the reader.
- *Analytical essays.* These demand that you step back from experience to conceptualize it and that you assert and support a viable claim. Analytical essays (also called *critical essays* or simply *papers*) generally adopt a thesis-

---

[4]Heilker, Paul. *The Essay: Theory and Pedagogy for an Active Form.* Urbana, IL: National Council of Teachers of English, 1996, p. 183.

driven structure and value logical argument and critical reflection. They often explore ideas, consider context, invite response to readings, draw connections, or explain complex phenomena.

- *Persuasive essays.* These are aimed at shaping readers' beliefs or spurring an audience to action. Persuasive essays hinge on arguments that often rely on a range of appeals, including those based on logic and evidence, on the audience's preferences and emotions, and on the speaker's credibility. Although all essays are to some degree persuasive in nature, some are explicitly grounded in arguments intended to change the audience's beliefs or actions.

Even these three categories don't entirely capture the variety of essays one might encounter. In fact, you can put nearly any adjective in front of the word *essay* to shade its purpose and structure: descriptive essay, interpretive essay, reflective essay, research essay, literary essay, exploratory essay, and so on. The chapters that follow include various kinds of essay assignments and explain pragmatic strategies to help you complete them successfully.

This book is centered on the themes of writing, community, and social action. Reading selections are included to extend and challenge your thinking. Many of the writing assignments ask you to employ the essay genre; others ask you to think (and write) beyond the essay.

Nota Bene (From Latin, Meaning "Mark Well" or "Take Note")

From the start, save all the writing you do for this course. This includes not only papers you hand in but also notes, early drafts, journal entries, and so on. Keep it all. Near the end of the term you may be asked to assemble a portfolio or to write an essay reflecting on your coursework, both of which require reviewing samples of writing from the entire course.

Writing *about, for,* and *with* the Community

The fact is that few people (except for academics and professional writers) write essays after they leave college. Yet this doesn't mean that most people stop writing. In fact, most continue to write (and sometimes they even write *more*) to meet the demands of their personal, work, and civic lives. And it doesn't mean that the essay genre is disposable. In fact, for those who value exploring intellectual questions or expressing ideas, essays offer unique opportunities for sustained inquiry and reflection. One of the great gifts of college is that it offers the space and encouragement for such critical thinking and exploratory writing.

To acknowledge varieties of writing in addition to those traditionally valued in school, this book, particularly the later chapters, structures opportunities for you to write a range of documents that encourage awareness of social concerns, that meet the needs of workplace and public spheres, and that serve your community. These assignments, often called *service-learning*, demand an engagement with the local community. In this book, service-learning projects take three main approaches:

- Writing *about* community outreach experiences, local community problems, and social justice concerns.
- Writing *for* local nonprofit organizations, which involves generating real-world documents such as publicity materials or in-house research to assist community agencies in doing their work.
- Writing *with* local citizens to raise awareness of or to address community problems.

The hyphenated term *service-learning* emphasizes two complementary purposes for the approach: to provide a pragmatic service to the community and to engage in meaningful learning. The service energizes and deepens the learning, and the learning energizes and deepens the service. Another key element of service-learning is reflection: reflection on your own learning, reflection on your actions and choices, reflection on community problems and our shared culture. Future chapters invite you to reflect on your roles as both a writer and a citizen, as well as on social justice more generally.

Students usually find service-learning writing experiences gratifying, even as they find them demanding. Community writing projects present a compelling invitation to exercise writing as social action, and they often help participants to become more confident, versatile, and reflective writers.

ENDNOTE

The ideas presented in this chapter resurface throughout future chapters, sometimes explicitly (when, for example, you are asked to engage in a composing process that includes planning, peer review, and revision) and sometimes implicitly (in the sense that future assignments assume that writing functions as purposeful social action). So now it's time to write, reflect, and act.

2

Writing Your Life

Why do we tell stories about our lives? In what ways can writing from personal experience prompt reflection and enrich critical thinking? How can one craft compelling personal essays? Chapter 2 introduces the features and patterns typically found in autobiographical writing and shares strategies for composing a personal essay focused on one's own literacy history, ethical development, or community service experiences. This chapter also includes several engaging examples of personal writing by both students and professional writers.

———————

I have a great suspicion of autobiographical writing. So much of it reeks of self-indulgence and self-absorption, yet any serious engagement with the world involves a questioning of one's self.
—Cornel West, scholar and activist

The act of writing is the act of discovering what you believe.
—David Hare, playwright

Most people find rewards in telling their own stories, in sharing something of themselves with others. There is something fundamentally human about this, whether it happens in the course of a late-night talk between friends or in the pages of a personal essay. And even those who are somewhat suspicious of autobiographical writing—such as scholar and activist Cornel West, cited above—recognize the value of reflecting on one's own life as a prelude to healthy engagement with others. Writing about personal experience, then, provides a way to share compelling stories and to express meaningful ideas. It is also one way to heed the ancient Greek maxim "Know thyself."

Although narrative forms the bedrock for most personal writing, personal essays are not simply reports of one's history or retellings of any old stories. Good personal essays render textured experience but also help the reader make some sense of it. Personal essayists don't attempt to nail down every detail of a life; instead they select key turning points, encounters, and themes that seem ripe for expression. They then bring that selected experience close to the reader, explore the tensions inherent to it, and articulate or imply how and why it can be meaningful to readers.

WRITING TO DISCOVER

Personal essays are propelled by narratives of experience—by stories. Think for a few minutes about the people you know—family, friends, co-workers—who are great storytellers.

Speculate about what it is that makes their stories so engaging. Take notes in response to the following questions:

- What kinds of details do they use?
- How do they keep everyone's attention?
- How do they give the story energy and color?
- How much of their success is in *what* they say, and how much is in the *way* they say it?

Also consider the flip side: What makes a story come across as flat and lifeless?

Recall from Chapter 1 that essays generally move the reader from the *known* to the *new*. Personal essays do this in two ways: They share stories that are new to the reader and they suggest ways of seeing those narratives that reveal—implicitly or explicitly—their significance or meaning. As will be discussed later, you shouldn't confuse this second part with delivering a moral at the end of a story (even though many fine personal essays wrestle with moral issues).

The assignment and readings in this chapter invite you to reflect on your own history with writing, schooling, or ethical development. You have experience with writing, schooling, and growing—it may be good, bad, mixed, whatever. No matter the circumstances, you have a wealth of material on which to draw. Personal essays don't demand that you have exotic, action-packed, dramatic events to report. More often, they focus on everyday experiences that you, as a writer, *make* significant for your reader.

There are several overlapping aims for this essay unit. Your essay should:

- Demonstrate your competency in the personal essay format (a genre valued in humanistic disciplines such as English) and in strategies such as narration and description (which can be useful in many other kinds of writing).
- Allow your instructor and classmates to know you better as both a person and a writer. Moreover, reflecting on your life can prompt discussions

about literacy and about what it means to be a "good writer" or about ethics and what it means to be a "good person."

- Invite you to adopt a self-reflective posture. By asking you to question yourself and to articulate what you believe (recall the two epigraphs for this chapter), this essay starts a process of reflective thinking that is encouraged throughout this book.

If your instructor chooses, the topic of this assignment can be redirected to other themes. Whatever the topic, the same basic rhetorical strategies for crafting a personal essay and the same basic composing process of planning, drafting, gathering feedback, revising, and editing still apply.

PERSONAL ESSAY ASSIGNMENT
Autobiographical Reflections on Literacy, Ethics, or Service

For this essay, select one of the following:

- A turning point, a key event, or an encounter that reveals some aspect of yourself as a reader or writer
- A turning point in your ethical development
- A meaningful event that you experienced while involved in community service

Although you should keep the focus on your personal experience, the essay should speak to what readers can discover from your rendering of personal experience. The essay should be based on autobiographical narrative, develop a central tension and turn, and make use of literary devices such as description, setting, character, and figurative language.

Exploratory Writing: Mining Your Own History

Exploratory writing is for the purpose of generating ideas and exploring possibilities; at this stage you are not trying to compose an essay. The more creative and varied the possibilities you have at the outset, the better your final draft is likely to be. In the past you may have done this in many ways, such as by brainstorming, freewriting, or outlining. Later in this book you will employ these strategies, as well as several others. Exploratory writing may include lists, sketches, fragments of thoughts, stream-of-consciousness ramblings, tentative plans, and so on. At this idea stage, you shouldn't worry about grammar.

Although your exploratory writing may be shared with classmates, it will not be graded.

This writing is informal but important. (It isn't busy work—you'll use it.) Think of it as getting down data that you can work with later. The more you record now, the more you will have to select from when you write your essay.

Jot down responses to the prompts that follow. You should respond to all of them, but some may trigger more thoughts or seem more important to you than others. When that happens, write more fully. Useful ways of getting beyond first thoughts include describing specific events, scenes, writings, people, dialogues, and stories.

The following questions are keyed to the literacy autobiography option (that is, the first option in the assignment above). Feel free to adapt these questions to other purposes and topics if you are writing on one of the other assignment options.

- Think of times when writing has seemed hard or difficult or unpleasant. What made it so? List several specific instances that come to mind and then write more on two or three of them. What about times when writing seemed easier or more pleasant? Again, make a list, and then choose two or three for further reflection. What made those events rewarding?
- What is your first memory of reading or writing? Describe it.
- Think back to writings you have done, both in school and out of school. Which is one that you're particularly proud of? Describe it in detail. Why did you select this one?
- Think about a person who knows your writing or how you write. It might be a friend, teacher, relative, anyone. Who is that person? Write the name. What would that person say about your writing and/or about you as a writer? How would you respond to that? Try writing a hypothetical dialogue with that person, beginning with something that person says.
- Consider influences on you as a writer, positive and negative.

  Which influences come to mind (for example, people, events, memories)?
  What reading material was around when you grew up?
  Were any books or readings particularly memorable? List them.
  What kind of reading do you like now?
  In "Shitty First Drafts" (Chapter 1), Anne Lamott describes certain "voices in her head" that surface when she writes. Are there any such "voices" from your past that encourage or discourage you?
  Now that you've made a list, mark any entries that stand out to you. Write more about one of them. Why and how was it influential?

- Review lessons from school. List a few things you learned about writing in school. Come up with at least four, and more if you can. Pick one that has

been helpful and explain why. Pick one that has not been helpful and explain why.

- Consider at least one occasion for writing outside of school. Do you keep
  a journal? If so, why? Have you written any letters that are important to
  you? Have you ever written a speech, a song, or a poem? When and why?

- Think about times when reading or writing have allowed you to connect
  with other people in a meaningful way. Describe the connection and the
  kinds of texts that forged the connection (a letter? an email message? a
  poem? a song?). Now think about times when writing served as a way to
  change or break connections with people.

- Consider an event or a time that prompted you to change your writing
  style. What prompted that change? Describe your style before and after
  the event.

- Think about change over time. How has your writing changed over the
  long term? You might fill in the blanks of this prompt: "At first . . . Then . . .
  And then . . . And then . . . "

When you are done responding to these prompts, look over everything
you've written. Mark those sections or small bits that seem ripe for further inquiry. You might even share them with a friend or classmate.

You won't be able to use all this exploratory writing; if you did, your essay
would be scattered rather than focused. The point is to consider multiple possibilities before settling on any single topic. (Sometimes writers pick topics too
quickly, and they hurt themselves by not first considering options that could
yield better results.) If you find a promising nugget or two in your exploratory
writing, then you've already started composing your essay.

Reading Selections

Writers rely on other writers. That is, what we read can both spark and shape
our own writing.

The following selections are by authors who employ the first-person perspective to grapple with issues related to writing, schooling, and service. Five are personal essays by first-year college students (O'Konski, Montalvo, McMurtray,
Garber, and Martens), written in response to an assignment similar to the one
featured on page 27. Two are by professional writers (hooks and Rose), ex-
cerpted from their books.

As you read, consider not only how the pieces relate to, or contrast with,
your own experience but also what they reveal about how, as a culture, we teach
and value different kinds of literacy and different approaches to ethics.

Excerpt: bell hooks, *writing autobiography*

bell hooks grew up as Gloria Watkins in Kentucky and was educated at Stanford University. She is the author of several books on race, gender, cultural critique, and teaching, including Talking Back: Thinking Feminist, Thinking Black *(1988), from which the following text is selected.*

To me, telling the story of my growing up years was intimately connected with the longing to kill the self I was without really having to die. I wanted to kill that self in writing. Once that self was gone—out of my life forever—I could more easily become the me of me. It was clearly the Gloria Jean of my tormented and anguished childhood that I wanted to be rid of, the girl who was always wrong, always punished, always subjected to some humiliation or other, always crying, the girl who was to end up in a mental institution because she could not be anything but crazy, or so they told her. She was the girl who sat a hot iron on her arm pleading with them to leave her alone, the girl who wore her scar as a brand marking her madness. Even now I can hear the voices of my sisters saying "mama make Gloria stop crying." By writing the autobiography, it was not just this Gloria I would be rid of, but the past that had a hold on me, that kept me from the present. I wanted not to forget the past but to break its hold. This death in writing was to be liberatory.

Until I began to try and write an autobiography, I thought that it would be a simple task this telling of one's story. And yet I tried year after year, never writing more than a few pages. My inability to write out the story I interpreted as an indication that I was not ready to let go of the past, that I was not ready to be fully in the present. Psychologically, I considered the possibility that I had become attached to the wounds and sorrows of my childhood, that I held to them in a manner that blocked my efforts to be self-realized, whole, to be healed. A key message in Toni Cade Bambara's novel *The Salteaters*, which tells the story of Velma's suicide attempt, her breakdown, is expressed when the healer asks her "are you sure sweetheart, that you want to be well?"

There was very clearly something blocking my ability to tell my story. Perhaps it was remembered scoldings and punishments when mama heard me saying something to a friend or stranger that she did not think should be said. Secrecy and silence—these were central issues. Secrecy about family, about what went on in the domestic household was a bond between us—was part of what made us family. There was a dread one felt about breaking that bond. And yet I could not grow inside the atmosphere of secrecy that had pervaded our lives and the lives of other families about us. Strange that I had always challenged the secrecy, always let something slip that should not be known growing up, yet as a writer staring into the solitary space of paper, I was bound, trapped in the fear that a bond is lost or broken in the telling. I did not want to be the traitor, the teller of family secrets—and yet I wanted to be a writer. Surely, I told myself, I could write a purely imaginative work—a work that would not hint at personal private realities. And so I tried. But always there were the intruding traces, those elements of real life however disguised. Claiming the freedom to grow as an imaginative writer was connected for me with having the courage to open, to be able to tell the truth of one's life as I had experienced it in writing. To talk about one's life—that I could do. To write about it, to leave a trace—that was frightening.

The longer it took me to begin the process of writing autobiography, the further removed from those memories I was becoming. Each year, a memory seemed less and less clear. I wanted not to lose the vividness, the recall and felt an urgent need to begin the work and complete it. Yet I could not begin even though I had begun to confront some of the reasons I was blocked, as I am blocked just now in writing this piece because I am afraid to express in writing the experience that served as a catalyst for that block to move.

I had met a young black man. We were having an affair. It is important that he was black. He was in some mysterious way a link to this past that I had been struggling to grapple with, to name in writing. With him I remembered incidents, moments of the past that I had completely suppressed. It was as though there was something about the passion of contact that was hypnotic, that enabled me to drop barriers and thus enter fully, rather re-enter those past experiences. A key aspect seemed to be the way he smelled, the combined odors of cigarettes, occasionally alcohol, and his body smells. I thought often of the phrase "scent of memory," for it was those smells that carried me back. And there were specific occasions when it was very evident that the experience of being in his company was the catalyst for this remembering.

Two specific incidents come to mind. One day in the middle of the afternoon we met at his place. We were drinking cognac and dancing to music from the radio. He was smoking cigarettes (not only do I not smoke, but I usually make an effort to avoid smoke). As we held each other dancing those mingled odors of alcohol, sweat, and cigarettes led me to say, quite without thinking about it, "Uncle Pete." It was not that I had forgotten Uncle Pete. It was more that I had forgotten the childhood experience of meeting him. He drank often, smoked cigarettes, and always on the few occasions that we met him, he held us children in tight embraces. It was the memory of those embraces—of the way I hated and longed to resist them—that I recalled.

Another day we went to a favorite park to feed ducks and parked the car in front of tall bushes. As we were sitting there, we suddenly heard the sound of an oncoming train—a sound which startled me so that it evoked another long-suppressed memory: that of crossing the train tracks in my father's car. I recalled an incident where the car stopped on the tracks and my father left us sitting there while he raised the hood of the car and worked to repair it. This is an incident that I am not certain actually happened. As a child, I had been terrified of just such an incident occurring, perhaps so terrified that it played itself out in my mind as though it had happened. These are just two ways this encounter acted as a catalyst breaking down barriers enabling me to finally write this long-desired autobiography of my childhood.

Each day I sat at the typewriter and different memories were written about in short vignettes. They came in a rush, as though they were a sudden thunder-storm. They came in a surreal, dreamlike style which made me cease to think of them as strictly autobiographical because it seemed that myth, dream, and real-ity had merged. There were many incidents that I would talk about with my sib-lings to see if they recalled them. Often we remembered together a general out-line of an incident but the details were different for us. This fact was a constant reminder of the limitations of autobiography, of the extent to which autobiogra-phy is a very personal story telling—a unique recounting of events not so much as they have happened but as we remember and invent them. One memory that I would have sworn was "the truth and nothing but the truth" concerned a wagon that my brother and I shared as a child. I remembered that we played with this toy only at my grandfather's house, that we shared it, that I would ride it and my brother would push me. Yet one facet of the memory was puzzling, I remembered always returning home with bruises or scratches from this toy. When I called my mother, she said there had never been any wagon, that we had shared a red wheelbarrow, that it had always been at my grandfather's house because there were sidewalks on that part of town. We lived in the hills where there were no sidewalks. Again I was compelled to face the fiction that is a part of all retelling, remembering. I began to think of the work I was doing as both fiction and autobiography. It seemed to fall in the category of writing that Audre Lorde, in her autobiographically-based work *Zami*, calls bio-mythography. As I wrote, I felt that I was not as concerned with accuracy of detail as I was with evoking in writing the state of mind, the spirit of a particular moment.

The longing to tell one's story and the process of telling is symbolically a ges-ture of longing to recover the past in such a way that one experiences both a sense of reunion and a sense of release. It was the longing for release that com-pelled the writing but concurrently it was the joy of reunion that enabled me to see that the act of writing one's autobiography is a way to find again that aspect of self and experience that may no longer be an actual part of one's life but is a living memory shaping and informing the present. Autobiographical writing was a way for me to evoke the particular experience of growing up southern and black in segregated communities. It was a way to recapture the richness of southern black culture. The need to remember and hold to the legacy of that ex-perience and what it taught me has been all the more important since I have since lived in predominately white communities and taught at predominately white colleges. Black southern folk experience was the foundation of the life around me when I was a child; that experience no longer exists in many places where it was once all of life that we knew. Capitalism, upward mobility, assimilation of other values have all led to rapid disintegration of black folk experience or in some cases the gradual wearing away of that experience.

Within the world on my childhood, we held onto the legacy of a distinct black culture by listening to the elders tell their stories. Autobiography was experienced most actively in the art of telling one's story. I can recall sitting at Baba's (my grandmother on my mother's side) at 1200 Broad Street—listening to people come and recount their life experience. In those days, whenever I brought a playmate to my grandmother's house, Baba would want a brief outline of their autobiography before we would begin playing. She wanted not only to know who their people were but what their values were. It was sometimes an awesome and terrifying experience to stand answering these questions or witness another playmate being subjected to the process and yet this was the way we would come to know our own and one another's family history. It is the absence of such a tradition in my adult life that makes the written narrative of my girlhood all the more important. As the years pass and these glorious memories grow much more vague, there will remain the clarity contained within the written words.

Conceptually, the autobiography was framed in the manner of a hope chest. I remembered my mother's hope chest, with its wonderful odor of cedar and thought about her taking the most precious items and placing them there for safekeeping. Certain memories were for me a similar treasure. I wanted to place them somewhere for safekeeping. An autobiographical narrative seemed an appropriate place. Each particular incident, encounter, experience had its own story, sometimes told from the first person, sometimes told from the third person. Often I felt as though I was in a trance at my typewriter, that the shape of a particular memory was decided not by my conscious mind but by all that is dark and deep within me, unconscious but present. It was the act of making it present, bringing it into the open, so to speak, that was liberating.

From the perspective of trying to understand my psyche, it was also interesting to read the narrative in its entirety after I had completed the work. It had not occurred to me that bringing one's past, one's memories together in a complete narrative would allow one to view them from a different perspective, not as singular isolated events but as part of a continuum. Reading the completed manuscript, I felt as though I had an overview not so much of my childhood but of those experiences that were deeply imprinted in my consciousness. Significantly, that which was absent, left out, not included also was important. I was shocked to find at the end of my narrative that there were few incidents I recalled that involved my five sisters. Most of the incidents with siblings were with me and my brother. There was a sense of alienation from my sisters present in childhood, a sense of estrangement. This was reflected in the narrative. Another aspect of the completed manuscript that is interesting to me is the way in which the incidents describing adult men suggest that I feared them intensely, with the exception of my grandfather and a few old men. Writing the autobiographical narrative enabled me to look at my past from a different perspective and to use this knowledge as a means of self-growth and change in a practical way.

In the end I did not feel as though I had killed the Gloria of my childhood. Instead I had rescued her. She was no longer the enemy within, the little girl who had to be annihilated for the woman to come into being. In writing about her, I reclaimed that part of myself I had long ago rejected, left uncared for, just as she had often felt alone and uncared for as a child. Remembering was part of a cycle of reunion, a joining of fragments, "the bits and pieces of my heart" that the narrative made whole again.   ■

Responding to Reading

1. hooks starts her piece with a rather shocking few sentences. What effect does that have on readers? How do these sentences about writing and killing help set the stage for the conclusions she ultimately draws?

2. hooks writes that "The longing to tell one's story and the process of telling is symbolically a gesture of longing to recover the past in such a way that one experiences both a sense of reunion and a sense of release." What does she mean by this?

3. Consider how writing is similar to and different from other ways of recording and recovering the past, such as through sharing stories orally and through photography and video.

4. In the final two paragraphs, hooks recounts a few key functions that writing personal narrative serves for her. What are they?

Student Essay: Richard O'Konski, *The Monster Under the Bed*

When he wrote this essay, Richard O'Konski was a first-year student planning to major in computer engineering.

A h, sleep. What a wonderful place. A place where our imagination comes alive and dances atop a flurry of wild ideas. Red polka dotted creatures with five legs come out of their caverns to play hide-and-go-seek with us. Worlds collide in brilliant showers of light while at the same time a new planet forms. Everyday objects become beautiful, animated spectacles. But when I was a kid, there was always one thing that kept my imagination from running wild—one thing that kept me from my sleep and my dreams—and yet for some strange reason, the one thing that hindered me was produced by that very same imagination that was locked in the closet with the hopelessly mangled key—for lying in wait for me every night before I climbed under the covers was the creature under the bed.

The creature under the bed was a secret. Nobody knew what it looked like. Nobody knew if it was a big, slimy, one-eyed, one-armed creature with giant fangs and blood dripping from its child-sized mouth—or if it was merely a man lying in wait with a blade clutched in his powerful hand, waiting to slice open the throat of any child who just wanted to dream. It was a secret—but every kid out there knew about it. Some may have even claimed to see it. But nobody truly did, because it didn't exist. It was a figment of our very vivid imaginations. Unfortunately, though, our fear of the creature under the bed was very real. The creature may have been escapable, but our fear was not. Our fear met with us every night. It tormented us, teased us, tortured us—simply to make reaching the dreamy goal of sleep a little more difficult to attain. It became part of our lives, and shook our souls. It grabbed us and warned us, "Don't look under the bed! You don't want to know what's down there." And then it grinned an evil smile and left us shaking. "Should I look under the bed? Maybe I should look just to make sure. But I don't want to look! I'm so afraid! What's down there?!" And maybe every once in a while we would get the nerve to look under the bed, but . . . no, the monster was never there. It was just our fear of the monster that was always there.

Why are we so afraid? Why does fear have such an impact on us, as to make us dream up ridiculous stories? Why do we have to be so scared? Because we don't know. We don't know what's waiting for us under the bed. We don't know what lies in wait for us—about what the future holds for us. There's an uncertainty. And what scares people more than anything? Uncertainty. The idea that we just don't know. That's what scares us so much.

We may somehow get an idea in our minds that we may have gotten off television or in a book somewhere that just stuck with us. And our minds take that idea and twist it into strange shapes and find holes in it and realize that it isn't complete. There's something that just isn't right about it. And then our minds twist that idea some more and turn it into something that, even for a split second, may seem very real. And then the uncertainty comes in. Pretty soon, that uncertainty turns into fear, and that once playful idea turns into the most frightening nightmare.

That's what happened to me. That's what happened to my writing.

As I see it, writing is a wonderful tool. It allows us to free our imaginations and solve the most complicated problems. It allows us to dream up those five-legged creatures with the purple horn and the bloody fangs. It's what allows us to discover our true inner selves. It's what allows us to be us—just like our dreams.

But just as there was that creature under the bed waiting for us to sleep, there's a creature in my mind, just waiting for me to write. And I know it's there. It's harassing me. It's laughing at me. It's trying to scare me. And it's doing a pretty darn good job.

Ever since I can remember beginning to write, there has always been this hatred of writing. I've always loathed the moment when it came time to write an essay or research paper, and it's not necessarily because I'm bad at it—I've actually had some teachers that were quite fond of it—it's because I'm afraid of it. I'm afraid of what people will think of it. I'm afraid of what grade I'll get on it. But most of all, I'm afraid of what people will think of me after they read it.

I've noticed in our society that in many cases, most people are not too fond of those who are different. It doesn't usually like those who don't conform and fit in with the "normal" people. Unfortunately for me, I've always felt that I haven't fit into this group of conforming, normal people. I've never fulfilled what our society expects of me as a male: I don't like sports; I don't care about drinking and partying all the time; I don't care about cars; and I just don't care about "being a real man's man." None of these things have ever been a part of my life. Unfortunately, this is what I feel people expect me to be, and that's why it's so hard for me to tell people in my writing, "That just isn't me."

I've been forgetting something, though—something that I know too well: fear is not an impasse; it's a challenge. It is something in life that must be dealt with and must be overcome. I can't just submit to my fear. How could the Wright brothers invent the airplane if they gave up? How could such a government as ours exist if the founders just gave up? How could I have ever defeated the creature under the bed if I merely gave up? I couldn't have defeated it, and that's why I didn't give up. I didn't give up then, and I'm not going to give up now.

And I know how I'm going to do it. I just need to keep in mind something I realized as a kid. The monster peering from under the bed is not real. The monster that inhabits my mind is not real. It's all a figment of my imagination. It's just a fleeting idea that came upon me, like a leaf blowing in the wind that happened to fall at my feet. I decided to pick that leaf up, turn it over in my hand, and feel the coarse texture of it, but pretty soon I had to throw the leaf back into the air, where the wind could once again pick it up and deliver it elsewhere. That's the key in my struggle. I just need to forget. I looked fear in the face—I let it intimidate me like a bully. Now I just need to walk away and never look back.

My fear of writing is the monster under the bed. It is that creature in the closet. It is any fictitious creature that plagued my young mind. And just like I forgot about the monster with time, so I need to forget about that fear of writing. I let the fear consume me for too long. I let the fear write for me for too long. I have been afraid for too long. I need to forget about the monsters under the bed and write for myself. ∎

Responding to Reading

1. In his first two paragraphs, O'Konski creates a colorful description of sleep and of childhood visions. Why does he do this? What effect does it have on readers?

2. Can you relate to any of O'Konski's fears about writing? How?

3. Many personal essays recount a moment or a process of change. How does the author of this essay express a change in himself? Locate the pivotal turning point(s) in the essay.

Student Essay: Eileen Montalvo, *Replanting My Roots*

When she wrote this essay, Eileen Montalvo was a first-year college student planning to major in education. Names of people described in the essay have been changed.

I remember the day that the delicate issue of race was introduced into my life. One would assume that being born brown in a predominantly white society would have been the beginning of my exploration in the subject. I never had to confront the issue, however, until kindergarten, when a girl refused to play with the toys because a "brown and dirty" girl was among their presence. My friends defended me, but the feeling of inferiority still plagues me at times.

For most of my years in school, I felt forced to abandon my Puerto Rican roots to fit the "American" ideal. I never talked to my friends about racial incidents that happened to me in fear that I would be belittled. I never spoke Spanish to my family around others in fear that we might be humiliated. At school, my teachers emphasized not writing about issues that were too controversial, in an attempt to keep everyone happy; unfortunately for me, that included issues concerning race. Needless to say, personal essays were among my most hated of writing assignments. To write about my experiences would involve admitting that I was not the same as everyone else, and hearing people say, "There she goes again." Despite my attempts to leave my roots behind, that fact remained that I was still Hispanic, and that fact alone outcasted me from being an "American."

It wasn't until my senior year in high school that I realized what I had thrown away in an attempt to reach such a subjective ideal. That year, I won the Martin Luther King Jr. Leadership Award along with other students from my school. We had to write an essay about how the teachings and/or life of Martin Luther King Jr. had an impact on our lives. I asked my friends how they would respond to this question. They said: "Do I look black to you? I don't think my life would be different one way or another." "He was a good man. Did you get the assignment done for Physics?"

How do you respond to such comments? I just looked at them and said, "Oh."

While the responses from my peers were, in some respects, *insulting*, I kept all comments that I had to myself. I tried to make excuses for their comments and lack of sensitivity. The next day, I went to sit with my usual group of friends during lunch. As I approached the table, I heard Rich, a fellow member of our group, rambling about an incident that had occurred earlier.

"Man, some Mexican guy was holding up the line. The lunch lady was trying to tell him that he didn't have enough cash, but did he move? NO!! He just kept talking to her in Spanish! Hello! Learn English!! Those Mexicans are so lazy—they want our money and jobs, but they don't want to learn our language! Oh, hey Eileen!! You see, Eileen's cool, she speaks English!"

I felt the blood rushing to my face. My body became tense. I could feel 101 different thoughts of anger and disgust come pouring out of my mouth. I controlled myself, knowing that if I were to let that happen, I would seriously hurt Rich. Instead, I turned around and walked away.

That evening, I stood in front of the mirror for what seemed hours. I stared at the contour of my eyes, the shape of my nose, the color of my skin. I felt the texture of my dark brown hair. I looked like the same people my friends had spoken so arrogantly about. The language they spoke was the first language I learned. My family migrated to the United States for the same reasons as theirs—a better way of life. I realized that my friends were speaking arrogantly about me—of my roots, of my background, of my language! They didn't like the qualities that made me different—only the ones that I had adapted from them. I sat down at my desk and released my frustrations and realizations. I wrote about the dream that Martin Luther King Jr. had, and how we are still struggling with issues of race and equality. I finally understood how Martin Luther King Jr.'s mission was similar to my own. Through my essay, I wanted the reader to feel emotions that they never allowed themselves to experience, and if that included being uncomfortable, so be it. I wanted to be so brutally honest that everyone, including myself, would have to ask themselves, "Have I ever treated someone in a manner less than humane? Have I denied someone else of their heritage to make myself more comfortable?"

I spent days and nights writing my essay with the little knowledge that I had gained in 18 years. The essay could only be a page long, but I made sure that every word and phrase counted. I knew that I had accomplished my goal when people from different racial and ethnic backgrounds found themselves as both the giver and receiver of prejudice after reading my essay. Some, however, refused to accept that racism is an issue that people need to deal with on a daily basis. I often heard, "Oh, Eileen. You're reading too much out of the situation.

Not everyone is a racist!" I must agree, not everyone is a racist; but we are all still responsible for how we treat others and respond to their life experiences.

Writing this essay was the first step in reevaluating who I really wanted to become, as well as in helping me accept and love the small things that I can never change. I had to force myself to be objective about my own insecurities and weaknesses when it came to racial issues. It is considerably easier to find flaws in others, but acknowledging and fixing these flaws in yourself is an incredibly difficult, yet empowering, experience. I became more accepting of other cultures different from my own. It also helped me replant the roots that I had tried to tear from my foundation in hopes of being "normal." The most beautiful lesson for me, however, is that through writing, whether it be poetry, essays, or just fragments, you can completely indulge in every aspect of what it is to be you. You can portray yourself in any light, in any way, and feel every emotion that comes with self-discovery. ■

Responding to Reading

1. In paragraph 2, Montalvo describes the kinds of writing not valued in her school. What are they? Why is this significant?

2. What function does writing the Martin Luther King, Jr., essay serve for Montalvo? How is this similar to or different from most school writing?

3. What is the main claim embedded in the essay? Where and how is it expressed?

4. Consider Montalvo's essay in relation to the bell hooks text. Does writing serve similar purposes for Montalvo as it does for hooks? If so, in what particular ways?

Excerpt: Mike Rose, I *Just Wanna Be Average*

Mike Rose is a professor at UCLA who is particularly interested in the factors that help and hinder student learning. Rose has published widely on literacy, schooling, and education, and the following selection is from his widely acclaimed book Lives on the Boundary.

It took two buses to get to Our Lady of Mercy. The first started deep in South Los Angeles and caught me at midpoint. The second drifted through neighborhoods with trees, parks, big lawns, and lots of flowers. The rides were long but were livened up by a group of South L.A. veterans whose parents also thought that Hope had set up shop in the west end of the county. There was Christy Biggars, who, at sixteen, was dealing and was, according to rumor, a pimp as well. There were Bill Cobb and Johnny Gonzales, grease-pencil artists extraordi- naire, who left Nembutal-enhanced swirls of "Cobb" and "Johnny" on the cor- rugated walls of the bus. And then there was Tyrrell Wilson. Tyrrell was the coolest kid I knew. He ran the dozens like a metric halfback, laid down a rap that outrhymed and outpointed Cobb, whose rap was good but not great—the curse of a moderately soulful kid trapped in white skin. But it was Cobb who would sneak a radio onto the bus, and thus underwrote his patter with Little Richard, Fats Domino, Chuck Berry, the Coasters, and Ernie K. Doe's mother-in- law, an awful woman who was "sent from down below." And so it was that Christy and Cobb and Johnny G. and Tyrrell and I and assorted others picked up along the way passed our days in the back of the bus, a funny mix brought to- gether by geography and parental desire.

Entrance to school brings with it forms and releases and assessments. Mercy relied on a series of tests, mostly the Stanford-Binet, for placement, and some- how the results of my tests got confused with those of another student named Rose. The other Rose apparently didn't do very well, for I was placed in the vo- cational track, a euphemism for the bottom level. Neither I nor my parents real- ized what this meant. We had no sense that Business Math, Typing, and English–Level D were dead ends. The current spate of reports on the schools crit- icizes parents for not involving themselves in the education of their children. But how would someone like Tommy Rose, with his two years of Italian schooling, know what to ask? And what sort of pressure could an exhausted waitress apply? The error went undetected, and I remained in the vocational track for two years. What a place.

My homeroom was supervised by Brother Dill, a troubled and unstable man who also taught freshman English. When his class drifted away from him, which was often, his voice would rise in paranoid accusations, and occasionally he would lose control and shake or smack us. I hadn't been there two months when one of his brisk, face-turning slaps had my glasses sliding down the aisle. Physical education was also pretty harsh. Our teacher was a stubby ex-lineman who had played old-time pro ball in the Midwest. He routinely had us grabbing our ankles to receive his stinging paddle across our butts. He did that, he said, to make men of us. "Rose," he bellowed on our first encounter; me standing geeky in line in my baggy shorts. " 'Rose'? What the hell kind of name is that?"

"Italian, sir," I squeaked.

"Italian! Ho. Rose, do you know the sound a bag of shit makes when it hits the wall?"

"No, sir."

"Wop!"

Sophomore English was taught by Mr. Mitropetros. He was a large, bejeweled man who managed the parking lot at the Shrine Auditorium. He would crow and preen and list for us the stars he'd brushed against. We'd ask questions and glance knowingly and snicker, and all that fueled the poor guy to brag some more. Parking cars was his night job. He had little training in English, so his lesson plan for his day work had us reading the district's required text, *Julius Caesar*, aloud for the semester. We'd finished the play way before the twenty weeks was up, so he'd have us switch parts again and again and start again: Dave Snyder, the fastest guy at Mercy, muscling through Caesar to the breathless squeals of Calpurnia, as interpreted by Steve Fusco, a surfer who owned the school's most envied paneled wagon. Week ten and Dave and Steve would take on new roles, as would we all, and render a water-logged Cassius and a Brutus that are beyond my powers of description.

Spanish I—taken in the second year—fell into the hands of a new recruit. Mr. Montez was a tiny man, slight, five foot six at the most, soft-spoken and delicate. Spanish was a particularly rowdy class, and Mr. Montez was as prepared for it as a doily maker at a hammer throw. He would tap his pencil to a room in which Steve Fusco was propelling spitballs from his heavy lips, in which Mike Dweetz was taunting Billy Hawk, a half-Indian, half-Spanish, reed-thin, quietly explosive boy. The vocational track at Our Lady of Mercy mixed kids traveling in from South L.A. with South Bay surfers and a few Slavs and Chicanos from the harbors of San Pedro. This was a dangerous miscellany: surfers and hodads and South-Central blacks all ablaze to the metronomic tapping of Hector Montez's pencil.

One day Billy lost it. Out of the corner of my eye I saw him strike out with his right arm and catch Dweetz across the neck. Quick as a spasm, Dweetz was out of his seat, scattering desks, cracking Billy on the side of the head, right behind the eye. Snyder and Fusco and others broke it up, but the room felt hot and close and naked. Mr. Montez's tenuous authority was finally ripped to shreds, and I think everyone felt a little strange about that. The charade was over, and when it came down to it, I don't think any of the kids really wanted it to end this way. They had pushed and pushed and bullied their way into a freedom that both scared and embarrassed them.

Students will float to the mark you set. I and the others in the vocational classes were bobbing in pretty shallow water. Vocational education has aimed at increasing the economic opportunities of students who do not do well in our schools. Some serious programs succeed in doing that, and through exceptional teachers—like Mr. Gross in *Horace's Compromise*—students learn to develop hypotheses and troubleshoot, reason through a problem, and communicate effectively—the true job skills. The vocational track, however, is most often a place for those who are just not making it, a dumping ground for the disaffected. There were a few teachers who worked hard at education; young Brother

Slattery, for example, combined a stern voice with weekly quizzes to try to pass along to us a skeletal outline of world history. But mostly the teachers had no idea of how to engage the imaginations of us kids who were scuttling along at the bottom of the pond.

And the teachers would have needed some inventiveness, for none of us was groomed for the classroom. It wasn't just that I didn't know things—didn't know how to simplify algebraic fractions, couldn't identify different kinds of clauses, bungled Spanish translations—but that I had developed various faulty and inadequate ways of doing algebra and making sense of Spanish. Worse yet, the years of defensive tuning out in elementary school had given me a way to escape quickly while seeming at least half alert. During my time in Voc. Ed., I developed further into a mediocre student and a somnambulant problem solver, and that affected the subjects I did have the wherewithal to handle: I detested Shakespeare; I got bored with history. My attention flitted here and there. I fooled around in class and read my books indifferently—the intellectual equivalent of playing with your food. I did what I had to do to get by, and I did it with half a mind.

But I did learn things about people and eventually came into my own socially. I liked the guys in Voc. Ed. Growing up where I did, I understood and admired physical prowess, and there was an abundance of muscle here. There was Dave Snyder, a sprinter and halfback of true quality. Dave's ability and his quick wit gave him a natural appeal, and he was welcome in any clique, though he always kept a little independent. He enjoyed acting the fool and could care less about studies, but he possessed a certain maturity and never caused the faculty much trouble. It was a testament to his independence that he included me among his friends—I eventually went out for track, but I was no jock. Owing to the Latin alphabet and a dearth of *R*s and *S*s, Snyder sat behind Rose, and we started exchanging one-liners and became friends.

There was Ted Richard, a much-touted Little League pitcher. He was chunky and had a baby face and came to Our Lady of Mercy as a seasoned street fighter. Ted was quick to laugh and he had a loud, jolly laugh, but when he got angry he'd smile a little smile, the kind that simply raises the corner of the mouth a quarter of an inch. For those who knew, it was an eerie signal. Those who didn't found themselves in big trouble, for Ted was very quick. He loved to carry on what we would come to call philosophical discussions: What is courage? Does God exist? He also loved words, enjoyed picking up big ones like *salubrious* and *equivocal* and using them in our conversations—laughing at himself as the word hit a chuckhole rolling off his tongue. Ted didn't do all that well in school—baseball and parties and testing the courage he'd speculated about took up his time. His textbooks were *Argosy* and *Field and Stream*, whatever newspapers he'd find on the bus stop—from the *Daily Worker* to pornography—

conversations with uncles or hobos or businessmen he'd meet in a coffee shop, *The Old Man and the Sea*. With hindsight, I can see that Ted was developing into one of those rough-hewn intellectuals whose sources are a mix of the learned and the apocryphal, whose discussions are both assured and sad.

And then there was Ken Harvey. Ken was good-looking in a puffy way and had a full and oily ducktail and was a car enthusiast . . . a hodad. One day in religion class, he said the sentence that turned out to be one of the most memorable of the hundreds of thousands I heard in those Voc. Ed. years. We were talking about the parable of the talents, about achievement, working hard, doing the best you can do, blah-blah-blah, when the teacher called on the restive Ken Harvey for an opinion. Ken thought about it, but just for a second, and said (with studied, minimal affect), "I just wanna be average." That woke me up. Average? Who wants to be average? Then the athletes chimed in with the clichés that make you want to laryngectomize them, and the exchange became a platitudinous melee. At the time, I thought Ken's assertion was stupid, and I wrote him off. But his sentence has stayed with me all these years, and I think I am finally coming to understand it.

Ken Harvey was gasping for air. School can be a tremendously disorienting place. No matter how bad the school, you're going to encounter notions that don't fit with the assumptions and beliefs that you grew up with—maybe you'll hear these dissonant notions from teachers, maybe from the other students, and maybe you'll read them. You'll also be thrown in with all kinds of kids from all kinds of backgrounds, and that can be unsettling—this is especially true in places of rich ethnic and linguistic mix, like the L.A. basin. You'll see a handful of students far excel you in courses that sound exotic and that are only in the curriculum of the elite: French, physics, trigonometry. And all this is happening while you're trying to shape an identity, your body is changing, and your emotions are running wild. If you're a working-class kid in the vocational track, the options you'll have to deal with this will be constrained in certain ways: you're defined by your school as "slow"; you're placed in a curriculum that isn't designed to liberate you but to occupy you, or, if you're lucky, train you, though the training is for work the society does not esteem; other students are picking up the cues from your school and your curriculum and interacting with you in particular ways. If you're a kid like Ted Richard, you turn your back on all this and let your mind roam where it may. But youngsters like Ted are rare. What Ken and so many others do is protect themselves from such suffocating madness by taking on with a vengeance the identity implied in the vocational track. Reject the confusion and frustration by openly defining yourself as the Common Joe. Champion the average. Rely on your own good sense. Fuck this bullshit. Bullshit, of course, is everything you—and the others—fear is beyond you: books, essays, tests, academic scrambling, complexity, scientific reasoning, philosophical inquiry.

The tragedy is that you have to twist the knife in your own gray matter to make this defense work. You'll have to shut down, have to reject intellectual stimuli or diffuse them with sarcasm, have to cultivate stupidity, have to convert boredom from a malady into a way of confronting the world. Keep your vocabulary simple, act stoned when you're not or act more stoned than you are, flaunt ignorance, materialize your dreams. It is a powerful and effective defense—it neutralizes the insult and the frustration of being a vocational kid and, when perfected, it drives teachers up the wall, a delightful secondary effect. But like all strong magic, it exacts a price.

My own deliverance from the Voc. Ed. world began with sophomore biology. Every student, college prep to vocational, had to take biology, and unlike the other courses, the same person taught all sections. When teaching the vocational group, Brother Clint probably slowed down a bit or omitted a little of the fundamental biochemistry, but he used the same book and more or less the same syllabus across the board. If one class got tough, he could get tougher. He was young and powerful and very handsome, and looks and physical strength were high currency. No one gave him any trouble.

I was pretty bad at the dissecting table, but the lectures and the textbook were interesting; plastic overlays that, with each turned page, peeled away skin, then veins and muscle, then organs, down to the very bones that Brother Clint, pointer in hand, would tap out on our hanging skeleton. Dave Snyder was in big trouble, for the study of life—versus the living of it—was sticking in his craw. We worked out a code for our multiple-choice exams. He'd poke me in the back: once for the answer under *A*, twice for *B*, and so on; and when he'd hit the right one, I'd look up to the ceiling as though I were lost in thought. Poke: cytoplasm. Poke, poke: methane. Poke, poke, poke: William Harvey. Poke, poke, poke, poke: islets of Langerhans. This didn't work out perfectly, but Dave passed the course, and I mastered the dreamy look of a guy on a record jacket. And something else happened. Brother Clint puzzled over this Voc. Ed. kid who was racking up 98s and 99s on his tests. He checked the school's records and discovered the error. He recommended that I begin my junior year in the College Prep program. According to all I've read since, such a shift, as one report put it, is virtually impossible. Kids at that level rarely cross tracks. The telling thing is how chancy both my placement into and exit from Voc. Ed. was; neither I nor my parents had anything to do with it. I lived in one world during spring semester, and when I came back to school in the fall, I was living in another.

Switching to College Prep was a mixed blessing. I was an erratic student. I was undisciplined. And I hadn't caught onto the rules of the game: why work hard in a class that didn't grab my fancy? I was also hopelessly behind in math. Chemistry was hard; toying with my chemistry set years before hadn't prepared me for the chemist's equations. Fortunately, the priest who taught both chemistry and second-year algebra was also the school's athletic director. Membership on the track team covered me; I knew I wouldn't get lower than a C. U.S. history was taught pretty well, and I did okay. But civics was taken over by a football coach who had trouble reading the textbook aloud—and reading aloud was the centerpiece of his pedagogy. College Prep at Mercy was certainly an improvement over the vocational program—at least it carried some status—but the social science curriculum was weak, and the mathematics and physical sciences were simply beyond me. I had a miserable quantitative background and ended up copying some assignments and finessing the rest as best I could. Let me try to explain how it feels to see again and again material you should once have learned but didn't.

You are given a problem. It requires you to simplify algebraic fractions or to multiply expressions containing square roots. You know this is pretty basic material because you've seen it for years. Once a teacher took some time with you, and you learned how to carry out these operations. Simple versions, anyway. But that was a year or two or more in the past, and these are more complex versions, and now you're not sure. And this, you keep telling yourself, is ninth- or even eighth-grade stuff.

Next it's a word problem. This is also old hat. The basic elements are as familiar as story characters: trains speeding so many miles per hour or shadows of buildings angling so many degrees. Maybe you know enough, have sat through enough explanations, to be able to begin setting up the problem: "If one train is going this fast . . . " or "This shadow is really one line of a triangle . . . " Then: "Let's see . . . " "How did Jones do this?" "Hmmmm." "No." "No, that won't work." Your attention wavers. You wonder about other things: a football game, a dance, that cute new checker at the market. You try to focus on the problem again. You scribble on paper for a while, but the tension wins out and your attention flits elsewhere. You crumple the paper and begin daydreaming to ease the frustration.

The particulars will vary, but in essence this is what a number of students go through, especially those in so-called remedial classes. They open their textbooks and see once again the familiar and impenetrable formulas and diagrams and terms that have stumped them for years. There is no excitement here. *No* excitement. Regardless of what the teacher says, this is not a new challenge. There is, rather, embarrassment and frustration and, not surprisingly, some anger in being reminded once again of long-standing inadequacies. No wonder so many students finally attribute their difficulties to something inborn, organic: "That part of my brain just doesn't work." Given the troubling histories many of these students have, it's miraculous that any of them can lift the shroud of hopelessness sufficiently to make deliverance from these classes possible.

Through this entire period, my father's health was deteriorating with cruel momentum. His arteriosclerosis progressed to the point where a simple nick on his shin wouldn't heal. Eventually it ulcerated and widened. Lou Minton would come by daily to change the dressing. We tried renting an oscillating bed—which we placed in the front room—to force blood through the constricted arteries in my father's legs. The bed hummed through the night, moving in place to ward off the inevitable. The ulcer continued to spread, and the doctors finally had to amputate. My grandfather had lost his leg in a stockyard accident. Now my father too was crippled. His convalescence was slow but steady, and the doctors placed him in the Santa Monica Rehabilitation Center, a sun-bleached building that opened out onto the warm spray of the Pacific. The place gave him some strength and some color and some training in walking with an artificial leg. He did pretty well for a year or so until he slipped and broke his hip. He was confined to a wheelchair after that, and the confinement contributed to the diminishing of his body and spirit.

I am holding a picture of him. He is sitting in his wheelchair and smiling at the camera. The smile appears forced, unsteady, seems to quaver, though it is frozen in silver nitrate. He is in his mid-sixties and looks eighty. Late in my junior year, he had a stroke and never came out of the resulting coma. After that, I would see him only in dreams, and to this day that is how I join him. Sometimes the dreams are sad and grisly and primal: my father lying in a bed soaked with his suppuration, holding me, rocking me. But sometimes the dreams bring him back to me healthy: him talking to me on an empty street, or buying some pictures to decorate our old house, or transformed somehow into someone strong and adept with tools and the physical.

Jack MacFarland couldn't have come into my life at a better time. My father was dead, and I had logged up too many years of scholastic indifference. Mr. MacFarland had a master's degree from Columbia and decided, at twenty-six, to find a little school and teach his heart out. He never took any credentialing courses, couldn't bear to, he said, so he had to find employment in a private system. He ended up at Our Lady of Mercy teaching five sections of senior English. He was a beatnik who was born too late. His teeth were stained, he tucked his sorry tie in between the third and fourth buttons of his shirt, and his pants were chronically wrinkled. At first, we couldn't believe this guy, thought he slept in his car. But within no time, he had us so startled with work that we didn't much worry about where he slept or if he slept at all. We wrote three or four essays a month. We read a book every two to three weeks, starting with the *Iliad* and ending up with Hemingway. He gave us a quiz on the reading every other day. He brought a prep school curriculum to Mercy High.

MacFarland's lectures were crafted, and as he delivered them he would pace the room jiggling a piece of chalk in his cupped hand, using it to scribble on the board the names of all the writers and philosophers and plays and novels he was weaving into his discussion. He asked questions often, raised everything from

Zeno's paradox to the repeated last line of Frost's "Stopping by Woods on a Snowy Evening." He slowly and carefully built up our knowledge of Western intellectual history—with facts, with connections, with speculations. We learned about Greek philosophy, about Dante, the Elizabethan world view, the Age of Reason, existentialism. He analyzed poems with us, had us reading sections from John Ciardi's *How Does a Poem Mean?*, making a potentially difficult book accessible with his own explanations. We gave oral reports on poems Ciardi didn't cover. We imitated the styles of Conrad, Hemingway, and *Time* magazine. We wrote and talked, wrote and talked. The man immersed us in language.

Even MacFarland's barbs were literary. If Jim Fitzsimmons, hung over and irritable, tried to smart-ass him, he'd rejoin with a flourish that would spark the indomitable Skip Madison—who'd lost his front teeth in a hapless tackle—to flick his tongue through the gap and opine, "good chop," drawing out the single "o" in stinging indictment. Jack MacFarland, this tobacco-stained intellectual, brandished linguistic weapons of a kind I hadn't encountered before. Here was this *egghead*, for God's sake, keeping some pretty difficult people in line. And from what I heard, Mike Dweetz and Steve Fusco and all the notorious Voc. Ed. crowd settled down as well when MacFarland took the podium. Though a lot of guys groused in the schoolyard, it just seemed that giving trouble to this particular teacher was a silly thing to do. Tomfoolery, not to mention assault, had no place in the world he was trying to create for us, and instinctively everyone knew that. If nothing else, we all recognized MacFarland's considerable intelligence and respected the hours he put into his work. It came to this: the troublemaker would look foolish rather than daring. Even Jim Fitzsimmons was reading *On the Road* and turning his incipient alcoholism to literary ends.

There were some lives that were already beyond Jack MacFarland's ministrations, but mine was not. I started reading again as I hadn't since elementary school. I would go into our gloomy little bedroom or sit at the dinner table while, on the television, Danny McShane was paralyzing Mr. Moto with the atomic drop, and work slowly back through *Heart of Darkness*, trying to catch the words in Conrad's sentences. I certainly was not MacFarland's best student; most of the other guys in College Prep, even my fellow slackers, had better backgrounds than I did. But I worked very hard, for MacFarland had hooked me. He tapped my old interest in reading and creating stories. He gave me a way to feel special by using my mind. And he provided a role model that wasn't shaped on physical prowess alone, and something inside me that I wasn't quite aware of responded to that. Jack MacFarland established a literacy club, to borrow a phrase of Frank Smith's, and invited me—invited all of us—to join.

There's been a good deal of research and speculation suggesting that the acknowledgment of school performance with extrinsic rewards—smiling faces, stars, numbers, grades—diminishes the intrinsic satisfaction children experience by engaging in reading or writing or problem solving. While it's certainly true that we've created an educational system that encourages our best and brightest to become cynical grade collectors and, in general, have developed an obsession with evaluation and assessment, I must tell you that venal though it may have been, I loved getting good grades from MacFarland. I now know how subjective grades can be, but then they came tucked in the back of essays like bits of scientific data, some sort of spectroscopic readout that said, objectively and publicly, that I had made something of value. I suppose I'd been mediocre for too long and enjoyed a public redefinition. And I suppose the workings of my mind, such as they were, had been private for too long. My linguistic play moved into the world; . . . these papers with their circled, red B-pluses and A-minuses linked my mind to something outside it. I carried them around like a club emblem.

One day in the December of my senior year, Mr. MacFarland asked me where I was going to go to college. I hadn't thought much about it. Many of the students I teach today spent their last year in high school with a physics text in one hand and the Stanford catalog in the other, but I wasn't even aware of what "entrance requirements" were. My folks would say that they wanted me to go to college and be a doctor, but I don't know how seriously I ever took that; it seemed a sweet thing to say, a bit of supportive family chatter, like telling a gangly daughter she's graceful. The reality of higher education wasn't in my scheme of things: no one in the family had gone to college; only two of my uncles had completed high school. I figured I'd get a night job and go to the local junior college because I knew that Snyder and Company were going there to play ball. But I hadn't even prepared for that. When I finally said, "I don't know," MacFarland looked down at me—I was seated in his office—and said, "Listen, you can write."

My grades stank. I had A's in biology and a handful of B's in a few English and social science classes. All the rest were C's—or worse. MacFarland said I would do well in his class and laid down the law about doing well in the others. Still, the record for my first three years wouldn't have been acceptable to any four-year school. To nobody's surprise, I was turned down flat by USC and UCLA. But Jack MacFarland was on the case. He had received his bachelor's degree from Loyola University, so he made calls to old professors and talked to somebody in admissions and wrote me a strong letter. Loyola finally accepted me as a probationary student. I would be on trial for the first year, and if I did okay, I would be granted regular status. MacFarland also intervened to get me a loan, for I could never have afforded a private college without it. Four more years of religion classes and four more years of boys at one school, girls at another. But at least I was going to college. Amazing.

In my last semester of high school, I elected a special English course fashioned by Mr. MacFarland, and it was through this elective that there arose at Mercy a fledgling literati. Art Mitz, the editor of the school newspaper and a very smart guy, was the kingpin. He was joined by me and by Mark Dever, a quiet boy who wrote beautifully and who would die before he was forty. MacFarland occasionally invited us to his apartment, and those visits became the high point of our apprenticeship: we'd clamp on our training wheels and drive to his salon.

He lived in a cramped and cluttered place near the airport, tucked away in the kind of building that architectural critic Reyner Banham calls a *dingbat*. Books were all over: stacked, piled, tossed, and crated, underlined and dog eared, well worn and new. Cigarette ashes crusted with coffee in saucers or spilling over the sides of motel ashtrays. The little bedroom had, along two of its walls, bricks and boards loaded with notes, magazines, and oversized books. The kitchen joined the living room, and there was a stack of German newspapers under the sink. I had never seen anything like it: a great flophouse of language furnished by City Lights and Café le Metro. I read every title. I flipped through paperbacks and scanned jackets and memorized names: Gogol, *Finnegans Wake*, Djuna Barnes, Jackson Pollock, *A Coney Island of the Mind*, F. O. Matthiessen's *American Renaissance*, all sorts of Freud, *Troubled Sleep*, Man Ray, *The Education of Henry Adams*, Richard Wright, *Film as Art*, William Butler Yeats, Marguerite Duras, *Redburn, A Season in Hell, Kapital*. On the cover of Alain-Fournier's *The Wanderer* was an Edward Gorey drawing of a young man on a road winding into dark trees. By the hotplate sat a strange Kafka novel called *Amerika*, in which an adolescent hero crosses the Atlantic to find the Nature Theater of Oklahoma. Art and Mark would be talking about a movie or the school newspaper, and I would be consuming my English teacher's library. It was heady stuff. I felt like a Pop Warner athlete on steroids.

Art, Mark, and I would buy stogies and triangulate from MacFarland's apartment to the Cinema, which now shows X-rated films but was then L.A.'s premier art theater, and then to the musty Cherokee Bookstore in Hollywood to hobnob with beatnik homosexuals—smoking, drinking bourbon and coffee, and trying out awkward phrases we'd gleaned from our mentor's bookshelves. I was happy and precocious and a little scared as well, for Hollywood Boulevard was thick with a kind of decadence that was foreign to the South Side. After the Cherokee, we would head back to the security of MacFarland's apartment, slaphappy with hipness.

Let me be the first to admit that there was a good deal of adolescent passion in this embrace of the avant-garde: self-absorption, sexually charged pedantry, an elevation of the odd and abandoned. Still it was a time during which I absorbed an awful lot of information: long lists of titles, images from expressionist paintings, new wave shibboleths, snippets of philosophy, and names that read like Steve Fusco's misspellings—Goethe, Nietzsche, Kierkegaard. Now this is hardly the stuff of deep understanding. But it was an introduction, a phrase book, a Baedeker to a vocabulary of ideas, and it felt good at the time to know all these words. With hindsight I realize how layered and important that knowledge was.

It enabled me to do things in the world. I could browse bohemian bookstores in far-off, mysterious Hollywood; I could go to the Cinema and see events through the lenses of European directors; and, most of all, I could share an evening, talk that talk, with Jack MacFarland, the man I most admired at the time. Knowledge was becoming a bonding agent. Within a year or two, the persona of the disaffected hipster would prove too cynical, too alienated to last. But for a time it was new and exciting: it provided a critical perspective on society, and it allowed me to act as though I were living beyond the limiting boundaries of South Vermont Street.   ■

Responding to Reading

1. How does Rose use description to make his narrative come alive? Pick two specific places where you find his descriptions of people and/or events lively and engaging.

2. How does the vocational curriculum shape the actions and attitudes of Rose and his fellow students? Note a few examples and then look for patterns.

3. In paragraph 11, Rose writes, "Students will float to the mark you set." What does he mean by this? What are the implications of such thinking for the "tracking" systems found in many high schools?

4. How does Rose's own view of schooling and writing change? Map out the "before" view, the turning point, and the "after" view. Through this personal narrative, what is Rose trying to convey about larger issues of learning and schooling?

5. How does Rose mix storytelling with analysis?

Student Essay: Pat McMurtray,
Problem Child 3: My Version

When he wrote this essay, Pat McMurtray was a first-year student planning to major in architecture. The names of people and places in this essay have been changed.

Work can be tough, we all know that. And without purpose, work can be impossible to do. I had always thought that the toughest work was schoolwork, but I was wrong. The toughest work for me was teaching the schoolwork that even I wouldn't want to do. Luckily for me, I got the opportunity to find purpose in this task and it not only became bearable, but also fun.

At Rockland High School we had to do community service hours every year. In my senior year we got a month off, so that we could volunteer full time at a local charity or community center. I chose to work at the Stiller Center, a school for special children. Not just for special children, but for "problem children." The truth is that the kids *had* problems, not were problems. The boys were from broken homes and had parents in jail or rehab. Many of them had been beaten or molested or had seen their parents beat each other. Still others had complex mental disorders for which they had to take specific medication. They had special workers to keep an eye on eight-year-olds who were so traumatized that they needed this "suicide watch." The lists of problems, disorders, and issues are too long to list. I was told that I was not allowed to defend myself; some of the boys were really violent. I was told not to bring anything from the outside that would bother the children because I could start a riot. Most of these boys were boarders at the school, with drill sergeants for teachers; the school was more like a prison than any school I had ever been to.

I was afraid to go to the Stiller Center. I was worried that these kids were going to end up like all of the stories that I had heard about. It was terrifying to walk into the giant corridor that was blocked first by a code-lock door and then by a giant metal detector. The halls were filled with the screams of children. It sounded more like a haunted house than a school to me; wails and moans of temper-tantrums rang through the halls. I saw boys being restrained for misbehavior; the teachers had them pinned to the ground or wrapped up in a corner to keep them from hurting themselves or others. Security was so tight that I had to get a picture ID to be allowed on the premises without a guide. It felt like I was walking through a prison. I knew as soon as I walked into Mrs. Molloy's classroom that I was in for an uphill battle. All of their little eyes were on me, looking for a sign of weakness. The first week was really tough, as I was constantly fighting the boys, trying to get them to do their work and behave. I told them to study and they'd laugh, I'd work with them but I'd do all the work, I bribed them and all they did was fill in the blanks so they could get credit and candy, but they never did any real work.

I was surprised to find a woman like Mrs. Molloy in a place like this. She was the sweetest, most unintimidating person in the world, not like all the other "wardens." She was the picture perfect little old lady. She gave the little boys candy and was always nice to them no matter what had happened. The odd thing was that the boys actually had respect for her, more so than for the other teachers who were stern. Instead of the utter defiance in the other rooms, the boys just seemed indifferent towards their work. The boys did not get much done in her classroom. Most of the time they just caused trouble; their days were spent throwing gummy bears at each other and watching tapes of Barney. It was odd that no one in the center was worried about the children misbehaving in her room; every other room had an extra person just to restrain the children. Mrs. Molloy just had a way with the children.

I, however, had to try and find a way with the children. To me all the boys were troublemakers. Corey was the biggest troublemaker of them all. This scrappy little black kid walked around like he was the king of the world. No one seemed to recognize his self-proclaimed authority. He never got to have the "party time," the fun break that all the kids get on Fridays, because he was never good enough during the week. I was warned by the entire faculty to watch out because he was a little con man and would try to use me if he could. Everyone kept a close eye on Corey. There was never a moment in his day where he was alone. He stole extra candy and hid everyone's books. He took all the toys and wouldn't let anyone else play with them. Try as I might, it looked impossible for me to control Corey. I tried to be nice, but he took me as weak. I tried to be tough, but he saw me as the authority and shut himself off.

It took me two weeks before I finally found a way to get Corey's attention and respect: basketball. Corey loved basketball and hadn't been beaten by anyone in the entire school for over a year. One day we played and I was beating him badly when I took a dive and let him win. For the rest of that day he was bragging to everyone. But after everyone had gone home or to the dorms he said, "That was cool. Nobody ever done something likes that for me. Thanks bud!" And wouldn't you know it, but the ringleader of all the "problem kids" gave me the biggest hug I ever had. I never felt so important in my entire life. With thirty seconds of conversation Corey had put all of the last week's fears and worries a galaxy away. From that instant I knew that I had chosen the right place to volunteer and that I was going to make the most of every minute that I was going to spend there. Mrs. Molloy told me later that Corey's dad had been in jail for eight years and hadn't talked to his son since he was one and a half. I knew what she was trying to say. That's when it all hit me. These kids needed me.

From that day on things were different. I was done trying to impress a bunch of nine and ten year olds—no, I was there to make a difference, make their lives fun, and be a good role model. From there on out I stayed late and came early. I skipped breaks and volunteered for extra work, just so I could be with these guys. I volunteered to take them to the library, and I gave up my lunch break to eat with them. The kids found a new favorite game: human monkey bars and I was the only toy they needed for it. The first week lasted forever, but the next three went by all too fast. I don't think I'll ever forget the great bunch of kids that I met there. To me Corey, Brian, Ollie, Alan, and Dominic became part of my family. In fact, this Christmas break I plan on going back to see them all.

Everyone has problems, including the kids. I had a problem too, but with the boys' help I fixed mine. I can still see all of their faces and the giant poster of all their handprints waving goodbye. It brings a tear to my eye. I finally realized how important role models are and how important it is for me to set an example, especially in the toughest of situations. Saying goodbye to those kids was one of the toughest things I have ever done. Now I feel like I'm always going to be missing a small part of my family. ∎

Responding to Reading

1. In this essay the narrator undergoes a change of attitude. Locate the most important turning point(s) in the narrative.

2. Notice how the writer uses colorful details to help describe his characters. Find two or three sentences that do a particularly good job of helping readers to see and hear characters.

3. This essay plays on multiple meanings of the word *problem*. How many different "problems" are represented, and how does the assigning of "problem" status change in the course of the narrative?

Student Essay: Allison Garber, *Faith Like Small Children*

Allison Garber was a first semester freshman majoring in Liberal Studies at Azusa Pacific University when she wrote this essay for a Freshman Writing Seminar on Community Service Learning. She plans to pursue a career in elementary school teaching. The names of people and places in the essay have been changed.

Getting up at six-thirty every morning was not my idea of the perfect summer. But I loved that as soon as I got to work, bunches of kids would jump on my back, hanging from every part of my body. They would tell me how much they love me, and the love I received from these kids is what made my whole summer worthwhile. For nine weeks of my twelve-week summer, I worked on staff at Cedar Crest Day Camp. My job was not an easy task. It wasn't fun working twelve hours a day with no breaks. The horrific working conditions included intense heat, screaming kids, messy clean-ups, and the few angry parents who just had to speak with you at the end of your exhausting day. Constantly, friends and family would ask me why I did it, and I would tell them all the same thing—simply because I love it.

Have you even been friends with a seven-year-old? I'm talking about a true friendship. I came to the point where these kids became more than just kids, but they became real people. I had never come to know such wonderful people who were so happy and bold in their faith. But I didn't learn this all at once, and I didn't just jump into relationships with these kids. It was a process that started with just one special child: Kelsey Lane.

It was seven-thirty AM, week three of camp, and I was exhausted from the previous two weeks. I managed to stumble in that morning with a smile on my face and a positive attitude to start another week of camp. After our regular Monday morning meeting, the rest of the staff and I made our way to the gym to play with the kids before camp officially started.

I walked around the noisy gym; I looked around at the hundred and thirty kids. The rambunctious children were running, chasing other kids; some were even chasing staff members. There were balls flying through the air, kids screaming, and kids having fun. Some kids sat along the side of the gym walls playing cards and other games, and some were crying as they said good-bye to their parents. That morning I walked past the children and observed all I saw. I was taking it all in, as I had never been around so many children with so many different personalities. But as I looked along the gym wall, one child stood out to me—it was Kelsey.

I watched a group of girls playing a card game, and one of the girls stood up in the middle of the game. Her hair was blonde and tangled, but through all of the tangles it still looked beautiful. She began to wiggle as she stood, and red lips started to slowly open. She began to dance around singing a silly song with no meaning whatsoever. You could hear her sweet laughter throughout the entire gym. Kelsey's smile beamed so brightly you could feel the joy inside her heart. I instantly knew that this girl was different. That particular week I happened to be in charge of the seven-year-olds and Kelsey had been placed in my group.

That afternoon I took my group into a Sunday school room where we would have our daily unit time. Our group performed the regular activities as everyone went around in a circle saying their name.

When it was Kelsey's turn, she stood up and with her bright smile and amazing glow, she addressed the other children and said, "Hi! My name is Kelsey Lane and I am seven years old. I am a Christian and Jesus lives inside of my heart. He is with me all the time. He died on the cross for me because he loves me and he wants me to go to heaven and be with him. I want all of you to know that he died for you too, because he loves you."

Astonished, I looked at the little girl and replied, "Kelsey, that is so wonderful. Can you share with the children how Jesus came into your heart?"

Kelsey's face began to grin as she proceeded to tell her story.

"Well, one day at Sunday school, my teacher asked us if we wanted Jesus to come into our heart. I really wanted him to, so we said a prayer."

Kelsey bowed her little head and closed her eyes. She folded her angelic hands and then began to pray.

"Dear Jesus, forgive me for my sins. I am sorry for all of the bad things I have done. Please come into my heart, because I love you. Amen."

The classroom was silent. We all looked at Kelsey in amazement, including me.

"Thank you so much for sharing, Kelsey. That was a beautiful prayer."

After Kelsey sat down, I took advantage of the time to share more about Christ with the kids.

That afternoon when camp was over, I was very tired and dirty, but when I got home I put all of my priorities aside and spent time with God. I began to think about my life, about the children, and especially about Kelsey. I began to imagine what it's like to be seven, in a room full of kids I don't know, but yet have the boldness to speak as greatly as Kelsey did. What would make this girl share her innocent faith and simple testimony with a room full of complete strangers? At the age of seven, this girl could do something that I have struggled with my entire life. That day when Kelsey was speaking, her words came out so naturally; she didn't force herself to share, but she wanted to. If was as if God was speaking through this seven-year-old girl. He was speaking not only to the kids, but to me as well.

The next few weeks Kelsey and I became very close. Kelsey was a girl that had fun everywhere she was, whether she was stuck on a three hour bus ride or walking around in one hundred and five degree weather at the zoo. This girl had no complaints, no matter what the situation was. She was one of the only children at day camp that I never saw cry. Not only did I become close to Kelsey, I got to know all of her friends as well. I have never met a group of girls so loving and accepting as these girls. They were absolutely amazing.

There were many kids I met this summer. Almost all of the children I liked, but there were others that I really grew to love. Kelsey was a child that truly changed something in me. She taught me how to fully be myself and hold nothing back. She taught me not to be afraid to share my faith. I learned to truly allow God to speak through me, and to trust in the words he gives me. Throughout the seven weeks I knew Kelsey, God truly used her in my life. He showed me that sometimes He wants us to be childlike, and to have faith like small children. ∎

Responding to Reading

1. How does the reader characterize herself and convey her perspective on the camp in the first paragraph? Compare this "old self" and "old perspective on camp" to the "new self" and "new perspective on camp" that emerges by the end of the essay.

2. Notice how the author uses direct quotations and dialogue in the middle section of the essay. What advantages does this have over simply summarizing the events and conversations?

3. Consider the role of religious faith in the author's personal development. In what ways does her faith change? What, for her, is the relationship of religious belief to daily work? Support your claims with specific passages from the essay.

4. In both this essay and in McMurtray's, children are central characters. What roles do they play in each narrator's growth?

Student Essay: Emily Martens, *Traveling Away from Everything Known*

When she wrote this essay, Emily Martens was a first-year student planning to major in art.

I was on a plane to California, enjoying my first commercial airplane flight, reading my magazine and gazing out from my window seat in luxurious comfort. Along with me were twelve fellow teenagers from my youth group and our four leaders who elected to travel to Mexico in order to minister to the children of Ensenada. Everyone was talking loudly and fidgeting, joking and laughing; excitement crackled in the air, barely contained. I had isolated myself from most of the assembly and sat silently staring at my tense reflection in the glass. I was out of place in our group. Even though there were a meager twelve of us, we had already sanctioned ourselves into cliques. Besides that growing awkwardness within the group, I didn't speak Spanish. Not many of the other individuals did either. We had our translator, Alistair, with us for that, but it still contributed to my sensation of uneasiness.

Eventually we landed and made it to the hotel. I tried not to focus on the discomfort, tried to take my mind off of it with the beautiful scenery around me. I had never seen anything like it before, dozens of palm trees reaching for the sky and their elegantly cascading fronds blowing in the cool ocean breeze. There were trees with delicate, purple flowers on them and dark, towering magnolias with their graceful, snowy-white blossoms. Vines of bougainvillea were everywhere, buds opening in the intense California sunshine. The sky was clear that morning as we started the long journey to the Baja Peninsula, traveling in two rented RVs. On the drive from Los Angeles, I had a lot of time to reflect on why I was actually on this trip. One may think, shouldn't I have done that before I decided to go on it? Truth to be told, I went because I've always had this curiosity about missions work. I had always wondered why we as churches feel we absolutely must change those people's minds. Was it ethical to change someone that was perfectly happy the way they were?

We crossed the border, but even before that, the poverty was staggering. You think you're going to be prepared for it, but you're not. There are little huts amid the dust and dirt, scattered like the sparse, brown shrubbery around them. Planks and boards were seemingly propped up against one another to form dwellings. Roofs were made of corrugated tin and doorways were covered with hanging cloths. The shacks were thrown together, and some of them were held up by miracles. Care hadn't been taken to make them presentable; there were no lawns in front, no beds of native flowers, no palm trees. Harsh land surrounded the shanties, broken only by the occasional clothesline. The ocean was right there, but nothing was green; it lapped against the barren shores continually in vain. The beaches were littered with people's garbage and waste, and the water was unhealthy to even swim in.

Finally, we reached Ensenada itself. It is set on a hill, and upon approach, I saw the boatyard with all of the gigantic, rusted cranes and immobile ships. I felt like they signified the town's potential and its inability to attain it. We began to drive through town, first viewing the nice tourist section. There were hotels and opulent restaurants with neon signs, the BMWs and Bentleys parked in the large lots designated for visitors by more than just the sign at the entrance. Tall, majestic palm trees lined the streets, along with gracious flowers bending low to the ground.

We gradually navigated the traffic, and drove through the rest of the town. It was like night and day. There were little, white houses strewn throughout the hills that made up the city itself. Little tin outbuildings were added on to a lot of them. Laundry was flapping in the breeze, and little children tossed around balls and jumped rope. Men stood around with their mustaches and hats pulled low, talking to each other. Squat palm trees interspersed the broken sidewalks. The RVs continued traveling until we reached our base, about five miles outside of town. To reach our camp, we had to drive on a rut-filled highway, and then down nothing more than two dusty tracks. The two tracks passed through the hills and even vineyards of sorts, and the hovels of those who tended them.

Early the next morning, we woke up to the cold sunshine, got dressed, and went into town to start our first day of vacation Bible school. We made it to the little church we were to use, and were greeted by a little, wrinkled Mexican. His faced cracked into a wide grin, displaying white teeth against his dark skin. His eyes lit up when they spied us, and I could almost feel the years melt off of his tired body. He didn't care that his church was falling down, that he was old, that we didn't speak Spanish; he was just happy to see us, glad that we might help him repair the church, and give the children a little break of sorts.

The little ones started gathering around the church building, dressed in clothes that were probably from the United States in the eighties. Their faces were beaming, their small, grubby hands reached for ours. They laughed at our inability to communicate, taking it in stride and overcoming that small, insignificant barrier quickly. They immediately began to play with us, jumping around and running in the streets and in front of the church. There was a pudgy little boy with dark, curly hair and a sweatshirt and sweatpants on. A little girl dressed in a simple cotton dress with her hair flowing down around her shoulders brought her jump rope. They didn't care about their social position the way kids in my school did when they were small, didn't care about who wore what, who got good grades, who was the best at kickball, that they had nothing compared with other people. They just found delight in their own existence, in simple little actions and games, eating snacks, making crafts, in everyday life. One day with these uncomplicated people was all it took to reshape things in my life that had been there for as long as I can remember.

These children grew up in the church, and would continue to grow up in the church after we left. They didn't need us to come in there and preach to them or save them. We entertained them momentarily with our stories, examples, lessons, crafts, games and songs. We shared our lives with these children, but they remained as happily unaffected and innocent as before we came. They were as secure in their own religion as anyone can be at that age.

I looked at my own group, and the culture they represented. We were filled with pettiness and cruelty and caring only about ourselves. We fussed and argued the whole week, ignoring the needs of those who we were to serve. The cliques in the group couldn't get over their differences to work together. There had been constant in-fighting the whole entire week. I felt opposed to some of the guys who refused to take anything seriously and weren't prepared, and it made me angry that the rest of the group and the leaders ignored this and wouldn't say anything. I spoke up once, and was called down. Steve, the youth pastor, said he didn't want to start a conflict, but he just wouldn't acknowledge the one that was there, wouldn't acknowledge any of the other conflicts that were there. They remained unresolved with this attitude, and distracted us from focusing on the ministry we were there for.

I left Mexico feeling like a violator. I felt like I had invaded something beautiful and sacred, plundering it for no good reason. I went to Mexico not even knowing the language, and not knowing much about myself. I knew about the Bible, its stories and God's love, but I didn't have any practical knowledge about any of these things; they didn't have to be tested in my religiously unified community.

When I left Mexico, I took so much more from the children than I gave to them. I found that I had to discover about true selflessness, about untainted love, pure joy, contentment, and security for myself; about people and their own religion, God's immeasurable love for everyone, and how to see and feel that love. The cookie cutter values learned from my religious institution were my guide and a point of comparison. I took the vague definitions and guidelines I learned and then applied my conscience, and real life experiences. I'm not saying that doing whatever works is acceptable, but I found that I could have blind faith in something for only so long before it became challenged and changed or secured and strengthened. I learned that joy can be found in simple things, and I justified and intensified my knowledge about love for others, about being unconditional in everything, giving one's all, and that the meaning of happiness is contentment. I simultaneously tore down all of my previous knowledge about missions, about different religions being right or wrong, and replaced it with the things I saw. I don't feel right trying to change other people that are perfectly happy the way they are, secure in their own religion and their beliefs. I know now that religious security is often an illusion. ∎

Responding to Reading

1. One of the ways Martens provides structure and energy to the essay is by including several contrasts. Note specific places where and describe how she draws contrasts between places, people, and beliefs.

2. Locate two passages where visual images draw readers into the narrative. Which details does the writer choose to share? Why are they effective?

3. How does Martens's essay complicate the role of missionary work? Which aspects of this kind of service work seem laudable to you? Which seem problematic to you?

4. Martens grapples with the connections between religion, service, and social justice. How does her representation of those connections compare to how Garber represents them?

Reading into Writing

Several common themes link the readings in the previous section, including writing and literacy, school and institutionalized learning, social environment, race and class, hopes and fears, and ethics and spirituality. The questions in this section are aimed at helping you explore connections among the various readings in preparation for your own writing.

The personal essay you will be assigned to write later in this chapter need not revisit the themes addressed in the preceding readings, but you might want to explore similar issues or even particular concerns raised in the readings. The following questions focus on the content of the previous essays—*what* is written. The next section focuses on the rhetorical features of the personal essay genre—*how* such essays are crafted.

1. How is personal experience located in community or social life? Why are time and place important, even when one is writing about personal, intimate topics?

2. hooks writes that "bringing one's past, one's memories together in a complete narrative would allow one to view them from a different perspective." How are these various writers using narrative to see themselves from another perspective? How do they help readers see from new perspectives?

3. How and why do hooks's and Montalvo's attitudes about whether to address certain topics in writing shift or get challenged by key experiences? Likewise, how do specific, transformative events serve as catalysts for writing and personal reflection?

4. Rose and McMurtray both reflect on children who are often overlooked by or are ill suited to the institutions they inhabit. How are the children described in those reading selections shaped by those institutions? Why write about such people and events?

5. Garber and Martens articulate connections between religion, social action, and personal development. How are ethics, spirituality, and community action linked for these writers and for you?

6. The pieces by Rose, McMurtray, Garber, and Martens all prominently feature children or adolescents. In some of those readings, adults influence the lives and perceptions of younger people; in others, the younger people influence the lives and perceptions of the adults. What in particular makes these intergenerational relationships significant and transformative for the characters involved?

7. What other connections, patterns, or contrasts among the readings strike you as being significant?

Rhetorical Features of the Personal Essay

As outlined in Chapter 1, most essays share a few basic characteristics: They center on one main topic, they develop a claim or tension, and they move readers from the *known* to the *new*. But different kinds of essays express these characteristics differently. Although each essay is unique, we can identify the conventions and rhetorical features common to a particular *kind* of essay, such as the personal essay. Rhetorical features are not absolute rules; rather, they speak to the expectations that readers bring to a particular kind of genre and the effects that particular strategies have on readers. Writers should be aware of both the specific strategies at hand and their readers' expectations.

The personal essays and the narrative excerpts above are a far cry from the thesis-driven analytical essays that we often associate with school writing. Look them over and consider the ways that the selections are similar. The topics are different, so you need to look at the broader strategies that the writers employ. In other words, rather than focus only on *what* the essays are saying, examine *how* the essays are constructed. When you do that, you'll recognize several commonalities. What follows are discussions of three such commonalities, three rhetorical features associated with the personal essay: narrative base; tension, turn, and resolution; and literary devices.

Narrative Base

Personal essays are grounded in narrative, in story. This stands in contrast to a thesis-driven essay, where the claim–support structure is front and center ("This essay will prove that . . . "). Just because an essay is structured as a narrative doesn't mean that it has no claim. Rather, the claim is often embedded in the story, implied, or delayed.

Most narratives proceed chronologically, but they don't need to. In fact, flashbacks and jumps in time are often effective narrative strategies. Some personal essays employ a "frame" as part of the narrative structure. For example, several of the reading selections above open by announcing the writer's present situation, shift into telling a story from the past, and then return to the present to reflect on the story. In these cases, the opening and closing sections (set in the present) frame the central narrative (set in the past).

Tension, Turn, and Resolution

Not just any story will do. Unless a narrative has *tension*, it is just an aimless string of events. (Be careful not to equate tension with suspense.) In an autobiographical essay, the writer develops tension between two or more ideas, people, worldviews, etc. In personal essays, two tensions are especially common:

- Old self versus new self
- Old perspective versus new perspective

Notice, for example, how O'Konski, the author of "The Monster Under the Bed," develops a contrast between an "old self" who harbors a childlike fear of writing and a "new self" who grapples maturely with that fear. Recall how Garber contrasts her "old self" and "old perspective on camp" with the "new self" and "new perspective on camp" that develop out of her encounter with a special child. Likewise, Martens contrasts her "old perspective" on religion and outreach with a "new perspective" that emerges during her trip to Mexico.

A tension usually demands a *turn*—a moment of realization or change. For example, as she describes the key events of her visit and reflects on her own past, Martens helps the reader understand *how* and *why* her attitude turns. She doesn't just tell the reader, "I changed my mind." She shows the process by which her mind changes, and in doing so she reveals and supports her claim about the need to scrutinize one's motives for engaging in community outreach.

As essays turn and then move toward closure, the main tension is often resolved or reconciled. For example, in "Replanting My Roots," Montalvo resolves a tension between ignoring her ethnic heritage and embracing her roots by showing how she acknowledged ("replanted") her newfound cultural awareness and integrated it more fully into her identity. Resolution, however, does not mean a fairytale ending or a lesson tacked on to the end of the narrative.

Literary Devices

Particular literary devices can help you craft a successful personal essay. Among the most important are description, setting, character, and figurative language.

Description.   Because personal essays invite readers to share in the writer's experience, they must re-create that experience in detail. This makes the common maxim "Show, don't tell" apt advice for autobiographical essays. One way to "show" is to use *sensory detail.* For example, at one point in her essay "Replanting My Roots," Montalvo expresses anger at another character, Rich. But she doesn't just *tell* the reader "I was mad at Rich." Instead, she *shows* her feelings by writing, "I felt the blood rushing to my face. My body became tense. I could feel 101 different thoughts of anger and disgust come pouring out of my mouth. I controlled myself, knowing that if I were to let that happen, I would seriously hurt Rich." This showing description allows readers to *participate* in the scene, whereas simply telling would have kept readers at arm's length.

As you enhance your descriptions with sensory detail, be attentive to all five senses: sight, smell, touch, sound, and taste. Also, understand that description for the sake of description is a waste of time. Rather, you should use description selectively to help develop and illustrate the central tension of an essay.

PRACTICE: *Show and Tell*

Consider how you would convert the following "tell" sentences into "show" passages.

Example: The teacher bored the students. (*telling*)

As Mr. Norton's monotone voice droned on about differential equations, eyelids grew heavy. Norton didn't even notice the guys in the back row hiding their closed eyes under the brims of their baseball caps. Toward the end of class, Ed's head bobbed forward, followed by a wheezing snore. (*showing*)

1. The children were excited to see me.
2. The room was ugly and smelled strange.
3. It was an amazing concert.

Setting.   The writer needs to put the reader into a setting, and this demands description. For example, notice how Martens helps readers see the poverty of the Mexican town by including specific visual details:

> We began to drive through town, first viewing the nice tourist section. There were hotels and opulent restaurants with neon signs, the BMWs and Bentleys parked in the large lots designated for visitors by more than just the sign at the entrance. Tall, majestic palm trees lined the streets, along with gracious flowers bending low to the ground. We gradually navigated the traffic, and drove through the rest of the town. It was like night and day. There were little, white houses strewn throughout the hills that made up the city itself. Little tin outbuildings were added on to a lot of them. Laundry was flapping in the breeze, and little children tossed around balls and jumped rope.

This description of setting also sets up contrasts between rich and poor, first world and third world, native and outsider—all central themes of the essay. Martens uses setting not only to provide context but also to help develop key tensions in the essay.

Character.   Good narratives feature credible characters—characters that readers can see and hear. In an autobiographical narrative, the most important character is *you*. But there may, of course, be others. Again, description is key to creating characters. Go back and review how Rose introduces each of his characters. He doesn't have room to include exhaustive descriptions of each, so he chooses a few telling details. Of Jack MacFarland, Rose writes: "Mr. MacFarland had a master's degree from Columbia and decided, at twenty-six, to find a little school and teach his heart out. . . . He was a beatnik who was born too late. His teeth were stained, he tucked his sorry tie in between the third and fourth buttons of his shirt, and his pants were chronically wrinkled." Rose carefully selects a few details that reveal a sense of MacFarland. When you are introducing characters, then, you should ask, Which selected details will convey a sense of this individual as a whole person?

Another way to breathe life into characters is to give them voice. The most common way to do this is to directly quote characters and to put them into dialogue with other characters, or even with themselves. Dialogue, whether interpersonal or internal, can be an effective tactic for showing key features of characters and for revealing how pivotal tensions are unfolding. Notice how Garber enlivens her essay by directly quoting a child's exclamation about her faith, followed by a dialogue between the child and the narrator. Here the characters become three-dimensional people with real voices who connect with each other in a palpable way. As with setting, you should use dialogue strategically. For example, if you are featuring a conflict or connection between characters, you should put those characters into direct dialogue when the tension is most intense or poignant.

Figurative Language.   Figurative language can help develop characters and tensions, highlight connections that might otherwise go unnoticed, imbue a moment with just the right associations and emotions, or deliver a jolt of energy to a text. Similes and metaphors are among the most common kinds of figurative language. For example, hooks likens autobiography to a hope chest, and this metaphor attaches to personal writing a sense of domestic warmth. Sometimes an extended analogy is more appropriate, as when, to illustrate his fear of writing, O'Konski renders a colorful description of a monster under the bed. He could have just written, "I was afraid of writing," but would that have been nearly as effective?

Title Brainstorming

A title creates your reader's first impression. A limp title, such as "My Writing Experiences," predisposes the reader to boredom; an engaging title, such as "The Monster Under the Bed," invites the reader to dive in. Titles should do two things: give an honest sense of what is to follow and hook the reader's interest.

Try out several kinds of titles before settling on one. Jot down a list of possible titles that conform to each of the following formats:

- A one-word title
- A title with an active verb
- A title with a colon (e.g., *Star Trek: The Next Generation*, "Children in Poverty: Who's to Blame?")
- An ironic, witty, or wordplay title
- A title in the form of a question
- A key image or phrase from the essay as a title
- A character's name as part of a title

Review your list and put a check next to the two titles that you find most promising. Share them with a classmate to get some feedback.

The Peer Workshop: Sharing Drafts with Others

Most professional writers share with others drafts of their work-in-progress. Sometimes this happens early in the writing process, when ideas are just coming into being and the voice of another can spur creativity or guide planning.

Sometimes sharing later in the writing process is appropriate; at that point a fresh perspective can assist the author in revising and editing. Often, writers gather feedback at many points in the composing process. Writers can use peer workshops to tap the collective intelligence of the writing class to improve everyone's thinking and writing.

WRITING TO DISCOVER

List occasions when, in the past, you have shared your in-process writing with others. Have any English teachers structured peer workshops as part of courses? Or did you, for example, share a draft of your college application essay with anyone? Have you worked on a school newspaper where an editor reviewed submissions? Have you ever asked for writing help from a parent, friend, teacher, or tutor?

After creating your list, sort through it and put a + next to those situations you found most helpful and a − next to those you found least helpful.

Finally, come up with at least three *specific practices* common to the helpful situations and at least three *specific problems* common to the others. Share your findings with a classmate. As a whole class, try to arrive at practices and guidelines that lead to high-quality peer review.

Three key guidelines for peer workshops follow; if they're not already included on the list compiled by your class, add them:

- *Create an environment of respect.* This means more than being nice to each other (although being nice is important). Each writer deserves to have his or her work reviewed carefully and completely; to breeze through a draft and offer scant response (positive or negative) is a sign of disrespect. Harsh criticism is out of bounds; constructive suggestions are welcome. Rather than judge or prescribe, it is often best to frame your responses in the first person (e.g., "I get confused here" rather than "The draft is confusing" or "To be convinced, I need more hard evidence" rather than "Add more").

- *Be specific.* Blanket praise or summary judgments tend to be of little use to writers. Some general comments are fine, but most remarks should be detailed. Make reference to specific bright spots and specific troublesome parts. (This doesn't mean fussing over grammar and wording but rather attending to meaning and expression.) Offer detailed advice for cutting and adding.

- *Think revision.* Remember that your feedback should propel revision. Rather than adopt either a hands-off or judgmental stance, think of yourself as a coach offering doable advice for the next draft.

The bottom line is that peer workshops, when done well, can help you improve your writing. But when they are done poorly, workshops are a waste of time.

Becoming a good peer editor takes practice. One way to practice is to select one of the student essays from this chapter and use the peer review questions below to guide the response you could offer the writer.

Revision Versus Editing

Keep in mind the difference between *revision* and *editing*. Revision, true to the root of the word, entails *re-seeing* the purpose, arrangement, and development of the draft. It involves rethinking on a large scale—and to emphasize this, some people use the terms *global revision, conceptual revision,* or *deep revision*. In practice, this may mean moving around large chunks of text, adding substantial passages, cutting sections that don't fit, and posing challenging questions.

Whereas revision concerns macrostructure, *editing* concerns microstructure. It focuses on the sentence level and involves matters of style, usage, and grammar. Because getting bogged down in sentence-level issues too early can stifle revision, many writers find it helpful to defer editing until late in the composing process. Yet careful editing is essential. A poorly edited document may not only distract and annoy readers but may also lead many readers to unfavorable judgments (unfair or not) about the document as a whole and about the intellect of the writer.

Peer Review Questions

In groups of two or three, share drafts either by reading them aloud (in turn) or by exchanging them. As you listen or read, respond to the questions below, and then write detailed responses:

1. Which *specific* ideas, words, phrases, or images struck you as particularly memorable and promising?

2. Which *specific* things struck you as confusing or as needing more elaboration?

3. What is the main tension in the draft?

4. Where does the writer use descriptions to show rather than tell? Where would more sensory description, dialogue, or detail help the reader more fully engage with the narrative?

5. Do the descriptions directly contribute to the main tension of the essay? How?

6. What other literary devices (i.e., setting, character, figurative language) does the writer use? Which of these need more emphasis or development? How could the writer use each literary device more strategically?
7. As a reader, what do you want to hear more about?

The Revision Plan

After completing a peer review workshop, look over the responses to your draft and mark those bits of commentary and advice that you find compelling. Remember that just because you get advice doesn't mean you need to take it. You should consider everything, but as the writer, you still steer the ship.

Taking into account the peer responses as well as your own emerging ideas, write a revision plan in the form of a bulleted list. This writing can be informal, but it is important. It will serve as a reminder when you revisit the draft.

The Process Note

When you are preparing to hand in a final draft, your instructor may ask for a *process note*, which is an informal reflection on the experience of writing the essay. Among the questions you should consider when writing a process note are the following:

- What was it like for you to draft and revise this essay? What were your biggest struggles? easiest parts?
- What do you think are the strongest aspects of your essay?
- If you had more time, what would you work on?
- Is there anything your instructor should keep in mind while reading your essay?

ENDNOTE

The chapters that follow this one focus on additional genres and contexts for writing. Strategies for writing compelling narratives are useful even when you are composing essays that follow a thesis-driven structure or documents in community settings. After all, expressing one's perspective, giving shape to experience, crafting an engaging story line, and employing description are tools that a versatile writer should have on hand.

What Is Literacy?

Defining *literacy* may at first seem a simple task. But, in fact, it is quite complex. What are the different kinds of literacies? How do they relate to each other? And what are the practical consequences of defining literacy one way rather than another? Because Chapters 1 and 2 raise questions about reading and writing, and because many service-learning courses involve tutoring or other literacy work, this section raises key questions about the nature of literacy.

By exploring the various purposes for and processes of writing, Chapters 1 and 2 implicitly and explicitly raise questions about literacy. While a dictionary might define *literacy* as "the ability to read and write," that commonplace definition doesn't do justice to the multiple ways that literacy is either addressed in academic scholarship or practiced in everyday life. Each of the readings in this section expresses and explains some basic characteristics of literacy, and therefore helps set the stage for further discussion. Together, the readings challenge some common conceptions about literacy and suggest ways to account for its variety and complexity.

Literacy tutoring is the central activity of many service-learning courses. Such training is often conducted through programs such as America Reads or through any number of initiatives that focus on serving children, adults, recent immigrants, or prison populations. This section is particularly relevant to participants in such programs.

WRITING TO DISCOVER

Write your own one-paragraph definition of literacy. Don't settle for an overly general definition such as "the ability to read and write." Rather, get as specific as you can: the ability to read what? write what? do what?

Another way to approach this is to describe what knowledge and which skills, in your view, characterize a literate person versus an illiterate person.

To help conceptualize literacy, scholars often speak of different *kinds* of literacies. Some common terms include:

- *Functional literacy.* A working facility for adapting to the basic reading and writing demands of work and civic life. The abilities to fill out a job application, follow on-the-job instructions, perform rote reading and writing tasks, and vote are often considered benchmarks of functional literacy.

- *Cultural literacy.* The ability to accumulate and employ the knowledge, habits, and codes that are characteristic of those who are "cultured." Efforts to promote cultural literacy are critiqued by some as being elitist and championed by others as being essential to forming a shared or common culture.

- *Academic literacy.* The capacity to negotiate the demands of schooling. This usually includes proficiency in abstract thinking, in common academic genres (such as the essay), and in advanced reading. It also entails a working knowledge of the explicit and implied "rules" of classroom practice and test taking.

- *Critical literacy.* An aptitude for comprehending how individuals relate to the social, political, and economic systems in which they are situated. Culminating in what is often called "critical consciousness," critical literacy emphasizes the analysis of power relations and the critique of structural injustice.

Although the readings in this section do not offer practical advice on how to tutor people in reading and writing, they can be used to help examine the motives, practices, and possibilities of particular literacy initiatives.

Excerpt: Paulo Freire, *The Banking Concept of Education*

Paulo Freire was a Brazilian educator whose work on literacy has garnered a worldwide following. Freire helped to develop literacy programs in several countries through international organizations such as the United Nations and The World Council of Churches. Freire authored many books on education and social action, the most famous being Pedagogy of the Oppressed, *from which the passage below is taken.*

A careful analysis of the teacher–student relationship at any level, inside or outside the school, reveals its fundamentally *narrative* character. This relationship involves a narrating Subject (the teacher) and the patient, listening objects (the students). The contents, whether values or empirical dimensions of reality, tend in the process of being narrated to become lifeless and petrified. Education is suffering from narration sickness.

The teacher talks about reality as if it were motionless, static, compartmentalized, and predicable. Or else he expounds on a topic completely alien to the existential experience of the students. His task is to "fill" the students with the contents of his narration—contents which are detached from reality, disconnected from the totality that engendered them and could give them significance. Words are emptied of their concreteness and become a hollow, alienated, and alienating verbosity.

The outstanding characteristic of this narrative education, then, is the sonority of words, not their transforming power. "Four times four is sixteen; the capital of Pará is Belém." The student records, memorizes, and repeats these phrases without perceiving what four times four really means, or realizing the true significance of "capital" in the affirmation "the capital of Pará is Belém," that is, what Belém means for Pará and what Pará means for Brazil.

Narration (with the teacher as narrator) leads the students to memorize mechanically the narrated content. Worse yet, it turns them into "containers," into "receptacles" to be "filled" by the teacher. The more completely she fills the receptacles, the better a teacher she is. The more meekly the receptacles permit themselves to be filled, the better students they are.

Education thus becomes an act of depositing, in which the students are the depositories and the teacher is the depositor. Instead of communicating, the teacher issues communiqués and makes deposits which the students patiently receive, memorize, and repeat. This is the "banking" concept of education, in which the scope of action allowed to the students extends only as far as receiving, filing, and storing the deposits. They do, it is true, have the opportunity to become collectors or cataloguers of the things they store. But in the last analysis, it is the people themselves who are filed away through the lack of creativity, transformation, and knowledge in this (at best) misguided system. For apart from inquiry, apart from the praxis, individuals cannot be truly human. Knowledge emerges only through invention and re-invention, through the restless, impatient, continuing, hopeful inquiry human beings pursue in the world, with the world, and with each other.

In the banking concept of education, knowledge is a gift bestowed by those who consider themselves knowledgeable upon those whom they consider to know nothing. Projecting an absolute ignorance onto others, a characteristic of the ideology of oppression, negates education and knowledge as processes of inquiry. The teacher presents himself to his students as their necessary opposite; by considering their ignorance absolute, he justifies his own existence. The students, alienated like the slave in the Hegelian dialectic, accept their ignorance as justifying the teacher's existence—but, unlike the slave, they never discover that they educate the teacher.

The *raison d'être* of libertarian education, on the other hand, lies in its drive towards reconciliation. Education must begin with the solution of the teacher-student contradiction, by reconciling the poles of the contradiction so that both are simultaneously teachers *and* students.

This solution is not (nor can it be) found in the banking concept. On the contrary, banking education maintains and even stimulates the contradiction through the following attitudes and practices, which mirror oppressive society as a whole:

a.   the teacher teaches and the students are taught;
b.   the teacher knows everything and the students know nothing;
c.   the teacher thinks and the students are thought about;
d.   the teacher talks and the students listen—meekly;
e.   the teacher disciplines and the students are disciplined;
f.   the teacher chooses and enforces his choice, and the students comply;
g.   the teacher acts and the students have the illusion of acting through the action of the teacher;
h.   the teacher chooses the program content, and the students (who were not consulted) adapt to it;
i.   the teacher confuses the authority of knowledge with his or her own professional authority, which she and he sets in opposition to the freedom of the students;
j.   the teacher is the Subject of the learning process, while the pupils are mere objects.

It is not surprising that the banking concept of education regards men as adaptable, manageable beings. The more students work at storing the deposits entrusted to them, the less they develop the critical consciousness which would result from their intervention in the world as transformers of that world. The more completely they accept the passive role imposed on them, the more they tend simply to adapt to the world as it is and to the fragmented view of reality deposited in them.

The capability of banking education to minimize or annul the students' creative power and to stimulate their credulity serves the interests of the oppressors, who care neither to have the world revealed nor to see it transformed. The oppressors use their "humanitarianism" to preserve a profitable situation. Thus they react almost instinctively against any experiment in education which stimulates the critical faculties and is not content with a partial view of reality but always seeks out the ties which link one point to another and one problem to another. ■

Responding to Reading

1. Discuss times when you have experienced education in the "banking" model. How did it make you feel?

2. What assumptions about students are made in the banking model of education? What kinds of students does it create? What kind of student–learning does the banking model depend on?

3. According to Freire, how does banking education compare to liberatory education?

4. What, for Freire, would a truly educated or literate person understand and be able to do?

Essay: Sylvia Scribner, *Literacy in Three Metaphors*

Educated at Smith College and The New School for Social Research, Sylvia Scribner was a social scientist who wrote extensively in the fields of learning, cognition, education, and literacy.

Although literacy is a problem of pressing national concern, we have yet to discover or set its boundaries. This observation, made several years ago by a leading political spokesman (McGovern 1978), echoes a long-standing complaint of many policymakers and educators that what counts as literacy in our technological society is a matter "not very well understood" (Advisory Committee on National Illiteracy 1929).

A dominant response of scholars and researchers to this perceived ambiguity has been to pursue more rigorously the quest for definition and measurement of the concept. Many approaches have been taken (among them, Adult Performance Level Project 1975; Bormuth 1975; Hillerich 1976; Kirsch and Guthrie 1977–78; Miller 1973; Powell 1977), and at least one attempt (Hunter and Harman 1979) has been made to put forward an "umbrella definition." Each of these efforts has identified important parameters of literacy, but none has yet won consensual agreement (for a thoughtful historical and conceptual analysis of shifting literacy definitions, see Radwin [1978]).

The definitional controversy has more than academic significance. Each formulation of an answer to the question "What is literacy?" leads to a different evaluation of the scope of the problem (i.e., the extent of *il*literacy) and to different objectives for programs aimed at the formation of a literate citizenry. Definitions of literacy shape our perceptions of individuals who fall on either side of the standard (what a "literate" or "nonliterate" is like) and thus in a deep way affect both the substance and style of educational programs. A chorus of clashing answers also creates problems for literacy planners and educators. This is clearly evident in the somewhat acerbic comments of Dauzat and Dauzat (1977, p. 37), who are concerned with adult basic education: "In spite of all of the furor and the fervor for attaining literacy . . . few have undertaken to say what they or anyone else means by literacy. Those few professional organizations, bureaus and individuals who have attempted the task of explaining 'what is literacy?' generate definitions that conflict, contradict but rarely complement each other. . . . These 'champions of the cause of literacy' crusade for a national effort to make literacy a reality without establishing what that reality is."

What lies behind the definitional difficulties this statement decries? The authors themselves provide a clue. They suggest that literacy is a kind of reality that educators should be able to grasp and explain, or, expressed in more classical terms, that literacy has an "essence" that can be captured through some Aristotelian-like enterprise. By a rational process of discussion and analysis, the "true" criterial components of literacy will be identified, and these in turn can become the targets of education for literacy.

Many, although by no means all, of those grappling with the problems of definition and measurement appear to be guided by such a search for the "essence"—for the "one best" way of conceptualizing literacy. This enterprise is surely a useful one and a necessary component of educational planning. Without denigrating its contribution, I would like to suggest, however, that conflicts and contradictions are intrinsic to such an essentialist approach.

Consider the following. Most efforts at definitional determination are based on a conception of literacy as an attribute of *individuals;* they aim to describe constituents of literacy in terms of individual abilities. But the single most compelling fact about literacy is that it is a *social* achievement; individuals in societies without writing systems do not become literate. Literacy is an outcome of cultural transmission; the individual child or adult does not extract the meaning of written symbols through personal interaction with the physical objects that embody them. Literacy abilities are acquired by individuals only in the course of participation in socially organized activities with written language (for a theoretical analysis of literacy as a set of socially organized practices, see Scribner and Cole [1981]). It follows that individual literacy is relative to social literacy. Since social literacy practices vary in time (Resnick [1983] contains historical studies) and space (anthropological studies are in Goody [1968]), what qualifies as individual literacy varies with them. At one time, the ability to write one's name was a hallmark of literacy; today in some parts of the world, the ability to memorize a sacred text remains the modal literacy act. Literacy has neither a static nor a universal essence.

The enterprise of defining literacy, therefore, becomes one of assessing what counts as literacy in the modern epoch in some given social context. If a nation-society is the context, this enterprise requires that consideration be given to the functions that the society in question has invented for literacy and their distribution throughout the populace. Grasping what literacy "is" inevitably involves social analysis: What activities are carried out with written symbols? What significance is attached to them, and what status is conferred on those who engage in them? Is literacy a social right or a private power? These questions are subject to empirical determination. But others are not: Does the prevailing distribution of literacy conform to standards of social justice and human progress? What social and educational policies might promote such standards? Here we are involved, not with fact but with considerations of value, philosophy, and ideology similar to those that figure prominently in debates about the purposes and goals of schooling. Points of view about literacy as a social good, as well as a social fact, form the ground of the definitional enterprise. We may lack consensus on how best to define literacy because we have differing views about literacy's social purposes and values.

These differing points of view about the central meaning of literacy warrant deeper examination. In this essay, I will examine some of them, organizing my discussion around three metaphors: literacy as adaptation, literacy as power, and literacy as a state of grace. Each of these metaphors is rooted in certain assumptions about the social motivations for literacy in this country, the nature of existing literacy practices, and judgments about which practices are critical for individual and social enhancement. Each has differing implications for educational policies and goals. I will be schematic in my discussion; my purpose is not to marshal supporting evidence for one or the other metaphor but to show the boundary problems of all. My argument is that any of the metaphors, taken by itself, gives us only a partial grasp of the many and varied utilities of literacy and of the complex social and psychological factors sustaining aspirations for and achievement of individual literacy. To illustrate this theme, I will draw on the literacy experiences of a Third World people who, although remaining at an Iron Age level of technology, have nevertheless evolved varied functions for written language; their experience demonstrates that, even in some traditional societies, literacy is a "many-meaninged thing."

LITERACY AS ADAPTATION

This metaphor is designed to capture concepts of literacy that emphasize its survival or pragmatic value. When the term "functional literacy" was originally introduced during World War I (Harman 1970), it specified the literacy skills required to meet the tasks of modern soldiering. Today, functional literacy is conceived broadly as the level of proficiency necessary for effective performance in a range of settings and customary activities.

This concept has a strong commonsense appeal. The necessity for literacy skills in daily life is obvious; on the job, riding around town, shopping for groceries, we all encounter situations requiring us to read or produce written symbols. No justification is needed to insist that schools are obligated to equip children with the literacy skills that will enable them to fulfill these mundane situational demands. And basic educational programs have a similar obligation to equip adults with the skills they must have to secure jobs or advance to better ones, receive the training and benefits to which they are entitled, and assume their civic and political responsibilities. Within the United States, as in other nations, literacy programs with these practical aims are considered efforts at human resource development and, as such, contributors to economic growth and stability.

In spite of their apparent commonsense grounding, functional literacy approaches are neither as straightforward nor as unproblematic as they first appear. Attempts to inventory "minimal functional competencies" have floundered on lack of information and divided perceptions of functionality. Is it realistic to try to specify some uniform set of skills as constituting functional literacy for all adults? Two subquestions are involved here. One concerns the choice of parameters for defining a "universe of functional competencies." Which literacy tasks (e.g., reading a newspaper, writing a check) are "necessary," and which are "optional"? The Adult Performance Level Project test (1975), one of the best conceptualized efforts to specify and measure competencies necessary for success in adult life, has been challenged on the grounds that it lacks content validity: "The APL test fails to meet this [validity] criterion . . . not necessarily because test development procedures were technically faulty, but because it is not logically possible to define this universe of behaviors [which compose functional competence] without respect to a value position which the test developers have chosen not to discuss" (Cervero 1980, p. 163).

An equally important question concerns the concept of uniformity. Do all communities and cultural groups in our class-based and heterogeneous society confront equivalent functional demands? If not, how do they differ? Some experts (e.g., Gray 1965; Hunter and Harman 1979) maintain that the concept of functional literacy makes sense only with respect to the proficiencies required for participation in the actual life conditions of particular groups or communities. But how does such a relativistic approach mesh with larger societal needs? If we were to consider the level of reading and writing activities carried out in small and isolated rural communities as the standard for functional literacy, educational objectives would be unduly restricted. At the other extreme, we might not want to use literacy activities of college teachers as the standard determining the functional competencies required for high school graduation. Only in recent years has research been undertaken on the range of literacy activities practiced in different communities or settings within the United States (e.g., Heath 1980, 1981; Scribner 1982*a*), and we still know little about how, and by whom, required literacy work gets done. Lacking such knowledge, public discussions fluctuate between narrow definitions of functional skills pegged to immediate vocational and personal needs, and sweeping definitions that virtually reinstate the ability to cope with college subject matter as the hallmark of literacy. On the other hand, adopting different criteria for different regions or communities would ensure the perpetuation of educational inequalities and the differential access to life opportunities with which these are associated.

Adapting literacy standards to today's needs, personal or social, would be shortsighted. The time-limited nature of what constitutes minimal skill is illustrated in the "sliding scale" used by the U. S. Bureau of Census to determine literacy. During World War I, a fourth-grade education was considered sufficient to render one literate; in 1947, a U. S. Census sample survey raised that figure to five years; and by 1952 six years of school was considered the minimal literacy threshold. Replacing the school-grade criterion with a functional approach to literacy does not eliminate the time problem. Today's standards for functional competency need to be considered in the light of tomorrow's requirements. But not all are agreed as to the nature or volume of literacy demands in the decades ahead. Some (e.g., Naisbitt 1982) argue that, as economic and other activities become increasingly subject to computerized techniques of production and information handling, even higher levels of literacy will be required of all. A contrary view, popularized by McLuhan (1962, 1964) is that new technologies and communication media are likely to reduce literacy requirements for all. A responding argument is that some of these technologies are, in effect, new systems of literacy. The ability to use minicomputers as information storage and retrieval devices requires mastery of symbol systems that build on natural language literacy; they are second-order literacies as it were. One possible scenario is that in coming decades literacy may be increased for some and reduced for others, accentuating the present uneven, primarily class-based distribution of literacy functions.

From the perspective of social needs, the seemingly well-defined concept of functional competency becomes fuzzy at the edges. Equally as many questions arise about functionality from the individual's point of view. Functional needs have not yet been assessed from the perspective of those who purportedly experience them. To what extent do adults whom tests assess as functionally illiterate perceive themselves as lacking the necessary skills to be adequate parents, neighbors, workers? Inner-city youngsters may have no desire to write letters to each other; raising one's reading level by a few grades may not be seen as a magic ticket to a job; not everyone has a bank account that requires the mastery of unusual forms (Heath 1980). Appeals to individuals to enhance their functional skills might founder on the different subjective utilities communities and groups attach to reading and writing activities.

The functional approach has been hailed as a major advance over more traditional concepts of reading and writing because it takes into account the goals and settings of people's activities with written language. Yet even tender probing reveals the many questions of fact, value, and purpose that complicate its application to educational curricula.

We now turn to the second metaphor.

LITERACY AS POWER

While functional literacy stresses the importance of literacy to the adaptation of the individual, the literacy-as-power metaphor emphasizes a relationship between literacy and group or community advancement.

Historically, literacy has been a potent tool in maintaining the hegemony of elites and dominant classes in certain societies, while laying the basis for increased social and political participation in others (Resnick 1983; Goody 1968). In a contemporary framework, expansion of literacy skills is often viewed as a means for poor and politically powerless groups to claim their place in the world. The International Symposium for Literacy, meeting in Persepolis, Iran (Bataille 1976), appealed to national governments to consider literacy as an instrument for human liberation and social change. Paulo Freire (1970) bases his influential theory of literacy education on the need to make literacy a resource for fundamental social transformation. Effective literacy education, in his view, creates a critical consciousness through which a community can analyze its conditions of social existence and engage in effective action for a just society. Not to be literate is a state of victimization.

Yet the capacity of literacy to confer power or to be the primary impetus for significant and lasting economic or social change has proved problematic in developing countries. Studies (Gayter, Hall, Kidd, and Shivasrava 1979; United Nations Development Program 1976) of UNESCO's experimental world literacy program have raised doubts about earlier notions that higher literacy rates automatically promote national development and improve the social and material conditions of the very poor. The relationship between social change and literacy education, it is now suggested (Harman 1977), may be stronger in the other direction. When masses of people have been mobilized for fundamental changes in social conditions—as in the USSR, China, Cuba, and Tanzania—rapid extensions of literacy have been accomplished (Gayter et al. 1979; Hammiche 1976; Scribner 1982b). Movements to transform social reality appear to have been effective in some parts of the world in bringing whole populations into participation in modern literacy activities. The validity of the converse proposition—that literacy per se mobilizes people for action to change their social reality—remains to be established.

What does this mean for us? The one undisputed fact about illiteracy in America is its concentration among poor, black, elderly, and minority-language groups—groups without effective participation in our country's economic and educational institutions (Hunter and Harman 1979). Problems of poverty and political powerlessness are, as among some populations in developing nations, inseparably intertwined with problems of access to knowledge and levels of literacy skills. Some (e.g., Kozol 1980) suggest that a mass and politicized approach to literacy education such as that adopted by Cuba is demanded in these conditions. Others (e.g., Hunter and Harman 1979) advocate a more action-oriented approach that views community mobilization around practical, social, and political goals as a first step in creating the conditions for effective literacy instruction and for educational equity.

The possibilities and limits of the literacy-as-power metaphor within our present-day social and political structure are not at all clear. To what extent can instructional experiences and programs be lifted out of their social contexts in other countries and applied here? Do assumptions about the functionality and significance of literacy in poor communities in the United States warrant further consideration? Reder and Green's (1984) research and educational work among West Coast immigrant communities reveals that literacy has different meanings for members of different groups. How can these cultural variations be taken into account? How are communities best mobilized for literacy—around local needs and small-scale activism? or as part of broader political and social movements? If literacy has not emerged as a priority demand, should government and private agencies undertake to mobilize communities around this goal? And can such efforts be productive without the deep involvement of community leaders?

LITERACY AS A STATE OF GRACE

Now we come to the third metaphor. I have variously called it literacy as salvation and literacy as a state of grace. Both labels are unsatisfactory because they give a specific religious interpretation to the broader phenomenon I want to depict—that is, the tendency in many societies to endow the literate person with special virtues. A concern with preserving and understanding scripture is at the core of many religious traditions, Western and non-Western alike. As studies by Resnick and Resnick (1977) have shown, the literacy-as-salvation metaphor had an almost literal interpretation in the practice of post- Luther Protestant groups to require of the faithful the ability to read and remember the Bible and other religious material. Older religious traditions—Hebraic and Islamic—have also traditionally invested the written word with great power and respect. "This is a perfect book. There is no doubt in it," reads a passage from the Qur'an. Memorizing the Qur'an—literally taking its words into you and making them part of yourself—is simultaneously a process of becoming both literate and holy.

The attribution of special powers to those who are literate has its ancient secular roots as well. Plato and Aristotle strove to distinguish the man of letters from the poet of oral tradition. In the perspective of Western humanism, literateness has come to be considered synonymous with being "cultured," using the term in the old-fashioned sense to refer to a person who is knowledgeable about the content and techniques of the sciences, arts, and humanities as they have evolved historically. The term sounds elitist and archaic, but the notion that participation in a literate—that is, bookish—tradition enlarges and develops a person's essential self is pervasive and still undergirds the concept of a liberal education (Steiner 1973). In the literacy-as-a-state-of-grace concept, the power and functionality of literacy is not bounded by political or economic parameters but in a sense transcends them; the literate individual's life derives its meaning and significance from intellectual, aesthetic, and spiritual participation in the accumulated creations and knowledge of humankind, made available through the written word.

The self-enhancing aspects of literacy are often given a cognitive interpretation (Greenfield and Bruner 1969; Olson 1977). For centuries, and increasingly in this generation, appeals have been made for increased attention to literacy as a way of developing minds. An individual who is illiterate, a UNESCO (1972) publication states, is bound to concrete thinking and cannot learn new material. Some teachers of college English in the United States (e.g., Farrell 1977) urge greater prominence for writing in the curriculum as a way of promoting logical reasoning and critical thinking. Literate and nonliterate individuals presumably are not only in different states of grace but in different stages of intellectual development as well. Although evidence is accumulating (Scribner and Cole 1981) refuting this view, the notion that literacy per se creates a great divide in intellectual abilities between those who have and those who have not mastered written language is deeply entrenched in educational circles of industrialized countries.

The metaphor of literacy-as-grace, like the others, has boundary problems. For one thing, we need to know how widely dispersed this admiration of book knowledge is in our society. To what extent are beliefs about the value of literateness shared across social classes and ethnic and religious groups? How does book culture—more accurately, how do book cultures—articulate with the multiple and diverse oral cultures flourishing in the United States? Which people value literacy as a preserver of their history or endow their folk heroes with book learning? Are there broad cultural supports for book learning among wide sectors of the population? McLuhan and others have insisted that written literacy is a vestige of a disappearing "culture." Is this point of view defensible? And if so, what implications does it pose for our educational objectives?

I have described some current views of the meaning of literacy in terms of three metaphors. I have tried to indicate that each metaphor embraces a certain set of, sometimes unexamined, values; moreover, each makes assumptions about social facts in our society—the utilities of literacy and the conditions fostering individual attainment of literacy status. These metaphors are often urged on us as competitive; some choice of one or the other does in fact seem a necessary starting point for a definitional enterprise. But for purposes of social and educational planning, none need necessarily become paramount at the expense of the others; all may have validity. [Scribner goes on to discuss her research on the social meaning of literacy among the Vai, a West African People.]

NOTE
This paper is based on a planning document for research on literacy that I prepared when associate director of the National Institute of Education. Eugene Radwin made many helpful comments on that document and contributed a number of bibliographic references cited here.

REFERENCES
Adult Performance Level Project. *Adult Functional Competency: A Summary.* Austin: University of Texas, Division of Extension, 1975.

Advisory Committee on National Illiteracy. "Report." *School and Society* 30 (1929): 708.

Anzalone, S., and S. McLaughlin. *Literacy for Specific Situations.* Amherst: University of Massachusetts, Center for International Education, 1982.

Bataille, L., ed. *A Turning Point for Literacy: Proceedings of the International Symposium for Literacy, Persepolis, Iran, 1975.* Oxford: Pergamon Books, 1976.

Bormuth, J. R. "Reading Literacy: Its Definition and Assessment." In *Toward a Literate Society: The Report of the Committee on Reading of the National Academy of Education,* edited by J. B. Carroll and J. S. Chall. New York: McGraw-Hill Book Co., 1975.

Cervero, R. M. "Does the Texas Adult Performance Level Test Measure Functional Competence?" *Adult Education* 30 (1980): 152–65.

Dauzat, S. J., and J. Dauzat. "Literacy in Quest of a Definition." *Convergence* 10 (1977): 37–41.

Farrell, L. J. "Literacy, the Basics, and All that Jazz." *College English* 38 (1977): 443–59.

Freire, P. *Cultural Action for Freedom* (Monograph Series no. 1). Cambridge, Mass.: Harvard Educational Review, 1970.

Cayter, M., B. Hall, J. R. Kidd, and V. Shivasrava. *The World of Literacy: Policy, Research, and Action.* Toronto: International Development Centre, 1979.

Goody, J., ed. *Literacy in Traditional Societies.* Cambridge: Cambridge University Press, 1968.

Gray, W. *The Teaching of Reading and Writing: An International Survey.* Chicago: Scott, Foresman & Co./UNESCO, 1965.

Greenfield, P. M., and J. S. Bruner. "Culture and Cognitive Growth." In *Handbook of Socialization: Theory and Research,* edited by D. A. Goslin. New York: Rand McNally & Co., 1969.

Hair, P. E. H. "Notes on the Discovery of the Vai Script." *Sierra Leone Language Review* 2 (1963): 36—49.

Hammiche, B. "Functional Literacy and Educational Revolution." In *A Turning Point for Literacy: Proceedings of the International Symposium for Literacy, Persepolis Iran, 1975,* edited by L. Bataille. Oxford: Pergamon Press, 1976.

Harman, D. "Review of *The Experimental World Literacy Program.*" *Harvard Educational Review* 47 (1977): 444–46.

Heath, S. B. "The Functions and Uses of Literacy." *Journal of Communication* 30 (1980): 123–33.

Heath, S. B. "Toward an Ethnohistory of Writing in American Education." In *Writing: The Nature, Development and Teaching of Written Communication,* vol. 1, edited by M. F. Whiteman. Hillsdale, N. J.: Lawrence Erlbaum Associates, 1981.

Hillerich, R. L. "Toward an Assessable Definition of Literacy." *English Journal* 65 (1976): 50–55.

Holsoe, S. E. "Slavery and Economic Response among the Vai." In *Slavery in Africa: Historical and Anthropological Perspectives,* edited by S. Miers and I. Kopytoff. Madison: University of Wisconsin Press, 1977.

Hunter, C. S. J., and D. Harman. *Adult Illiteracy in the United States.* New York: McGraw-Hill Book Co., 1979.

Kirsch, I., and J. T. Guthrie. "The Concept and Measurement of Functional Literacy." *Reading Research Quarterly* 13 (1977–78): 485–507.

Kozol, J. *Prisoners of Silence: Breaking the Bonds of Adult Illiteracy in the United States.* New York: Continuum Publishing Corp., 1980.

McGovern, G. *Congressional Record* (September 1978), p. 14,834.

McLuhan, M. *The Gutenberg Galaxy.* Toronto: University of Toronto Press, 1962.

McLuhan, M. *Understanding Media: The Extensions of Man.* New York: McGraw-Hill Book Co., 1964.

Miller, G. A., ed. *Linguistic Communication: Perspectives for Research.* Newark, Del.: International Reading Association, 1973.

Naisbett, J. *Megatrends: Ten New Directions Transforming Our Lives.* New York: Warner Books, 1982.

Olson, D. R. "From Utterance to Text: The Bias of Language in Speech and Writing." *Harvard Educational Review* 47 (1977): 257–81.

Powell, W. R. "Levels of Literacy. "*Journal of Reading* 20 (1977): 488–92.

Radwin, E. "Literacy—What and Why." Unpublished manuscript, Harvard University, 1978.

Reder, S., and K. R. Green. "Literacy as a Functional Component of Social Structure in an Alaska Fishing Village." *International Journal of the Sociology of Language* 42 (1983): 122–41.

Resnick, D. P., ed. *Literacy in Historical Perspective.* Washington, D. C.: Library of Congress, 1983.

Resnick, D. P., and L. B. Resnick. "The Nature of Literacy: An Historical Exploration." *Harvard Educational Review* 47 (1977): 370–85.

Scribner, S. "Industrial Literacy" (Final Report to the Ford Foundation). New York: CUNY, Graduate School and University Center, 1982. (*a*)

Scribner, S. "Observations on Literacy Education in China." *Linguistic Reporter* 25 (1982): 1–4.(*b*)

Scribner, S., and M. Cole. *The Psychology of Literacy.* Cambridge, Mass.: Harvard University Press, 1981.

Steiner, G. "After the Book." In *The Future of Literacy,* edited by R. Disch. Englewood Cliffs, N. J.: Prentice-Hall, Inc. 1973.

United Nations Development Program. *The Experimental World Literacy Programme: A Critical Assessment.* Paris: UNESCO, 1976.

UNESCO. *Regional Report on Literacy.* Teheran: UNESCO, 1972.

Wagner, D. A., B. M. Messick, and J. Spratt. "Studying Literacy in Morocco." In *The Acquisition of Literacy: Ethnographic Perspectives,* edited by B. B. Schieffelin and P. Gilmore. Norwood, N. J.: Ablex, in press. ∎

Responding to Reading

1. Why bother defining literacy? What might be some practical consequences of defining literacy in one way versus another way?

2. Using both your own words and passages from the text, describe the key characteristics of each of the three metaphors for literacy.

3. How do Scribner's metaphors for literacy expand, confirm, or contradict your preconceived assumptions about literacy?

4. If you are working with a literacy program, consider which of Scribner's metaphors seems to prevail in the design and execution of the program.

5. Given Scribner's framework (or even thinking beyond it), what is your own preferred metaphor for literacy?

Essay: Andrea Fishman, *Becoming Literate*: A *Lesson from the Amish*

Andrea Fishman lived on an Amish farm in Pennsylvania while studying the roles of reading and writing among the Amish, and this research led to her book Amish Literacy: What and How It Means. *Currently a member of the English Department at West Chester University in Pennsylvania, Fishman is interested in issues related to literacy, literature, writing, and education.*

One clear, frost-edged January Sunday night, two families gathered for supper and an evening's entertainment. One family—mine—consisted of a lawyer, a teacher, and their twelve-year-old son; the other family—the Fishers—consisted of Eli and Anna, a dairy farmer and his wife, and their five children, ranging in age from six to seventeen. After supper in the Fisher's large farm kitchen—warmed by a wood stove and redolent of the fragrances of chicken corn soup, homemade bread, and freshly baked apples—the table was cleared and an additional smaller one set up to accommodate games of Scrabble, double Dutch solitaire, and dominoes. As most of us began to play, adults and children randomly mixed, Eli Fisher, Sr., settled into his brown leather recliner with the newspaper, while six-year-old Eli, Jr., plopped on the corner of the couch nearest his father with a book.

Fifteen or twenty minutes later, I heard Eli, Sr., ask his son, "Where are your new books?" referring to a set of outgrown Walt Disney books we had brought for little Eli and his seven-year-old brother, Amos. Eli, Jr., pointed to a stack of brightly colored volumes on the floor, from which his father chose *Lambert, the Sheepish Lion*. As Eli, Jr., climbed onto the arm of the recliner and snuggled against his father, Eli, Sr., began reading the book out loud in a voice so commandingly dramatic that soon everyone was listening to the story, instead of playing their separate games. Broadly portraying the roles of both Lambert and his lioness mother and laughing heartily at the antics of the cub who preferred cavorting with the sheep to stalking with the lions, Eli held his enlarged audience throughout the rest of the story.

As most of us returned to our games when he finished reading, Eli, Sr., asked of anyone and everyone, "Where's the *Dairy*?" Daniel, the Fishers' teenage son, left his game and walked toward his father. "It's in here," he said, rummaging through the newspapers and magazines in the rack beside the couch until he found a thick newsletter called *Dairy World*, published by the Independent Buyers Association, to which Eli belonged.

Eli leafed through the publication, standing and walking toward the wood stove as he did. Leaning against the wall, he began reading aloud without preface. All conversation stopped as everyone once again attended to Eli's loudly expressive reading voice, which said:

> A farmer was driving his wagon down the road. On the back was a sign which read: "Experimental Vehicle. Runs on oats and hay. Do not step in exhaust."

Everyone laughed, including Eli, Sr., who then read the remaining jokes on the humor page to his attentive audience. All our games forgotten, we shared the best and the worst riddles and jokes we could remember until it was time for bed.

Occasions like this one occur in many homes and have recently attracted the interest of family literacy researchers (Heath; Taylor; Wells). The scene at the Fishers could have been the scene in any home where parents value reading and writing and want their children to value them as well. It would not be surprising if Eli and Anna, like other literacy-oriented parents, read bedtime stories to their children, helped with their homework, and encouraged them to attain high school diplomas, if not college degrees. But Eli and Anna do none of these things: they read no bedtime stories, they are annoyed if their children bring schoolwork home, and they expect their children to go only as far in school as they did themselves, as far as the eighth grade.

So, although Eli and Anna appeared on that Sunday night to be ideal pro-literacy parents, they may not be, according to commonly described standards, and one significant factor may account for their variations from the supposed ideal: Eli and Anna are not mainstream Americans but are Old Order Amish, raising their family according to Old Order tradition and belief. The Sunday night gathering I just described took place by the light of gas lamps in a house without radio, stereo, television, or any other electrical contrivance. Bedtime in that house is more often marked by singing or silence than by reading. Schoolwork rarely enters there because household, field, and barn chores matter more. And the Fisher children's studying is done in a one-room, eight-grade, Old Order school taught by an Old Order woman who attended the same kind of school herself. So while Eli, Jr., like his siblings, is learning the necessity and the value of literacy, what literacy means to him and the ways in which he learns it may differ in both obvious and subtle ways from what it means and how it's transmitted to many mainstream children, just as Eli's world differs from theirs, both obviously and subtly.

As suggested earlier, Eli, Jr., lives in a house replete with print, from the kitchen bulletin board to the built-in bookcases in the playroom to the tables and magazine rack in the living room. There are children's classics and children's magazines. There are local newspapers, shoppers' guides, and other adult periodicals. And there are books of children's Bible stories, copies of the King James Version of the Bible, and other inspirational volumes, none of which mark the Fishers' home as notably different from that of many other Christian Americans.

Yet there are differences, easily overlooked by a casual observer but central to the life of the family and to their definition of literacy. One almost invisible difference is the sources of these materials. Eli and Anna attempt to carefully control the reading material that enters their home. Anna buys books primarily from a local Christian bookstore and from an Amish-operated dry goods store, both of which she trusts not to stock objectionable material. When she sees potentially interesting books in other places—in the drugstore, in the book and card shop, or at a yard sale—she uses the publisher's name as a guide to acceptable content. Relatives and friends close to the family also supply appropriate titles both as gifts and as recommendations, which Anna trusts and often chooses to follow up.

Another, slightly more visible difference comes in the form of books and periodicals around the Fisher house that would not be found in many mainstream, farm, or Christian homes. Along with the local newspaper in the rack beside the couch are issues of *Die Botschaft*, which describes itself as "A Weekly Newspaper Serving Old Order Amish Communities Everywhere." On the desk is a copy of *The Amish Directory*, which alphabetically lists all the Amish living in Pennsylvania and Maryland by nuclear family groups, giving crucial address and other information, along with maps of the eighty-seven church districts included.

On top of the breakfront in the sitting area are copies of songbooks, all in German: some for children, some for adults, and one––the *Ausbund*— for everyone, for this is the church hymnal, a collection of hymns written by tortured and imprisoned sixteenth-century Anabaptists about their experiences and their faith. Kept with these songbooks is a German edition of the Bible and a copy of the *Martyrs Mirror*, an oversized, weighty tome full of graphic descriptions in English of the tortured deaths of early Anabaptists, each illustrated by a black-and-white woodcut print.

Despite what may seem to be the esoteric nature of these texts, none remain in their special places gathering dust, for all are used regularly, each reinforcing in a characteristic way the Amish definition of literacy and each facilitating the image Eli, Jr., has of himself as literate.

Because singing is central to Amish religious observance and expression, the songbooks are used frequently by all members of the family. Because singing requires knowing what is in the text and because Amish singing, which is unaccompanied and highly stylized, requires knowing how to interpret the text exactly as everyone else does, the songbooks represent a kind of reading particularly important to the community, a kind that must be mastered to be considered literate. Yet because singing may mean holding the text and following the words as they appear or it may mean holding the text and following the words from memory or from others' rendition, children of Eli's age and younger all participate, appearing and feeling as literate as anyone else.

Functioning similarly are the German Bible and the *Martyrs Mirror*. Though only the older Fishers read that Bible, they do so regularly and then share what they've read with their children. It is the older Fishers, too, who read the *Martyrs Mirror*, but that text Eli, Sr., usually reads aloud during family devotions, so that Anna and all the children, regardless of age, participate similarly through his oral presentations.

While it may seem easier to accept such variant definitions of reading in shared communal situations like these, the participation of Eli, Jr., was equally welcome and equally effective in shared individual reading. When individual oral reading was clearly text-bound, as it is during family devotions, Eli was always enabled to participate in ways similar to his brothers' and sisters', making him a reader like them. When all the Fishers took turns reading the Bible aloud, for example, someone would read Eli's verse aloud slowly, pausing every few words, so that he could repeat what was said and thereby take his turn in the rotation.

When the older children were assigned Bible verses or *Ausbund* hymn stanzas to memorize, Eli was assigned the same one as Amos, the sibling closest in age. Their assignment would be shorter and contain less complex vocabulary than the one the older children got, yet Amos and Eli would also practice their verse together, as the older children did, and would take their turns reciting, as the older children did, making Eli again able to participate along with everyone else.

Because oral reading as modeled by Eli, Sr., is often imitated by the others, Eli, Jr., always shared his books by telling what he saw or knew about them. No one ever told him that telling isn't the same as reading, even though they may look alike, so Eli always seemed like a reader to others and felt like a reader himself.

When everyone else sat reading or playing reading-involved games in the living room after supper or on Sunday afternoons, Eli did the same, to no one's surprise, to everyone's delight, and with universal, though often tacit, welcome and approval. When the other children received books as birthday and Christmas presents, Eli received them too. And when he realized at age six that both of his brothers had magazine subscriptions of their own, Eli asked for and got one as well. Eli never saw his own reading as anything other than real; he did not see it as make-believe or bogus, and neither did anyone else. So, despite the fact that before he went to school Eli, Jr., could not read according to some definitions, he always could according to his family's and his own.

Just as all the Fishers read, so they all write, and just as Eli was enabled to define reading in a way that made him an Amish reader, so he could define writing in a way that made him an Amish writer. Letter writing has always been a primary family activity and one central to the Amish community. Anna writes weekly to *Die Botschaft*, acting as the scribe from her district. She, Eli, Sr., and sixteen-year-old Sarah all participate in circle letters, and the next three children all write with some regularity to cousins in other Amish settlements.

Yet, no matter who is writing to whom, their letters follow the same consistently modeled Amish format, beginning with "Greetings . . . ," moving to recent weather conditions, then to family and community news of note, and ending with a good-bye and often a philosophical or religious thought. I've never seen anyone in the community instructed to write this way, but in the Fisher family, letters received and even letters written are often read out loud, and though this oral sharing is done for informative rather than instructive purposes, it provides an implicit model for everyone to follow.

With all the other family members writing letters, reading them out loud, and orally sharing those they have received, Eli, Jr., wanted to write and receive letters, too, and no one said he couldn't. When he was very young, he dictated his messages to Sarah and drew pictures to accompany what she wrote down for him. Then, even before he started school, Eli began copying the dictated messages Sarah recorded, so that the letters would be in his own hand, as the drawings were.

Other forms of writing also occur in the Fisher household for everyone to see and use. Greeting cards, grocery lists, bulletin board reminders, and bedtime notes from children to absent parents were all part of Eli's life to some extent, and his preschool writing and drawing always adorned the refrigerator, along with the school papers of his brothers and sisters.

In addition, the Fishers played writing-involved games—including Scrabble and Boggle—in which everyone participated, as the family revised the rules to suit their cooperative social model and their definition of literacy. In any game at the Fishers, the oldest person or persons playing may assist the younger ones.

No question of fairness arises unless only some players go unaided. Older players, too, may receive help from other players or from onlookers. Score is always kept, and, while some moves are ruled illegal, age or aid received neither bars nor assures a winner. Eli, Jr., therefore, has always played these games as well as anyone else.

Obviously, Eli, Jr., learned a great deal about literacy from all these preschool experiences, but what he learned went far beyond academic readiness lessons. More important, Eli learned that literacy is a force in the world—his world—and it is a force that imparts power to all who wield it. He could see for himself that reading and writing enable people as old as his parents and as young as his siblings to fully participate in the world in which they live. In fact, it might have seemed to him that, to be an Amish man, one must read and write, and to be a Fisher, one must read and write as well.

So, even before the age of six, Eli began to recognize and acquire the power of literacy, using it to affiliate himself with the larger Amish world and to identify himself as Amish, a Fisher, a boy, and Eli Fisher, Jr. However, what enabled Eli to recognize all these ways of defining and asserting himself through literacy was neither direct instruction nor insistence from someone else. Rather, it was the ability that all children have long before they can read and write print text, the ability, as Friere puts it, "to read the world." "It is possible," Friere asserts, "to view objects and experiences as texts, words, and letters, and to see the growing awareness of the world as a kind of reading, through which the self learns and changes" (6). Eli, Jr., clearly illustrates this understanding of how children perceive and comprehend the seemingly invisible text of their lives. What he came to understand and accept this way were the definition and the role of print literacy as his society and culture both consciously and tacitly transmit them.

When Eli, Jr., began school, therefore, he was both academically and socially ready to begin. To smooth the transition from home to school, Eli's teacher—like most in Old Order schools—held a "preschool day" in the spring preceding his entry to first grade. On that day, Eli and Mary, the two prospective first-graders in Meadow Brook School, came to be initiated as "scholars." Verna, their teacher, had moved the two current first-graders to other seats, clearing the two desks immediately in front of hers for the newcomers; all that day Mary and Eli sat in the first-grade seats, had "classes," and did seatwork like all the other children. They seemed to know they were expected to follow the rules, to do what they saw others doing, to practice being "scholars," and Verna reinforced that notion, treating those two almost as she would anyone else.

To begin one lesson, for example, "Let's talk about bunnies," she instructed, nodding her head toward the two littlest children, indicating that they should stand beside her desk. She then showed them pictures of rabbits, with the word *bunnies* and the number depicted indicated in word and numeral on each picture. After going through the pictures, saying, "three bunnies," "four bunnies," and having the children repeat after her, Verna asked three questions and got three choral answers.

"Do bunnies like carrots?" she asked.
"Yes," the two children answered together.
"Do they like lettuce?"
"Yes."
"Do they sometimes get in Mother's garden?"
"Yes."

Were it not for some enthusiastic head nodding, Eli, Jr., and Mary could have been fully matriculated students.

When she was ready to assign seatwork, Verna gave the preschoolers pictures of bunnies to color and asked, "What do we do first? Color or write our names?"

"Write our names," the pair chorused, having practiced that skill earlier in the day.

"Yes, we always write our names first. Go back to your desk, write your name, then color the picture. Do nothing on the back of the paper." And the children did exactly that, doing "what we do" precisely "the way we do it."

Verna also conducted what she called a reading class for the two preschoolers, during which they sat, and she held an open picture book facing them. Talking about the pictures, Verna made simple statements identifying different aspects of and actions in the illustrations. After each statement Verna paused, and the children repeated exactly what she had said. The oral text accompanying one picture said:

Sally is eating chips and watching TV.
Sally has a red fish.
Sally has spilled the chips.

After "reading" the text this way, the children answered questions about it.

"What does Sally have?" Verna asked.
"A fish," they replied.
"What color is her fish?"
"Red."
"Did Sally spill the chips?"
"Yes."
"Did the cat eat the chips?"
"Yes."

While the content of this lesson seems incongruous, I know, its form and conduct fit the Meadow Brook model perfectly. Precise recall and yeses are all that the questions demand. Even the last question, while not covered in the "reading," requires recognition of only what happens in the picture.

What happened in Meadow Brook School that day—and what would happen in the eight school years to follow—reinforced, extended, and rarely contradicted what Eli already knew about literacy. Reading and writing at school allowed him to further affiliate and identify himself with and within his social group. While his teacher occasionally gave direct instructions, those instructions tended to be for activities never before seen or experienced: otherwise, Eli and Mary knew to follow the behavioral and attitudinal lead of the older children and to look to them for assistance and support, just as they looked to the teacher. In other words, reading the school world came as naturally to these children as reading the world anywhere else, and the message in both texts was emphatically the same.

Most important here, however, may be the remarkable substantive coherence that Meadow Brook School provided, a coherence that precluded any conflict over what, how, or even whether to read and write. Eli's experience as a Fisher had taught him that reading comes in many forms—secular and religious, silent and oral, individual and communal—and they all count. Through his at-home experience, Eli had also learned which other, more specific, less obvious abilities count as reading in his world. He had learned to value at least four significant abilities: (1) the ability to select and manage texts, to be able to find his mother's letter in *Die Botschaft* or to find a particular verse in the Bible; (2) the ability to empathize with people in texts and to discern the implicit lessons their experiences teach: to empathize with Lambert the lion, who taught the possibility of peaceful coexistence, and to empathize with the Anabaptist martyrs, who taught the rightness of dying for one's faith; (3) the ability to accurately recall what was read, to remember stories, riddles, and jokes or to memorize Bible and hymn verses; and (4) the ability to synthesize what is read in a single text with what is already known or to synthesize information across texts in Amish-appropriate ways.

When Eli got to school, he found a similar definition of reading in operation. He and Mary were helped to select and manage text. Their attention was directed toward what mattered in the text and away from what did not. They were helped to discover the single right answer to every question. They had only to recall information without interpreting or extending it in any significant way. And they were expected to empathize with the people in Verna's lunchtime oral reading without questioning or hypothesizing about what had happened or what would happen next.

Similarly, before Eli went to school, he knew what counted as writing in his world, just as he knew what counted as reading. He learned at home that being able to write means being able to encode, to copy, to follow format, to choose content, and to list. And, when he arrived at school, this same definition, these same abilities, were all that mattered there, too.

While the dimensions of reading and writing that count at Meadow Brook and elsewhere in Eli's life seem little different from those that count in mainstream situations—a terrifying fact, I would suggest—it is important to recognize that several mainstream-valued skills are completely absent from the Amish world as I've experienced it. Critical reading—individual analysis and interpretation—of the sort considered particularly important by most people who are mainstream-educated or mainstream educators is not valued by the Amish because of its potentially divisive, counterproductive power.

Literary appreciation, too, is both irrelevant and absent because the study of text-as-object is moot. How a writer enables a reader to empathize with his characters doesn't matter; only the ability to empathize matters. Text, whether biblical or secular, is perceived not as an object but as a force acting in the world, and it is the impact of that force that counts.

When it comes to writing, the existing Amish definition also differs in what is absent, rather than what is present. While grammar, spelling, and punctuation do count for the Old Order, they do so only to the extent that word order, words, and punctuation must allow readers to read—that is, to recognize and make sense of their reading. If a reader readily understands the intention of an adjective used as an adverb, a singular verb following a plural noun, a sentence fragment, or a compound verb containing a misplaced comma, the Amish do not see these as errors warranting attention, despite the fact that an outside reader may.

Equally irrelevant in Old Order schools is the third-person formal essay—the ominous five-paragraph theme—so prevalent in mainstream classrooms. Amish children never learn to write this kind of composition, not because they are not college-bound but because the third-person-singular point of view assumed by an individual writer is foreign to this first-person-plural society; thesis statements, topic sentences, and concepts like coherence, unity, and emphasis are similarly alien.

One final distinction separates the Amish definition of literacy from that of many mainstream definitions: the absence of originality as a desirable feature. Not only do community constraints limit the number of appropriate topics and forms an Amish writer may use, but original approaches to or applications of those topics and forms is implicitly discouraged by the similarity of models and assignments and by the absence of fiction as an appropriate personal genre. All aspects of community life reward uniformity; while writing provides an outlet for individual expression and identification, singular creativity stays within community norms.

For Eli Fisher, Jr., then, the definition of literacy he learned at home was consistent with the one he found at school, though it differed in several important ways from those of most MLA members, for example. Yet for Eli, as for Friere, "deciphering the word flowed naturally from reading the immediate world" (7). From reading his world, this six-year-old derived a complete implicit definition that told him what literacy is and whether literacy matters. I can't help but wonder, however, what would have happened had Eli gone to school and been told, explicitly or through more powerful behaviors, that he really didn't know what counted as reading and writing, that his reading and writing were not real but other unknown or alien varieties were. What would have happened had his quiet imitative behavior made him invisible in the classroom or, worse yet, made his teacher assume that he was withdrawn, problematic, or less than bright? What if his work were devalued because it was obviously copied or just unoriginal? What if he had been called on to perform individually in front of the class, to stand up and stand out? Or what if he had been asked to discuss private issues in public? Or to evaluate what he read?

Had any of these things happened, I suspect that Eli would have had to make some difficult choices that would have amounted to choosing between what he had learned and learned to value at home and what he seemed expected to learn at school. To conform to his teacher's demands and values, he would have had to devalue or disavow those of his parents—a demand that public schools seem to make frequently of children from cultural or socioeconomic groups differing from those of their teachers or their schools, a demand that seems unfair, uncalled for, and unnecessary, not to mention counterproductive and destructive.

Eli Fisher's experience suggests, therefore, that those of us who deal with children unlike ourselves need to see our classrooms and our students differently from the way we may have seen them in the past. We need to realize that students, even first-graders, have been reading the world—if not the word—for at least five, six, or seven years; they come to school not devoid of knowledge and values but with a clear sense of what their world demands and requires, including what, whether, and how to read and write, though their understandings may differ significantly from our own. We need to realize that our role may not be to prepare our students to enter mainstream society but, rather, to help them see what mainstream society offers and what it takes away, what they may gain by assimilating and what they may lose in that process. Through understanding their worlds, their definitions of literacy, and their dilemmas, not only will we better help them make important literacy-related decisions, but we will better help ourselves to do the same.

WORKS CITED

Freire, Paulo. "The Importance of the Act of Reading." *Journal of Education* Winter 1983: 5-10.
Heath, Shirley Brice. *Ways with Words: Language, Life, and Work in Communities and Classrooms.* Cambridge: Cambridge UP, 1983.
Taylor, Denny. *Family Literacy.* Portsmouth: Heinemann, 1983.
Wells, Gordon. *The Meaning Makers.* Portsmouth: Heinemann, 1986. ∎

Responding to Reading

1. What are the key features of Amish literacy? What counts for literacy in that particular community? In what particular ways does that conception of literacy accord with and depart from your own?

2. Fishman references Freire twice. Review those sections. How does she use Freire, and particularly his concept of "reading the world," to inform the essay?

3. Review the final three paragraphs, in which Fishman reflects on the potential consequences of mainstream school practices for children like Eli, Jr. What is Fishman's main point here? Should it have any bearing on how literacy tutors do their work?

Poem: Audre Lorde, *Learning to Write*

Audre Lorde was a poet, an essayist, and a novelist who was raised in New York. Educated at Hunter College and Columbia University, Lorde published several books of poetry and prose and served as the poet laureate of New York from 1991 to 1992. She died of breast cancer in 1992.

Is the alphabet responsible
for the book
in which it is written
that makes me peevish and nasty
and wish I were dumb   again?

We practiced drawing our letters
digging into the top of the desk
and old Sister Eymard
rapped our knuckles
until they bled
she was the meanest of all
and we knew she was crazy
but none of the grownups
would listen to us
until she died in a madhouse.

I am a bleak heroism of words
that refuse
to be buried alive
with the liars.

Responding to Reading

1. What is the prevailing tone of this poem? How is it conveyed?

2. Examine the poem's title. Why is it significant? Using evidence from the poem, consider what kind(s) of "writing" Lorde is evoking. In what ways could the title be interpreted as serious? ironic?

3. Discuss several of the key tensions in this poem: between old and young, between teacher and student, between schooled reading/writing and the "heroism of words," between lies and truth, between constraint and freedom, and so on.

4. At the end of her essay on Amish literacy, Andrea Fishman suggests a potential rift between the literacy valued by students and that valued by their teachers. How is this evident in Lorde's poem?

5. Note how this poem represents matters of authority—both teacher authority and religious authority. How does it compare to how Fishman describes the nature of teacher and religious authority among the Amish and to how Freire imagines the ideal teacher–student relationship?

6. What does this poem suggest about learning to write? about schooling? about teaching? about the nature of language?

ASSIGNMENT OPTIONS

PROPOSAL ESSAY

Drawing on the readings in this section, propose your ideal vision of literacy instruction. Be sure to consider the realistic constraints to that vision and to anticipate the objections that others might raise against it.

CONNECTING READING TO SERVICE

How do these theoretical essays inform your own work as a tutor? In what ways do they help you see new or different things? In what ways do they make your work harder or more complicated? Draw on the readings and on your own specific experiences to introduce, illustrate, and/or support your main points.

3

Exploring Community

What brings a community together? How can communities nurture us? And how can they at the same time constrain us? The readings in this chapter reflect on the nature of community and on the ways that our participation in communities shapes our lives, both individually and collectively. The main assignments ask you to describe and analyze a particular community that is important to you and to define community as a concept.

Communities help shape our identities and provide a context for our actions. To better understand them is to better understand ourselves. Dictionary definitions try to nail down the meaning of *community*. But the term remains slippery, and rightly so. Community is both an abstract concept and a lived enterprise. It both begs definition and defies easy compartmentalization. This chapter encourages deliberation on the meanings and manifestations of *community*, inviting you to see it from multiple perspectives and to arrive at your own definition.

If you are currently engaged in community service, or preparing for it, you should be aware of the basic architecture of community before you embark on that work. This chapter examines patterns in community life. Along with Chapter 6, it forms one of the foundations for responsible community action. It also raises several key ideas that resurface in Chapter 4.

Community: 1. a body of individuals organized as a unit or manifesting some unifying trait: (a) state, commonwealth; (b) the people living in a particular region; (c) a group of people marked by a common characteristic but living within a larger society; (d) any group sharing interests or pursuits; (e) a body of persons united by historical consciousness or by common social, economic and political interests. 2. society at large; the public. 3. common or joint ownership, tenure, experience, or pertinence; common character; shared activity.

—**Adapted from** *Merriam-Webster's Collegiate Dictionary*

Right now you belong to several overlapping communities. Some are small—family, group of friends, church, workplace, fraternity or sorority, club, team; some large—town, neighborhood, university; some larger still—city, state, political party, ethnic group, nation. Some are at once local and global. One might be a member of a local church congregation and also part of that denomination's worldwide following; or an architect might see her everyday workplace as a vital community and also value membership in the broader profession of architecture.

Some communities are hard to define. Do we consider the individuals from all over the world who share a chat room on the Web a community? Should the fans of a particular music group, for example, be considered a community?

How else do Americans "collectivize" themselves as members of groups? We often display outward signs of our membership in communities. We don a cap with a sport team's logo or put a college sticker on a car's rear window. These announce, "I identify with this team" or "I belong to this educational community." There are myriad other signals of community membership: a ring, a yarmulke, a veil, a cross, a tattoo, a pink triangle, a red, white, and blue ribbon, a uniform, a business suit, a lab coat. However, many community markers are not visible. We often know nothing of the familial, social, political, religious, and personal affiliations of the people we pass on the street.

WRITING TO DISCOVER

List at least six communities—large and small, formal and informal—to which you belong. When you are done, share your list with a classmate.

Then pick two. For each, write a paragraph that describes how and why that community matters to you.

Most of the time we don't think deliberately about the nature of community; we simply go about participating in communities as part of daily life. But key events can bring matters of community to the forefront of attention. The tragic events of September 11, 2001, have prompted a dramatic revival of questions about the nature of the United States as a national community. American flags on houses, in windows, and on lapels signal patriotism and announce membership in a national community. Meanwhile, tensions between inclusion and exclusion, freedom and constraint, rights and responsibilities—which are always tugging at each other in both local and national communities—have become much more visible.

ASSIGNMENT OPTIONS

ANALYZING A PARTICULAR COMMUNITY

Write an essay that describes, defines, and analyzes a particular community of which you are a part or about which you are particularly curious. It could be a community defined by geography (e.g., home town, neighborhood, campus, city), a group or collective with which you have long identified (perhaps defined by ethnicity, race, religion, identity, interest, profession, etc.), or a community that you have entered recently or hope to enter soon (e.g., college, dorm, service-learning site, peer social group, club, fraternity). The essay should include analysis of language practices.

Drawing on experience, observation, and research, include a textured description of the community that is comprehensible to outsiders. Include analysis of the key community tensions and language practices. Some guiding questions include the following:

- What factors define the group (geography, age, interests, ethnicity, shared history, etc.)?
- What is the history of the community? How does that history shape current practices and attitudes?
- What is the typical process of entering the community?
- What language practices are common to the community (special terms, habits of communication, etc.)? How do talk and writing reflect certain kinds of group membership?
- What other patterns of sameness are evident within the community (dress, rituals, values, behaviors, etc.)?
- How does the community deal with difference?
- What are the rewards and costs of membership?
- How does the community express and negotiate key tensions?
- How might people from alternate perspectives (i.e., insider vs. outsider) define the community differently from one another?

Readings from this chapter will help you apply such questions to a particular community.

DEFINING COMMUNITY

Drawing on the readings in this chapter, craft an extended definition of *community*. Follow the guidelines and rhetorical strategies for extended definitions explained in the chapter, and use examples and experience to support your claims.

Community Tensions

Communities are dynamic rather than static. Consciously or not, each community, whether large or small, must negotiate between forces of togetherness and separateness, collective values and individual preferences, connection to the past and movement toward the future. Because tensions constitute a natural part of community life, recognizing them is a fruitful place to begin our analysis.

Excerpt: David L. Kirp, *Almost Home: America's Love–Hate Relationship with Community*

David L. Kirp is a professor of public policy at the University of California, Berkeley. The following is drawn from the introduction to his most recent book.

On a warm September afternoon a few weeks into the fall 1999 term, Berkeley's Sproul Plaza teems with life. Students scurry between classes or head toward Telegraph Avenue. The quintessentially Berkeley characters are on the scene—the preacher cajoling, the man with the fake microphone crooning off-key, and the drummer pounding away.

In this scruffy square, the cultural revolution had its tumultuous start with the Free Speech Movement. But now that seems like ancient history. Mario Savio, the personification of the Movement, has been transformed into an icon, his death mourned by a chancellor whose predecessor sicced the police on him. When compared to the 1960s, the occasional protests over the demise of affirmative action or the university's unwillingness to let its teaching assistants unionize are timid affairs. A small circle embedded in the Plaza is inscribed with the words, "This Space is the Territory of No Nation," but to the oblivious passerby, that circle—with the utopian fantasy that it represents—is just part of the pavement.

On this Indian summer day, student organizations are recruiting new members. Tables have been set up along the edge of Sproul Plaza—an astonishing one hundred and seventy-six tables—manned by students who together represent a benign Babel. Campus Greens are here as well as Campus Republicans. So are the Undergraduate Minority Business Association and the Pre-Med Honor Society; the New Life Christian Club, the Asian Baptists, and the Bahia Club; the Taiwanese Student Association and La Familia; Cal Dykes and Chi Phi; the Golden Bear Victory Fellowship and Food Not Bombs; Swingin' Out and Take Back the Night. The hockey team hopes to convert roller-bladers into goalies; the debating society hopes to lure silver-tongued orators.

Students wander slowly past these tables, as if window-shopping for an identity, deciding how to choose among their multiple selves. One of them might be black and Latino, a practicing Catholic, a Go player and a soccer nut. Another could be a lesbian whose politics are libertarian and whose passion is square dancing.

Literally thousands of personal decisions about which groups to join, or whether to join at all, will be made this afternoon and in the coming days. Out of this crucible of choice will emerge small communities rooted in common interests—a network of associations that closely resembles the vision of democracy made small that Alexis de Tocqueville found so distinctive and so praiseworthy.

Directly underneath Sproul Plaza, a very different scene is being played out. In a darkened room as claustrophobic as a prison cell and as hushed as a cloister, students sit hunched over the latest generation of electronic games, Tomb Raider or Quake or Warcraft. They are intent on the task at hand, deadly earnest as they commit virtual mayhem on the bad guys and the evil empires. No one is talking—indeed, there is no sound at all except the electronically created voice of the machines. The civil society that is in the process of being formed in the Plaza is just a few feet away, but the psychological distance can be reckoned in light years.

These are two distinct worlds, two very different conceptions of the individual: the citizen and the solitary self. But when the students emerge from the electronic cave, blinking in the dazzling sunshine, some of them will join the crowds checking out the myriad campus organizations. And some of those who are staffing the tables on the Plaza will find their way downstairs. They find the pleasure both in solitary pursuits and sociability—and in having the chance to choose between these pleasures, to construct the shape of their lives.

*   *   *

The pull and tug of isolation and communion, freedom and commitment, contained in this vignette tells a tale of America in miniature.

There is a ton of prose on the idea of community, and mostly it is passionately opinionated. Community is praised and damned—a haven in a heartless world or a prison of conformity; a place where habits of the heart are nurtured or a seedbed of intolerance; a place to which you can't return or a place from which you'd gladly flee. The word *community* itself is a Rorschach blot upon which myriad hopes and fears are projected.   ∎

In this passage, Kirp offers both grounded examples and abstract generalizations (a rhetorical strategy that good essayists often employ). In doing so, he emphasizes the nature of community and its role in shaping our identities, as well as the power of individuals to make choices that shape their own identities.

WRITING TO DISCOVER

Kirp writes of "two distinct worlds, two very different conceptions of the individual." What are the "worlds"? How do both relate to your life? Do you identify more with one "world" than the other? Do you negotiate both? How?

What does Kirp mean when he writes that "The word *community* itself is a Rorschach blot upon which myriad hopes and fears are projected"?

When and how in daily life do you use the word *community*?

Kirp uses the example of the students in and below the plaza to illustrate the oppositions he names in the final paragraph. In doing so, he points to some of the tensions that surface in all kinds of communities, tensions that you, too, may have recognized or felt at one time or another. In a simplified form, two of the key tensions Kirp mentions are:

Engaged citizen ◄──────► Solitary self

Community as nurturing ◄──────► Community as constraining

A number of other tensions underwrite these two oppositions. Consider how the following concepts, commitments, and values push and pull at each other:

Common good ◄──────► Individual freedom

Shared goals ◄──────► Personal opportunities

Responsibilities ◄──────► Rights

Shared norms and values ◄──────► Self-expression and individualism

Common life ◄──────► Privacy

Consensus ◄──────► Dissent

There are attractive, perhaps indispensable, characteristics of community on both sides of the arrows. And, happily, in both our everyday practice and our local and national politics, we find ways to blend and negotiate such competing forces. Thus, such mapping of tensions is not intended to force stark "either/or" choices or encourage absolutist stances; rather, seeing the tensions helps us to discern which aspects are emphasized or favored when particular definitions of *community* are advanced.

When describing and defining a community to which you belong, you need to understand and analyze such tensions and their consequences. To assist you in this, the readings in this chapter demonstrate how several perceptive thinkers describe, define, and analyze community.

WRITING TO DISCOVER

Consider two communities—one formal and one informal—on which you could potentially focus in your essay. For each, jot down at least two characteristics that make the group distinctive.

Also write a few sentences in response to each of the following questions:

- How did you come to be a member of the community?
- What binds the members together?
- Which tensions or conflicts tug at the community?

Excerpt: Tracy Kidder, A *Moral Place*

Tracy Kidder is a Pulitzer Prize–winning author of several nonfiction books, including The Soul of the New Machine, House, Among Schoolchildren, *and* Old Friends. *The following is an excerpt from Kidder's 1999 book* Hometown, *which examines Northampton, a town in western Massachusetts. Notice how Kidder blends his own personal observations with some retelling of history and many direct quotations from local residents.*

In the days before it had a town clock, Northampton paid a citizen to sound a trumpet, calling all to Sunday Meeting. Attendance was required. Proper Sabbath behavior was enforced by tithing-men, each one of whom was also charged with checking on the morals of a dozen families. They carried black canes tipped with brass as symbols of their office. In Northampton nowadays, local ordinances policed a great deal of what went on outdoors, such as skateboarding and street music, and the tobacco control coordinator prowled around with a camera, looking for violations of the ban against smoking in restaurants. Even downtown, for all its flamboyance, had a serious air. Off and on, little groups stood in front of Memorial Hall, protesting international arms dealing and whatever war was current. Battles against homelessness, racism, domestic abuse, the burning of black churches in the South, were carried on from pamphlet-laden tables in Pulaski Park, and in lectures and discussion groups inside the

Unitarian Society and the First Church. In spite of the nightly masquerades and all the luxuries for sale, Northampton was a moral place.

On a billboard out by the Interstate, an ad for a Main Street shop read, STUFF YOU WANT; below that someone had written, in artfully drippy red paint, WHILE OUR GHETTOS BLEED. That message had lingered for months. The fading graffito on the back wall of Thorne's Marketplace—GENTRIFICATION IS WAR, FIGHT BACK—had remained undisturbed for years. On Main Street, inside the shop that caters to recreational runners, a middle-aged customer tells the clerk that he must be fitted to only one brand of sneaker. "It's the only kind that isn't made by sweatshop labor in China," he explains. In a dress and accessories shop a block away, a woman gazes longingly at a pair of shoes—black with a gold-colored adornment like a snaffle bit on top. Then she turns away. Of course, she could afford the shoes, she tells her husband that night. But she doesn't actually *need* them, and there are so many problems in the world—starving children, threatened species, political prisoners—that she can't help but think the money would be better spent elsewhere. Besides, she says, smiling sheepishly, she's afraid she'd feel pretentious wearing fancy shoes in Northampton. People who dyed their hair green were more comfortable here, it seemed, than people who bought leather pumps.

Downtown had a tone, and the tone had a history. It probably stretched back to the Puritans' sumptuary laws, which were intended to keep average citizens from aping the rich. There were exceptions, of course, but anecdotes from the town's annals suggest that by the time of the Revolution the rich of Northampton were endeavoring not to look too different from everyone else. In the early 1800s a resident recorded in his diary a story he'd heard, an object lesson on this theme: In 1775 or thereabouts, a young tradesman came to seek his fortune in Northampton. He carried letters of introduction to the town's leading men. First he visited the famous soldier Seth Pomeroy, hero of the French and Indian Wars, soon to fight, at the age of sixty-five, at the battle of Bunker Hill. "But to his surprise found Col. Pomeroy clothed with a leather apron and arms naked, busy at the Anvil. . . " Then he called on a Major Hawley. He found him living in an old, plain house, sitting in a ratty old armchair.

> The young man had doubts whether this man could be the famous Major Hawley and received the affirmative reply that his name was Hawley—the young man presented his letter of introduction and soon found the Great Man and that Greatness did not consist in splendid buildings or courtly dress and was taught the useful lesson of not judging a man by his outward dress.

Timothy Dwight, the president of Yale, visited Northampton in the early 1800s and noticed a peculiarity about the town's three hundred homes. "A considerable number of the houses are ordinary, many are good, and not a small proportion are handsome," he wrote. But the handsome ones weren't situated together. The rich hadn't settled down in exclusive neighborhoods, the way Dwight seemed to think they should. The handsome houses were "so scattered on the different streets as to make much less impression on the eye than even inferior buildings in many other places."

During the 1980s Northampton had indulged in a spree, extravagant by local standards, with money and real estate. But the boom had ended now. Many of the bon vivants of the eighties had moved away, been indicted, or simply calmed down. And the wealthy had generally become retiring again. Gossip had punished ostentation in the past. It still did today. The rich were especially vulnerable, because they were greatly outnumbered. For years the town's median income had stood below the Massachusetts average, and as of the 1990 federal census, only seventy-nine households, fewer than one percent, considerably less than the national average, had incomes of $150,000 or more. Wealthy people here tended to live on remote hilltops, far away from inquiring eyes, or else discreetly, in houses with plain exteriors but interiors that contained kitchens good enough for restaurants, and private libraries, and art collections of great worth. The wealthy of Northampton drove good cars but not the very best. They didn't have live-in servants, though some maintained the equivalents of staffs, in caterers, cleaners, gardeners. One tier below, there was a much larger prosperous class, the upper middle by local standards—academics, business owners, various professionals. Many people had given up a little something to live here, forsaking their chances to maximize profits.

As long as they avoided ostentation, people could be wealthy in Northampton and still be called "progressive." In fact, the combination was likely. One way to achieve it was to open one's house to fundraisers for a worthy cause. Mayor Ford once remarked, "It does seem to me that the rich here are quite benign." Of course, she was a beneficiary of fund-raisers, but she had a point. In Northampton inequality was more muted than in many American places.

Not that unanimity prevailed. A while ago the progressive forces had gone too far for some, and now the town was fighting over a proposed local statute, called the Domestic Partnership Ordinance, a gay rights initiative of sorts.

In other places, this kind of argument usually came mixed with practical questions about municipal finance and economic fairness, about discrimination in the workplace and freedom from harassment. Not in Northampton. The ordinance would allow an unmarried couple, whether heterosexual or homosexual, to license themselves as domestic partners at city hall for a ten-dollar fee. In return, one partner would have the right to view the school records of the other partner's child, with the partner's written permission. But anyone could do that already. One domestic partner would also have the right to visit the other in any city-owned jail or hospital. But Northampton didn't own a hospital, and the only jail under its control was the lockup at the police station, which didn't allow visitors of any sort. So the ordinance would grant rights that either didn't exist or that everyone already possessed. It wouldn't cost the town a penny. Maybe in other places the DPO wouldn't have seemed worth arguing about. But it had any number of symbolic meanings here. It set the town up for an election of great purity, an election about principle alone.

"This has always been a tolerant community," some natives liked to say. But not all that long ago, in the 1950s, the police had arrested a Smith College professor named Newton Arvin, winner of the National Book Award for a biography of Melville. His crime was possessing pictures of scantily clad young men. Exposed as a homosexual, and too weak to resist pressure from police, Arvin snitched on some of his best gay friends, was retired from Smith, and checked himself into the state mental hospital.

Gay-bashing in Northampton seems to have grown, along with the numbers of openly gay residents, until the early 1980s, when Judge Ryan, then the district attorney, prosecuted a man for making harassing phone calls to a local lesbian. Ordinarily the culprit would have gotten a stern warning, but the people who spoke for gay residents had been demanding action. Ryan pressed to have the man be given jail time. The judge remembered that case with mixed feelings. "He was just some poor slob and we made an example of him. But it seemed to work."

A place often gets known for one of its parts. In tabloids as far away as England, Northampton was now described as overrun by lesbians, teeming with weird and florid sexuality. The city census didn't ask the citizens what kind of sex they preferred, but a careful, between-the-lines analysis by the city planner suggested that lesbians constituted only one of many sizable minorities in town. Perhaps they only seemed more numerous than retired persons, because here they felt safe enough to come out of hiding. Several churches now performed gay marriages and the *Gazette* carried the announcements alongside traditional ones. Lesbians had become some of the city's sturdiest burghers. They ran thriving businesses. They served on civic boards. Three of the city's cops were openly gay, after all, and so were two city councillors. The first cop to come out had found FAGGOT written on his locker, but that was years ago, and if some people on the force still didn't like the idea of gay colleagues, they knew better than to say so. The First Church, scion of the Puritan church, had, after a little struggle, officially declared itself to be "open and affirming"—that is, to people of all sexual persuasions.

Nowadays so many people in Northampton, both gay and straight, referred to their significant others as "my partner" that you might have thought it was almost entirely a town of lawyers. So when the council proposed the Domestic Partnership Ordinance, it hadn't seemed likely to arouse much opposition. But an organization called Northampton for Traditional Values hastily assembled, and in no time at all they collected three thousand signatures, forcing the ordinance onto the ballot.

Tommy O'Connor watched from a little distance. He thought the DPO gave gay people here a way of sort of getting married, a state that he approved of. "It'd be kind of nice for them," he said. What he didn't like about the ordinance was its licensing of unmarried heterosexuals—another assault, he felt, on the sanctity of marriage. And what he disliked much more was that this seemed like an attempt to rub new lifestyles in old-timers' faces. This wasn't a simple argument between newcomers and natives, between Noho and Hamp, but elections make an issue two-sided. He felt that newcomers were trying to declare that they'd taken over. He lived across the border now. He didn't have a vote. If he had, he'd have voted against the ordinance.

The opposition, Northampton for Traditional Values, declined grand public debate. In lieu of real public discourse, lawn signs sprouted up all over town and the papers printed hundreds of letters to the editor. The backers of the DPO said, among many other things, that the DPO would represent a start, one small stand against the scorn and persecution that gay people had forever suffered. They said their cause was civil rights. Nonsense, said the opposition. The ordinance didn't ask for tolerance, which gay people here already had, but for official recognition, corporate approval, of gay and out-of-wedlock cohabitation. It asked the town to vote for lifestyles that many people here could tolerate but not in good conscience affirm. That seemed to be the essence of the argument at its most decorous. Both sides, of course, uttered meaner thoughts behind closed doors.

The camps held strategy sessions. They conducted phone-banking. The proponents even did some sophisticated polling. They raised far more money than the opposition, and no wonder. They had better fund-raisers: name tags, cocktails, and elevating surroundings. At one pro-DPO fundraiser, cocktails ended with the bright sound of a bell, and the host, standing on a rug that looked like a work of art, said to the crowd, "This Tibetan bell can be heard for miles, and sometimes even in the kitchen." Short, inspiring speeches followed.

On election day, people who listened to National Public Radio the rest of the year tuned into the 1400 Team. You could hear Ron Hall's voice coming out of car windows and through doorways all morning. It rained that afternoon. Campaigners stood their ground, lining streets outside the polling places, holding up their competing signs: VOTE NO ON 1 and VALUE ALL FAMILIES. Many actually looked cheerful.

"This is democracy," said one sign-holder, as waterfalls of rain spilled off his hat.

"As good as it gets," said another.

For the first time in Northampton's history, the votes were counted electronically, so the results came in much earlier than ever before. Against most expectations, Northampton for Traditional Values had prevailed—but by a margin so narrow that the contest looked like a dead heat.

Two religious services followed the vote. The winners held theirs on election night in the World War II Club, a smoky bar on Conz Street. When the returns were announced, someone cried, "It's a miracle. Hallelujah!" A group of about thirty gathered in a circle, holding hands, bowing their heads, while Father Honan of St. Mary's said a prayer. "We had a cause worth fighting for," he said afterward. Then the father raised up a glass, thanking the electorate and, presumably, God.

The losers put on a more elaborate service. They called it "A Healing Ceremony." It was held two weeks after the election, in the grand hall of the Unitarian church—by far the loveliest in a town full of churches. It has a vaulted ceiling, as tall as the Sistine Chapel's. It looks like a religious place without religion's somber side. The place is warm and bright and airy. The pews are comfortable, the architecture neoclassical, with authentic Tiffany windows fifteen feet tall and Corinthian columns. The place seems designed less for worship than for thought.

A photographic exhibit of gay and lesbian families hung on the walls, and the crowd—the majority female—filled up every pew. Victoria Safford, the Unitarian's pastor, the local rabbi, three different Christian ministers—Congregational, Episcopal, Methodist—and several lay speakers mounted the high pulpit in turn and offered consolation. As they spoke, sounds of sniffling, now and then of weeping, came from the congregation. The hall was full of handkerchiefs. But one lesbian couple was giggling softly, and whispering loud enough to attract the attention of someone nearby.

"Shhh. You shouldn't laugh in church."

"She's a recovering Catholic."

They giggled a little more and then composed their faces. They at least seemed to have emerged from grief. Perhaps the music helped. First the assembly sang a Unitarian hymn, one that doesn't mention God, called "We Sing Now Together":

We sing of community in the making
In every far continent, region and land

Then Andrea Ayvazian, for many years a lecturer on racism, now a seminary student, and the owner of one of the town's finest voices, stood near the Steinway and sang a more modern sort of song. Her lovely, deep voice filled the hall. She gestured with her arms, pulling the congregation with her, sing-along style. She could have worked a crowd in Las Vegas, but the song belonged in

New Northampton. It was entitled, "How Could Anyone." It began, "How could anyone ever tell you you are anything less than beautiful." Andrea wore an enormous smile. "Sing with me," she called, and after another verse or two, she asked, "Is it too low for you?"

It was not. The congregation had the hang of it by then, but Andrea's voice could still be heard, shining among the rest. "How could anyone fail to notice your loving is a miracle," she sang. "Now get angry!" She showed them how. "*Don't* let *anyone ever* tell you you are *anything* less than beautiful. *Don't* let *anyone ever* tell you you are less than whole." She called for "one more *don't*" and then let her voice begin to fall. Still filling up the nave, it fell toward the vocal embodiment of great calm after a storm: "How could anyone ever tell you you are less than beautiful. . . "

Of course, in a democracy, if one group of people asks the electorate questions such as "Do you agree with us?" and "Do you like us?" they ought to be prepared to hear them answer, "No." But it would be a while before some women in Northampton stopped bursting into tears and a while before many others could look at fellow citizens without wondering, "Which way did you vote?"

Liberalism had seemed to be in season here. It had seemed like the political philosophy against which all others had to struggle, or else shut up. But now it looked as if Northampton's current residents stay almost equally divided in their strong opinions about their town, about how people ought to conduct their private lives inside it, about the way Northampton defined tolerance, about who owned the place. Was the town destined to remain forever split in two camps, forever scowling at each other? Only if less than half of a town can be said to define it. As usual, a majority of the adult population hadn't even bothered to vote.

■

Responding to Reading

1. Kidder builds his narrative around the vote over the Domestic Partnership Ordinance. Other than "those for" and "those against," which other tensions are evident? Which broader values, attitudes, or histories are in play? Make the key tensions visible by presenting them as terms on each side of a double-headed arrow.

2. Why does Kidder devote so much time to the town's history? How does this inform the reader's understanding of the community and its actions?

3. How does Kidder's own perspective shape his writing? Are there places where you see him sympathizing with some constituencies over others? In what ways does your attitude about your home community shape how you describe it to others?

4. Why does Kidder title this piece "A Moral Place"? In what way(s) is it moral? To whom is it moral?

Excerpts: Alexis de Tocqueville, *Democracy in America*

Alexis de Tocqueville was a French aristocrat who traveled to the United States in 1831 to see and write about the young country. He published his reflections in a two-volume work titled Democracy in America, *which has long been heralded as among the most perceptive commentaries on American culture. In fact, politicians still routinely quote de Tocqueville in their speeches.*

Alexis de Tocqueville ranges widely in his reflections on democracy, discussing the forces that shape the particular character of American community—a Puritan heritage, a multiracial society, a democratic spirit born of a citizen revolution, a constitution emphasizing civil rights, a government premised on checks and balances, a capitalist economic system, the frontier ideal of rugged individuality, the American affinity for civic associations, and so on. de Tocqueville was also particularly interested in how the American experiment in democracy compared to the traditional aristocratic systems of Europe.

What follows are excerpts from *Democracy in America*, Volume 2, first published in 1840. This version is translated from the French by Delba Winthrop and edited by Harvey C. Mansfield. The entire text of *Democracy in America* is also available in digital format at Project Gutenberg (http://promo.net/pg).

CHAPTER 2: ON INDIVIDUALISM IN DEMOCRATIC COUNTRIES

I have brought out how, in centuries of equality, each man seeks his beliefs in himself; I want to show how, in the same centuries, he turns all his sentiments toward himself alone.

Individualism is a recent expression arising from a new idea. Our fathers knew only selfishness.

Selfishness is a passionate and exaggerated love of self that brings man to relate everything to himself alone and to prefer himself to everything.

Individualism is a reflective and peaceable sentiment that disposes each citizen to isolate himself from the mass of those like him and to withdraw to one side with his family and his friends, so that after having thus created a little society for his own use, he willingly abandons society at large to itself.

Selfishness is born of a blind instinct; individualism proceeds from an erroneous judgment rather than a depraved sentiment. It has its source in the defects of the mind as much as in the vices of the heart.

Selfishness withers the seed of all the virtues; individualism at first dries up only the source of public virtues; but in the long term it attacks and destroys all the others and will finally be absorbed in selfishness.

Selfishness is a vice as old as the world. It scarcely belongs more to one form of society than to another.

Individualism is of democratic origin, and it threatens to develop as conditions become equal.

In aristocratic peoples, families remain in the same state for centuries, and often in the same place. That renders all generations so to speak contemporaries. A man almost always knows his ancestors and respects them; he believes he already perceives his great-grandsons and he loves them. He willingly does his duty by both, and he frequently comes to sacrifice his personal enjoyments for beings who no longer exist or who do not yet exist.

In addition, aristocratic institutions have the effect of binding each man tightly to several of his fellow citizens.

Classes being very distinct and immobile within an aristocratic people, each of them becomes for whoever makes up a part of it a sort of little native country, more visible and dearer than the big one.

As in aristocratic societies all citizens are placed at a fixed post, some above the others, it results also that each of them always perceives higher than himself a man whose protection is necessary to him, and below he finds another whom he can call upon for cooperation.

Men who live in aristocratic centuries are therefore almost always bound in a tight manner to something that is placed outside of them, and they are often disposed to forget themselves. It is true that in these same centuries the general notion of *those like oneself* is obscure and that one scarcely thinks of devoting oneself to the cause of humanity; but one often sacrifices oneself for certain men.

In democratic centuries, on the contrary, when the duties of each individual toward the species are much clearer, devotion toward one man becomes rarer: the bond of human affections is extended and loosened.

In democratic peoples, new families constantly issue from nothing, others constantly fall into it, and all those who stay on change face; the fabric of time is torn at every moment and the trace of generations is effaced. You easily forget those who have preceded you, and you have no idea of those who will follow you. Only those nearest have interest.

As each class comes closer to the others and mixes with them, its members become indifferent and almost like strangers among themselves. Aristocracy had made of all citizens a long chain that went from the peasant up to the king; democracy breaks the chain and sets each link apart.

As conditions are equalized, one finds a great number of individuals who, not being wealthy enough or powerful enough to exert a great influence over the fates of those like them, have nevertheless acquired or preserved enough enlightenment and goods to be able to be self-sufficient. These owe nothing to anyone, they expect so to speak nothing from anyone; they are in the habit of always considering themselves in isolation, and they willingly fancy that their whole destiny is in their hands.

Thus not only does democracy make each man forget his ancestors, but it hides his descendants from him and separates him from his contemporaries; it constantly leads him back toward himself alone and threatens finally to confine him wholly in the solitude of his own heart.

*   *   *

CHAPTER 4: HOW THE AMERICANS COMBAT INDIVIDUALISM WITH FREE INSTITUTIONS

Despotism, which in its nature is fearful, sees the most certain guarantee of its own duration in the isolation of men, and it ordinarily puts all its care into isolating them. There is no vice of the human heart that agrees with it as much as selfishness: a despot readily pardons the governed for not loving him, provided that they do not love each other. He does not ask them to aid him in leading the state; it is enough that they do not aspire to direct it themselves. He calls those who aspire to unite their efforts to create common prosperity turbulent and restive spirits, and changing the natural sense of words, he names those who confine themselves narrowly to themselves good citizens.

Thus the vices to which despotism gives birth are precisely those that equality favors. These two things complement and aid each other in a fatal manner.

Equality places men beside one another without a common bond to hold them. Despotism raises barriers between them and separates them. It disposes them not to think of those like themselves, and for them it makes a sort of public virtue of indifference.

Despotism, which is dangerous in all times, is therefore particularly to be feared in democratic centuries.

It is easy to see that in these same centuries men have a particular need of freedom.

When citizens are forced to be occupied with public affairs, they are necessarily drawn from the midst of their individual interests, and from time to time, torn away from the sight of themselves.

From the moment when common affairs are treated in common, each man perceives that he is not as independent of those like him as he at first fancied, and that to obtain their support he must often lend them his cooperation.

When the public governs, there is no man who does not feel the value of public benevolence and who does not seek to capture it by attracting the esteem and affection of those in the midst of whom he must live.

Several of the passions that chill and divide hearts are then obliged to withdraw to the bottom of the soul and hide there. Haughtiness dissimulates; contempt does not dare come to light. Selfishness is afraid of itself.

Under a free government, since most public functions are elective, men who by the loftiness of their souls or the restiveness of their desires are cramped in private life, feel every day that they cannot do without the populace surrounding them.

It then happens that through ambition one thinks of those like oneself, and that often one's interest is in a way found in forgetting oneself. I know that one can object to me here with all the intrigues that arise in an election, the shameful means the candidates often make use of, and the calumnies their enemies spread. These are occasions for hatred, and they present themselves all the more often as elections become more frequent.

These evils are undoubtedly great, but they are passing, whereas the goods that arise with them stay.

The longing to be elected can momentarily bring certain men to make war on each other, but in the long term this same desire brings all men to lend each other a mutual support; and if it happens that an election accidentally divides two friends, the electoral system brings together in a permanent manner a multitude of citizens who would have always remained strangers to one another. Freedom creates particular hatreds, but despotism gives birth to general indifference.

The Americans have combated the individualism to which equality gives birth with freedom, and they have defeated it.

The legislators of America did not believe that, to cure a malady so natural to the social body in democratic times and so fatal, it was enough to accord to the nation as a whole a representation of itself; they thought that, in addition, it was fitting to give political life to each portion of the territory in order to multiply infinitely the occasions for citizens to act together and to make them feel every day that they depend on one another.

This was wisely done.

The general affairs of a country occupy only the principal citizens. They assemble in the same places only from time to time; and as it often happens that afterwards they lose sight of each other, lasting bonds among them are not established. But when it is a question of having the particular affairs of a district regulated by the men who inhabit it, the same individuals are always in contact and they are in a way forced to know each other and to take pleasure in each other.

Only with difficulty does one draw a man out of himself to interest him in the destiny of the whole state, because he understands poorly the influence that the destiny of the state can exert on his lot. But should it be necessary to pass a road through his property, he will see at first glance that he has come across a relation between this small public affair and his greatest private affairs, and he will discover, without anyone's showing it to him, the tight bond that here unites a particular interest to the general interest.

Thus by charging citizens with the administration of small affairs, much more than by leaving the government of great ones to them, one interests them in the public good and makes them see the need they constantly have for one another in order to produce it.

One can capture the favor of a people all at once by a striking action; but to win the love and respect of the populace that surrounds you, you must have a long succession of little services rendered, obscure good offices, a constant habit of benevolence, and a well-established reputation of disinterestedness.

Local freedoms, which make many citizens put value on the affection of their neighbors and those close to them, therefore constantly bring men closer to one another, despite the instincts that separate them, and force them to aid each other.

In the United States, the most opulent citizens take much care not to isolate themselves from the people; on the contrary, they constantly come close to them, they gladly listen to them and speak to them every day. They know that the rich in democracies always need the poor, and that in democratic times one ties the poor to oneself more by manners than by benefits. The very greatness of the benefits, which brings to light the difference in conditions, causes a secret irritation to those who profit from them; but simplicity of manners has almost irresistible charms: their familiarity carries one away and even their coarseness does not always displease.

At first this truth does not penetrate the minds of the rich. They ordinarily resist it as long as the democratic revolution lasts, and they do not accept it immediately even after this revolution is accomplished. They willingly consent to do good for the people, but they want to continue to hold them carefully at a distance. They believe that is enough; they are mistaken. They would thus ruin themselves without warming the hearts of the population that surrounds them. It does not ask of them the sacrifice of their money, but of their haughtiness.

One would say that in the United States there is no imagination that does not exhaust itself in inventing the means of increasing wealth and satisfying the needs of the public. The most enlightened inhabitants of each district constantly make use of their enlightenment to discover new secrets appropriate to increasing the common prosperity; and when they have found any, they hasten to pass them along to the crowd.

When examining up close the vices and weakness often displayed in America by those who govern, one is astonished at the growing prosperity of the people—and one is wrong. It is not the elected magistrate who makes American democracy prosper; but it prospers because the magistrate is elective.

It would be unjust to believe that the patriotism of the Americans and the zeal that each of them shows for the well-being of his fellow citizens have nothing real about them. Although private interest directs most human actions, in the United States as elsewhere, it does not rule all.

I must say that I often saw Americans make great and genuine sacrifices for the public, and I remarked a hundred times that, when needed, they almost never fail to lend faithful support to one another.

The free institutions that the inhabitants of the United States possess and the political rights of which they make so much use recall to each citizen constantly and in a thousand ways that he lives in society. At every moment they bring his mind back toward the idea that the duty as well as the interest of men is to render themselves useful to those like them; and as he does not see any particular reason to hate them, since he is never either their slave or their master, his heart readily leans to the side of benevolence. One is occupied with the general interest at first by necessity and then by choice; what was calculation becomes instinct; and by dint of working for the good of one's fellow citizens, one finally picks up the habit and taste of serving them.

Many people in France consider equality of conditions as the first evil and political freedom as the second. When they are obliged to submit to the one, they strive at least to escape the other. And I say that to combat the evils that equality can produce there is only one efficacious remedy: it is political freedom.

CHAPTER 5: ON THE USE THAT THE AMERICANS MAKE OF ASSOCIATION IN CIVIL LIFE

I do not wish to speak of those political associations with the aid of which men seek to defend themselves against the despotic action of a majority or against the encroachments of royal power. I have already treated this subject elsewhere. It is clear that if each citizen, as he becomes individually weaker and consequently more incapable in isolation of preserving his freedom, does not learn the art of uniting with those like him to defend it, tyranny will necessarily grow with equality.

Here it is a question only of the associations that are formed in civil life and which have an object that is in no way political.

The political associations that exist in the United States form only a detail in the midst of the immense picture that the sum of associations presents there.

Americans of all ages, all conditions, all minds constantly unite. Not only do they have commercial and industrial associations in which all take part, but they also have a thousand other kinds: religious, moral, grave, futile, very general and very particular, immense and very small; Americans use associations to give fêtes, to found seminaries, to build inns, to raise churches, to distribute books, to send missionaries to the antipodes; in this manner they create hospitals, prisons, schools. Finally, if it is a question of bringing to light a truth or developing a sentiment with the support of a great example, they associate. Everywhere that, at the head of a new undertaking, you see the government in France and a great lord in England, count on it that you will perceive an association in the United States.

In America I encountered sorts of associations of which, I confess, I had no idea, and I often admired the infinite art with which the inhabitants of the United States managed to fix a common goal to the efforts of many men and to get them to advance to it freely.

I have since traveled through England, from which the Americans took some of their laws and many of their usages, and it appeared to me that there they were very far from making as constant and as skilled a use of association.

It often happens that the English execute very great things in isolation, whereas there is scarcely an undertaking so small that Americans do not unite for it. It is evident that the former consider association as a powerful means of action; but the latter seem to see in it the sole means they have of acting.

Thus the most democratic country on earth is found to be, above all, the one where men in our day have most perfected the art of pursuing the object of their common desires in common and have applied this new science to the most objects. Does this result from an accident or could it be that there in fact exists a necessary relation between associations and equality?

Aristocratic societies always include within them, in the midst of a multitude of individuals who can do nothing by themselves, a few very powerful and very wealthy citizens; each of these can execute great undertakings by himself.

In aristocratic societies men have no need to unite to act because they are kept very much together.

Each wealthy and powerful citizen in them forms as it were the head of a permanent and obligatory association that is composed of all those he holds in dependence to him, whom he makes cooperate in the execution of his designs.

In democratic peoples, on the contrary, all citizens are independent and weak; they can do almost nothing by themselves, and none of them can oblige those like themselves to lend them their cooperation. They therefore all fall into impotence if they do not learn to aid each other freely.

If men who live in democratic countries had neither the right nor the taste to unite in political goals, their independence would run great risks, but they could preserve their wealth and their enlightenment for a long time; whereas if they did not acquire the practice of associating with each other in ordinary life, civilization itself would be in peril. A people among whom particular persons lost the power of doing great things in isolation, without acquiring the ability to produce them in common, would soon return to barbarism.

Unhappily, the same social state that renders associations so necessary to democratic peoples renders them more difficult for them than for all others.

When several members of an aristocracy want to associate with each other they easily succeed in doing so. As each of them brings great force to society, the number of members can be very few, and, when the members are few in number, it is very easy for them to know each other, to understand each other, and to establish fixed rules.

The same facility is not found in democratic nations, where it is always necessary that those associating be very numerous in order that the association have some power.

I know that there are many of my contemporaries whom this does not embarrass. They judge that as citizens become weaker and more incapable, it is necessary to render the government more skillful and more active in order that society be able to execute what individuals can no longer do. They believe they have answered everything in saying that. But I think they are mistaken.

A government could take the place of some of the greatest American associations, and within the Union several particular states already have attempted it. But what political power would ever be in a state to suffice for the innumerable multitude of small undertakings that American citizens execute every day with the aid of an association?

It is easy to foresee that the time is approaching when a man by himself alone will be less and less in a state to produce the things that are the most common and the most necessary to his life. The task of the social power will therefore constantly increase, and its very efforts will make it vaster each day. The more it puts itself in place of associations, the more particular persons, losing the idea of associating with each other, will need it to come to their aid: these are causes and effects that generate each other without rest. Will the public administration in the end direct all the industries for which an isolated citizen cannot suffice? and if there finally comes a moment when, as a consequence of the extreme division of landed property, the land is partitioned infinitely, so that it can no longer be cultivated except by associations of laborers, will the head of the government have to leave the helm of state to come hold the plow?

The morality and intelligence of a democratic people would risk no fewer dangers than its business and its industry if the government came to take the place of associations everywhere.

Sentiments and ideas renew themselves, the heart is enlarged, and the human mind is developed only by the reciprocal action of men upon one another.

I have shown that this action is almost nonexistent in a democratic country. It is therefore necessary to create it artificially there. And this is what associations alone can do.

When the members of an aristocracy adopt a new idea or conceive a novel sentiment, they place it in a way next to themselves on the great stage they are on, and in thus exposing it to the view of the crowd, they easily introduce it into the minds or hearts of all those who surround them.

In democratic countries, only the social power is naturally in a state to act like this, but it is easy to see that its action is always insufficient and often dangerous.

A government can no more suffice on its own to maintain and renew the circulation of sentiments and ideas in a great people than to conduct all its industrial undertakings. As soon as it tries to leave the political sphere to project itself on this new track, it will exercise an insupportable tyranny even without wishing to; for a government knows only how to dictate precise rules; it imposes the sentiments and the ideas that it favors, and it is always hard to distinguish its counsels from its orders.

This will be still worse if it believes itself really interested in having nothing stir. It will then hold itself motionless and let itself be numbed by a voluntary somnolence.

It is therefore necessary that it not act alone.

In democratic peoples, associations must take the place of the powerful particular persons whom equality of conditions has made disappear.

As soon as several of the inhabitants of the United States have conceived a sentiment or an idea that they want to produce in the world, they seek each other out; and when they have found each other, they unite. From then on, they are no longer isolated men, but a power one sees from afar, whose actions serve as an example; a power that speaks, and to which one listens.

The first time I heard it said in the United States that a hundred thousand men publicly engaged not to make use of strong liquors, the thing appeared to me more amusing than serious, and at first I did not see well why such temperate citizens were not content to drink water within their families.

In the end I understood that those hundred thousand Americans, frightened by the progress that drunkenness was making around them, wanted to provide their patronage to sobriety. They had acted precisely like a great lord who would dress himself very plainly in order to inspire the scorn of luxury in simple citizens. It is to be believed that if those hundred thousand men had lived in France, each of them would have addressed himself individually to the government, begging it to oversee the cabarets all over the realm.

There is nothing, according to me, that deserves more to attract our regard than the intellectual and moral associations of America. We easily perceive the political and industrial associations of the Americans, but the others escape us; and if we discover them, we understand them badly because we have almost never seen anything analogous. One ought however to recognize that they are as necessary as the first to the American people, and perhaps more so.

In democratic countries the science of association is the mother science; the progress of all the others depends on the progress of that one.

Among the laws that rule human societies there is one that seems more precise and clearer than all the others. In order that men remain civilized or become so, the art of associating must be developed and perfected among them in the same ratio as equality of conditions increases.   ■

Responding to Reading

1. How does de Tocqueville's conception of individualism differ from selfishness? Further, what is the relationship between democracy and individualism?

2. How do de Tocqueville's reflections on individualism (made over 150 years ago) relate to your perceptions of contemporary U.S. culture?

3. How does de Tocqueville's work anticipate and echo Kirp's reflections on the events of Sproul Plaza in Berkeley, California?

4. Why is the U.S. practice of gathering in free associations so important to de Tocqueville? What are its costs and benefits?

5. What does de Tocqueville mean when, at the end of Chapter 5, he writes: "In democratic countries the science of association is the mother science; the progress of all the others depends on the progress of that one"?

Essay: John McKnight, *Redefining* Community

John McKnight is the Director of the Community Studies Program at the Center for Urban Affairs and Policy Research at Northwestern University in Evanston, Illinois. He has authored many works, including a guide for community development titled Community Building from the Inside Out. *The following is from his book,* The Careless Society.

It was in a small New England town that I first understood the limits of community services. The town was located in a state with one of the most humane and progressive systems for serving people who are labeled developmentally disabled. Very few were in large institutions, small group homes had proliferated, sheltered workshops were being dismantled, and a serious effort was under way in the schools to bring labeled children into the regular classrooms. In this town, I was taken to one of the group homes. The home was physically indistinguishable from the other houses on the street. Living in the house were five middle-aged men, most of whom had lived there for nearly ten years.

It was with considerable pride that an agency director and a public official took me to visit these men. They wanted me to see how their clients were "a part of the community" and the beneficiaries of an effective program of community services. When the opportunity came to talk to each of the men, I inquired about their lives, experiences, and relationships in the town. To my surprise, the response of each man made clear that they had almost no social relationships with their neighbors or the other citizens of the town. None of them could identify a close local friend or neighbor, and none were involved in any kind of organization, association, or club. When I asked the staff members whether they knew of any social relationships the men had in the community, they were unable to identify any other than a few shopkeepers.

Later I learned, by talking with other people within the state human service system, that the isolated circumstances of these five men tended to be the rule rather than the exception. Nonetheless, they were described as "deinstitutionalized," as being "in the community," and as receiving "community services." That was when I first realized that all of this community language obscured the basic fact that these men were completely isolated from community while surrounded by community services.

One wonders how it is possible, in a small town of 5,000 people, to find a typical house and have five residents live there for ten years without any effective community relationships. Yet human service systems designed to provide what are called "community services" often have managed to do just that.

Perhaps the issue can be clarified by defining "community services" more accurately. I would not want to suggest that these are services that will "make people part of community." Rather, I mean to point out that services provided in small towns or neighborhoods should not be called community services if they do not involve people in community relationships. Indeed, what are now called community services are often the major barriers to involvement in the community. Let's say, then, that the system in this state is now providing *local services*, not community services. And that the relocation of those services to local places has had almost no positive effect on the participation of labeled people in community life.

This failure of integration clearly limits the lives of the labeled people themselves. But the exclusion also limits the experience of local citizens. Most community members have infrequent opportunities to be joined in their common life by people who have been given one of the labels established by the service industry. Indeed, the common life of North America is so segregated that the absence of experience with those who are excluded has led many citizens to imagine that labeled people are somehow inappropriate for community life. Many have come to believe that labeled people are so incapacitated that their lives literally depend upon separate and expert attention. Having accepted this proposition, most citizens lead lives in which they can only imagine, never see or talk to, labeled people.

WHAT IS COMMUNITY?

How can incorporation of labeled people into community life be achieved? Before we can respond to that question, we must ask: What do we mean by community?

There is no universally accepted definition. However, one is so practically useful that it can become central to the work of those concerned about the incorporation of labeled people into community life.

I am referring to an understanding laid out by Alexis de Tocqueville, the French count who visited the United States in 1831. What he found was that European settlers were creating a society different from the one they knew in Europe: communities formed around an uncustomary social invention, small groups of common citizens coming together to form organizations that solve problems.

Tocqueville observed three features in how these groups operated. First, they were groups of citizens who decided they had the power to decide what was a problem. Second, they decided they had the power to decide how to solve the problem. Third, they often decided that they would themselves become the key actors in implementing the solution. From Tocqueville's perspective, these citizen associations were a uniquely powerful instrument being created in America, the foundation stones of American communities.

It should seem obvious that communities are collective associations. They are more than and different from a series of friendships. One can have a friendship with a labeled person in an institution, for example, but that does not mean the person has been incorporated into the community. A community is more than just a place. It comprises various groups of people who work together on a face-to-face basis in public life, not just in private.

The kinds of associations that express and create community take several forms. Many of them are relatively formal, with names and with officers elected by the members. They may be the American Legion, the church bowling league, or the local peace fellowship.

A second kind of association is not so formal. It usually has no officers or name. Nonetheless, it represents a gathering of citizens who solve problems, celebrate together, or enjoy their social compact. These associations could be a poker club, a coffee klatch, or a gathering of neighbors who live on the block. The fact that they do not have a formal name and structure should not obscure the fact that they are often the sites of critical dialogue, opinion formation, and decision-making that influence the values and problem-solving capacities of citizens. Indeed, many Americans are primarily influenced in their decision-making and value formation by these informal groups.

A third form of association is less obvious because one could describe the place where it occurs as an enterprise or business. However, much associational activity takes place in restaurants, beauty parlors, barbershops, bars, hardware stores, and other places of business. People gather in these places for interaction as well as transaction. In the eighteenth century, some of the most basic discussions about the formation of the government of the United States and its Constitution occurred in inns and taverns, and similar settings provide the backdrop for some of the most fundamental associational life today.

These three types of associations represent the community from which most labeled people are excluded, and into which they need to be incorporated if they are to become active citizens at the associational center of a democratic society.

INCLUDING THE EXCLUDED

Once we have understood the nature of the community of associations, we can begin to look at ways to incorporate excluded people into this community life. Some people who have been excluded forge a path back into community on their own. This is usually a heroic struggle that requires great commitment and persistence. And while we know that this escape into inclusion is infrequent, it is equally clear that life in the community is the dream of many of those labeled people whose lives are surrounded by nothing but services.

A second point of entry into community life is created by family and friends, who almost always have a vision for the labeled individual that reaches beyond access to community services. They see that the good life is not just a fully serviced life, but a life filled with the care, power, and continuity that come from being part of a community.

A third point of entry into community is the one I would like to focus on in this article. It is a process involving individuals who assume a special responsibility for guiding excluded people out of service and into the realm of the community. In varying degrees, this phenomenon occurs in many places.

Northwestern University's Center for Urban Affairs and Policy Research has engaged in a continuing study of the initiatives of these individuals who serve as "community guides." The guides are unique, unschooled in their efforts, and informed by their own individual creativity and insight. While it is difficult to generalize about these people, it is possible to describe some patterns of their work.

BUILDING COMMUNITY RELATIONSHIPS

Effective guides do not just introduce one person to another: They bring a person into the web of associational life that can act as a powerful force in that person's life. And they bring the individual into life as a citizen by incorporating him into relationships where his capacities can be expressed—where he is not simply defined by his "deficiencies."

Most guides are people with a special eye for the gift, the potential, the interest, the skills, the smile, the capacity of those who are said to be "in special need." Focusing upon these strengths, they introduce people into community life. Several guides we interviewed had previously worked in service systems, and told us they had not realized that their entire understanding of the people they called clients was focused upon "fixing" them. They report that their most basic change in attitude, allowing them to be a guide, was to stop trying to "fix" people.

A second attribute of most, but not all, effective guides is that they are well-connected in the interrelationships of community life. They have invested much of life's energy and vitality in associational activity. Because of these connections, they are able to make a variety of contacts quickly because "they know people who know other people." This is why most guides come from community life rather than service systems. A person interested in human services can spend money and receive training that will give the capacity to fix others. There is, however, no school, program, curriculum, or money that can connect a person to associational community life. Instead, this capacity grows stronger from years of experience and contribution to community life.

The third common characteristic of community guides is that they achieve their ends because they are trusted by their community peers, and not because they have institutional authority. This point is a correlate of the second. If guides are well connected, it is because they are trusted, and that trust is the result of their having invested their lives and commitments in the lives of others in the informal web of associational life.

In working through a framework of trust, the guides do not identify themselves with systems. They do not say that they are from the Department of Mental Deficiency, Division of Experimentation, Bureau of Community Programs. Instead, they say, "I'm a friend of your sister Mary, and she said that I should ask you about the choir that you direct. I have a friend who loves to sing and has a beautiful voice, and I think that you might like to have her in your choir." In this way, the guide is introducing an excluded person based on her capacity to sing. She is making the introduction through a relationship with a trusted relative. She is seeking engagement of the excluded person in an association of community life—a local choir. In two sentences, the guide is able to bring together the capacity, the connectedness, and the trust that are the visible pathways into community life.

The fourth characteristic of almost all community guides is that they believe strongly that the community is a reservoir of hospitality that is waiting to be offered. It is their job to lead someone to ask for it.

This belief in a hospitable community is a critical ingredient in the work of successful guides. Their vivacious expectations of success make it clear that they are "making an offer you can't refuse" when they introduce an excluded person to a citizen active in associational life. They are not apologetic or begging or asking for charity or help. Instead, they are enthusiastically presenting the gift of an excluded person to the hospitality of a person active in the community.

In our experience, we have found that guides' belief in a hospitable community is well founded. Indeed, many guides find that their belief in the community grows even greater as they consistently find that there is a broad community readiness to incorporate people who have been excluded. This is not to say that every person in every neighborhood is hospitable—we all know this is not the case. But the guides we interviewed report that the great majority of people they have encountered are receptive and open to diversity. It is the obvious task of the guide to relate to this part of the community rather than to focus on those who are negative or resistant.

Unfortunately, many people in human service systems have had negative experiences as they have tried to parachute small institutions called group homes into neighborhoods. Frequently, the local residents will resist this professional vision of "community integration." However, the very same neighbors, asked to meet and involve one person named Sam Jones who has been labeled developmentally disabled, will frequently welcome that person into their collective life. Just as every individual has capacities and deficiencies, every community has hospitality and rejection. A community guide knows the terrain of hospitality and avoids the pitfall of rejection.

A fifth characteristic of most effective community guides is that they learn that they must say goodbye to the person they guide into community life. This is not a natural step. Nonetheless, most guides report that they have learned that in order for the fullness of community hospitality to be expressed and the excluded person to be wholly incorporated as a citizen, they must leave the scene. They are guides, not servants.

POLICY PATHS TO INCLUSION

While most guides are people who do not need "policies" to guide them and are, in fact, unsure of what a policy is, there are those in human service systems who need policies in order to understand practice. For such policy and system operatives, it is possible to summarize the work of guides in the following policy statement: "It is our policy to reduce dependence on human services by increasing interdependence in community life through a focus on the gifts and capacities of people who have been excluded from community life because of their labels."

Contained in this policy statement is the recognition that there are many dependency-creating human services. It is those services that the guides attempt to replace with associational life. However, it is also clear that there are human services that do not create dependence and could be designed to support community life, such as income supplements, independent living aides, and specialized medical services. There has been very little systematic study in this area. A preliminary hypothesis is that services that are heavily focused on deficiency tend to be pathways out of community and into the exclusion of serviced life. We need a rigorous examination of public investments so that we can distinguish between services that lead people out of community and into dependency and those activities that support people in community life.

Finally, we are reminded that the policy statement indicates that it is our goal to "increase interdependence in community life." It is critical here that we emphasize the word *interdependence*. The goal is not to create independence—except from social service systems. Rather, we are recognizing that every life in community is, by definition, interdependent—filled with trusting relationships and empowered by the collective wisdom of citizens in discourse.

Community is about the common life that is lived in such a way that the unique creativity of each person is a contribution to the other. The crisis we have created in the lives of excluded people is that they are disassociated from their fellow citizens. We cannot undo that terrible exclusion by a thoughtless attempt to create illusory independence. Nor can we undo it by creating a friendship with a person who lives in exclusion.

Our goal should be clear. We are seeking nothing less than a life surrounded by the richness and diversity of community. A collective life. A common life. An everyday life. A powerful life that gains its joy from the creativity and connectedness that come when we join in association to create an inclusive world.   ■

Responding to Reading

1. In his opening anecdote, why does McKnight bristle at the use of the term *community services* and the phrase *a part of the community?*

2. McKnight makes reference to Alexis de Tocqueville. How does he use de Tocqueville's ideas to inform his essay?

3. For McKnight, what are the key elements of a healthy community? What kinds of relationships would one find in his ideal community?

4. According to McKnight, what factors or influences can corrupt or weaken community? What are some ways that communities can go astray?

What Is Community? A Roundtable

Susan Faludi (journalist/feminist): The ideal community for Americans is often an escape from political engagement. Europeans are so much more engaged. Community here is running away to the suburbs. The media has become our psuedocommunity. People don't belong, but if they're part of a sound bite, they feel part of a larger world. It's a false idea of the media as a public forum, an idea encouraged by politicians. People take their intimate stories on TV talk shows, replacing political engagement and community, which would actually bind people, with psychology and therapy.

Frances Moore Lappe (activist/writer/political theorist): People are looking for community in all the wrong places. It's not goodwill and like-mindedness, it's daily experience in workplaces and neighborhoods and churches and civic groups. The Sonoma County Faith-Based Community Organizing Project is a prime example of concerned people coming together—farmworkers, African-Americans, whites of all classes, professionals, nuns, accountants, lawyers. They got together candidates for the school board, for example, and judged them on how well they listened to constituents' concerns. It's a two-way process of public officials accepting accountability and citizens taking an active role.

Noam Chomsky (linguist/political analyst): Community is PR bullshit designed in the 1930s by the corporations, when they became terrified by the collapse of their society brought on by the Wagner Act and the labor movement. They developed new techniques to control the population and inculcate the concept of living together in harmony—all Americans, all working together: the sober workman, the hardworking executive, the housewife. And Them—the outsiders trying to disrupt. Community is a bit of a joke. Only labor has succeeded. That's why business hates unions. They can create real community and democracy.

Barbara Kingsolver (novelist): There's no shame in depending on each other. There's a heroism in ordinariness and connectedness and using relationship skills to get through difficult times, as opposed to the isolated heroism of the cowboy. Look at things in your living room or refrigerator and realize that they were made by thousands of people on different continents. The lemons we buy at the grocery connect us with a food chain, with people coming up from Mexico, being sprayed by pesticides. It's easier to see just a lemon, but only when we see the whole line can we feel connectedness and responsibility.

Theodore Roszak (historian): Our culture builds bigger and bigger-bigger forces, corporations, trading alliances. The thrust toward the global in government, communications, and business goes against the human need for smaller, face-to-face communities. There is a disintegrative quality to reaching out beyond neighborhood and nationality ties. When computer networks are organized and we have 500 TV channels, common culture will disintegrate; we will have small enclaves for smaller groups. I can't predict what kind of community it will be, but the new community will be in reaction to the crushing bigness of systems.

These passages were culled from interviews by Michael Krasny, the host of "Forum," a West Coast public affairs radio show and a regular contributor to *Mother Jones* magazine. For more information, see "What Is Community?" (http://www.motherjones. com/mother_jones/MJ94/krasny.html).

Reading into Writing

Several common themes link the readings in this chapter: the complex and often conflicted nature of community, the potentials and limits of civic association, the gaps between ideals and reality, the human hunger for belonging and connection, the persistence of divisive and self-centered forces, our collective capacity for both helpful and hurtful action.

The following questions raise concerns that cut across the readings and point to the kinds of issues with which you might grapple when composing your essay:

1. Did these readings (and your discussions of them) challenge, confirm, or change your views in any way? If so, how?
2. In their pieces, both Kirp and McKnight cite de Tocqueville admiringly. Why do you think his reflections, recorded nearly two centuries ago, still pertain? What about de Tocqueville's analysis struck you as enduring? What struck you as outdated?
3. Different visions of community imply different rights, roles, and responsibilities for everyday citizens. Consider the different versions of community presented in the readings and what each of them demands from a citizen such as you.
4. Are new technologies such as the Internet and wireless communications changing how we experience community? If so, how?
5. Does your generation view community differently than other generations? How? Why?

6. List at least three direct quotations from the readings that you find appealing or that might prove useful to your essay.

Rhetorical Strategies for the Community Analysis Essay

The essay you write for the assignment in this chapter should build on experience and observation, although it must ultimately push beyond description to include analysis. Because you are a participant in the community you are describing and analyzing, the essay can be narrated in the first person (i.e., "*I*"). This also means that although the essay will be thesis driven, many of the rhetorical strategies outlined in Chapter 2—such as narrative base, tension/ turn, "showing," literary devices—will prove useful.

Several basic strategies, including the following, will be helpful for both generating content and for scaffolding your analysis:

- Identifying patterns of sameness
- Recognizing differences
- Using direct observations
- Sharpening definitions

Identifying Patterns of Sameness

The *com-* in *community* is derived from the Latin for "with," and it shares that prefix with words such as *common* and *compatible*. Communities generally have some elements that members share *with* each other, some unifying characteristics, some patterns of sameness.

We often think of community as being defined by geography. For example, because we grow up in a certain town, we gain membership into that community because we live there (and perhaps, at some point, we leave it behind to join another geographic community). Although geography is often a defining aspect of community, it is not the only one. Shared language can bind a community across regions and countries. We might also be affiliated with a community of co-workers on the job or with a group of others who share a concern about a particular issue or problem (a community of cancer survivors, for example).

We choose some of our communities (e.g., a fraternity), but not others (e.g., our race). Moreover, our membership in some communities changes as we move through life: A college community might be central during student days but less so later; a community of fellow skateboarders might be important in one period, of fellow parents at a later stage in life.

The following box lists some factors that can provide the glue for communities.

Factors That Can Unify Communities

Geography	Interests
History/shared experience	Rituals
Age	Values
Gender	Commitments
Social class	Problems
Race and/or ethnicity	Goals
Customs	Beliefs and attitudes
Traditions	Ideals
Language practices	Economic practices
Religious beliefs/practices	Shared suffering/trauma

When identifying patterns of sameness, the following questions help advance analysis; to generate ideas for your essay, apply each of them to the community you are studying:

- Starting with the factors listed in the box above, what specific characteristics are shared by members of the community? What behaviors and attitudes are common?
- How does one become a member of the community? Is it voluntary or involuntary? Are there formal or informal initiation processes or rituals?
- What is the history of the community?
- What groups or individuals are included, and what groups or individuals are underrepresented or excluded entirely?
- Do any markers or codes—formal or informal—signal membership?
- Is the membership static or fluid? long term or short term?
- What are some of the distinguishing communication practices? Are there distinctive ways that members talk, write, or employ nonverbal forms of language? Is there a specialized dialect, vocabulary, shorthand, or system of naming?
- How are the identities of the members shaped by the beliefs and practices of the community?

The community that you choose to examine for your essay can be rather loosely defined—for example, a group of friends that goes camping together regularly—or more clearly defined by more formal institutional and cultural factors—for example, the Pennsylvania Amish community that Fishman describes in her essay "Becoming Literate: A Lesson from the Amish," included in the special section "What Is Literacy?"

Belonging to a community can provide great comfort and nurturance. Think of times when you've found solace or support (or even just plain fun) among a group that echoed and encouraged your interests, values, and aspirations. Consider the rewards of belonging to a network that helps to shape your identity and sustain your well-being.

WRITING TO DISCOVER

Select two communities to which you belong and list the three most significant unifying factors and patterns of sameness.

Use the "Factors That Can Unify Communities" box and the questions above to propel your thinking and discussion.

Recognizing Differences

Even the tightest communities house differences. We can see this at the level of the family. Individuals within the same family—sharing a common cultural background, shared experiences, and close relationships—often manifest different attitudes, beliefs, and behaviors. Just as in the natural world, in a community, diversity is ever present and, indeed, can be a source of considerable strength and vitality. Therefore, as part of analyzing community, you need to recognize the trends toward difference that counterbalance the trends toward unity.

In some communities, difference and diversity are welcomed; in others, they are discouraged. As we identify the unifying factors in communities, it is essential to ask

- How does a particular community deal with those who depart from normative behavior or prevailing values?
- How does the community welcome or discourage individual or marginal perspectives?
- What are the consequences of community for those who have little power?

WRITING TO DISCOVER

Recall a time when you felt constrained by a particular community. How did your own identity, history, habits, beliefs, or preferences depart from the dominant character of the community? How did you handle the situation? Also consider how, in general, communities should deal with members who depart from the prevailing norms and values of the majority.

Now consider the community about which you plan to write. In what ways does it welcome and/or discourage difference?

In nearly every community, centripetal forces that trend toward sameness and centrifugal forces that trend toward difference remain in dynamic tension. They are crosscurrents in which we can drown or through which we can swim.

Using Direct Observations

When de Tocqueville wanted to discover the nature of the American national community, he couldn't do so by relying on books or the opinions of others. In order to arrive at fresh and insightful analysis, he took a tour of the United States to observe it first hand—see the towns and cities, listen to the people, attend events, take notes.

The essay assignment for this chapter asks you to adopt a similar stance, one that anthropologists call the *participant–observer*. Being a participant–observer means that personal experience will clearly inform and influence how you see and what you write; but you must also engage in systematic observation of a particular community. Such observations, recorded in field notes, will supply much of the data that will both shape and support the claims advanced in your analysis.

You may draw on memories of past events when writing the essay, but you should also do at least one direct observation of the chosen community. If you are writing about a fraternity, for example, you could select several key occasions—a dinner, a meeting, an ordinary day in the lounge—and record in textured detail what you see and hear. If you are writing about a neighborhood—even one with which you are intimately familiar—take the time to go there, sit down, observe, and take notes. Only through this kind of observation, through distancing yourself from the subject, will you recognize details that would be overlooked if you tried to rely solely on memory.

Field notes demand a system, even if a simple one. Because memory is notoriously unreliable, you should take notes while you observe or immediately afterward. You should record what you actually hear—not just summarize conversations. You should describe events in vivid detail—not just summarize what happens in a sentence or two. Notice, for example, that when Kirp describes Sproul Plaza at Berkeley, he doesn't just say, "There were lots of different student groups and it was busy." Instead, he names the specific groups and describes the particular people, sounds, sights, and happenings. Likewise, Kidder describes Northampton, Massachusetts, in detail, allowing readers to actually see it, meanwhile weaving in direct quotations and dialogue, allowing readers to hear voices.

The following template offers a simple but effective format for taking field notes. One column is for recording direct observations; another is for reflections on those observations. Some sample notes have been filled in by a student who is writing about the group of people he works with at a local chapter of Habitat for Humanity, which he considers an informal but significant community for him.

Date, Time, & Place	Observations	Reflections/Commentary/ Analysis
Sat., 10/18, 8:30am, Habitat for Humanity work site	*Jim, site supervisor and a local contractor who knows what he's doing in construction, was there when I arrived—he's always there first. I was next, followed soon after by Marla, Carl and Bill and two new people—local high school students. Then Edda showed up with the big thermos of coffee and we all had a cup, small talking about our Friday-night activities. (I don't really even like coffee, but I usually have a cup anyway.) Bill told a sexually explicit joke, and as usual, Edda (who is very religious) told him to hush and that (in a half-joking, half-serious tone), "You had better get yourself to church Sunday." The 2 new kids just kind of hung out on the edges, quiet, not getting our inside jokes.*	*The coffee is our morning ritual. Signals that we need to get going, but not right away. Without some of the banter and joking and catching up, it would just be a cold, early morning of work. The small talk gets people laughing and makes us feel like we are not just co-workers but friends, too. I wonder— why does Jim do this on weekends after doing the same thing all week?*
	We've been working on this site for four Saturdays now, and today we do the framing. As we start to lift the first wall around 10am, Ana, who will get this house, shows up. She apologized for being late—said something about a daycare mix-up with her kids' sitter. She's excited to get involved, even though she doesn't know much about construction, so she mostly does small stuff like cleaning up the site. The core group of us who are here nearly every week go right to our usual tasks, almost automatically.	*Having a frame up by the end of the day gives us a sense of concrete accomplishment. We can see the skeleton of a home and are reminded why we're doing this with a weekend day instead of sitting around watching sports like most of my friends.*

Save your field notes. Some instructors will ask you to hand them in with your essays.

Like field notes, interviews can also provide evidence for your analysis. If you opt to conduct an interview, first see the detailed interviewing advice outlined in Chapter 4. Especially if circumstances do not allow for direct observation of your chosen community (if, for example, writing about your home community when you are at college away from home), testimony gleaned from interviewing other members or observers of that community (whether in person, over the phone, or via email) can be particularly valuable.

Sharpening Definitions

We often think of definitions as being short and compact, as is the case with dictionary definitions. Such definitions are also termed *denotations*—attempts to nail down the exact meaning of a word. Of course, words also have *connotations*—associations that color a given word. For example, the denotation of the word *cuddle* is "to hug closely," but it carries connotations of warmth and intimacy. Conversely, the word *cheap* may literally mean "inexpensive," but it can also connote shoddiness. Such short uses of definition are certainly useful, particularly when you are deliberating about word choice in a sentence; but other ways of defining also merit our attention. This section addresses two modes useful in writing essays: *stipulative* and *extended* definitions.

Stipulative Definitions.   Have you ever argued with a friend, reached a dead end, and then realized that you were working from different assumptions about the meanings of key terms? Have you ever said, "Well, yes, but it depends on what you mean by . . ."?

Such breakdowns reveal a failure to *stipulate* in advance the meaning of a key term. If I were to start an essay by claiming that half of the adults in a particular community are illiterate, I should define what I mean by "illiterate" and how I arrived at the percentage. It is the writer's job to anticipate which terms need to be defined, and this requires careful audience analysis. (However, if a writer were to play it too safe and define every word, readers would be bored or distracted.) You need to define words or concepts that might cause misunderstanding or that you use in a special way.

Articulating a definition is a way to avoid misunderstanding or to build common ground on which the writer and reader can meet. The rhetorician Kenneth Burke claimed that fundamental to persuasion is identification, and by this he meant that the writer and reader must find some way to connect, to stand on common ground, to identify with each other. Creating a definition shared by writer and reader is one way to forge such an identification. Such a stipulative definition usually constitutes but one part of a larger argument.

In constructing an effective argument related to community or community action, you might first want to define how you are deploying the term *community*. Otherwise, you could be building a structure on shifting sands.

Extended Definitions   Extended definitions, in the form of essays, are longer than either dictionary or stipulative definitions because they require deliberation, development, and detail.

When writing a definition essay on a given topic, one answers a very basic question: What is it? Or, put differently, How would you characterize it? The central purpose is to *explain*.

Some essays adopt as their sole purpose explanation through definition. For example, when faced with the question What is success? some might define it as having a well-paying job and a nice home. Some might define it in terms of personal and familial relationships. Some might define it as making a significant contribution to society or to the arts. Some might define it in relationship to religious faith. Your job as an essayist would be to craft an extended definition by marshaling reason, examples, and evidence to explain your perspective on the term in question.

Guiding Questions

The following questions can help in both generating and sharpening ideas for extended-definition essays. Consider, for example, how the questions might apply if you were writing an essay about your participation in a community of people who meet each weekend to build houses with Habitat for Humanity.

- Within what category does the word or topic fit?
  Habitat for Humanity is a national voluntary/philanthropic organization with local chapters.

- How is it distinguished from others conventionally associated with that same category?
  Unlike many philanthropic organizations, Habitat focuses exclusively on housing. Among the characteristics that make it special and distinctive are . . .

- How does your definition compare to or depart from commonplace understandings? Consider both denotation and connotations.
  Many people may understand Habitat as an organization that builds houses for poor and low-income people, but what they don't understand is . . . What I have learned from working with Habitat for three years is . . .

- What are its core characteristics? What are its special characteristics?
  The mission of Habitat is . . . Its core values include emphasis on the dignity and self-reliance that come with private ownership of one's own home, the process of cooperative and pragmatic action, the principle of helping people to help themselves. . . . In my experience working with the local chapter, I have found that . . .

- Which examples help support and illustrate the chosen definition?
  As an example of helping people to help themselves, Habitat policies require that prospective home owners devote significant time to working on the construction crew. The organization also . . . I recall a time when . . .

- Which respected authorities support all or part of your definition?
  Research done by XYZ suggests that Habitat's efforts have proven effective in ABC ways. Former President Jimmy Carter devotes his energies to the organization because . . . Local Habitat chapter leader Ed Lawrence says that he sees Habitat as . . .

- What is *not* covered by the definition?
  Habitat practices differ from federal housing programs in that . . . The bonds that people form while building the houses often result in friendships that . . .

- How is your definition related to, shaped by, or dependant on context and history? Does your definition change if the context or the audience changes?
  Habitat was founded in response to particular economic circumstances that include . . .

- Has the meaning of the word or topic changed over time? How?
  When it started, Habitat was . . . and now it is . . .

- Who might object to your definition? How can you anticipate and address such objections in advance?
  Different people might see Habitat differently. For example, there is a prayer that is standard practice when a house is completed. I've noticed that for some volunteers this is very important, as it complements their spiritual motivations for service—they'd probably define Habitat as at least in part a religious or mission activity. For some others—committed to housing but not themselves religious—the prayer makes them uncomfortable. This difference suggests that . . .

- What are the *implications* of your definition? What actions or attitudes would follow if your audience accepted your definition? In other words, why does explaining your definition matter?
  How people perceive the organization may affect their willingness to join or to donate money . . .

Use these questions to spark thinking and writing, to help develop raw material for the analysis or definition essays. These questions are designed as *heuristics*—that is, as tools for helping you generate and clarify ideas. They are all related to the key question propelling the essay: What is it? However, you still need to organize your material, fill in content gaps that may not be covered by the prompts above, and provide all the connective tissue that makes for a coherent essay.

Peer Review Questions

The following questions can help guide peer workshops:

1. Where would including more detail and description give readers a better understanding of the community or group?

2. Where does the writer identify patterns of sameness (unifying factors) and difference in the community?

3. How does the writer discuss tensions at work in the community?

4. Is there any analysis of the language practices distinctive to the group? If not, where might that be inserted?

5. Does the writer provide specific examples to support claims? Where might more examples be helpful?

6. Has the writer considered how people from various viewpoints perceive the community?

7. How does the writer employ strategies for definition?

8. Does the text use any quotations from or references to the readings to help inform and advance the analysis?

ENDNOTE

Communities are complex organisms. Although many communities will always, to some degree, resist easy categorization, by stepping back to examine them we can more effectively and ethically act within them.

The chapters that follow build on several of the principles outlined in this chapter. For example, the next chapter examines another kind of community—the community formed by an academic discipline—and subsequent chapters prepare and guide writers in conducting community-based writing projects. In order to handle such projects successfully and responsibly, one should understand the characteristics and complexities of community life.

4

Writing in Academic Communities

How does writing function in college life? How and why does writing vary across academic disciplines? This chapter introduces the idea of the "discourse community," emphasizes the social and contextual nature of writing, and applies these two concepts to discovering how writing functions in academic majors and disciplines. The writing assignment—an empirical report—invites you to examine language practices in your chosen field of study. Completing this assignment also lays the foundation for writing a similar report in Chapter 7.

Communication is integral to community. As demonstrated in Chapter 3, how particular communities use language is one of the ways that they define and distinguish themselves. Speaking, listening, reading, writing, and viewing are vital not only to neighborhoods and nations but also to professions and academic disciplines. This chapter focuses on communication practices—and particularly writing practices—that occur within academic communities. The readings and exercises will guide you as you investigate a particular discipline's communication habits. That, in turn, should prove useful as you move forward in your major field of study.

Scholars have developed terms such as *discourse community, community of practice,* and *activity system* to help describe the ways writing works in a particular discipline or profession and to help discern the ways language practices vary across settings, contexts, and disciplines. This chapter describes what a discourse community is and explains its consequences as you learn to write across contexts. It then asks you to apply the principle of the discourse community to academic life, and particularly to the writing you are likely to do in a college major.

The suggested genre for the writing assignment in this chapter is the empirical research report, a format common to the sciences and social sciences. This chapter introduces the conventions of the genre and features one academic article that uses it.

ASSIGNMENT
Research Report: Investigating an Academic Discourse Community

For this report you should investigate the language practices of an academic discipline—preferably that of your own major or prospective major. Research will involve interviewing experts in that discourse community, examining documents produced within that community, and articulating well-supported conclusions that you can share with the rest of the class.

Format: Empirical research report (explained later in this chapter)

Research: Conduct at least two interviews: one with a faculty person in the discipline and one with an upper-division student in the discipline. (You may conduct more interviews, if you wish.) With instructor permission, you can team up with others in the class to conduct these interviews, although each person should write his or her own report.

           Collect several examples of writing in the discourse community and analyze them.

           Read "A Stranger in Strange Lands: One Student Writing Across the Curriculum" (which appears as a reading later in this chapter) and consider how you might use that research in developing your report.

What Is a Discourse Community?

Most professions demand effective communicators and specialized modes of communication. This is evident when you switch on a TV show such as *ER*. When a patient is wheeled in, the machines beeping and buzzing, the doctors and nurses automatically launch into medical work and talk. Everyone seems to know his or her role; no one slows down to instruct or explain. They toss around terms such as *epi, foley,* and *lavage;* they order a "CBC" or a "chem 7." We know it's an emergency; we know they're working to assess and treat the patient; we get the gist of what they're doing. But still, we are outsiders. We don't have a grasp on the medical knowledge; we haven't been schooled in that language. What is immediately clear to the doctors and nurses is opaque to us. We're just not part of that professional culture. This doesn't mean that medical professionals and ordinary folks can't communicate in everyday situations. But most of us—unless trained and mentored for years—cannot participate fully in the specialized activity system of doctors and nurses, the *discourse community* of medicine.

Discourse refers to communication practices. It is a more expansive term than *writing* or even *language* in that it covers many media (e.g., writing, speaking, digital text, gestures, cultural codes, visual images), includes both everyday and special language events, and refers not only to static texts but also to language in action.

A *discourse community* is a group of people who are unified by similar patterns of language use, shared assumptions, common knowledge, and parallel habits of interpretation. This is also sometimes referred to as a "community of practice." Some discourse communities are rather small (a handful of nuclear physicists spread around the world who exchange research in a highly specialized academic journal), some larger (an ethnic neighborhood in which members share a history, language, public space, local institutions such as schools, and a local newspaper), and some larger still (a nation, such as the United States, unified by a shared history, mass media, a government, a sense of national identity). As Chapter 3 demonstrates, communities are complex organisms. Patterns of sameness unify and distinguish a community; likewise, differences and tensions emerge. Not all members of a discourse community communicate exactly the same way, of course, but they do generally share several discernable linguistic characteristics.

Most of us belong to several overlapping discourse communities. However, this chapter examines only academic disciplines—biology or English or electrical engineering, for example—as distinct discourse communities, as distinct activity systems, each with different motives, conventions, habits, and ways of communicating. Because this book concentrates on writing, this chapter gives only passing attention to speaking, viewing, and nonverbal communication; it instead centers on how writers and written texts function within academic communities.

A common belief is that once one learns the rules for writing, one can write pretty much anything. There is also a perception that "good writing" reflects a fairly fixed set of skills and standards that apply consistently across most circumstances. Yet even an "A" in first-year composition doesn't carry any guarantee that one will be a successful writer in a chosen discipline. And in fact, perfect sentence-level skills—while certainly good to have—would be but little consolation if today you were asked to write a legal brief, an engineering proposal, or a master's thesis in history. Such acts of writing require knowing what kinds of evidence matter in a chosen field and which don't. They demand knowing which values and habits prevail as well as understanding what makes people in a particular community nod yes in affirmation or wince in disapproval.

Much of the research on writing confirms this view: Writing is about much more than mastering grammar and usage (although these are indeed important). Successful writing also demands a working familiarity with the values, habits, conventions, and tacit knowledge that prevail in a particular discourse community. Learning to write means entering a discourse community or an activity system—becoming a member, or at least an apprentice. Once one earns membership, writing becomes a tool for action within the community.

Entering a new discourse community can be like learning a foreign language. Keeping this analogy in mind can be helpful; but you should also understand that coming to participate in a discourse a community involves more than acquiring a technical vocabulary. One also needs to learn the culture that forms the context for that vocabulary.

In the reading selection below, Nancy Sakamoto employs a game metaphor. Like the foreign language analogy, this one is also useful, as it suggests that entering a discourse community means getting to know the rules of a new game (both the explicit and implicit ones) and practicing (often for years) before really getting the swing of things.

Essay: Nancy Sakamoto, *Conversational Ballgames*

Nancy Sakamoto was born in the United States, graduated from UCLA, and lived in Japan for 24 years. She is the author of Polite Fictions: Why Japanese and Americans Seem Rude to Each Other.

After I was married and had lived in Japan for a while, my Japanese gradually improved to the point where I could take part in simple conversations with my husband and his friends and family. And I began to notice that often, when I joined in, the others would look startled, and the conversational topic would come to a halt. After this happened several times, it became clear to me that I was doing something wrong. But for a long time, I didn't know what it was.

Finally, after listening carefully to many Japanese conversations, I discovered what my problem was. Even though I was speaking Japanese, I was handling the conversation in a western way.

Japanese-style conversations develop quite differently from western-style conversations. And the difference isn't only in the languages. I realized that just as I kept trying to hold western-style conversations even when I was speaking Japanese, so my English students kept trying to hold Japanese-style conversations even when they were speaking English. We were unconsciously playing entirely different conversational ballgames.

A western-style conversation between two people is like a game of tennis. If I introduce a topic, a conversational ball, I expect you to hit it back. If you agree with me, I don't expect you simply to agree, and do nothing more. I expect you to add something—a reason for agreeing, another example, or an elaboration to carry the idea further. But I don't expect you always to agree. I am just as happy if you question me or challenge me, or completely disagree with me. Whether you agree or disagree, your response will return the ball to me.

And then it is my turn again. I don't serve a new ball from my original starting line. I hit your ball back again from where it has bounced. I carry your idea further, or answer your questions or objections, or challenge or question you. And so the ball goes back and forth, with each of us doing our best to give it a new twist, an original spin, or a powerful smash.

And the more vigorous the action, the more interesting and exciting the game. Of course, if one of us gets angry, it spoils the conversation, just as it spoils a tennis game. But getting excited is not at all the same as getting angry. After all, we are not trying to hit each other. We are trying to hit the ball. So long as we attack only each other's opinions, and do not attack each other personally, we don't expect anyone to get hurt. A good conversation is supposed to be interesting and exciting.

If there are more than two people in the conversation, then it is like doubles in tennis, or like volleyball. There's no waiting in line. Whoever is nearest and quickest hits the ball, and if you step back, someone else will hit it. No one stops the game to give you a turn. You're responsible for taking your own turn.

But whether it's two players or a group, everyone does his best to keep the ball going, and no one person has the ball for very long.

A Japanese-style conversation, however, is not at all like tennis or volleyball. It's like bowling. You wait for your turn. And you always know your place in line. It depends on such things as whether you are older or younger, a close friend or a relative stranger to the previous speaker, in a senior or junior position, and so on.

When your turn comes, you step up to the starting line with your bowling ball, and carefully bowl it. Everyone else stands back and watches politely, murmuring encouragement. Everyone waits until the ball has reached the end of the alley, and watches to see if it knocks down all the pins, or only some of them, or none of them. There is a pause, while everyone registers your score.

Then, after everyone is sure that you have completely finished your turn, the next person in line steps up to the same starting line, with a different ball. He doesn't return your ball, and he does not begin from where your ball stopped. There is no back and forth at all. All the balls run parallel. And there is always a suitable pause between turns. There is no rush, no excitement, no scramble for the ball.

No wonder everyone looked startled when I took part in Japanese conversations. I paid no attention to whose turn it was, and kept snatching the ball halfway down the alley and throwing it back at the bowler. Of course the conversation died. I was playing the wrong game.

This explains why it is almost impossible to get a western-style conversation or discussion going with English students in Japan. I used to think that the problem was their lack of English language ability. But I finally came to realize that the biggest problem is that they, too, are playing the wrong game.

Whenever I serve a volleyball, everyone just stands back and watches it fall, with occasional murmurs of encouragement. No one hits it back. Everyone waits until I call on someone to take a turn. And when that person speaks, he doesn't hit my ball back. He serves a new ball. Again, everyone just watches it fall.

So I call on someone else. This person does not refer to what the previous speaker has said. He also serves a new ball. Nobody seems to have paid any attention to what anyone else has said. Everyone begins again from the same starting line, and all the balls run parallel. There is never any back and forth. Everyone is trying to bowl with a volleyball.

And if I try a simpler conversation, with only two of us, then the other person tries to bowl with my tennis ball. No wonder foreign English teachers in Japan get discouraged.

Now that you know about the difference in the conversational ballgames, you may think that all your troubles are over. But if you have been trained all your life to play one game, it is no simple matter to switch to another, even if you know the rules. Knowing the rules is not at all the same thing as playing the game.

Even now, during a conversation in Japanese I will notice a startled reaction, and belatedly realize that once again I have rudely interrupted by instinctively trying to hit back the other person's bowling ball. It is no easier for me to "just listen" during a conversation, than it is for my Japanese students to "just relax" when speaking with foreigners. Now I can truly sympathize with how hard they must find it to try to carry on a western-style conversation.

If I have not yet learned to do conversational bowling in Japanese, at least I have figured out one thing that puzzled me for a long time. After his first trip to America, my husband complained that Americans asked him so many questions and made him talk so much at the dinner table that he never had a chance to eat. When I asked him why he couldn't talk and eat at the same time, he said that Japanese do not customarily think that dinner, especially on fairly formal occasions, is a suitable time for extended conversation.

Since Westerners think that conversation is an indispensable part of dining, and indeed would consider it impolite not to converse with one's dinner partner, I found this Japanese custom rather strange. Still, I could accept it as a cultural difference even though I didn't really understand it. But when my husband added, in explanation, that Japanese consider it extremely rude to talk with one's mouth full, I got confused. Talking with one's mouth full is certainly not an American custom. We think it very rude, too. Yet we still manage to talk a lot and eat at the same time. How do we do it?

For a long time, I couldn't explain it, and it bothered me. But after I discovered the conversational ballgames, I finally found the answer. Of course! In a western style conversation, you hit the ball, and while someone else is hitting it back you take a bite, chew, and swallow. Then you hit the ball again, and then eat some more. The more people there are in the conversation, the more chances you have to eat. But even with only two of you talking you still have plenty of chances to eat.

Maybe that's why polite conversation at the dinner table has never been a traditional part of Japanese etiquette. Your turn to talk would last so long without interruption that you'd never get a chance to eat.   ■

Responding to Reading

1. Have you ever been in a situation like the one Sakamoto describes, in which you did not know the unwritten rules of a culture or group? (This does not have to involve travel abroad—it can also apply to other situations.)

2. Why didn't Sakamoto immediately realize her mistaken habits of communication?

3. What role does Sakamoto's husband play in her cultural education? What role does personal experience play? What other factors help her arrive at realizations about communication?

4. Sakamoto uses personal narrative and the extended metaphors of tennis, bowling, and volleyball to frame her essay. How effective are these rhetorical strategies? What other approaches could the author have taken?

Discourse Communities, Disciplines, and "Good" Writing

Sakamoto's experience illustrates that learning the surface vocabulary of a language does not ensure that one will be able to communicate effectively. Just as with conversation, successful writing is usually about more than learning explicit rules. Rather, it demands becoming an apprentice to a particular culture. Note that "culture" can refer not just to national cultures (such as that of the Japanese) but also to academic culture (such as that of biologists) or professional cultures (such as that of lawyers) or any number of subcultures (such as that of Green Bay Packers fans).

Learning to write is a social process. Entering a new community of practice can be a slow and difficult process, and novices cannot simply dive in and expect to swim as experts. In fact, expertise usually cannot be achieved only by study; it generally takes a good deal of experience or apprenticeship on the job, acting within the discourse community itself (which is why, for example, doctors not only attend medical school but also undergo years as interns and residents).

Still, one meaningful thing that a newcomer to a community can do is increase his or her awareness of how language functions in a discourse community. As a student, you can learn some of the unstated rules of disciplinary communities and thus avoid misunderstanding later. The assignment for this chapter provides a framework for researching a particular discourse community: that of your prospective major in college. This will put you one step ahead of the game as you progress in that major.

As you and your classmates undertake this assignment, you will come to realize that there is no universal standard for "good" writing in the university. Rather, each discipline constitutes a community of practice or an activity system that uses writing in its own way and for its own motives. Writing as a physicist, for example, is quite different from writing as a literary critic, which in turn is quite different from writing as a nurse, and so on. Although some basic skills such as standard grammar hold relatively consistent across the university, each discipline has its own traditions, conventions, and standards to which the members of that community conform (or, perhaps, against which they rebel). Successful college writers recognize the differences among the discourse communities and act in light of that awareness.

WRITING TO DISCOVER

Sketch three columns on a page and at the top of each write the title of a recent academic course in which you had to do a significant amount of writing, whether in the form of essays, papers, exams, journals, or other projects. Below each course title, first write the actual texts that you can remember writing while in that course. Then write the rules for successful writing in that class. These should include explicit rules—such as course or grading policies—and unwritten rules—such as the assumed norms for writing in that course or perceptions about what the teacher wanted. Note where the expectations for the writing in the three classes overlap and where they differ.

Research Article: Lucille McCarthy, *Stranger in Strange Lands: One Student Writing Across the Curriculum*

Lucille McCarthy is a researcher and professor who has published many studies on learning and writing in college. She wrote the following article, which was published in a scholarly journal, for researchers in the field of composition studies. You might find it difficult, and the specialized terminology and citations of previous scholarship will be unfamiliar. That's okay. Stick with it.

Because this reading selection is difficult, try a systematic note-taking method to help get a handle on it. For each cluster of two to four paragraphs, make marginal notes on the most significant content for that section, the rhetorical function of that section, and any questions or connections that the section raises in your mind. That is, for each chunk of text, ask three questions:

- What is the main idea(s) of this section? What does it *say?*
- What is the function of this section in the larger developing argument? What does this section *do* to advance the argument?
- What *connections* or *questions* are worth noting?

As you will see, this model for note-taking is already provided for the first few sections. Pick up with your own marginal notes, using the same format, where those end. This kind of reading and reflection can be slow, but it improves comprehension.

Abstract. This study asks questions about the nature of writing processes in classrooms. As students go from one classroom to another, they are presented with new speech situations, and they must determine what constitute appropriate ways of speaking and writing in each new territory. How do students, in the course of the semester, figure out what the writing requirements are in that discipline and for that teacher, and how do they go about producing it? In order to answer these questions the researcher followed one college student's writing experiences in one class per semester during his freshman and sophomore years. Follow-up data were collected during his junior year. Four research methods were used: observation, interviews, composing-aloud protocols, and text analysis. Conclusions are drawn from the data about how this student figured out what constituted acceptable writing in each classroom, and how he worked to produce it. Also presented are conclusions about what enhanced or denied his success in communicating competently in unfamiliar academic territories. Affecting his success were unarticulated social aspects of classroom contexts for writing as well as explicitly stated requirements and instructions.

Idea: *Dave, a student, is the focus of this study on college writing.*

Function: *McCarthy probably uses Dave in the introduction to her article because readers can relate to him.*

Connections: *Dave seems like an average student—I can relate to what he says about figuring out what teachers want and them all wanting different things. The "rules of the game" reference reminds me of the game metaphors in the "Conversational Ballgames" reading.*

Dave Garrison, a college junior and the focus of the present study, was asked how he would advise incoming freshmen about writing for their college courses. His answer was both homely and familiar.

"I'd tell them," he said, "first you've got to figure out what your teachers want. And then you've got to give it to them if you're gonna' get the grade." He paused a moment and added, "And that's not always so easy."

No matter how we teachers may feel about Dave's response, it does reflect his sensitivity to school writing as a social affair. Successful students are those who can, in their interactions with teachers during the semester, determine what constitute appropriate texts in each classroom: the content, structures, language, ways of thinking, and types of evidence required in that discipline and by that teacher. They can then produce such a text. Students who cannot do this, for whatever reason—cultural, intellectual, motivational—are those who fail, deemed incompetent communicators in that particular setting. They are unable to follow what Britton calls the "rules of the game" in each class (1975, p. 76). As students go from one classroom to another they must play a wide range of games, the rules for which, Britton points out, include many conventions and presuppositions that are not explicitly articulated.

Idea: *The study looks at Dave's writing in 3 different classes. Each different class is like a new, strange land for Dave.*

Function: *Summarizes the study; introduces the metaphor ("stranger in strange lands") used in the title.*

Connections: *The "newcomer in a foreign country" phrase also reminds me of the Sakamoto reading—in her case Japan, in this case new subject courses. The "strange lands" thing seems true. I sometimes feel that way—lost, disoriented—when taking a new course with a new teacher.*

In this article, writing in college is viewed as a process of assessing and adapting to the requirements in unfamiliar academic settings. Specifically, the study examined how students figured out what constituted appropriate texts in their various courses and how they went about producing them. And, further, it examined what characterized the classroom contexts which enhanced or denied students' success in this process. This study was a 21-month project which focused on the writing experiences of one college student, Dave, in three of his courses, Freshman Composition in the spring of his freshman year, and, in his sophomore year, Introduction to Poetry in the fall and Cell Biology in the spring. Dave, a biology/pre-med major, was typical of students at his college in terms of his SAT scores (502 verbal; 515 math), his high school grades, and his white, middle-class family background.

As I followed Dave from one classroom writing situation to another, I came to see him, as he made his journey from one discipline to another, as a stranger in strange lands. In each new class Dave believed that the writing he was doing was totally unlike anything he had ever done before. This metaphor of a newcomer in a foreign country proved to be a powerful way of looking at Dave's behaviors as he worked to use the new languages in unfamiliar academic territories. Robert Heinlein's (1961) science fiction novel suggested this metaphor originally. But Heinlein's title is slightly different; his stranger is in a *single* strange land. Dave perceived himself to be in one strange land after another.

BACKGROUND TO THE STUDY

The theoretical underpinnings of this study are to be found in the work of sociolinguists (Hymes, 1972a, 1972b; Gumperz, 1971) and ethnographers of communication (Basso, 1974; Heath, 1982; Szwed, 1981) who assume that language processes must be understood in terms of the contexts in which they occur. All language use in this view takes place within speech communities and accomplishes meaningful social functions for people. Community members share characteristic "ways of speaking," that is, accepted linguistic, intellectual, and social conventions which have developed over time and govern spoken interaction. And "communicatively competent" speakers in every community recognize and successfully employ these "rules of use," largely without conscious attention (Hymes, 1972a, pp. xxiv–xxxvi).

A key assumption underlying this study is that writing, like speaking, is a social activity. Writers, like speakers, must use the communication means considered appropriate by members of particular speech or discourse communities. And the writer's work, at the same time, may affect the norms of the community. As students go from one class to another, they must define and master the rules of use for written discourse in one classroom speech community after another. And their writing can only be evaluated in terms of that particular community's standards.

*   *   *

The ultimate aim of this study is to contribute to our understanding of how students learn to write in school. Findings from this study corroborate the notion that learning to write should be seen not only as a developmental process occurring within an individual student, but also as a social process occurring in response to particular situations.

METHODS

The research approach was naturalistic. I entered the study with no hypotheses to test and no specially devised writing tasks. Rather, I studied the writing that was actually being assigned in these classrooms, working to understand and describe that writing, how it functioned in each classroom, and what it meant to people there. My purpose was to get as rich a portrait as possible of Dave's writing and his classroom writing contexts. To this end I combined four research tools: observation, interviews, composing-aloud protocols, and text analysis. The data provided by the protocols and text analysis served to add to, cross-check, and refine the data generated by observation and interviews. Using this triangulated approach (Denzin, 1978), I could view Dave's writing experiences through several windows, with the strengths of one method compensating for the limitations of another.

The Courses

The college is a private, co-educational, liberal arts institution located in a large, northeastern city. Of its 2600 students nearly half are business, accounting, and computer science majors. Yet over half of students' courses are required liberal arts courses, part of the core curriculum. Two of Dave's courses in this study are core courses: Freshman Composition and Introduction to Poetry. The third, Cell Biology, is a course taken by biology majors; it was Dave's third semester of college biology. All three were one-semester courses. In the descriptions of these courses that follow, I use pseudonyms for the teachers.

In Freshman Composition, which met twice a week for 90 minutes, students were required to write a series of five, similarly structured essays on topics of their choice. These two or four page essays were due at regular intervals and were graded by the professor, Dr. Jean Carter. Classes were generally teacher-led discussions and exercises, with some days allotted for students to work together in small groups, planning their essays or sharing drafts. Dr. Carter held one individual writing conference with each student at mid semester.

Introduction to Poetry is generally taken by students during their sophomore year, and it, like Freshman Composition, met for 90 minutes twice a week. In this class students were also required to write a series of similar papers. These were three to six page critical essays on poems that students chose from a list given them by their professor, Dr. Charles Forson. These essays, like those in Freshman Composition, were due at regular intervals and were graded by the professor. The Poetry classes were all lectures in which Dr. Forson explicated poems. However, one lecture early in the semester was devoted entirely to writing instruction.

Cell Biology, which Dave took in the spring of his sophomore year, met three times a week, twice for 90-minute lectures and once for a three-hour lab. In this course, like the other two, students were required to write a series of similar short papers, three in this course. These were three to five page reviews of journal articles which reported current research in cell biology. Students were to summarize these articles, following the five-part scientific format in which the experiment was reported. They were then to relate the experiment to what they were doing in class. These reviews were graded by the professor, Dr. Tom Kelly.

The Participants

The participants in this study included these three professors, Drs. Carter, Forson, and Kelly. All were experienced college teachers who had taught these courses before. All talked willingly and with interest about the writing their students were doing, and both Dr. Carter and Dr. Forson invited me to observe their classes. Dr. Kelly said that it would not be productive for me to observe in his Cell Biology course because he spent almost no time talking directly about writing, so pressed was he to cover the necessary course material.

The student participants in this study were Dave and two of his friends. I first met these three young men in Dr. Carter's Freshman Composition class where I was observing regularly in order to learn how she taught the course, the same one I teach at the college. As I attended that course week after week, I got to know the students who sat by me, Dave and his friends, and I realized I was no longer as interested in understanding what my colleague was teaching as I was in understanding what these students were learning. As the study progressed, my focus narrowed to Dave's experiences, although none of the three students knew this. The contribution of Dave's friends to this study was to facilitate my understanding of Dave. At first, in their Freshman Composition class, these students saw my role as a curious combination of teacher and fellow student. As the study progressed, my role became, in their eyes, that of teacher/inquirer, a person genuinely interested in understanding their writing. In fact, my increasing interest and ability to remember details of his writing experiences seemed at times to mystify and amuse Dave.

At the beginning of this study Dave Garrison was an 18 year old freshman, a biology pre-med major who had graduated the year before from a parochial boys' high school near the college. He described himself as a "hands-on" person who preferred practical application in the lab to reading theory in books. Beginning in his sophomore year, Dave worked 13 hours a week as a technician in a local hospital, drawing blood from patients, in addition to taking a full course load. He "loved" his hospital work, he said, because of the people and the work, and also because difficulties with chemistry have made him worry about being accepted in medical school. In the hospital he was getting an idea of a range of possible careers in health care. The oldest of four children, Dave lived at home and commuted 30 minutes to campus. He is the first person in his family to go to college, though both of his parents enjoy reading, he said, and his father writes in his work as an insurance salesman. When Dave and I first met, he told me that he did not really like to write and that he was not very good, but he knew that writing was a tool he needed, one that he hoped to learn to see better.

Instrumentation and Analytic Procedures

[Here McCarthy devotes 15 paragraphs to describing the methods for her study, which include classroom observations, interviews, "protocols" during which Dave voices what he is thinking while writing, and analysis of Dave's tests and papers.]

Validity of the findings and interpretations in this study was ensured by employing the following techniques. (1) Different types of data were compared.

(2) The perspectives of various informants were compared. (3) Engagement with the subject was carried on over a long period of time during which salient factors were identified for more detailed inquiry. (4) External checks on the inquiry process were made by three established researchers who knew neither Dave nor the professors. These researchers read the emerging study at numerous points and questioned researcher biases and the bases for interpretations. (5) Interpretations were checked throughout with the informants themselves. (See Lincoln & Guba, 1985, for a discussion of validity and reliability in naturalistic inquiry.)

RESULTS AND DISCUSSION

Information from all data sources supports three general conclusions, two concerning Dave's interpretation and production of the required writing tasks and one concerning social factors in the classrooms that influenced him as he wrote. First, although the writing tasks in the three classes were in many ways similar, Dave interpreted them as being totally different from each other and totally different from anything he had ever done before. This was evidenced in the interview, protocol, and text analysis data.

Second, certain social factors in Freshman Composition and Cell Biology appeared to foster Dave's writing success in them. Observation and interview data indicated that two unarticulated aspects of the classroom writing contexts influenced his achievement. These social factors were (1) the functions that writing served for Dave in each setting, and (2) the roles that participants and students' texts played there. These social factors were bound up with what Dave ultimately learned from and about writing in each class.

Third, Dave exhibited consistent ways of figuring out what constituted appropriate texts in each setting, in his terms, of "figuring out what the teacher wanted." Evidence from the interviews and protocols shows that he typically drew upon six information sources, in a process that was in large part tacit. These information sources included teacher-provided instructional supports, sources Dave found on his own, and his prior knowledge.

The Writing Assignments: Similar Tasks, Audiences, and Purposes

My analysis of the assignments, combined with the observation and interview data, showed that the writing in the three classes was similar in many ways. It was, in all cases, informational writing for the teacher-as-examiner, the type of writing that Applebee found comprised most secondary school writing (1984). More specifically, the task in Cell Biology was a summary, and in Freshman Composition and Poetry it was analysis, closely related informational uses of writing. Dave's audiences were identified as teacher-as-examiner by the fact that all assignments were graded and that Dave, as he wrote, repeatedly wondered how his teacher would "like" his work.

Further similarities among the writing in the three courses included the purpose that the professors stated for having their students write. All three said that the purpose was not so much for students to display specific information, but rather for students to become competent in using the thinking and language of their disciplines.

*   *   *

Thus in all three courses Dave's tasks were informational writing for the teacher-as-examiner. All were for the purpose of displaying competence in using the ways of thinking and writing appropriate to that setting. And in all three courses Dave wrote a series of similar short papers, due at about three-week intervals, the assumption being that students' early attempts would inform their subsequent ones, in the sort of trial-and-error process that characterizes much language learning. Further, the reading required in Poetry and Cell Biology, the poems and the journal articles, were equally unfamiliar to Dave. We might expect, then, that Dave would view the writing for these three courses as quite similar, and, given an equal amount of work, he would achieve similar levels of success. This, however, is not what happened.

Dave's Interpretation of the Writing Tasks

The Writer's Concerns While Composing.   In spite of the similarities among the writing tasks for the three courses, evidence from several sources shows that Dave interpreted them as being totally different from each other and totally different from anything he had ever done before. Dave's characteristic approach across courses was to focus so fully on the particular new ways of thinking and writing in each setting that commonalities with previous writing were obscured for him. And interwoven with Dave's conviction that the writing for these courses was totally dissimilar was his differing success in them. Though he worked hard in all three courses, he made B's in Freshman Composition, D's and C's in Poetry, and A's in Cell Biology.

The protocol data explain in part why the writing for these classes seemed so different to Dave. Dave's chief concerns while composing for each course were very different. His focus in Freshman Composition was on textual coherence. Fifty-four percent of his expressed concerns were for coherence of thesis and subpoints, coherence within paragraphs, and sentence cohesion. By contrast, in Poetry, though Dave did mention thesis and subpoints, his chief concerns were not with coherence, but with the new ways of thinking and writing in that setting. Forty-four percent of his concerns focused on accurately interpreting the poem and properly using quotes. In Cell Biology, yet a new focus of concerns is evident. Seventy-two percent of Dave's concerns deal with the new rules of use in that academic discipline. His chief concerns in Biology were to accurately understand the scientific terms and concepts in the journal article and then to accurately rephrase and connect these in his own text, following the same five-part structure in which the published experiment was reported. It is no wonder that the writing for these classes seemed very different to Dave. As a newcomer in each academic territory, Dave's attention was occupied by the new conventions of interpretation and language use in each community.

The same preoccupations controlled his subsequent work on the papers. In each course Dave wrote a second draft, which he then typed. In none of these second drafts did Dave see the task differently or make major changes. He is, in this regard, like the secondary students Applebee (1984) studied who were unable, without teacher assistance, to revise their writing in more than minor ways. And Dave revised none of these papers after the teachers had responded.

We can further fill out the pictures of Dave's composing for the three classes by combining the protocol findings with the observation and interview data. In his first protocol session, in April of his freshman year, Dave composed the first draft of his fourth paper for Freshman Composition, an essay in which he chose to analyze the wrongs of abortion. To this session Dave brought an outline of this thesis and subpoints. He told me that he had spent only 30 minutes writing it the night before, but that the topic was one he had thought a lot about. As he composed, Dave was most concerned with, and apparently very dependent upon, his outline, commenting on it, glancing at it, or pausing to study it 14 times during the 30 minutes of composing. Dave's next most frequently expressed concerns were for coherence at paragraph and sentence levels, what Dr. Carter referred to as coherence of mid-sized and small parts. These were the new "rules of use" in this setting. Dave told me that in high school he had done some "bits and pieces" of writing and some outlines for history, but that he had never before written essays like this. The total time Dave spent on his abortion essay was five hours.

In Dave's Poetry protocol session seven months later, in November of his sophomore year, he composed part of the first draft of his third and last paper for that class, a six-page analysis of a poem called "Marriage" by contemporary poet Gregory Corso. To this session he brought two pages of notes and his *Norton Anthology of Poetry* in which he had underlined and written notes in the margins beside the poem. He told me that he had spent four hours (of an eventual total of 11) preparing to write: reading the poem many times and finding a critical essay on it in the library. During his pre-writing and composing, Dave's primary concern was to get the right interpretation of the poem, "the true meaning" as he phrased it. And as Dave wrote, he assumed that his professor knew the true meaning, a meaning, Dave said, that "was there, but not there, not just what it says on the surface." Further, Dave knew that he must argue his interpretation, using not his own but the poet's words; this was his second most frequently expressed concern.

As Dave composed, he appeared to be as tied to the poem as he had been to his outline in Freshman Composition the semester before. He seemed to be almost *physically* attached to the *Norton Anthology* by his left forefinger as he progressed down the numbers he had marked in the margins. He was, we might say, tied to the concrete material, the "facts" of the poem before him. Dave never got his own essay structure; rather, he worked down the poem, explicating from beginning to end. In the retrospective interview he said, "I didn't really have to think much about my thesis and subs because they just come naturally now.... But anyway it's not like in Comp last year. Here my first paragraph is the introduction with the thesis, and the stanzas are the subpoints." Dave's preoccupation with the poem and the new conventions of interpreting and quoting poetry resulted in a paper that was not an analysis but a summary with some interpretation along the way. His focus on these new rules of use appeared to limit his ability to apply previously learned skills, the thesis-subpoint analytical structure, and kept him working at the more concrete summary level.

This domination by the concrete may often characterize newcomers' first steps as they attempt to use language in unfamiliar disciplines (Williams, 1985). Dave's professor, Dr. Forson, seemed to be familiar with this phenomenon when he warned students in his lecture on writing: "You must remember that the poet ordered the poem. You order your essay with your own thesis and subtheses. Get away from 'Next.... Next'." But if Dave heard this in September, he had forgotten it by November. Dave's experience is consonant with Langer's (1984) finding that students who know more about a subject as they begin to write are likely to choose analysis rather than summary. And these students receive higher scores for writing quality as well.

In his writing for Cell Biology the following semester, Dave's concerns were again focused on the new and unfamiliar conventions in this setting. Before writing his last paper, a four-page review of an experiment on glycoprotein reported in *The Journal of Cell Biology,* Dave spent three hours preparing. (He eventually spent a total of eight hours on the review.) He had chosen the article in the library from a list the professor had given to students and had then read the article twice, underlining it, making notes, and looking up the definitions of unfamiliar terms. To the protocol session Dave brought these notes, the article, and a sheet on which he had written what he called "Dr. Kelly's guidelines," the five-part scientific experiment format that Dr. Kelly wanted students to follow: Background, Objectives, Procedures, Results, and Discussion.

In his composing aloud, Dave's chief concerns in Biology were, as in Poetry the semester before, with the reading, in this case the journal article. But here, unlike Poetry, Dave said the meaning was "all out on the table." In Poetry he had had to interpret meaning from the poem's connotative language; in Biology, by contrast, he could look up meanings, a situation with which Dave was far more comfortable. But as he composed for Biology, he was just as tied to the journal article as he had been to the poem or to his outline in previous semesters. Dave paused frequently to consult the article, partially covering it at times so that his own paper was physically closer to what he was summarizing at that moment.

Dave's first and second most commonly expressed concerns during the Biology protocol session were for rephrasing and connecting parts of the article and for following Dr. Kelly's guidelines. These were, in essence, concerns for coherence and organization, what Dave was most concerned with in Freshman Composition. But the writing for Biology bore little relation in Dave's mind to what he had done in Freshman Composition. In Biology he was indeed concerned about his organization, but here it was the five-part scientific format he had been given, very different, it seemed to him, than the thesis/subpoint organization he had had to create for his freshman essays. In fact, until I questioned him about it at the end of the semester, Dave never mentioned the freshman thesis/subpoint structure. And the concerns for coherence at paragraph and sentence levels that had been so prominent as he wrote for Freshman Composition were replaced in Biology by his concern for rephrasing the article's already coherent text. In Freshman Composition Dave had talked about trying to get his sentences and paragraphs to "fit" or "flow" together. In Biology, however, he talked about trying to get the article into his own words, about "cutting," "simplifying," and "combining two sentences." Again, it is no wonder that Dave believed that this writing was totally new. It took one of Dave's friend's and my prodding during an interview to make Dave see that he had indeed written summaries before. Lots of them.

The Nature of Cooperation in the Three Courses. The text analysis data provide further insight into why Dave perceived the writing in these courses as so dissimilar. The data provide information about what was, in Grice's terms, essential to maintaining the Cooperative Principle in these written exchanges. Analyses of the teachers' responses to Dave's papers show that his concerns in each class generally did match theirs. Put differently, Dave had figured out, though not equally well in all classes, what counted as "cooperation" in each context, and what he had to do to be deemed a competent communicator here. (See Table 1.)

Analysis of Dave's finished essay for Freshman Composition suggests that his concerns for textual coherence were appropriate. Dave knew that to keep the Cooperative Principle in force in Dr. Carter's class, he had to pay special attention to fulfilling the condition of *Manner*, to making himself clear, using appropriate forms of expression. He succeeded and was deemed cooperative by Dr.

TABLE 1 *Teachers' Responses to Dave's Papers*

	Quality	Quantity	Relevance	Manner	Grade
	Number of Responses Indicating				
	Violations of Conditions for Cooperation				
Composition	0	0	0	2	18/20
Poetry	8	0	0	11	C+
Cell Biology	0	0	0	14	96

Carter when she responded to his contribution with a telegraphic reply on the first page: "18/20." Apart from editing two words in Dave's text, she made no further comments, assuming that Dave and she shared an understanding of what constituted cooperation in her class and of what her numbers meant. (She had explained to students that she was marking with numbers that semester in an attempt to be more "scientific," and she had defined for them the "objective linguistic features of text" to which her numbers referred.) Dave did understand the grade and was, of course, very pleased with it.

In an interview, Dr. Carter explained her grade to me. "Though his content isn't great," she said, "his paper is coherent, not badly off at any place. . . . He gave a fair number of reasons to develop his paragraphs, he restated his point at the end, and there is no wasted language. It's not perfectly woven together, but it's good." Though Dr. Carter mentioned the "reasons" Dave gave as evidence for his contentions, she was concerned not so much with their meaning as with their cohesiveness. Cooperation in this setting thus depended upon fulfilling the condition of *Manner*. Dave knew this and expected only a response to how well he had achieved the required form, not to the content of his essay.

In his writing for Poetry the following semester, Dave was attempting to keep the Cooperative Principle in force by paying special attention to two conditions, *Quality* and *Manner*. That is, first he was attempting to say what was true and give adequate evidence, and, second, he was attempting to use proper forms of expression. This is evidenced in the interview and protocol as well as the text data. Analysis of Dr. Forson's 19 responses to Dave's paper shows that Dave's concerns matched those of his teacher, that Dave had figured out, though only in part, what counted as cooperation in that setting. Dr. Forson's responses all referred to violations of the same conditions Dave had been concerned with fulfilling, *Quality* and *Manner*. In seven of his eight marginal notes and in an endnote, Dr. Forson disagreed with Dave's interpretation and questioned his evidence, violations of the *Quality* condition. Mina Shaughnessy (1977) says that such failure to properly coordinate claims and evidence is perhaps the most common source of misunderstanding in academic prose. The ten mechanical errors that Dr. Forson pointed out were violations of the condition of *Manner,* violations which may jeopardize the Cooperative Principle in many academic settings. Dave's unintentional violations in Poetry of the *Quality* and *Manner* conditions jeopardized the Cooperative Principle in that exchange, resulting in the C+ grade.

Dr. Kelly's responses to Dave's writing in Biology were, like those in Freshman Composition, much briefer than Dr. Forson's. Dr. Kelly's 14 marks or phrases all pointed out errors in form, unintentional violations of the Gricean condition of *Manner.* But these were apparently not serious enough to jeopardize the aims of the written conversation in Biology; Dave's grade on the review was 96.

This application of Grice's rubric for spoken conversation to student-teacher written interaction gives further insight into the differences in these classroom contexts for writing. It is evident that successfully maintaining the Cooperative Principle was a more complicated business in Poetry than in Freshman Composition or Biology. In Biology, Dave was unlikely to violate the condition of *Quality,* as he did in Poetry, because he was only summarizing the published experiment and thus only had to pay attention to the condition of *Manner.* In Poetry, by contrast, he was called upon to take an interpretive position. This assumed that he had already summarized the poem. He had not. Thus his analytical essay took the form of a summary, as we have seen. In Biology, on the other hand, the writing was supposed to be a summary that then moved to a comparison of the summarized experiment to what was going on in class.

For Dave, the latter assignment was more appropriate. Novices in a field may need the simpler summary assignment that helps them understand the new reading, the new language that they are being asked to learn. They may then be ready to move to analysis or critique. One wonders if Dave's success in Poetry would have been enhanced if he had been asked to write out a summary of the poem first. He could then have worked from that summary as he structured his own critical essay.

Similarly, in Freshman Composition, Dave was unlikely to violate the condition of *Quality,* to say something untrue or provide inadequate evidence for his claim. Though Dave did have to provide evidence for his subpoints, he was not evaluated for his content, and thus he concentrated on the condition of *Manner.* Further, the writing in Freshman Composition did not require Dave to master unfamiliar texts as it did in both Poetry and Biology. And for Dave the task of integrating new knowledge from his reading into his writing in those courses was his salient concern, as we have seen.

The apparent absence of attention paid in any of these classes to fulfilling the conditions of *Quality* or *Relation* is puzzling. Perhaps Dave's prior school writing experience had trained him to include the right amount of information *(Quantity)* and stay on topic *(Relation).*

The text analysis data, then, show that what counted as cooperation in these three classes was indeed quite different. Dr. Forson, in his extensive responses, apparently felt it necessary to reteach Dave how people think and write in his community. This is understandable in light of Dave's numerous unintentional violations of the Cooperative Principle. Further, though Dr. Forson told students that he was being objective, finding the meaning of the poem in the text, he told me that his responses to students' papers were to argue his interpretation of the poem and, thus, to justify his grade.

The differing language and forms of these professors' responses probably also added to Dave's sense that in each classroom he was in a new foreign land. Response style may well be discipline-specific as well as teacher-specific, with responses in literary studies generally more discursive than in the sciences. Further, Dr. Forson's responses were in the informal register typically used by an authority speaking to a subordinate (Freedman, 1984). His responses to Dave's paper included the following: "You misfire here." "I get this one. Hurrah for me!" "Pardon my writing. I corrected this in an automobile." The informality, and the word "corrected" in particular, leave little doubt about the authority differential between Dr. Forson and Dave. By contrast, Dave seemed to interpret the numerical grade in Biology as more characteristic of a conversation between equals. In a comment that may say more about the classroom interaction than their written interaction, Dave spoke of Dr. Kelly's brief responses to his review: "Yeah. He's like that. He treats us like adults. When we ask him questions, he answers us." Dave's apparent mixing of his spoken and written interaction with Dr. Kelly emphasizes the point that students' and teachers' writing for each other in classrooms is as fully contextualized as any other activity that goes on there.

Before Dave turned in his last papers in Poetry and Biology, I asked him to speculate about the grade he would get. When he handed in his six-page paper on the Corso poem, "Marriage," on which he had spent eleven hours, he told me that he hoped for an A or B: "I'll be really frustrated on this one if the grade's not good after I've put in the time on it." A week later, however, he told me in a resigned tone and with a short laugh that he'd gotten a C+. By contrast, when he turned in his last review in Biology, he told me he knew he would get an A. When I questioned him, he replied, "I don't know how I know. I just do." And he was right: his grade was 96. Dave obviously understood far better what constituted cooperation in Biology than he did in Poetry.

Social Aspects of the Classrooms that Influenced Dave's Writing

Why was Dave's success in writing in these classrooms so different? The answers to this question will illuminate some of the dimensions along which school writing situations differ and thus influence student achievement. It would be a mistake to think that the differing task structure was the only reason that Dave was more successful in Biology and Freshman Composition than he was in Poetry. Assignments are, as I have suggested, only a small part of the classroom interaction, limited written exchanges that reflect the nature of the communication situation created by participants in that setting. Two unarticulated qualities in the contexts for writing in Freshman Composition and Biology appeared to foster Dave's success in those classes. These were (1) the social functions Dave's writing served for him in those classes, and (2) the roles played by participants and by students' texts there.

The Functions Dave Saw His Writing as Accomplishing. It has been argued that the social functions served by writing must be seen as an intrinsic part of the writing experience (Clark & Florio, 1983; Hymes, 1972a, 1972b; Scribner & Cole, 1981). Evidence from interviews and observations indicates that the writing in Freshman Composition and Biology was for Dave a meaningful social activity, meaningful beyond just getting him through the course. Further, Dave and his teachers in Freshman Composition and Biology mutually understood and valued those functions. This was not the case in Poetry. The data show a correlation not only between meaningful social functions served by the writing and Dave's success with it, but also between the writing's social meaning and Dave's ability to remember and draw upon it in subsequent semesters.

In Freshman Composition Dave's writing served four valuable functions for him. He articulated all of these:

1. Writing to prepare him for future writing in school and career
2. Writing to explore topics of his choice
3. Writing to participate with other students in the classroom
4. Writing to demonstrate academic competence

In Biology Dave also saw his writing as serving four valuable functions:

1. Writing to learn the language of Cell Biology, which he saw as necessary to his career
2. Writing to prepare him for his next semester's writing in Immunology
3. Writing to make connections between his classwork and actual work being done by professionals in the field
4. Writing to demonstrate academic competence

Evidence from interviews and observation shows that Dr. Carter and Dr. Kelly saw writing in their classes as serving the same four functions that Dave did.

On the other hand, in Poetry, though Dave's professor stated four functions of student writing, Dave saw his writing as serving only one function for him: writing to demonstrate academic competence. Dave, always the compliant student, did say after he had received his disappointing grade in Poetry that the writing in Poetry was probably good for him: "Probably any kind of writing helps you." Though he may well be right, Dave actually saw his writing for Poetry as serving such a limited function—evaluation of his skills in writing poetry criticism for Dr. Forson—that he was not really convinced (and little motivated by the notion) that this writing would serve him in any general way.

Dave contended that any writing task was easy or difficult for him according to his interest in it. When I asked him what he meant by interesting, he said, "If it has something to do with my life. Like it could explain something to me or give me an answer that I could use now." Writing must have, in other words, meaningful personal and social functions for Dave if it is to be manageable, "easy," for him. These functions existed for Dave in Freshman Composition and Biology, providing the applications and personal transaction with the material that may be generally required for learning and forging personal knowledge (Dewey, 1949; Polanyi, 1958).

Dave's Poetry class, however, served no such personally meaningful functions. Six weeks after the Poetry course was finished, I asked Dave some further questions about his last paper for that course, the discussion of the Corso poem on which he had worked 11 hours. He could remember almost nothing about it. When I asked him to speculate why this was, he said, "I guess it's because I have no need to remember it." By contrast, when I asked Dave in the fall of his junior year if his Cell Biology writing was serving him in his Immunology course as he had expected, he said, "Yes. The teacher went over how to write up our labs, but most of us had the idea anyway from last semester because we'd read those journal articles. We were already exposed to it."

Of course the functions of his writing in Biology served Dave better than in Poetry in part because he was a biology major. The writing for Cell Biology fit into a larger whole: his growing body of knowledge about this field and his professional future. The material in Cell Biology was for Dave a comprehensible part of the discipline of Biology which was in turn a comprehensible part of the sciences. Dave was, with experience, gradually acquiring a coherent sense of the language of the discipline, how biologists think and speak and what it is they talk about. And his understanding of the language of biology was accompanied by an increasing confidence in his own ability to use it. Both of these are probably necessary foundations for later, more abstract and complex uses of the language (Piaget, 1952; Perry, 1970; Williams, 1985).

In the required one-semester Poetry class, however, the poems seemed to Dave to be unrelated to each other except for commonly used poetic devices, and his writing about them was unrelated to his own life by anything at all beyond his need to find the "true meaning" and get an acceptable grade. Dave's different relationship to the languages of these disciplines was shown when he said, "In Biology I'm using what I've *learned.* It's just putting what I've learned on paper. But in Poetry, more or less each poem is different, so it's not *taught* to you. You just have to figure it out from that poem itself and hope Dr. Forson likes it." Nor, in Poetry, was Dave ever invited to make personally meaningful connections with the poems. And he never did it on his own, no doubt in part because he was so preoccupied with the new ways of thinking and speaking that he was trying to use.

In Freshman Composition the social function of writing that was perhaps most powerful for Dave was writing to participate with other students in the classroom. In his peer writing group Dave, for the first time ever, discussed his writing with others. Here he communicated personal positions and insights to his friends, an influential audience for him. That an important social function was served by these students' work with each other is suggested by their clear memory, a year and a half later, both of their essays and of each other's reactions to them.

The four social functions that Dave's writing in Freshman Composition accomplished for him enhanced his engagement with and attitude toward the writing he did in that class. This engagement is reflected in Dave's memory not only of his essays and his friends' reactions to them, but also in his memory and use of the ideas and terms from that course. When Dave talked about his writing during his sophomore and junior years, he used the process terms he had learned in Freshman Composition: prewriting, revision, and drafts. He also used other language he had learned as a freshman, speaking at times about his audience's needs, about narrowing his topic, about connecting his sentences, providing more details, and choosing his organizational structure. This is not to say that Dave had mastered these skills in every writing situation nor that he always accurately diagnosed problems in his own work. In fact, we know that he did not. It is to say, however, that Dave did recognize and could talk about some of the things that writing does involve in many situations. Thus, the value of this course for Dave lay not so much in the thesis/subpoint essay structure. Rather, Dave had, as a result of his experiences in Freshman Composition, learned that writing is a process that can be talked about, managed, and controlled.

Thus the social functions that writing served for Dave in each class were viewed as an intrinsic part of his writing experiences there. Where these functions were numerous and mutually understood and valued by Dave and his teacher, Dave was more successful in figuring out and producing the required discourse. And then he remembered it longer. In Poetry, where his writing served few personally valued ends, Dave did less well, making a C on the first paper, a D on the second, and a C+ on the third. It should be noted, in addition, that grades themselves serve a social function in classrooms: defining attitudes and roles. Dave's low grades in Poetry probably further alienated him from the social communication processes in that classroom community and helped define his role there.

The Roles Played by the Participants and by Students' Texts.   Other social aspects of these classroom contexts for writing which affected Dave's experiences were the roles played by the people and texts in them. Such roles are tacitly assigned in classroom interaction and create the context in which the student stranger attempts to determine the rules of language use in that territory. Here we will examine (1) Dave's role in relation to the teacher, (2) Dave's role in relation to other students in the class, and (3) the role played by the students' texts there.

Dave's Role in Relation to the Teacher.   This is a particularly important role relationship in any classroom because it tacitly shapes the writer-audience relation that students use as they attempt to communicate appropriately. In all three classes Dave was writing for his teachers as pupil to examiner. However, data from several sources show that there were important variations in the actual "enactments" (Goffman, 1961) of this role-relationship.

In Composition, both Dave and his professor played the role of writer. Throughout the semester Dr. Carter talked about what and how she wrote, the long time she spent in prewriting activities, the eight times she typically revised her work, and the strategies she used to understand her audience in various situations. She spoke to students as if she and they were all writers working together, saying such things as "I see some of you write like I do," or "Let's work together to shape this language." And, as we have seen, she structured the course to provide opportunities for students to play the role of writer in their peer groups. She also asked them to describe their writing processes for several of their essays. Dave told me in an interview during his junior year, "In high school I couldn't stand writing, but in Comp I started to change because I knew more what I was doing. I learned that there are steps you can go through, and I learned how to organize a paper." As a freshman, Dave understood for the first time something of what it feels like to be a writer.

In Biology both Dave and his teacher, Dr. Kelly, saw Dave as playing the role of newcomer, learning the language needed for initiation into the profession. Dr. Kelly played the complementary role of experienced professional who was training Dave in the ways of speaking in that discipline, ways they both assumed Dave would learn in time.

In Poetry, on the other hand, Dave played the role of outsider in relationship to his teacher, the insider who knew the true meanings of poetry. And Dave stayed the outsider, unable ever to fully get the teacher's "true meaning." This outsider/insider relationship between Dave and Dr. Forson was created by a number of factors: (1) Their spoken and written interaction, (2) the few meaningful social functions served for Dave by the writing in that class, (3) the demanding nature of the analytic task, combined with (4) the limited knowledge Dave commanded in that setting, (5) the limited number of effective instructional supports, and (6) the low grades Dave got, which further alienated him from the communication processes in that class. (To the instructional supports provided in Poetry we will return below.) Because Dave's outsider role was not a pleasant one for him, he seemed increasingly to separate his thinking from his writing in Poetry, saying several times that he had the right ideas, the teacher just did not like the way he wrote them.

Dave's Role in Relationship to Other Students.   Students' relationships with each other, like those between students and teachers, are created as students interact within the classroom structures the teacher has set up. These classroom structures grow out of teachers' explicit and tacit notions about writing and learning. What specifically were the relationships among students in Freshman Composition, Biology, and Poetry?

In Composition, as we have seen, students shared their writing and responded to each other's work. The classroom structure reflected Dr. Carter's perhaps tacit notion that writing is a social as well as intellectual affair. However, in neither Poetry nor Biology was time built into the class for students to talk with each other about their writing. Dave lamented this as he wrote for Poetry early in his sophomore year, because, he said, he now realized how valuable the small group sessions had been in Freshman Composition the semester before.

In Biology, Dave told me students did talk informally about the journal articles they had selected and how they were progressing on their summaries. Dr. Kelly, who circulated during lab, was at times included in these informal talks about writing. And it is no surprise that students discussed their writing in this way in Biology in light of Dr. Kelly's notions about writing. It is, he believes, an essential part of what scientists do. He told me that it often comes as a rude shock to students that the way biologists survive in the field is by writing. He said, "These students are bright, and they can memorize piles of facts, but they're not yet good at writing. They know what science *is*," he told me, "but they don't know what scientists *do*." Thus, writing up research results is seen by Dr. Kelly as an integral part of a biologist's lab work. No wonder his students talked about it.

In Poetry, however, there was little talk of any kind among students. Classes were primarily lectures where Dr. Forson explicated poems and explained poetic devices. Only occasionally did he call on one of the 22 students for an opinion. This lack of student interaction in Poetry was in line with the image of the writer that Dr. Forson described for students, an image that may be widely shared in literary studies: A person alone with his or her books and thoughts. Dr. Forson did, however, tell students that he himself often got his ideas for writing from listening to himself talk about poems in class. Yet, in conversation with me, he said that he did not want students discussing the poems and their writing with each other because he feared they would not think for themselves. Dave picked up on this idea very clearly. It was not until the fall of his junior year that he admitted to me that he and his girlfriend had worked together on their papers. They had discussed the interpretations of the poems and how they might best write them, but he told me, they had been careful to choose different poems to write about so that Dr. Forson wouldn't know they had worked together. This absence of student interaction in Poetry may have contributed to the outsider role that Dave played in that class.

Throughout this study I was amazed at the amount of talk that goes on all the time outside class among students as they work to figure out the writing requirements in various courses. What Dave's experience in Poetry may suggest is that where student collaboration in writing is not openly accepted, it goes on clandestinely.

The Roles Played by Students' Texts.   What were students' texts called and how were they handled? Interview and observation data show that students' texts were treated quite differently in these three courses, and this affected how Dave saw the assignments, and, perhaps more important, how he saw himself as writer.

In Freshman Composition Dave wrote what he referred to as "essays"; in Biology, "reviews"; in Poetry, "papers." This latter term is commonly used, of course, but it is one that Emig (1983, p. 173) says suggests a low status text: "Paper"—as if there were no words on the sheet at all. In Poetry the high status texts, the ones that were discussed and interpreted, were the poems. Students' works were just more or less successful explications of those. Furthermore, in Poetry the one model essay the students read was written by the teacher. Though students were told they should think of their peers as their audience, in fact they never read each other's essays at all. Students' texts were, rather, passed only between student and teacher as in a private conversation.

In Biology, student texts enjoyed a higher status. Excellent student reviews were posted and students were encouraged to read them; they were to serve as models. Some student writers were thus defined as competent speakers in this territory, and the message was clear to Dave: This was a language that he too could learn given time and proper training.

And in Freshman Composition, of course, student texts were the *objects* of study. The class read good and flawed student texts from former semesters and from their own. This not only helped Dave with his writing, it also dignified student writing and elevated his estimation of his own work. Student texts were not, in short, private affairs between teacher and student; they were the subject matter of this college course.

Thus the roles that were enacted by teachers, students, and students' texts were quite different in each classroom and were an integral part of Dave's writing experiences there. The participants' interaction and the social functions that writing serves are important factors working to create the communication situation. And this communication situation, it has been suggested, is the fundamental factor shaping the success of writing instruction (Langer & Applebee, 1984, p. 171).

*   *   *

DISCUSSION

What, then, can be learned from Dave's experiences? First, this study adds to existing research which suggests that school writing is not a monolithic activity or global skill. Rather, the contexts for writing may be so different from one classroom to another, the ways of speaking in them so diverse, the social meanings of writing and the interaction patterns so different, that the courses may be for the student writer like so many foreign countries. These differences were apparent in this study not only in Dave's perceptions of courses but in his concerns while writing and in his written products.

Second, the findings of this study have several implications for our understanding of writing development. This study suggests that writing development is, in part, context-dependent. In each new classroom community, Dave in many ways resembled a beginning language user. He focused on a limited number of new concerns, and he was unable to move beyond concrete ways of thinking and writing, the facts of the matter at hand. Moreover, skills mastered in one situation, such as the thesis-subpoint organization in Freshman Composition, did not, as Dave insisted, automatically transfer to new contexts with differing problems and language and differing amounts of knowledge that he controlled. To better understand the stages that students progress through in achieving competence in academic speech communities, we need further research.

Dave's development across his freshman and sophomore years, where he was repeatedly a newcomer, may also be viewed in terms of his attitude toward writing. Evidence over 21 months shows that his notion of the purpose of school writing changed very little. Though there were, as we have seen, other functions accomplished for Dave by his writing in Freshman Composition and Biology, he always understood the purpose of his school writing as being primarily to satisfy a teacher-examiner's requirements. A change that did occur, however, was Dave's increased understanding of some of the activities that writers actually engage in and an increased confidence in his writing ability. As a freshman, he had told me that he did not like to write and was not very good, but by the fall of his junior year he sounded quite different. Because of a number of successful classroom experiences with writing, and an ability to forget the less successful ones, Dave told me, "Writing is no problem for me. At work, in school, I just do it."

Whether Dave will eventually be a mature writer, one who, according to Britton's (1975) definition, is able to satisfy his own purposes with a wide range of audiences, lies beyond the scope of this study to determine. We do know, however, that Dave did not, during the period of this study, write for a wide range of audiences. Nor did he, in these classes, define his own audiences, purposes, or formats, though he did in Freshman Composition choose his topics and in Poetry and Biology the particular poems and articles he wrote about. What this study suggests is that college undergraduates in beginning-level courses may have even less opportunity to orchestrate their own writing occasions than do younger students. Balancing teachers' and students' purposes is indeed difficult in these classrooms where students must, in 14 weeks, learn unfamiliar discourse conventions as well as a large body of new knowledge.

The findings of this study have several implications for the teaching of writing. They suggest that when we ask what students learn from and about writing in classrooms, we must look not only at particular assignments or at students' written products. We must also look at what they learn from the social contexts those classrooms provide for writing. In Freshman Composition, Dave learned that writer was a role he could play. In Biology, writing was for Dave an important part of a socialization process; he was the newcomer being initiated into a profession in which, he learned, writing counts for a great deal. From his writing in Poetry, Dave learned that reading poetry was not for him and that he could get through any writing task, no matter how difficult or foreign. This latter is a lesson not without its value, of course, but it is not one that teachers hope to teach with their writing assignments.

This study also raises questions about how teachers can best help student "strangers" to become competent users of the new language in their academic territory. Because all writing is context-dependent, and because successful writing requires the accurate assessment of and adaptation to the demands of particular writing situations, perhaps writing teachers should be explicitly training students in this assessment process. As Dave researched the writing requirements in his classroom, he drew upon six information sources in a process that was for him largely tacit and unarticulated. But Dave was actually in a privileged position in terms of his potential for success in this "figuring out" process. He had, after all, had years of practice writing in classrooms. Furthermore, he shared not only ethnic and class backgrounds with his teachers, but also many assumptions about education. Students from diverse communities may need, even more than Dave, explicit training in the ways in which one figures out and then adapts to the writing demands in academic contexts.

For teachers in the disciplines, "native-speakers" who may have used the language in their discipline for so long that is it partially invisible to them, the first challenge will be to appreciate just how foreign and difficult their language is for student newcomers. They must make explicit the interpretive and linguistic conventions in their community, stressing that theirs is one way of looking at reality and not reality itself. As Fish (1980) points out, "The choice is never between objectivity and interpretation, but between an interpretation that is unacknowledged as such and an interpretation that is at least aware of itself" (p. 179). Teachers in the disciplines must then provide student newcomers with assignments and instructional supports which are appropriate for first steps in using the language of their community. Designing appropriate assignments and supports may well be more difficult when the student stranger is only on a brief visit in an academic territory, as Dave was in Poetry, or when the student comes from a community at a distance farther from academe than Dave did.

Naturalistic studies like the present one, Geertz says, are only "another country heard from . . . nothing more or less." Yet, "small facts speak to large issues" (1973, p. 23). From Dave's story, and others like it which describe actual writers at work in local settings, we will learn more about writers' processes and texts and how these are constrained by specific social dynamics. Our generalizations and theories about writing and about how people learn to write must, in the final analysis, be closely tied to such concrete social situations.

REFERENCES

Applebee, A. (1984). *Contexts for learning to write: Studies of secondary school instruction.* Norwood, NJ: Ablex.

Basso, K. (1974). The ethnography of writing. In R. Bauman and J. Sherzer (Eds.), *Explorations in the ethnography of speaking.* (pp. 425–432). New York: Cambridge University Press.

Bazerman, C. (1981). What written knowledge does: Three examples of academic discourse. *Philosophy of the Social Sciences, 11,* 361–387.

Berkenkotter, C. (1983). Decisions and revisions: The planning strategies of a publishing writer. *College Composition and Communication, 34,* 156–169.

Bizzell, P. (1982). Cognition, convention, and certainty: What we need to know about writing. *PRE/TEXT, 3,* 213–243.

Bridweil, L. (1980). Revising strategies in twelfth grade students' transactional writing. *Research in the Teaching of English, 14,* 197–222.

Britton, J., Burgess, T., Martin, N., McLeod, A., & Rosen, H. (1975). *The development of writing abilities 11-18.* London: Macmillan.

Calkins, L. (1980). Research update: When children want to punctuate: Basic skills belong in context. *Language Arts, 57,* 567–573.

Clark, C., & Florio, S., with Elmore, J., Martin, J., & Maxwell, R. (1983). Understanding writing instruction: Issues of theory and method. In P. Mosenthal, L. Tamor, & S. Walmsley (Eds.), *Research on writing: Principles and methods.* (pp. 236–264). New York: Longman.

Cooper, M. (1986). The ecology of writing. *College English, 48,* 364–375.

Denzin, N. (1978). *Sociological methods.* New York: McGraw-Hill.

Dewey, J. (1949). *The child and the curriculum and the school and society.* Chicago: University of Chicago Press.

Dyson, A. (1984). Learning to write/learning to do school: Emergent writers' interpretations of school literacy tasks. *Research in the Teaching of English, 18,* 233–264.

Emig, J. (1983). *The web of meaning: Essays on writing, teaching, learning, and thinking.* Upper Montclair, NJ: Boynton/Cook.

Erikson, F. (1982). Taught cognitive learning in its immediate environments: A neglected topic in the anthropology of education. *Anthropology & Education Quarterly, 13* (2), 148–180.

Faigley, L. (1985). Nonacademic writing: The social perspective. In L. Odell & D. Goswami (Eds.), *Writing in nonacademic settings.* (pp. 231–248). New York: Guilford Press.

Fish, S. (1980). Interpreting the Variorium. In J. Tompkins (Ed.), *Reader response criticism: From formalism to post-structuralism.* Baltimore: Johns Hopkins University Press.

Florio, S., & Clark, C. (1982). The functions of writing in an elementary classroom. *Research in the Teaching of English, 16,* 115–130.

Flower, L., & Hayes, J. (1981). The pregnant pause: An inquiry into the nature of planning. *Research in the Teaching of English, 15,* 229–244.

Freedman, S. (1984). The registers of student and professional expository writing: Influences on teachers' responses. In R. Beach & L. Bridwell (Eds.), *New directions in composition research.* (pp. 334–347). New York: Guilford Press.

Freedman, S. (1985). *The acquisition of written language: Response and revision.* New York: Ablex.

Geertz, C. (1973). *The interpretation of cultures.* New York: Basic Books.

Gilmore, P., & Glatthorn, A. (1982). *Children in and out of school: Ethnography and education.* Washington, DC: Center for Applied Linguistics.

Goffman, E. (1961). *Encounters: Two studies in the sociology of interaction.* New York: Bobbs-Merrill.

Grice, H. (1975). *Logic and conversation.* 1967. William James Lectures, Harvard University. Unpublished manuscript, 1967. Excerpt in Cole and Morgan (Eds.), *Syntax and semantics, Vol. III: Speech acts.* (pp. 41–58). New York: Academic Press.

Guba, E. (1978). *Toward a method of naturalistic inquiry in educational evaluation.* Los Angeles: Center for the Study of Evaluation, University of California at Los Angeles.

Gumperz, J. (1971). *Language in social groups.* Stanford, CA: Stanford University Press.

Heath, S. B. (1982). Ethnography in education: Defining the essentials. In P. Gilmore & A. Glatthorn (Eds.), *Children in and out of school: Ethnography and education.* (pp. 33–55). Washington, DC: Center for Applied Linguistics.

Heinlein, R. (1961). *Stranger in a strange land.* New York: Putnam.

Herrington, A. (1985). Writing in academic settings: A study of the contexts for writing in two college chemical engineering courses. *Research in the Teaching of English, 19,* 331–359.

Hymes, D. (1972a). Introduction. In C. Cazden, V. P. John, & D. Hymes (Eds.), *Functions of language in the classroom.* (pp. xi–lxii). New York: Teachers College Press.

Hymes, D. (1972b). Models of the interaction of language and social life. In J. Gumperz & D. Hymes (Eds.), *Directions in sociolinguistics.* (pp. 35–71). New York: Holt, Reinhart, & Winston.

Kantor, K. (1984). Classroom contexts and the development of writing intuitions: An ethnographic case study. In R. Beach & L. Bridwell (Eds.), *New directions in composition research.* (pp. 72–94). New York: Guilford.

Langer, J. (1984). The effects of available information on responses to school writing tasks. *Research in the Teaching of English, 18,* 27–44.

Langer, J. (1985). Children's sense of genre: A study of performance on parallel reading and writing tasks. *Written Communication, 2,* 157–188.

Langer, J. (1986). Reading, writing, and understanding: An analysis of the construction of meaning. *Written Communication, 3,* 219–267.

Langer, J., & Applebee, A. (1984). Language, learning, and interaction: A framework for improving the teaching of writing. In A. Applebee (Ed.), *Contexts for learning to write: Studies of secondary school instruction.* (pp. 169–182). Norwood, NJ: Ablex.

Lincoln, Y., & Guba, E. (1985). *Naturalistic inquiry.* Beverly Hills, CA: Sage Publications.

Odell, L., & Goswami, D. (1985). *Writing in nonacademic settings.* New York: Guilford Press.

Perl, S. (1979). The composing process of unskilled college writers. *Research in Teaching of English, 13,* 317–336.

Perry, W. G. (1970). *Forms of intellectual and ethical development in the college years.* New York: Holt, Rinehart, and Winston.

Piaget, J. (1952). *The origins of intelligence in children.* New York: International Universities Press.

Pianko, S. (1979). A description of the composing processes of college freshman writers. *Research in the Teaching of English, 13,* 5–22.

Polanyi, M. (1958). *Personal knowledge: Towards a post-critical philosophy.* Chicago: University of Chicago Press.

Scribner, S. & Cole, M. (1981). Unpackaging literacy. In M. F. Whiteman (Ed.), *Variation in writing: Functional and linguistic-cultural differences.* (pp. 71–88). Hillsdale, NJ: Lawrence Erlbaum.

Shaughnessey, M. (1977). *Errors and expectations.* New York: Oxford University Press.

Spradley, J. (1979). *The ethnographic interview.* New York: Holt, Rinehart and Winston.

Spradley, J. (1980). *Participant observation.* New York: Holt, Rinehart and Winston.

Szwed, J. (1981). The ethnography of literacy. In M. F. Whiteman (Ed.), *Variation in writing: Functional and linguistic-cultural differences.* (pp. 13–23). Hillsdale, NJ: Lawrence Earlbaum.

Whiteman, M. F. (1981). *Variation in writing: Functional and linguistic-cultural differences.* Hillsdale, NJ: Lawrence Erlbaum.

Williams, J. (1985, March). *Encouraging higher order reasoning through writing in all disciplines.* Paper presented at the Delaware Valley Writing Council-PATHS Conference, Philadelphia. ■

Responding to Reading

1. As you travel from one course to another, have you ever felt like Dave? Share any examples that resonate with his experience.

2. In her title and throughout the piece, McCarthy employs the metaphor of entering a strange land. In "Conversational Ballgames" Sakamoto uses the metaphors of tennis and other ballgames. How do these metaphors help or hinder your comprehension? How do you use metaphors in your writing?

3. What does the form of this article tell you about the interests and values of its audience? Why does McCarthy devote so much attention to describing her methods? What do you suspect that the readers of *Research in the Teaching of English,* the journal in which the piece originally appeared, consider valid evidence?

4. Select two or three short passages that you find particularly important. Compare them to those chosen by your classmates.

5. McCarthy writes: "Because all writing is context-dependent, and because successful writing requires the accurate assessment of and adaptation to the demands of particular writing situations, perhaps writing teachers should be explicitly training students in this assessment process." What does she mean by this? Do you agree? If so, why? If not, how should writing instructors teach?

6. Is there any way that you can apply McCarthy's findings to your own writing in college? How?

Gathering Data: Analyzing Documents

Empirical reports often draw on a whole range of data, such as systematic observations, measurements, the results of experiments, and computations. There are two main ways that you should gather data for your report on a disciplinary discourse community: by analyzing documents and by interviewing experts. This section addresses how to analyze documents and the next section addresses how to conduct interviews.

One way to learn about a culture is to study its artifacts (as anthropologists and archeologists do). Correspondingly, to learn about a discourse community, one should study the texts produced in and by it. Some (but not necessarily all) of this work should be done before you conduct your interviews because this will help you better prepare for the interviews.

For this assignment, you should review and analyze several different kinds of documents, including the following:

- *Articles in scholarly and professional journals.* Every discipline has at least one scholarly journal, and most have many. It is through these publications that researchers share their findings and engage in scholarly exchange. Journals are often quite specialized and difficult for newcomers to read. But don't despair; in reviewing articles, you need not understand the content in full.

  Try this process: Look for the section of your library where periodicals for your chosen field are located. If you can't find it, ask a reference librarian. Then scan 10–12 pieces of scholarly writing (preferably in several different journals in your chosen discipline). Then pick two or three to read completely and analyze. (If possible, look up scholarship by your prospective interviewee, and choose one of his or her pieces to read in full.)

- *Published guidelines for writers in your field.* Seek out handbooks, which are often sanctioned by disciplinary associations, that offer guidelines for writers in your particular field. Sometimes these are hefty books, such as the *Modern Language Association (MLA) Handbook,* which applies to English and foreign languages. Sometimes they are thin volumes or pamphlets. Sometimes they are brief guidelines for writers (often titled "Guidelines for Submissions") and can be found in scholarly journals themselves or on their Web sites.

- *Other documents.* Seek out information on what other kinds of writing academics or professionals in your chosen discipline do. This might include reports, letters, email correspondence, grant proposals, and so on. It might also include articles in popular periodicals. (*Psychology Today,* for example, is a popular-press outlet for research. As a publication, it differs from specialized academic journals in psychology.) If you can, get samples.

- *Websites.* Look up the home pages of national associations, the home pages of faculty members at your college and others, online course syllabi, and other sites related to your field.

- *Student writing.* Try to find both writing assignments (e.g., papers, tests, projects) for upper-division courses in the major and actual student texts (e.g., old papers, tests).

You might not be able to procure all these kinds of documents, but the more you have, the better. A larger data set usually yields more reliable results. If you have trouble locating documents, ask your interviewees for help; as experienced members of that community, they will be your best guides. Also seek the help of reference librarians.

Tips for Analysis

After you have gathered the documents listed above, you must analyze them. Here are some tips for doing so:

- *Keep an eye out for patterns.* What is repeated across several documents?

- *Consider the kinds of topics researched.* What do they have in common? Which topics are most popular?

- *Identify standard formats, genres, and rhetorical conventions.* Do all the articles follow the same basic format?

- *Assess what kinds of evidence are valued.* Is experimental or numerical data privileged? Are eloquent arguments valued? Are historical documents valued? Is previous scholarship valued? Also examine the kinds of sources most often cited by scholars in the field.

- *Notice the nature of verbal/visual integration.* Are charts, graphs, photos, equations, etc. integrated with the text? What role do they play?

- *Examine characteristics of style and tone.* Describe the prose style (spare or elaborate? accessible or opaque? long, fluid sentences or short, punchy ones? active or passive voice? first- or third-person perspective? etc.) Also assess the voice and tone (dispassionate? argumentative? defensive? even-tempered? elitist? distanced? warm?).

If you are puzzled by something, be sure to take note of it and save that question for your interviewees. They will be able guides in analyzing documents in their fields.

Gathering Data: Interviewing

You should interview at least one faculty member in your chosen discipline and at least one upper-division major. Interviewing a wider sample will create more credible results, so you might also consider interviewing more faculty members and undergraduates—and even graduate students, alumni, or professionals in the workplace.

Good interviews require preparation. If you think you can walk into an interview and wing it, you are taking the risk of both embarrassing yourself and failing to get the information you need.

One way to help prepare for and conduct an interview is to work with a classmate interested in the same discipline. Collaboration can alleviate the nervousness some people feel when conducting an interview. However, flying solo is fine, too.

Tips for Interviewing

As you prepare for your interviews, consider the following advice:

- *Prepare open-ended questions.* Closed-ended questions are those that can be answered with yes or no, such as "Do you like your job?" They lead to limited disclosure, whereas open-ended questions encourage elaboration and discussion. An open-ended alternative to "Do you like your job?" is "What do you enjoy about your job?" Notice how simply changing the structure of a question encourages an interviewee to share more:

Closed-ended Questions	Open-ended Questions
Does writing play a big role in your own work?	What kinds of writing do you do as part of your work?
When grading student writing, do you look for good grammar?	How do you grade student writing?

- *Be ready with follow-up questions.* Although you need to have prepared questions, you should not be too rigid. Sometimes you will want to invite further inquiry into a topic that seems promising. You can then ask,

"Can you say more about that?" or "Could you help me understand that better?"

- *Take notes or tape-record.* Don't trust your memory. Take notes, but not on everything, lest you have your head buried in a notebook the whole time. If you want to tape-record an interview, ask for permission to record before beginning the interview.

- *Be aware of your nonverbal cues.* Body language is important. You should lean forward, maintain eye contact, nod, and occasionally insert comments such as "Uh-huh," "Yes, I see," and "I hadn't thought of that" to signal your attentiveness.

- *Stay on track.* You have only a limited amount of time, and interviews can wander. Sometimes you need to steer the interview back to its purpose. Be polite but assertive.

- *Review anything that is still unclear.* Before you leave the interview, ask for clarification on key points.

A detailed agenda for an interview, including several suggested questions, is outlined in the following box.

Interview Preparation

BEFORE THE INTERVIEW

- Find out as much as possible about your interviewee (via websites, publications, etc.)
- Plan interview questions
- If collaborating, have a team plan
- When setting up the interview, communicate about its purpose and how long you expect it to take

ESTABLISHING RAPPORT

- Greet warmly and express appreciation for meeting
- Introduce yourself
- Remind the interviewee about the purpose of the interview
- Give your interviewee an invitation to talk about himself/herself by asking a question such as What drew you into the field of _____?

MAIN QUESTIONS

- If you haven't already gotten it from other sources (such as a personal website or a college catalog), inquire about background information (schooling, experience, credentials, etc.).
- Which subjects do you teach and research?
- What are your research methods?
- Can you describe how you move from research to writing? or how writing is integral to your research?
- What kinds of writing do you do as an anthropologist/engineer/etc.?
- Are there specific formats/genres? What are they? When is each used? Is there a format/genre that you use most frequently?
- Do you ever share your writing? Does anyone see it in the early stages? the later stages?
- Do you co-author any of your work? If so, with whom? How does that process work?
- Do you communicate in ways other than writing (visuals, drawings, graphs, tables, etc.)? Do you combine different media in the same document (e.g., graphs and writing)?
- Does technology play any role in your composing process?
- How would you describe the writing style that is most valued and practiced in your discipline?
- What kind of writing do you assign in your classes? What do you look for when you are assessing or grading student writing? (Do you have any examples of successful student writing?)
- What common mistakes or misunderstandings about writing do you see most often in your students?
- What do you want your students to understand about communication and writing before they graduate?
- Do professionals in this field do much writing after college? What kinds of writing do they do? What kinds of writers are most valued?

CLOSING STRATEGIES

- Invite a final thought, such as Can you think of anything we haven't covered?
- Ask for documents that could help you (assignments, student samples, etc.)
- Ask about other potential people to interview (undergrads, graduate students, other faculty members, recent graduates)
- Ask whether you can follow up later if you have more questions
- Let the interviewee know how helpful he or she has been
- Thank your interviewee for his or her time and generosity

The template in the "Interview Preparation" box is only a general outline. You might need to add, cut, or customize questions to fit your particular situation. Finally, don't forget to write a thank-you note within three days of the interview.

Practice Interview

There is no substitute for practice. To help prepare for an interview, you can conduct a mock interview. Classmates (and perhaps the instructor, too) can play the roles of interviewer and interviewee. Rehearse everything, from the knock on the door to the closing handshake.

You get only one shot at an interview. It is best to make your mistakes during a mock interview rather than during the real thing.

After you have gathered and analyzed all your documents and your interview notes, recall McCarthy's approach to her data. She writes, "I read and reread my field notes and interview transcripts looking for patterns and themes." You should do the same.

Rhetorical Features of the Empirical Research Report

Empirical research reports generally strive for objectivity and adopt a fairly consistent structure. "Empirical" denotes that conclusions are based on systematic observations and data collection rather than on personal insights or deductive reasoning. The purpose of such reports is usually to extend human knowledge and/or to support decision making. McCarthy's "A Stranger in Strange Lands" is a fine example of an empirical research report that is primarily aimed at extending knowledge about how students learn to write, but that also has some application for decision making (e.g., teachers can use her findings to make better decisions about instruction and curriculum).

The overall tone of your report should be dispassionate and evenhanded. Although many kinds of scientific writing frown upon using the personal pronoun *I*, in this report you can, if you wish, because revealing your personal role in gathering and analyzing the evidence can be an effective strategy. Notice how McCarthy engages in sound, objective analysis but still retains some of the appealing rhetorical strategies we find in personal essays, such as beginning with an anecdote (a description of and quote from Dave) and using the first person perspective judiciously ("As I followed Dave from one classroom writing situation to another . . . ").

Section headings signal the structure of McCarthy's article, and this format is fairly common—with some variations by discipline—in empirical and scientific reports. The skeleton of such reports is shown in the following box.

Empirical Research Report Structure

Abstract
Introduction
Objectives
Background
Methods
Facts/Results
Discussion
Conclusions
Recommendations

Because you will write a compressed version of a research report, it is wise to trim and simplify the structure (while still remaining true to the substance and purpose of empirical research). If you look at the student samples at the end of this chapter, you will notice that both have omitted the abstract (which is not necessary in a brief report) and each has combined (slightly differently) some of the report sections. A simplified structure, along with guiding questions for each section, is outlined in the following box.

Simplified Empirical Research Report Structure

Introduction and Objectives	Why is your research important? What are you trying to discover?
Method	How did you gather data? Was your research method sound?
Results/Facts	What are your results?
Discussion and Conclusions	How do you interpret your results? What is the significance of the results?
Recommendations	What are the implications of your findings? How can you/we act on them?

Be sure to consider the questions keyed to each section *from your reader's point of view.* Below are a few tips for addressing those questions as you construct each section. You can also flip to the student samples at the end of the chapter to see how two writers, Karen and Melissa, handle each section.

Introduction and Objectives

You have several options when introducing a report. McCarthy starts with a brief portrait of Dave, Karen makes a customized appeal to her audience (first-year students in college), and Melissa gets right to the point ("The purpose of this research was to . . . "). Whatever approach you choose, you should employ a few basic rhetorical strategies:

- *Announce the topic.* This can be done in the first sentence, and it needs to be delivered at least by midway through the first section.

- *Explain the relevance of your research.* Be clear about why your audience should care about this report. Perhaps it will extend the reader's knowledge of something pertinent; perhaps it will widen the reader's awareness; perhaps it will help the reader make decisions or meet particular goals.

- *Be explicit about the aims of your research.* People don't read empirical reports for fun; they read them to get something out of them. Therefore, the reader will want to know your objective (or objectives) at the outset.

Method

You should expect your readers to be skeptical (although not hostile). One essential step in winning confidence is convincing the audience that your research methods are sound, that they meet basic standards of rigor and completeness. You also need to be clear about any limitations that your methods place on the report's conclusions and recommendations. The key here is honest and full disclosure—be up front and don't try to hide anything from readers. The following are a few specific guidelines:

- *Explain how you collected your data.* If necessary, also explain why you opted for one particular method of collection over others.

- *Explain how you evaluated your data.* What criteria did you employ? What methods did you use?

- *Explain any limitations to your method.* You should anticipate your readers' concerns and potential objections and address them in advance.

- *Appeal to authorities who lend credibility to your method.* Karen and Melissa do this by explaining the qualifications of their interview subjects. McCarthy does it by citing published research.

Results/Facts

The "Results/Facts" section is fairly self-explanatory. Many kinds of empirical reports include tables and graphs in this section, but your report is not likely to include much numerical data or many visuals. Sometimes this section is combined with the "Discussion" section.

Discussion and Conclusions

Contrary to popular opinion, facts do not always speak for themselves. You need to help your reader make sense of the results you present. Highlight the most significant findings and patterns; explain any oddities in your results; and, most importantly, explain how your results relate to your original research objectives.

Recommendations

The "Recommendations" section is usually brief. It suggests what should be done, based on the research findings and your interpretation of them. Reports often include recommendations that are specific and immediate, as with an engineering report that suggests the correction of a design flaw in a machine. In your report, you can make recommendations to yourself, to fellow college students, or to prospective students who hope to enter your major. The recommendations can be immediate or long-term suggestions. You can also highlight the most important thing that you learned through your research. Sometimes the "Conclusions" and "Recommendations" sections are combined into a single section.

Student Research Reports: Karen, *Writing About Numbers: Writing Practices in Mathematics* and Melissa Lewis, *Beyond the Textbook: The Language of Historians*

When they wrote these reports, the authors were first-year students.

WRITING ABOUT NUMBERS: WRITING PRACTICES IN MATHEMATICS

Many freshman mathematics majors wonder why they need to take writing classes while in college. The general opinion is that mathematics majors must be able to play with numbers, not words. While there is not much writing in the field of mathematics, writing plays a distinct and important role.

BACKGROUND

After having read McCarthy's article "A Stranger in Strange Lands . . . ," I began to think about the writing practices in academic discourse communities. McCarthy's article explained that an average student had three different experiences while writing for three different classes. I decided to investigate the average writing experience of a student who majors in one field of study and how that experience is unique.

OBJECTIVES

Even though they do not realize it, mathematics majors need to know how to write. But must majors do not understand *why* they need to write. For the average student out of high school, mathematics is just numbers, not words. Before I began to research the writing that takes place in this field, I knew that I would be required to write some proofs, but I did not know of anything else I would need to write. The purpose of this report is to give myself and other potential mathematics majors an understanding of what we should be expected to write.

METHODS

To accomplish this, I set out to interview some prominent mathematicians. To gain an insight into writing that occurs at all levels of mathematics, I interviewed a junior (undergraduate), a third-year graduate student, and a professor of mathematics, all at Kansas State University.

I have known Allison Harper (the junior) for several years—we went to high school together. She has been a mathematics major since entering the university her freshman year. Allison has graded college algebra and calculus homework papers for the department. She currently grades differential equations papers.

I met Heather VanDyke this year. She is a third-year graduate student and graduated with a mathematics degree from this university. She has written two papers for the *Eastern Oregon University Science and Mathematics Journal* and currently teaches some college algebra courses while pursuing her master's degree. While interviewing Heather, I also received input from Sarah Jackson, a second-year graduate student.

Dr. David Surowski was my main source of information. He received his Ph.D. in 1975 from the University of Arizona and is currently the Director of Graduate Studies at Kansas State University. He specializes in algebra and has written numerous articles and reviews for mathematics journals. Since he has written more than my other two sources, he therefore was able to provide me with more feedback.

FACTS

When I asked Allison and Heather if they had written anything for mathematics, their immediate answer was "proofs." (These are short explanations of why a particular mathematical statement is true. Once a person has proved a statement, they are allowed to use that statement without questions being called on their work.) They explained that proofs are for homework and that all math majors will write proofs. This I already knew, for I had written some in high school. Allison said she had done lab reports and a very short research paper dealing with the use of technology in a high school setting. Heather said that she had not really done a research paper, but she had written two contest papers: one on how to set up a team of business people for optimum communication, and one on a grading system that takes into account the amount of effort a student expends (both for the *Eastern Oregon University Science and Mathematics Journal*). These were not really research, but thinking and then writing down the solution. She also said that her contest papers were poor examples of writing because she received the subject of each paper on Friday night, and the paper was due on the following Monday. "The actual writing," she said, "took place very late at night."

I asked Allison and Heather about general writing in mathematics. Allison said, "I plan on writing things for math, but I have to wait until I know more math." Heather's reply was somewhat different. She thinks that writing "doesn't apply very much to mathematics." Apparently, this is because math consists mainly of numbers, not words.

Dr. Surowski, on the other hand, was very enthusiastic about writing. Since his master's thesis, he has written around 30 papers and 80 reviews, mainly for the *American Mathematical Society Journal*. He gave me a long list of things that mathematicians need to write: papers, books, grant proposals, documents, and reports. He said that, unfortunately, most math majors do not write until they do their master's thesis, and even that is not required. For a master's degree, a student can choose to write a thesis or to take a very big math test.

As to the style in which mathematicians write, everyone I interviewed said that mathematics articles are written in a "linear, logical fashion," as explained by Heather, with each sentence directly proceeding from the previous sentence. While it may seem that in most pieces of writing this is true, often a work will repeat some ideas over and over again. In mathematics, once something has been said, it is assumed to be said, and the author can then go on to the next idea. Dr. Surowski went further and said that writing for mathematics uses a more precise language than writing for other topics. Allison said that writing for math is "technical." Also, some mathematicians use some symbols to replace common words. But even when one uses symbols, Dr. Surowski warns that writing with symbols must still follow the regular English grammar rules;

that is, one must be able to replace the symbols with the words for which they stand and have the sentence still make sense. (Most people have had at least some limited contact with regular mathematics symbols. The "equals sign," (=) for instance, is the most common example of a symbol. The corresponding replacement words are generally "is equal to," but may sometimes consist of the word "is.")

DISCUSSION/CONCLUSION

The reason the students and the doctor did not share views on writing is because the students have not been exposed to writing in the field, yet. So, as a math major, one can anticipate little formal writing, but when one does write, the thoughts must be stated clearly and be easy to follow. The fact that most mathematicians do not really begin to write until after the master's thesis is probably the reason for the myth that mathematicians do not write. In fact, Dr. Surowski believes that writing is crucial to mathematics. He contends that "writing is the culmination of mathematics": one does not do several complicated equations, obtain an answer and throw the results away; rather, one will write about the work one has done in order to share it with others.

If one uses symbols, one must be sure to be aware of precisely what the symbols stand for, and also be aware of the audience for whom one is writing. A person without a background in mathematical symbols will not be able to read an article that extensively incorporates symbols. Heather says that mathematicians must be able to "write for the audience." Dr. Surowski says that one "can't always be a mathematician when [one is] writing." This goes along with Linda Flower's opinion when, in her article "Writing for an Audience," she says "The ability to adapt your knowledge to the needs of the reader is often crucial to your success as a writer" (141).

RECOMMENDATIONS

Mathematics majors apparently do not *need* to study writing to get through college. But eventually mathematicians must write if they are to be serious mathematicians. Dr. Surowski would like to see more writing implemented earlier into the field. Math majors will need to know how to communicate later in life, and it would be a good idea to start writing as early as possible.

WORKS CITED

McCarthy, Lucille. "A Stranger in Strange Lands: A College Student Writing Across the Curriculum." *Research in the Teaching of English.* National Council of Teachers of English, 1987.

Flower, Linda. "Writing for an Audience." *Language Awareness Readings for College Writers.* Eds. Paul Eschholz, Alfred Rosa, Virginia Clark. Boston: Bedford, 2000. 139–41. ■

BEYOND THE TEXTBOOK: THE LANGUAGE OF HISTORIANS

INTRODUCTION AND OBJECTIVES OF RESEARCH

The purpose of this research was to investigate the language practices of the history academic discourse community. By studying the samples of established historians, a newcomer to the field would be successful in learning the accepted practices of the community. The writing style of historians is different than that of engineers or mathematicians. The history circle practices distinct traditions, conventions and standards that vary from other groups' styles. The majority of students think of their dusty American History textbook when they think of historic writing. But after researching the field, I have found a greater variety of writings that historians complete.

METHOD OF OBTAINING FACTS

For expediency purposes, I decided to join forces with a classmate, Evan Tritsch, in the research of this project. We set appointments for interviews with an assistant professor of history from Kansas State University and an undergraduate student majoring in history.

Professor Bonnie Lynn-Sherow received her Ph.D. from Northwestern University in 1998 in American History. Her fields of specialization are Agricultural, Environmental, North American Indian and Canadian History. She has published two journal articles on land tenure and agriculture, and several encyclopedia articles related to Indian peoples, as well as book reviews in *Kansas History, Agricultural History* and *The Journal of the West*.

Ms. Lory Stone is a senior majoring in history and women's studies, with a minor in French. Her projected graduation date is December 2000. Her future plans are to attend law school in fall 2001.

We first interviewed Ms. Stone at Kansas State University Hale Library, recording the questions and answers with a microcassette recorder. The interview lasted approximately twenty-five minutes. The interview with Professor Lynn-Sherow took place in her office in Eisenhower Hall 216 and was also recorded with the microcassette recorder. It lasted approximately thirty minutes. After each interview, I transcribed the recorded interview onto a word-processed document and made copies for Evan and myself.

We also obtained two writings from each interviewee as examples of their writing to analyze. From Professor Lynn-Sherow, we examined: a book review published in *Kansas History* in 1996 for the book *Sustainable Agriculture in the American Midwest: Lessons from the Past, Prospects for the Future*, a collection of essays edited by Gregory McIssac and William R. Edwards, and an article titled

"Beyond Winter Wheat: The USDA Extension Service and Kansas Wheat Production in the Twentieth Century" published in *Kansas History* in 2000. From Ms. Stone we collected: a paper written for her Women in European History class in the fall of 1998 titled "A Masterpiece Molded From Clay: The Mind of Mary Wollstonecraft" and an essay for her History of American Medicine class in the spring of 2000 depicting an imaginary scenario in which the writer plays the Surgeon General of the United States during the period of an imaginary fatal epidemic. After making copies of each work, I studied the data and made notations of the writing styles I assessed in each piece.

FACTS

Historical writing serves two functions: it is a tool for communication from one historian to another explaining their research and discoveries and it is a permanent record for those discoveries to be chronicled (Smith 8). Historians use language to seek new knowledge, describe and criticize situations or ideas and record the past, among other applications (Smith 12).

To be a successful historian, a person must be able to communicate clearly by using proper mechanics, typically present their argument or thesis in the first paragraph, support the argument or thesis with sound evidence using examples that make logical sense, and utilize a historical perspective that takes into account the outlook of the time period that the topic was in.

As an effect of Post-Modernism, a style that typically uses traditional, classical and sometimes even extreme modernist styles, historians have approached their writing with more of a personal voice. "If you read stuff written in the 1950s or 1960s, it sounds like the voice of God came down: 'This happened and then this happened.' You never know what the author's voice is or what their underlying bias is. Today you can pick up a book and know what the author's deep personal investment in the subject is," explains Professor Lynn-Sherow. The author's personal style depends on his or her own preference. "As for when I first began writing, my papers were more factual, and now my writing has more of my voice supported by facts," recounts Ms. Stone. "Because I focus on women a lot, and it's something I'm passionate about, my voice just comes through in my papers."

The writing process for historians includes an extended period of work. A topic for writing can be either topical or temporal, focusing on a specific person, group, ideology, or time period that interests the author. History allows the author to personalize their work by choosing a subject that they find intriguing or misrepresented. For example, Professor Lynn-Sherow specialized in Environmental History and American Indian History and her work, therefore, is a combination of these two fields. Ms. Stone is a double major in Women's Studies, and so she likes to specialize her topics on women and female issues in history.

After choosing a topic, the author must begin to search for information. The most valued source historians can find is information that is given as a first-hand account, called a primary source. Historians find difficulty during research when searching for these documents. Professional historians often travel great distances in order to explore archives that have not been thoroughly looked through. "Certain libraries will have certain things online, but historians rely a lot on browsing, the serendipitous finding of material people haven't found yet, and so you know they're not digitized yet," says Professor Lynn-Sherow. This makes their job more difficult. Student historians, under time constraints, are not always able to travel great distances in search of primary sources, but do have a chance to examine them through inter-library loan. Also, some classes will examine primary documents as their textbooks. Many historians find it beneficial to be fluent in other languages when studying a primary source written in another language. "I'm currently taking a class on 'France from 1500–1715' and it helps a lot to know French," tells Ms. Stone.

Proving the validity of a work can be challenging for historians. An important skill is in finding the biases of a particular author, or the motives he or she had when writing their account. Generally, the greater length of time the account was written from the event, the more likely the account is to become biased. Even an autobiographical account can't always be trusted. "A person's memory often changes over time and you know they're going to sugarcoat what they did because they want to make their life look better," describes Professor Lynn-Sherow. "Correspondence made at the time of the event will be more valid of a source."

All of this research can take years of data processing and organizing notes. Historians have their own approach to organizing their material, so that it is not lost. Some systematize it in boxes, file systems and computers, which is what Professor Lynn-Sherow prefers. The intent is to be able to perform cross-referencing through different sources by looking at several accounts that can prove that an event did happen. "I use a computer program that uses key words, so I can type 'Oklahoma' as a key word and it will bring up all of my stuff on Oklahoma," explains Professor Lynn-Sherow. "This way, I'm not plagiarizing or summarizing from one source."

After organizing notes and research on a subject, some historians take time in examining the information and deciding on how they wish to begin their writing. "You do all of the research, you have all of the raw data floating around in your head, and you let it stay there for a long time; sometimes it's just a couple weeks, sometimes it's several months. I know professors who have taken several years," comments Professor Lynn-Sherow. "I know when I'm ready to write when I wake up in the middle of the night and I'm writing sentences in my head."

Again, students don't always have the extent of time that allows professional historians to go into great depth. Ms. Stone recalls Junior Seminar class in which the entire grade was based on a paper that was worked on throughout the entire semester. "We had to choose our topic in the first week, but that didn't afford us much time to research it. My topic changed throughout the course of the semester," Ms. Stone describes. "By the end, while still focusing on women, my emphasis had changed."

After getting their thoughts and information down on paper, historians revise multiple drafts. The availability of the computer has greatly helped them in this area because of its speed and simplicity. "I used to handwrite my papers before because I thought it was easier to have it right there and be able to look at it. But, oh man, I never do that anymore. I'll write out the basic outline of where I want to go, but then I'll just type," tells Ms. Stone. Professor Lynn-Sherow has a similar story: "When I wrote my undergraduate papers, they were on the electric typewriter. Four or five drafts on the typewriter were oh so painful. Now to be able to word process has made things go much faster." Email has also held a new role for historians' writings. While co-authoring a chapter on World War I and the Indians at Fort Riley with a graduate student currently teaching at Houston State University, Professor Lynn-Sherow was able to send revisions to her associate through email. But with the speed of email comes a consequence. Reports Professor Lynn-Sherow: "Sometimes, it actually speeds things up faster than you want it to. If my partner finishes it real fast and sends it back to me, I haven't even had a chance to breathe. I want at least a week before seeing it again. Also, I think book review editors have cut down the time that they give to do reviews because now you can send reviews in attachment and they've taken off the mailing time."

Historians tend to work more independently than professionals in other fields do. While historians do utilize co-authoring, it is not practiced frequently. In fact, Ms. Stone has never participated in a writing not completely hers. "I've gotten feedback from other people, but I can't think of a paper where my name and someone else's were at the top," she relates. Professor Lynn-Sherow has combined her writing with another author on few occasions. When co-authoring, she has always divided the work up and "put it together like a sandwich." When explaining why it is sometimes looked down upon among historians, she explains, "I think that it tends to make your work look less your own and more difficult to convince people that your work as a scholar is serious."

DISCUSSION AND CONCLUSIONS

Historical writing is typically explanatory through telling information, but also includes some exploratory, by explaining ideas (Hairston 133). When writing most articles, historians understand that their audience is their own peers: professionals who have an understanding to the background of their writing (Flower 139). This can make their writing confusing and perplexing for readers with no knowledge of the subject. Some historians try to prevent this by receiving feedback from others outside of their field. Explains Professor Lynn-Sherow,

"I'll have colleagues from the [history] department read [my work] who have no ability to get the nuance in my field. If they can understand it then I've done a good job at communicating."

Not only must a successful historian be proficient in their writing skills, but also in their research and time-management skills. Writing in history takes great patience and organization and cannot be taken lightly. Research is the basis for all of its writings, and therefore, can only be made through extensive time and exploration.

The study of history can provide intensive analytical skills that I noticed a great deal of in the writings of both interviewees. Both writers form conclusions from the data they collected in a reflective way. They put great thought into their ideas and were able to assess problems to social and political issues. After presenting the supporting statistical data, Professor Lynn-Sherow writes: "The fact was that wheat scientists felt wholly threatened by the introduction of new federal programs into what had traditionally been a closed local system" (Lynn-Sherow 107). She analyzes the facts she had collected using a historical perspective, explaining how the scientist felt. Ms. Stone also utilizes analytical skills when creating her invented epidemic. In the paper she investigates three hypotheses by different scientists for a cure to a disease. She created three possible reasons for the causes of the epidemic and then pointed out well-thought-out criticisms to each hypothesis that make logical sense. The skill to analyze a situation and understand possible motives for its happening can be learnt through the lessons of history.

When reflecting on the importance of studying history, Ms. Stone rationalizes, "Everything that we do currently is related to the past. And if we study the past, we can figure out what's best for ourselves in the future."

Professor Lynn-Sherow tells how important it is for history students to understand the analytical and critical thinking skills the subject can give: "It forces them to be intellectually curious . . . and to think about new things, make connections. We'd like to think that we'd make an impact on the way people make decisions for the rest of their life. Self-analysis is what I really want them to do."

And so, when looking at the importance writing plays in the field of history, one can see that without it, history would not exist. "Historians want to put it in story form because that's the only way you will remember it," explains Professor Lynn-Sherow. Only through its study, can a generation pass on its knowledge and wisdom that it has learned through its experiences. Similarly, Ms. Stone relates why she was originally attracted to history: "It was a big story to me."

RECOMMENDATIONS

I learned a great deal about the history academic discourse community through this assignment. I am seriously interested in entering the community, and this research has helped me understand the writing process that historians labor over. I have learned that historic writing goes far beyond the usual textbooks. I would recommend greater time and concentration on the research of this topic to others interested in the field; perhaps interview more people from a greater variety of backgrounds and examine a greater variety of writings. Although this project has helped me in recognizing the style of historians, I do not feel that comfortable enough to reproduce it.

WORKS CITED

Flower, Linda. "Writing for an Audience." *Language Awareness: Readings for College Writers.* Edited by Paul Eschholz, Alfred Rosa, and Virginia Clark. Boston: Beford, 2000.

Hairston, Maxine. "What Happens When People Write?" *Language Awareness: Readings for College Writers.* Edited by Paul Escholz, Alfred Rosa, and Virginia Clark. Boston: Beford, 2000.

Lynn-Sherow, Bonnie. "Beyond Winter Wheat: The USDA Extension Service and Kansas Wheat Production in the Twentieth Century." *Kansas History* 2000. 23(1–2): 100–111.

———. "Review of *Sustainable Agriculture in the American Midwest: Lessons from the Past, Prospects for the Future,* edited by Gregory McIssac and William R. Edwards." Kansas History 1996. 19(2): 156

Smith, Frank. *Writing and the Writer.* Hillsdale, NJ: Erlbaum, 1982. 7–17.

Stone, Lory. "Epidemic Outbreak in Miami." 2000.

———. "A Masterpiece Molded From Clay: The Mind of Mary Wollstonecraft." 1998. ∎

Peer Review Questions

When your report is in the draft stage, it is wise to get the feedback of classmates. Try asking classmates the following questions:

1. Which specific parts of the draft seem strongest and most promising?
2. Did you learn anything new from reading the draft? If so, what?
3. Where in particular do you as a reader get lost or confused?
4. Does the draft include all the required sections? Which section(s) could use more development?
5. Which claims could use more evidence? Which discussions could use more elaboration?
6. Has the author gathered enough data to make reasonable conclusions? If not, note where more data would be helpful.
7. Do you find the recommendations convincing? Why or why not?
8. Consider the working title for the report. Is it both accurate and engaging? too boring? too offbeat? just right?
9. Offer two specific suggestions for the writer.

ENDNOTE

The idea of the discourse community as outlined in this chapter can be applied to many contexts. For example, thinking of a particular context as a discourse community and becoming more aware of its language practices can prove particularly useful when starting a new job (most workplaces, after all, can be thought of as discourse communities) or when preparing to write in community contexts.

5

Literature, Culture, and Social Reflection

Why read literature? How can literature function as social action? What are some pragmatic strategies for interpreting literature and analyzing social issues? This chapter features selected poems and short stories as both works of art and as windows on contemporary American culture. These reading selections open themselves to analysis as literary works, even as they raise important questions of social and economic justice.

We read because we cannot know enough people.
—Harold Bloom, literary critic

Every story is an act of trust between a writer and a reader; each story, in the end, is social. Whatever a writer sets down can harm or help the community of which he or she is a part.
—Barry Lopez, writer

One summer Robert Coles, a professor of psychiatry and medical humanities at Harvard University, was meeting with college students who had committed their summers to teaching and mentoring inner-city children in Boston. He recounts what happened:

Gradually, during the summer, many of the college students put [a] question to themselves: How could they educate *themselves* to listen better, comprehend a given world (its people, their assumptions, worries, fears, hopes), and thereby become more alert to various teaching possibilities, moments on the playground, in the classroom?

With that in mind, we discussed in detail a day or a week's events (some of them unnerving, even harrowing). Often the students wanted me to provide what I regarded as "technical" help—advice from a doctor trained to work with children. They asked others—lawyers, educators—for similar assistance. That was all to the good, but I often felt that what they most needed, what all of us need who are trying to engage many of our country's pressing and vexing social problems, was the wider perspective that literature can provide. . . . [Engaging with literary] readings reminded us of the particular humanity of the children— enabled us to think not only of abstractions (race, class, gender, ethnic background) but also of the problems each of us has as we grow up and try to figure our where we want to go in life, and why.[1]

Coles goes on to conclude that "Students need the chance to directly connect books to experience, ideas and introspection to continuing activity—through discussion in groups in which the thought and ideas that are so suggestively conveyed in fiction and in essays are brought to bear on the particular individuals who inhabit a world of hardship and pain." In large part, exploring such connections between fiction and community action is the aim of this chapter. For Coles, and indeed for many, both doing service and reading literature engage powerful and complementary callings that invite us into deeper reflection on ourselves, our relationships with others, and our shared culture.

WRITING TO DISCOVER

Think back to times in school when you have read and studied literature. Jot down a few experiences that you recall favorably—particular books, classes, moments. Now list a few that you found distasteful. With a classmate or together with the whole class, first explore the negative experiences, detailing reasons that made them negative. Then explore the positive experiences, likewise taking note of patterns.

Alternatively, describe your reading habits, both within and outside school. What kinds of reading do you do? What books have made an impression on you?

Reflection is a key word for literary study, as throughout history many have considered literature a reflection of reality. The Greek philosopher Aristotle called literature an act of *mimesis*, the process by which art "holds a mirror to nature," reflecting versions of life back at us. Films, TV shows, plays, novels, memoirs, stories, and poems all reflect and refract human realities and desires.

The role of literature as an art form has long been a topic of debate. It may be, as Aristotle suggests, a way to reflect experience. For some, it is an escape

---

[1]Coles, Robert. "Putting Head and Heart on the Line," *The Council Chronicle* (April 1995), p. 19.

from reality or mere entertainment. Alternatively, some people emphasize literature's role in explicit moral instruction, or its broader humanizing potential, to which Coles alludes. Others focus on literature as a way for us to express and order our emotions, or to render and reconcile our psychological conflicts and urges, or to tap the wellspring of our unconsciousness. Some see literature as an extension of the religious, oral, and mythical narratives that have ever defined, sustained, and enriched the human experience. Some revel in the aesthetic experience that good literature can deliver. Still others celebrate the potential that literature holds for opening multiple perspectives to readers, for allowing us to participate in the real and imagined lives of others.

This chapter acknowledges all these roles for literature, but it concentrates on an additional one: the potential of literature to help us better understand, and perhaps even change, our shared culture. This role is emphasized by Bertolt Brecht, the German writer and Nobel Prize winner, who once remarked, "Art is not a mirror held up to reality, but rather a hammer with which to shape it." To see art as an active tool rather than as a passive mirror is to see it as something with social power, something with the agency to shape minds and actions.

Consider the view of Brecht in relationship to music. We may see music primarily as reflecting our emotions (for example, all the songs about losing love that strike a chord with our own experiences of pain and anguish). Such songs mirror our own emotions, and we find this compelling. But music can also have both subtle and overt social functions. Think of the ways that some music— much folk or rap or reggae, for instance—raises our social consciousness or invites us to recognize and resist injustices. Such music still reflects powerful emotions and experiences, but it also invites an awareness of social problems—and awareness is a kind of social action.

In an interview, novelist Toni Morrison articulated a view similar to that of Brecht: "If anything I do, in the way of writing novels or whatever . . . isn't about the village or the community or about you, then it isn't about anything. I am not interested in indulging myself in some private exercise of my imagination . . . which is to say yes, the work must be political." Morrison suggests that we need to see literature not as private or transcendent but as enmeshed in history and culture. Reading literature can thus help us to cultivate what scholar Cy Knoblauch has called a "social imagination" and, perhaps, what philosopher Richard Rorty calls "social hope."

If the views of Brecht and Morrison are taken seriously, readers should respond to literature not as passive consumers but as active participants. Given this perspective, both literature itself and readers of literature perform *social action;* and as the Barry Lopez quote at the beginning of this chapter suggests, such acts of writing and reading can either help or harm communities.

In the end, you need not make an absolute choice between the mirror and hammer views on literature. Indeed, both views have merit. Instead, you should be aware of both perspectives. As you read each story and poem in this chapter, consider it a work of an individual imagination that invites you into the artfulness of the story; but also consider it a cultural tool for widening awareness, shaping the reader's consciousness, and, perhaps, prompting action.

ASSIGNMENT
Literary Analysis Essay

Drawing on one or a combination of the literary works in this chapter, write an essay that performs interpretation and/or criticism.

The essay should build on the strategies for reading literature outlined below and employ the rhetorical strategies for writing about literature and culture detailed later in the chapter.

A range of potential topics can be developed from the "Responding to Reading" questions that follow each work as well as from the "Writing to Discover" boxes.

Strategies for Reading Literature

In his book *Textual Power*, scholar and critic Robert Scholes describes three related but distinct levels of reading literary texts: reading, interpretation, and criticism. While these levels of reception are usually mingled as we respond to literature, breaking them into separate processes can clarify analysis.

Reading

At the reading level, the reader submits to the text, enters the story, and takes it all in (and hopefully enjoys it). Although this might seem like a passive process, it is, in fact, an active one: While reading a narrative, each person processes it in relationship to his or her own history and preconceptions, and therefore each reader "constructs" anew (in his or her mind) a version of the literary text.

The reading level is concerned with the literal events of narrative. At the reading level, you ask questions such as the following:

- What happens?
- Who is telling this story?
- What am I feeling and thinking? How does this text relate to my own experience?
- With whom do I identify?
- How are the conflicts unfolding?
- What strategies does the author use to construct the text?

Interpretation

Certain texts, such as the instructions for a VCR, don't encourage interpretation; others, especially literary texts, do. Most novels, poems, stories, and plays invite multiple interpretations. If we read closely and work from the specifics of the literal text, we can discover more general themes, tensions, ironies, symbols, and ideas. Scholes calls this process "text over text." That is, the "primary" text (i.e., the literal narrative) resides with other "secondary" texts (i.e., interpretations).

At the interpretative level, you ask questions such as the following:

- Beyond the literal events, what other meanings does the text encourage readers to explore?
- What is implied or suggested, even if not stated?
- What key themes is the author exploring?
- What tensions, oppositions, conflicts, and ironies propel the narrative?
- How does the author employ symbolism and symbolic action?
- How do the parts relate to the whole?
- What patterns are evident? Where is there repetition? To what effect are patterns and repetition used?

Criticism

The criticism level of responding considers the narrative in relationship to its social context. Criticism demands that the reader step outside the text and talk back to it. To engage in literary criticism does not mean that one has to be critical of the text—that is, bad-mouth or nitpick it. Rather, the reader adopts a critical distance. Conducting criticism requires an independent mind as well as a willingness to make claims and back them up. Scholes calls the process of criticism "text against text"—that is, your own writing responds to, or "against," the literary text.

At the level of criticism, you ask such questions as the following:

- How does the text relate to its historical context? to our contemporary cultural context?
- How does the text confirm, upset, or complicate my own values, commitments, and preferences (whether personal, aesthetic, political, or moral)?
- How does the text compare to other texts of its genre? to other kinds of texts?
- How can I apply particular literary, aesthetic, philosophical, social, economic, political, or ethical theories to the text?
- What are the social and ethical implications of this story? What perspectives are privileged?

As you read the stories and poems in this chapter, keep these three levels of reception in mind and use the questions above to prompt your thinking. Also realize that you can't answer all of the questions after one reading. On a first reading, you might simply enjoy the story or poem, letting it sweep you along in its imaginative energy. On second and third readings (as well as in your written responses and classroom discussions), you can more fully explore interpretive and critical questions.

A Case Study in Reading, Interpretation, and Criticism

What follows is an example of how the processes of reading, interpretation, and criticism can be applied to the poem "From Seven Floors Up." This is followed by another poem, "Jorge the Church Janitor Finally Quits," to which you can apply the same kind of analysis on your own.

Poem: Sharon Olds, *From Seven Floors Up*

Born in 1942 in San Francisco, Sharon Olds studied at Stanford University and received a master's degree from Columbia University. She is the author of several books of poetry, including Satan Says *(1980),* The Dead and the Living *(1983),* The Gold Cell *(1987),* The Father *(1992),* The Wellspring *(1995), and* Blood, Tin, Straw *(1999). She was named the New York State Poet in 1998, and she teaches at New York University.*

> He is pushing a shopping cart up the ramp
> out of the park. He owns, in the world,
> only what he has there—no sink, no water,
> no heat. When we had come out of the wilderness,
> after the week in the desert, in tents,   5
> and on the river, by canoe, and when I had my own
> motel-room, I cried for humble dreading
> joy in the shower, I kneeled and put
> my arms around the cold, clean
> toilet. From up here, his profile looks   10
> like Che Guevara's, in the last picture,
> the stitches like marks on a butcher's chart.
> Suddenly I see that I have thought that it could not
> happen to me, homelessness
> —like death, by definition it would not happen.   15
> And he shoulders his earth, his wheeled hovel,
> north, the wind at his back—November,
> the trees coming bare in earnest. November,
> month of my easy birth.   ■

Reading

A logical question to start with is Who is speaking? The narrator, we know from the title, is looking down from seven floors up, from an apartment building bordering a park, we discover. We have no clear indication of the narrator's gender (we might assume that it is a woman, like Olds, but there isn't any clear textual support for that assumption); but we know that the narrator is in a position of privilege (he or she has an apartment, speaks of travels, refers to "easy birth").

As for the narrative, the first two sentences show the speaker looking down on a homeless person pushing a cart, which, starting with line 4, prompts the memory of a camping and canoeing vacation, a "week in the desert," after which the narrator gratefully returns to the conveniences of modern amenities (the motel, the shower, the toilet). After this shift from present to past, the narrator shifts again to the present ("From up here"), where the homeless person again sparks a memory, this time of a picture of Che Guevara. (If you didn't know who Guevara was, you would need to investigate that, discovering that he was an Argentina-born Marxist who championed the dispossessed and played a visible role in Cuba's revolution in the 1950s.) Line 13, which begins with "Suddenly," marks a moment of introspection. Lines 16–18 report the departure of the homeless person into the park and the speaker's final reflection on her own life, her "easy birth."

Interpretation

Interpretation asks What does this text mean? Or, better, What are its meanings? Here we would explore themes (such as inequality and privilege), tensions (such as the contrasts between homelessness and security, urban "wilderness" and vacation "wilderness"), and character development (such as the speaker's growing realization of his or her own privilege).

In an interpretative mode, one would not simply find out who Che Guevara is but would question why the author has chosen this image (Guevara's revolutionary legacy, for example, speaks to the theme of inequality). One would also articulate how other images, literary devices, and particular components relate to the organic whole of the poem. For instance, one would look at the overlapping meanings of "November" in the final lines. One would identify how the movement between the past and the present propels the poem and leads to turning points in the narrator's understanding of self and world.

Criticism

Conducting criticism invites you to talk back to the text. How does the poem stir emotions, shape attitudes, or raise awareness in readers? To what end does it do these things? Does it prompt you to self-awareness of the sort depicted by the speaker? Is this art working more as a mirror or a hammer? both? something else altogether?

Questions of evaluation surface: Which interpretations are more convincing than others? Is the poem successful (which involves, of course, outlining criteria for success)?

Questions of intertextuality and genre beg attention: How does this text relate to other texts that deal with similar themes? How does this poem relate to other lyrical poems? to other poems about homelessness and privilege? to other works by Olds?

Questions of ethics can be posed: How much is the poem a private lament and how much is it a critique of economic and social systems? In what ways does the poem function as social action? Do we accept the speaker's views as voyeurism or as genuine self-reflection?

Poem: Martin Espada, *Jorge the Church Janitor Finally Quits*

Born in Brooklyn in 1957, Martin Espada has worked as a radio journalist, a mental patient advocate, and a tenant lawyer, and he is currently a professor of English at the University of Massachusetts. His books include The Immigrant Iceboy's Bolero *(1986),* Rebellion Is the Circle of a Lover's Hands *(1990), and* Imagine the Bread of Angels *(1996). Upon Espada's winning the PEN/Revson award for poetry, the judges remarked, "The greatness of Espada's art, like all great arts, is that it gives dignity to the insulted and the injured of the earth."*

No one asks
where I am from,
I must be
from the country of janitors,
I have always mopped the floor.   5
Honduras, you are a squatter's camp
outside the city
of their understanding.

No one can speak
my name,   10
I host the *fiesta*
of the bathroom,
stirring the toilet
like a punchbowl.
The Spanish of my name   15
is lost
when the guests complain
about toilet paper.

What they say
must be true: 20
I am smart,
but I have a bad attitude.

No one knows
that I quit tonight,
maybe the mop   25
will push on without me,

sniffing along the floor
like a crazy squid
with stringy gray tentacles.
They will call it Jorge.   ∎

Responding to Reading

Take notes on your response to this poem. First, pose questions related to reading; then move on to questions of interpretation; then on to criticism. When you are done, compare your notes to those of others.

WRITING TO DISCOVER

Take notes on the point of view from which each poem is narrated. What is distinctive about each perspective? In what ways are they similar? In what ways do they differ? What thoughts and emotions does each perspective evoke for you as a reader?

Alternatively, write your own poem, expressing how you "see" people whom our culture tends to overlook or dismiss. Or, you can adopt the perspective of someone who is overlooked.

Short Story: Toni Cade Bambara, *The Lesson*

Toni Cade Bambara was born in New York City in 1939 and was educated at Queens College and City College of New York. She worked not only as a writer but also as a welfare investigator, a community organizer, a literacy instructor, a college professor, and a director of plays and films. She published collections of short stories, including The Seabirds Are Still Alive and Other Stories *(1977), as well as novels, including* If Blessing Comes *(1987),* The Salt Eaters *(1980), and* Those Bones Are Not My Child *(published posthumously in 1999). She also edited a groundbreaking collection of African-American women's writing,* The Black Woman: An Anthology *(1970), as well as* Deep Sightings and Rescue Missions: Fiction, Essays, and Conversations *(1996). Bambara died of cancer in 1995. "The Lesson" is taken from* Gorilla, My Love *(1972). "The Lesson" is told in the engaging voice of a young girl, Sylvia, who is taken on a field trip from her poor New York City neighborhood to F.A.O. Schwarz, an upscale toy store on 5th Avenue, one of the city's most affluent streets.*

Back in the days when everyone was old and stupid or young and foolish and me and Sugar were the only ones just right, this lady moved on our block with nappy hair and proper speech and no makeup. And quite naturally we laughed at her, laughed the way we did at the junk man who went about his business like he was some big-time president and his sorry-ass horse his secretary. And we kinda hated her too, hated the way we did the winos who cluttered up our parks and pissed on our handball walls and stank up our hallways and stairs so you couldn't halfway play hide-and-seek without a goddamn gas mask. Miss Moore was her name. The only woman on the block with no first name. And she was black as hell, cept for her feet, which were fish-white and spooky. And she was always planning these boring-ass things for us to do, us being my cousin, mostly, who lived on the block cause we all moved North the same time and to the same apartment then spread out gradual to breathe. And our parents would yank our heads into some kinda shape and crisp up our clothes so we'd be presentable for travel with Miss Moore, who always looked like she was going to church, though she never did. Which is just one of the things the grownups talked about when they talked behind her back like a dog. But when she came calling with some sachet she'd sewed up or some gingerbread she'd made or some book, why then they'd all be too embarrassed to turn her down and we'd get handed out all spruced up. She'd been to college and said it only right that she should take responsibility for the young ones' education, and she not even related by marriage or blood. So they'd go for it. Specially Aunt Gretchen. She was the main gofer in the family. You got some ole dumb shit foolishness you want somebody to go for, you send for Aunt Gretchen. She been screwed into the go-along for so long, it's a blood-deep natural thing with her. Which is how she got saddled with me and Sugar and Junior in the first place while our mothers were in a la-de-da apartment up the block having a good ole time.

So this one day Miss Moore rounds us all up at the mailbox and it's puredee hot and she's knockin herself out about arithmetic. And school suppose to let up in summer I heard, but she don't never let up. And the starch in my pinafore scratching the shit outta me and I'm really hating this nappy-head bitch and her goddamn college degree. I'd much rather go to the pool or to the show where it's cool. So me and Sugar leaning on the mailbox being surly, which is a Miss Moore word. And Flyboy checking out what everybody brought for lunch. And Fat Butt already wasting his peanut-butter-and-jelly sandwich like the pig he is. And Junebug punchin on Q.T.'s arm for potato chips. And Rosie Giraffe shifting from one hip to the other waiting for somebody to step on her foot or ask her if she from Georgia so she can kick ass, preferably Mercedes'. And Miss Moore asking us do we know what money is, like we a bunch of retards. I mean real money, she say, like it's only poker chips or monopoly papers we lay on the grocer. So right away I'm tired of this and say so. And would much rather snatch Sugar and go to the Sunset and terrorize the West Indian kids and take their hair ribbons and their money too. And Miss Moore files that remark away for next week's lesson on brotherhood, I can tell. And finally I say we oughta get to the subway cause it's cooler and besides we might meet some cute boys. Sugar done swiped her mama's lipstick, so we ready.

So we heading down the street and she's boring us silly about what things cost and what our parents make and how much goes for rent and how money ain't divided up right in this country. And then she gets to the part about we all poor and live in the slums, which I don't feature. And I'm ready to speak on that, but she steps out in the street and hails two cabs just like that. Then she hustles half the crew in with her and hands me a five-dollar bill and tells me to calculate 10 percent tip for the driver. And we're off. Me and Sugar and Junebug and Flyboy hangin out the window and hollering to everybody, putting lipstick on each other cause Flyboy a faggot anyway, and making farts with our sweaty armpits. But I'm mostly trying to figure how to spend this money. But they all fascinated with the meter ticking and Junebug starts laying bets as to how much it'll read when Flyboy can't hold his breath no more. Then Sugar lays bets as to how much it'll be when we get there. So I'm stuck. Don't nobody want to go for my plan, which is to jump out at the next light and run off to the first bar-b-que we can find. Then the driver tells us to get the hell out cause we are there already. And the meter reads eighty-five cents. And I'm stalling to figure out the tip and Sugar say give him a dime. And I decide he don't need it bad as I do, so later for him. But then he tries to take off with Junebug foot still in the door so we talk about his mama something ferocious. Then we check out that we on Fifth Avenue and everybody dressed up in stockings. One lady in a fur coat, hot as it is. White folks crazy.

"This is the place," Miss Moore say, presenting it to us in the voice she uses at the museum. "Let's look in the windows before we go in."

"Can we steal?" Sugar asks very serious like she's getting the ground rules square away before she plays. "I beg your pardon," say Miss Moore, and we fall out. So she leads us around the windows of the toy store and me and Sugar screamin, "This is mine, that's mine, I gotta have that, that was made for me, I was born for that," till Big Butt drowns us out.

"Hey, I'm goin to buy that there."

"That there? You don't even know what it is, stupid."

"I do so," he say punchin on Rosie Giraffe. "It's a microscope."

"Whatcha gonna do with a microscope, fool?"

"Look at things."

"Like what, Ronald?" ask Miss Moore. And Big Butt ain't got the first notion. So here go Miss Moore gabbing about the thousands of bacteria in a drop of water and the somethinorother in a speck of blood and the million and one living things in the air around us is invisible to the naked eye. And what she say that for? Junebug go to town on that "naked" and we rolling. Then Miss Moore ask what it cost. So we all jam into the window smudgin it up and the price tag say $300. So then she ask how long'd take for Big Butt and Junebug to save up their allowances. "Too long," I say. "Yeh," adds Sugar, "outgrown it by that time." And Miss Moore say no, you never outgrow learning instruments. "Why, even medical students and interns and," blah, blah, blah. And we ready to choke Big Butt for bringing it up in the first damn place.

"This here costs four hundred eighty dollars," say Rosie Giraffe. So we pile up all over her to see what she pointin out. My eyes tell me it's a chunk of glass cracked with something heavy, and different-color inks dripped into the splits, then the whole thing put into a oven or something. But for $480 it don't make sense.

"That's a paperweight made of semi-precious stones fused together under tremendous pressure," she explains slowly, with her hands doing the mining and all the factory work.

"So what's a paperweight?" asks Rosie Giraffe.

"To weigh paper with, dumbbell," say Flyboy, the wise man from the East.

"Not exactly," say Miss Moore, which is what she say when you warm or way off too. "It's to weigh paper down so it won't scatter and make your desk untidy." So right away me and Sugar curtsy to each other and then to Mercedes who is more the tidy type.

"We don't keep paper on top of the desk in my class," say Junebug, figuring Miss Moore crazy or lyin one.

"At home, then," she say. "Don't you have a calendar and a pencil case and a blotter and a letter-opener on your desk at home where you do your home-work?" And she know damn well what our homes look like cause she nosys around in them every chance she gets.

"I don't even have a desk," say Junebug. "Do we?"

"No. And I don't get no homework neither," say Big Butt.

"And I don't even have a home," say Flyboy like he do at school to keep the white folks off his back and sorry for him. Send this poor kid to camp posters, is his speciality.

"I do," say Mercedes. "I have a box of stationery on my desk and a picture of my cat. My godmother bought the stationery and the desk. There's a big rose on each sheet and the envelopes smell like roses."

"Who want to know about your smelly-ass stationery," say Rosie Giraffe fore I can get my two cents in.

"It's important to have a work area all your own so that . . . "

"Will you look at this sailboat, please," say Flyboy, cuttin her off and pointin to the thing like it was his. So once again we tumble all over each other to gaze at this magnificent thing in the toy store which is just big enough to maybe sail two kittens across the pond if you strap them to the posts tight. We all start reciting the price tag like we in assembly. "Handcrafted sailboat of fiberglass at one thousand one hundred ninety-five dollars."

"Unbelievable," I hear myself say and am really stunned. I read it again for myself just in case the group recitation put me in a trance. Same thing. For some reason this pisses me off. We look at Miss Moore and she lookin at us, waiting for I dunno what.

"Who'd pay all that when you can buy a sailboat set for a quarter at Pop's, a tube of glue for a dime, and a ball of string for eight cents? It must have a motor and a whole lot else besides," I say. "My sailboat cost me about fifty cents."

"But will it take water?" say Mercedes with her smart ass.

"Took mine to Alley Pond Park once," say Flyboy. "String broke. Lost it. Pity."

"Sailed mine in Central Park and it keeled over and sank. Had to ask my father for another dollar."

"And you got the strap," laugh Big Butt. "The jerk didn't even have a string on it. My old man wailed on his behind."

Little Q.T. was staring hard at the sailboat and you could see he wanted it bad. But he too little and somebody'd just take it from him. So what the hell. "This boat for kids, Miss Moore?"

"Parents silly to buy something like that just to get all broke up," say Rosie Giraffe.

"That much money it should last forever," I figure.

"My father'd buy it for me if I wanted it."

"Your father, my ass," say Rosie Giraffe getting a chance to finally push Mercedes.

"Must be rich people shop here," say Q.T.

"You are a very bright boy," say Flyboy. "What was your first clue?" And he rap him on the head with the back of his knuckles, since Q.T. the only one he could get away with. Though Q.T. liable to come up behind you years later and get his licks in when you half expect it.

"What I want to know is," I says to Miss Moore though I never talk to her, I wouldn't give the bitch that satisfaction, "is how much a real boat costs? I figure a thousand get you a yacht any day."

"Why don't you check that out," she says, "and report back to the group?" Which really pains my ass. If you gonna mess up a perfectly good swim day least you could do is have some answers. "Let's go in," she say like she got something up her sleeve. Only she don't lead the way. So me and Sugar turn the corner to where the entrance is, but when we get there I kinda hang back. Not that I'm scared, what's there to be afraid of, just a toy store. But I feel funny, shame. But what I got to be shamed about? Got as much right to go in as anybody. But somehow I can't seem to get hold on the door, so I step away for Sugar to lead. But she hangs back too. And I look at her and she looks at me and this is ridicu-lous. I mean, damn, I have never ever been shy about doing nothing or going nowhere. But then Mercedes steps up and then Rosie Giraffe and Big Butt crowd in behind and shove, and next thing we all stuffed into the doorway with only Mercedes squeezing past us, smoothing out her jumper and walking right down the aisle. Then the rest of us tumble in like a glued-together jigsaw done all wrong. And people lookin at us. And it's like the time me and Sugar crashed into the Catholic church on a dare. But once we got in there and everything so hushed and holy and the candles and the bowin and the handkerchiefs on all the drooping heads, I just couldn't go through with the plan. Which was for me to run up to the altar and do a tap dance while Sugar played the nose flute and messed around in the holy water. And Sugar kept givin me the elbow. Then later teased me so bad I tied her up in the shower and turned it on and locked her in. And she'd be there till this day if Aunt Gretchen hadn't finally figured I was lying about the boarder takin a shower.

Same thing in the store. We all walkin on tiptoe and hardly touchin the games and puzzles and things. And I watched Miss Moore who is steady watchin us like she waitin for a sign. Like Mama Drewery watches the sky and sniffs the air and takes note of just how much slant is in the bird formation. Then me and Sugar bump smack into each other, so busy gazing at the toys, 'specially the sailboat. But we don't laugh and go into our fat-lady bump-stomach routine. We just stare at that price tag. Then Sugar run a finger over the whole boat. And I'm jealous and want to hit her. Maybe not her, but I sure want to punch somebody in the mouth.

"Watcha bring us here for, Miss Moore?"

"You sound angry, Sylvia. Are you mad about something?" Give me one of them grins like she tellin a grown-up joke that never turns out to be funny. And she's lookin very closely at me like maybe she plannin to do my portrait from memory. I'm mad, but I won't give her that satisfaction. So I slouch around the store bein very bored and say, "Let's go."

Me and Sugar at the back of the train watchin' the tracks whizzin by large then small then gettin gobbled up in the dark. I'm thinkin about this tricky toy I saw in the store. A clown that somersaults on a bar then does chin-ups just cause you yank lightly at his leg. Cost $35. I could see me askin my mother for a $35 birthday clown. "You wanna who that costs what?" she'd say, cockin her head to the side to get a better view of the hole in my head. Thirty-five dollars could buy new bunk beds for Junior and Gretchen's boy. Thirty-five dollars and the whole household could go visit Granddaddy Nelson in the country. Thirty-five dollars would pay for the rent and the piano bill too. Who are these people that spend that much for performing clowns and $1,000 for toy sailboats? What kinda work they do and how they live and how come we ain't in on it? Where we are is who we are, Miss Moore always pointin out. But it don't necessarily have to be that way, she always adds then waits for somebody to say that poor people have to wake up and demand their share of the pie and don't none of us know what kind of pie she talkin about in the first damn place. But she ain't so smart cause I still got her four dollars from the taxi and she sure ain't gettin it. Messin up my day with this shit. Sugar nudges me in my pocket and winks.

Miss Moore lines us up in front of the mailbox where we started from, seem like years ago, and I got a headache for thinkin so hard. And we lean all over each other so we can hold up under the draggy-ass lecture she always finishes us off with at the end before we thank her for borin us to tears. But she just looks at us like she readin tea leaves. Finally she say, "Well, what did you think of F.A.O. Schwarz?"

Rosie Giraffe mumbles, "White folks crazy."

"I'd like to go in there again when I get my birthday money," says Mercedes, and we shove her out the pack so she has to lean on the mailbox by herself.

"I'd like a shower. Tiring day," say Flyboy.

Then Sugar surprises me by saying, "You know, Miss Moore, I don't think all of us here put together eat in a year what that sailboat costs." And Miss Moore lights up like somebody goosed her. "And?" she say, urging Sugar on. Only I'm standin on her foot so she don't continue.

"Imagine for a minute what kind of society it is in which some people can spend on a toy what it would cost to feed a family of six or seven. What do you think?"

"I think," say Sugar pushing me off her feet like she never done before, cause I whip her ass in a minute, "that this is not much of a democracy if you ask me. Equal chance to pursue happiness means an equal crack at the dough, don't it?" Miss Moore is besides herself and I am disgusted with Sugar's treachery. So I stand on her foot one more time to see if she'll shove me. She shuts up, and Miss Moore looks at me, sorrowfully I'm thinkin. And somethin weird is going on, I can feel it in my chest.

"Anybody else learn anything today?" lookin dead at me. I walk away and Sugar has to run to catch up and don't even seem to notice when I shrug her arm off my shoulder.

"Well, we got four dollars anyway," she says.

"Uh hunh."

"We could go to Hascombs and get half a chocolate layer and then go to the Sunset and still have plenty money for potato chips and ice-cream sodas."

"Uh hunh."

"Race you to Hascombs," she say.

We start down the block and she gets ahead which is O.K. by me cause I'm goin to the West End and then over to the Drive to think this day through. She can run if she want to and even run faster. But ain't nobody gonna beat me at nuthin. ■

Responding to Reading

1. Why do you think Bambara chose to narrate her story from Sylvia's perspective? What effect does it have on the reader? How would the story have been different if it had been narrated from Miss Moore's point of view or from an omniscient point of view?

2. What details mark Miss Moore as an outsider to Sylvia's neighborhood? What are the consequences of her outsider status?

3. What "lesson" is Miss Moore trying to teach the children by taking them on the trip to the toy store? What is her philosophy or method of teaching? Are there any other lessons at play in the story?

4. As Sylvia is about to enter the toy store, she remarks, "But I feel funny, shame" (paragraph 40). Reread this paragraph and discuss where this feeling might come from. Have you ever felt that way about entering a place?

5. In paragraph 44 Sylvia says, "Where we are is who we are, Miss Moore always pointin out." What does this mean?

6. While in the store Sylvia expresses anger and gets "a headache for thinkin so hard." What prompts the anger and headache?

7. When Miss Moore is giving what Sylvia calls a "draggy-ass lecture" at the end of the visit, Sugar says, "this is not much of a democracy if you ask me. Equal chance to pursue happiness means an equal crack at the dough, don't it?" Sylvia is "disgusted with Sugar's treachery" and stands on her foot. Why? What is going on here?

8. Reread the final paragraph, in which Sylvia thinks to herself that she will "think this day through." Why does she react differently than Sugar? How (if at all) has Sylvia changed since the beginning of the story?

9. Recall the mirror and hammer views on art. Given this story, where do you think Bambara stands on the role of art? Provide evidence to support your view.

10. Narratives usually depend on character development. How does Sylvia develop? What are key turning points in her development? Support your claims with evidence from the text.

"The Lesson" and Economic Justice

"The Lesson" is an artful story in its own right. But it also beckons us to explore contemporary issues of social justice, particularly economic inequality and poverty. The collection of articles and statistical tables that follow attempt to contextualize the disparities of privilege that are alluded to in "The Lesson" as the children marvel at the wealthy world represented by the toy store. As you read this section, keep in mind Sylvia's retelling of Miss Moore's belief that "money ain't divided up right in this country" and Sugar's question, "Equal chance to pursue happiness means an equal crack at the dough, don't it?"

Working with Statistics

Narratives of individual experience—whether real or fictional—can be compelling. But we also need to look at the aggregate experience of communities, and statistical information is one important way to do that. Understanding the "big picture" with respect to statistical knowledge helps us to contextualize individual lives, just as listening to individual stories helps us to humanize what could otherwise be an impersonal collection of numbers.

We should keep in mind that statistics can be manipulated, which recalls a saying attributed by Mark Twain to former British Prime Minister Benjamin Disraeli: "There are three kinds of lies: lies, damn lies, and statistics." This witty overstatement raises a concern we face as both users and readers of statistical information: how to employ statistics accurately and ethically, and how to detect when others are using them misleadingly. For example, if I said that 75% of the sparrows in a particular forest nest in pine trees, you would likely assume that sparrows prefer pines. But what if 95% of the trees in that forest were pines? Omitting that crucial information would encourage a false conclusion.

Following a few guidelines can help one in using statistics critically and responsibly. This list is not exhaustive, but it's a start:

- Determine *who* has collected the data, *how* it was collected and is presented, and *why.* As for *who,* ask whether the person or institution collecting the data is credible. For example, the tables cited below are from the U.S. Census Bureau, which is a reliable institution (although some contend that the U.S. Census undercounts minorities and the poor). But if the source were either a conservative think tank or a liberal foundation, we would exercise greater skepticism, as a political bias can color the data. As for *how,* examine issues such as the size of the sample, the timeliness of the information, any possible survey biases or gaps, as well as the methods used to interpret and present the data. As for *why,* always ask *Cui bono?* or Who benefits? What interest does the source have in presenting the data?
- If you extract or highlight one number or statistic, examine how it relates to the larger data set. Is it part of a trend or pattern? Is it an anomaly?
- Brainstorm *multiple interpretations* of a statistic before settling on the one that you determine to be most sensible and ethical. If a cause–effect relationship is suggested, look for possible causes other than (or in addition to) the one featured.
- Ask yourself which data or which alternative information is omitted or underrepresented.
- Make your selection and interpretation of data visible to your reader. In other words, acquire the habit of *disclosure* by making your reader aware of where you got your statistics and how you are using them. Also, give your reader a path back to your source so that he or she has the opportunity to examine the primary material.

Statistics can help make sense of social phenomena, but raw numbers alone are of limited help. Statistics are generally plugged in to larger arguments as supporting evidence. When used responsibly, statistics are telling indicators of our collective life and, in turn, powerful resources for writers.

Examining U.S. Census Data on Poverty, Income, and Wealth

This section asks you to digest some complex statistical information on the demographics of social and economic life in the United States. Looking at tables full of numbers can be daunting and even dizzying. But don't despair. Here are some tips for reading tables:

- Read table *titles* carefully before diving into the numbers.
- Read the headings carefully to determine what *relationships* are being explored. For example, if there are dates in the left column, the table is usually tracking change across *time.* If different variables, such as ages or

racial groups, are in the left column, the table is usually tracking data by *category*.

- Give greater attention to the columns that detail *percentages* than to the ones that list raw numbers.
- Look for *patterns* and *trends*.

The following graph and table are drawn from U.S. Census Bureau data published in *Statistical Abstract of the United States*, 121st Edition (2001). To access the most up-to-date version of this information (and much more), go to http://www.census.gov/statab/www or consult the print version, which should be in the reference or government documents section of your library.

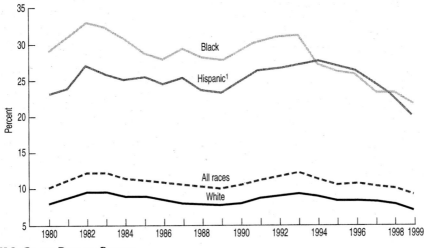

U.S. Census Data on Poverty

No. 685. Families Below Poverty Level and Below 125 Percent of Poverty by Race and Hispanic Origin: 1970 to 1999

[Families as of March of the following year. Based on Current Population Survey, see text, Sections 1 and 13, and Appendix III]

Year	Number below poverty level (1,000)				Percent below poverty level				Below 125 percent of poverty level	
	All races[1]	White	Black	His-panic[2]	All races[1]	White	Black	His-panic[2]	Number (1,000)	Percent
1970	5,260	3,708	1,481	(NA)	10.1	8.0	29.5	(NA)	7,516	14.4
1975	5,450	3,838	1,513	627	9.7	7.7	27.1	25.1	7,974	14.2
1976	5,311	3,560	1,617	598	9.4	7.1	27.9	23.1	7,647	13.5
1977	5,311	3,540	1,637	591	9.3	7.0	28.2	21.4	7,713	13.5
1978	5,280	3,523	1,622	559	9.1	6.9	27.5	20.4	7,417	12.8
1979[3]	5,461	3,581	1,722	614	9.2	6.9	27.8	20.3	7,784	13.1
1980	6,217	4,195	1,826	751	10.3	8.0	28.9	23.2	8,764	14.5
1981	6,851	4,670	1,972	792	11.2	8.8	30.8	24.0	9,568	15.7

Year	Number below poverty level (1,000)				Percent below poverty level				Below 125 percent of poverty level	
	All races[1]	*White*	*Black*	*His-panic[2]*	*All races[1]*	*White*	*Black*	*His-panic[2]*	*Number (1,000)*	*Percent*
1982	7,512	5,118	2,158	916	12.2	9.6	33.0	27.2	10,279	16.7
1983[4]	7,647	5,220	2,161	981	12.3	9.7	32.3	25.9	10,358	16.7
1984	7,277	4,925	2,094	991	11.6	9.1	30.9	25.2	9,901	15.8
1985	7,223	4,983	1,983	1,074	11.4	9.1	28.7	25.5	9,753	15.3
1986	7,023	4,811	1,987	1,085	10.9	8.6	28.0	24.7	9,476	14.7
1987[5]	7,005	4,567	2,117	1,168	10.7	8.1	29.4	25.5	9,338	14.3
1988	6,874	4,471	2,089	1,141	10.4	7.9	28.2	23.7	9,284	14.1
1989	6,784	4,409	2,077	1,133	10.3	7.8	27.8	23.4	9,267	14.0
1990	7,098	4,622	2,193	1,244	10.7	8.1	29.3	25.0	9,564	14.4
1991	7,712	5,022	2,343	1,372	11.5	8.8	30.4	26.5	10,244	15.3
1992[6]	8,144	5,255	2,484	1,529	11.9	9.1	31.1	26.7	10,959	16.1
1993	8,393	5,452	2,499	1,625	12.3	9.4	31.3	27.3	11,203	16.4
1994	8,053	5,312	2,212	1,724	11.6	9.1	27.3	27.8	10,771	15.5
1995	7,532	4,994	2,127	1,695	10.8	8.5	26.4	27.0	10,223	14.7
1996	7,708	5,059	2,206	1,748	11.0	8.6	26.1	26.4	10,476	14.9
1997	7,324	4,990	1,985	1,721	10.3	8.4	23.6	24.7	10,032	14.2
1998	7,186	4,829	1,981	1,648	10.0	8.0	23.4	22.7	9,714	13.6
1999	6,676	4,377	1,898	1,525	9.3	7.3	21.9	20.2	9,320	12.9

NA Not available. [1]Includes other races not shown separately. [2]Persons of Hispanic origin may be of any race. [3]Population controls based on 1980 census; see text, this section. [4]Beginning 1983, data based on revised Hispanic population controls and not directly comparable with prior years. [5]Beginning 1987, data based on revised processing procedures and not directly comparable with prior years. [6]Beginning 1992, based on 1990 population controls.

Source: U. S. Census Bureau, *Current Population Reports,* P60–210.

Responding to Reading

1. Examine the table and graph. Does any of the information surprise you? Before seeing the data, what would you have guessed the poverty rate was? Outside class, ask a few people what they estimate to be the percentage of families that fall below the poverty line. Compare the responses to reality.

2. How do you account for the poverty levels for Black and Hispanic families remaining so much higher than that of White families? Instead of settling on only one reason, speculate on multiple reasons for the disparity. Try this: "It might be because . . . or it might be because . . . or it might be because . . ." Come up with five potential reasons on your own, and then share your responses with a classmate.

3. Consider this statistical information in relationship to "The Lesson"? What "lessons" do the data reveal? How do these relate to Miss Moore's "lessons"?

4. How has the poverty rate for families changed since "The Lesson" was published in 1972?

No. 680. Children Below Poverty Level by Race and Hispanic Origin: 1970 to 1999

[Persons as of March of the following year. Covers only related children in families under 18 years old. Based on Current Population Survey; see text, Sections 1 and 13, Appendix III]

Year	Number below poverty level (1,000)					Percent below poverty level				
	All races[1]	White	Black	Asian and Pacific Islander	His-panic[2]	All races[1]	White	Black	Asian and Pacific Islander	His-panic[2]
1970	10,235	6,138	3,922	(NA)	(NA)	14.9	10.5	41.5	(NA)	(NA)
1975	10,882	6,748	3,884	(NA)	1,619	16.8	12.5	41.4	(NA)	33.1
1976	10,081	6,034	3,758	(NA)	1,424	15.8	11.3	40.4	(NA)	30.1
1977	10,028	5,943	3,850	(NA)	1,402	16.0	11.4	41.6	(NA)	28.0
1978	9,722	5,674	3,781	(NA)	1,354	15.7	11.0	41.2	(NA)	27.2
1979	9,993	5,909	3,745	(NA)	1,505	16.0	11.4	40.8	(NA)	27.7
1980	11,114	6,817	3,906	(NA)	1,718	17.9	13.4	42.1	(NA)	33.0
1981	12,068	7,429	4,170	(NA)	1,874	19.5	14.7	44.9	(NA)	35.4
1982	13,139	8,282	4,388	(NA)	2,117	21.3	16.5	47.3	(NA)	38.9
1983[3]	13,427	8,534	4,273	(NA)	2,251	21.8	17.0	46.2	(NA)	37.7
1984	12,929	8,086	4,320	(NA)	2,317	21.0	16.1	46.2	(NA)	38.7
1985	12,483	7,838	4,057	(NA)	2,512	20.1	15.6	43.1	(NA)	39.6
1986	12,257	7,714	4,037	(NA)	2,413	19.8	15.3	42.7	(NA)	37.1
1987[4]	12,275	7,398	4,234	432	2,606	19.7	14.7	44.4	22.7	38.9
1988	11,935	7,095	4,148	458	2,576	19.0	14.0	42.8	23.5	37.3
1989	12,001	7,164	4,257	368	2,496	19.0	14.1	43.2	18.9	35.5
1990	12,715	7,696	4,412	356	2,750	19.9	15.1	44.2	17.0	37.7
1991	13,658	8,316	4,637	348	2,977	21.1	16.1	45.6	17.1	39.8
1992[5]	14,521	8,752	5,015	352	3,440	21.6	16.5	46.3	16.0	39.0
1993	14,961	9,123	5,030	358	3,666	22.0	17.0	45.9	17.6	39.9
1994	14,610	8,826	4,787	308	3,956	21.2	16.3	43.3	17.9	41.1
1995	13,999	8,474	4,644	532	3,938	20.2	15.5	41.5	18.6	39.3
1996	13,764	8,488	4,411	553	4,090	19.8	15.5	39.5	19.1	39.9
1997	13,422	8,441	4,116	608	3,865	19.2	15.4	36.8	19.9	36.4
1998	12,845	7,935	4,073	542	3,670	18.3	14.4	36.4	17.5	33.6
1999	11,510	7,123	3,644	348	3,382	16.3	12.9	32.7	11.5	29.9

NA Not available. [1]Includes other races not shown separately. [2]Persons of Hispanic origin may be of any race. [3]Beginning 1983, data based on revised Hispanic population controls and not directly comparable with prior years. [4]Beginning 1987, data based on revised processing procedures and not directly comparable with prior years. [5]Beginning 1992, based on 1990 population controls.

Source: U. S. Census Bureau, *Current Population Reports* P60–210.
See also http://www.census.gov/prod/2000pubs/p60–210.pdf.

Responding to Reading

1. How does the data in this table (on children) compare to that in the first table (on families)?

2. Investigate the child poverty rates for countries other than the United States; look especially for comparisons with other industrialized nations. How do they compare to that of the United States? How do you account for the differences?

3. How does U.S. culture currently address the problem of child poverty? What possible social or governmental policies do you think should or should not be implemented? Why?

4. This data suggests that Black children, such as those in "The Lesson," are more than twice as likely as White children to be poor. Reflect on this statistic and offer several plausible explanations for how this has come to be.

Income & Wealth Distribution: U.S. Families, 1997

	Income	Wealth
Lowest 20%	4.2%	−0.5% (in debt)
2nd 20%	9.9%	1.0%
3rd 20%	15.7%	4.4%
4th 20%	23.0%	10.8%
Highest 20%	47.2%	84.3%

Source: Survey of Consumer Finances, Federal Reserve Board

Responding to Reading

1. Consider the differences between inequality of income and inequality of wealth (that is, a family's accumulated assets). How is disparity of income different from disparity of wealth? Why is the disparity of wealth greater than that of income? List several possible reasons.

2. Can anything be done about disparities of income and wealth? Should anything be done? If so, what and why? If nothing should be done, why? For some help in thinking through income and wealth disparities, see the following article online: "Inequality in America: The Recent Evidence," http://www.gwu.edu/~ccps/rcq/Inequality.html.

WRITING TO DISCOVER

- Relate Sugar's comments that "Equal chance to pursue happiness means an equal crack at the dough, don't it?" to the data presented in the preceding tables.
- The tables presented earlier suggest strong correlations between race and economics. How do you account for such broad and persistent patterns?

- Go to http://www.census.gov/statab/www to see the other data available from the government. In particular, take a look at Table No. 752, "Average Earnings of Year-Round, Full-Time Workers by Educational Attainment" (in Section 14, "Income, Expenditures, and Wealth"). What relationships are evident when you examine the relationship between education and income? How do the average incomes of males compare to those of females? How do you account for the disparities by gender?

Essay: Barbara Ehrenreich, Nickel-and-Dimed: On (Not) Getting By in America

Barbara Ehrenreich is a journalist and the author of several books, including The Snarling Citizen, The Worst Years of Our Lives: Irreverent Notes from a Decade of Greed, *and* Fear of Falling: The Inner Life of the Middle Class. *The following piece was originally published in* Harper's *magazine and has since been republished in* Nickel-and-Dimed: On (Not) Getting By in America *(2001), a book of essays that describe Ehrenreich's experiments in various low-wage jobs.*

One common response to "The Lesson," and to poverty in general, is "If poor and working-class people want to make it, all they need to do is work harder." Ehrenreich's experience complicates this claim, suggesting that an individual's work—even sustained labor by a diligent and intelligent person—often does not result in an escape from poverty.

At the beginning of June 1998 I leave behind everything that normally soothes the ego and sustains the body—home, career, companion, reputation, ATM card—for a plunge into the low-wage workforce. There, I become another, occupationally much diminished "Barbara Ehrenreich"—depicted on job-application forms as a divorced homemaker whose sole work experience consists of housekeeping in a few private homes. I am terrified, at the beginning, of being unmasked for what I am: a middle-class journalist setting out to explore the world that welfare mothers are entering, at the rate of approximately 50,000 a month, as welfare reform kicks in. Happily, though, my fears turn out to be entirely unwarranted: during a month of poverty and toil, my name goes unnoticed and for the most part unuttered. In this parallel universe where my father never got out of the mines and I never got through college, I am "baby," "honey," "blondie," and, most commonly, "girl."

My first task is to find a place to live. I figure that if I can earn $7 an hour—which, from the want ads, seems doable—I can afford to spend $500 on rent, or maybe, with severe economies, $600. In the Key West area, where I live, this pretty much confines me to flophouses and trailer homes—like the one, a pleasing fifteen-minute drive from town, that has no air-conditioning, no screens, no fans, no television, and, by way of diversion, only the challenge of evading the landlord's Doberman pinscher. The big problem with this place, though, is the rent, which at $675 a month is well beyond my reach. All right, Key West is expensive. But so is New York City, or the Bay Area, or Jackson Hole, or Telluride, or Boston, or any other place where tourists and the wealthy compete for living space with the people who clean their toilets and fry their hash browns.[1] Still, it is a shock to realize that "trailer trash" has become, for me, a demographic category to aspire to.

So I decide to make the common trade-off between affordability and convenience, and go for a $500-a-month efficiency thirty miles up a two-lane highway from the employment opportunities of Key West, meaning forty-five minutes if there's no road construction and I don't get caught behind some sun-dazed Canadian tourists. I hate the drive, along a roadside studded with white crosses commemorating the more effective head-on collisions, but it's a sweet little place—a cabin, more or less, set in the swampy backyard of the converted mobile home where my landlord, an affable TV repairman, lives with his bartender girlfriend. Anthropologically speaking, a bustling trailer park would be preferable, but here I have a gleaming white floor and a firm mattress, and the few resident bugs are easily vanquished.

Besides, I am not doing this for the anthropology. My aim is nothing so mistily subjective as to "experience poverty" or find out how it "really feels" to be a long-term low-wage worker. I've had enough unchosen encounters with poverty and the world of low-wage work to know it's not a place you want to visit for touristic purposes; it just smells too much like fear. And with all my real-life assets—bank account, IRA, health insurance, multiroom home—waiting indulgently in the background, I am, of course, thoroughly insulated from the terrors that afflict the genuinely poor.

No, this is a purely objective, scientific sort of mission. The humanitarian rationale for welfare reform—as opposed to the more punitive and stingy impulses that may actually have motivated it—is that work will lift poor women out of poverty while simultaneously inflating their self-esteem and hence their future value in the labor market. Thus, whatever the hassles involved in finding child care, transportation, etc., the transition from welfare to work will end happily, in greater prosperity for all. Now there are many problems with this comforting

---

[1]According to the Department of Housing and Urban Development, the "fair-market rent" for an efficiency is $551 here in Monroe County, Florida. A comparable rent in the five boroughs of New York City is $704; in San Francisco, $713; and in the heart of Silicon Valley, $808. The fair-market rent for an area is defined as the amount that would be needed to pay rent plus utilities for "privately owned, decent, safe, and sanitary rental housing of a modest (nonluxury) nature with suitable amenities."

prediction, such as the fact that the economy will inevitably undergo a downturn, eliminating many jobs. Even without a downturn, the influx of a million former welfare recipients into the low-wage labor market could depress wages by as much as 11.9 percent, according to the Economic Policy Institute (EPI) in Washington, D.C.

But is it really possible to make a living on the kinds of jobs currently available to unskilled people? Mathematically, the answer is no, as can be shown by taking $6 to $7 an hour, perhaps subtracting a dollar or two an hour for child care, multiplying by 160 hours a month, and comparing the result to the prevailing rents. According to the National Coalition for the Homeless, for example, in 1998 it took, on average nationwide, an hourly wage of $8.89 to afford a one-bedroom apartment, and the Preamble Center for Public Policy estimates that the odds against a typical welfare recipient's landing a job at such a "living wage" are about 97 to 1. If these numbers are right, low-wage work is not a solution to poverty and possibly not even to homelessness.

It may seem excessive to put this proposition to an experimental test. As certain family members keep unhelpfully reminding me, the viability of low-wage work could be tested, after a fashion, without ever leaving my study. I could just pay myself $7 an hour for eight hours a day, charge myself for room and board, and total up the numbers after a month. Why leave the people and work that I love? But I am an experimental scientist by training. In that business, you don't just sit at a desk and theorize; you plunge into the everyday chaos of nature, where surprises lurk in the most mundane measurements. Maybe, when I got into it, I would discover some hidden economies in the world of the low-wage worker. After all, if 30 percent of the workforce toils for less than $8 an hour, according to the EPI, they may have found some tricks as yet unknown to me. Maybe—who knows?—I would even be able to detect in myself the bracing psychological effects of getting out of the house, as promised by the welfare wonks at places like the Heritage Foundation. Or, on the other hand, maybe there would be unexpected costs—physical, mental, or financial—to throw off all my calculations. Ideally, I should do this with two small children in tow, that being the welfare average, but mine are grown and no one is willing to lend me theirs for a month-long vacation in penury. So this is not the perfect experiment, just a test of the best possible case: an unencumbered woman, smart and even strong, attempting to live more or less off the land.

*   *   *

On the morning of my first full day of job searching, I take a red pen to the want ads, which are auspiciously numerous. Everyone in Key West's booming "hospitality industry" seems to be looking for someone like me—trainable, flexible, and with suitably humble expectations as to pay. I know I possess certain traits that might be advantageous—I'm white and, I like to think, well-spoken and poised—but I decide on two rules: One, I cannot use any skills derived from my education or usual work—not that there are a lot of want ads for satirical essayists anyway. Two, I have to take the best-paid job that is offered me and of course do my best to hold it; no Marxist rants or sneaking off to read novels in the ladies' room. In addition, I rule out various occupations for one reason or another: Hotel front-desk clerk, for example, which to my surprise is regarded as unskilled and pays around $7 an hour, gets eliminated because it involves standing in one spot for eight hours a day. Waitressing is similarly something I'd like to avoid, because I remember it leaving me bone tired when I was eighteen, and I'm decades of varicosities and back pain beyond that now. Telemarketing, one of the first refuges of the suddenly indigent, can be dismissed on grounds of personality. This leaves certain supermarket jobs, such as deli clerk, or housekeeping in Key West's thousands of hotel and guest rooms. Housekeeping is especially appealing, for reasons both atavistic and practical: it's what my mother did before I came along, and it can't be too different from what I've been doing part-time, in my own home, all my life.

So I put on what I take to be a respectful-looking outfit of ironed Bermuda shorts and scooped-neck T-shirt and set out for a tour of the local hotels and supermarkets. Best Western, Econo Lodge, and HoJo's all let me fill out application forms, and these are, to my relief, interested in little more than whether I am a legal resident of the United States and have committed any felonies. My next stop is Winn-Dixie, the supermarket, which turns out to have a particularly onerous application process, featuring a fifteen-minute "interview" by computer since, apparently, no human on the premises is deemed capable of representing the corporate point of view. I am conducted to a large room decorated with posters illustrating how to look "professional" (it helps to be white and, if female, permed) and warning of the slick promises that union organizers might try to tempt me with. The interview is multiple choice: Do I have anything, such as child-care problems, that might make it hard for me to get to work on time? Do I think safety on the job is the responsibility of management? Then, popping up cunningly out of the blue: How many dollars' worth of stolen goods have I purchased in the last year? Would I turn in a fellow employee if I caught him stealing? Finally, "Are you an honest person?"

Apparently, I ace the interview, because I am told that all I have to do is show up in some doctor's office tomorrow for a urine test. This seems to be a fairly general rule: if you want to stack Cheerio boxes or vacuum hotel rooms in chemically fascist America, you have to be willing to squat down and pee in front of some health worker (who has no doubt had to do the same thing herself). The wages Winn-Dixie is offering—$6 and a couple of dimes to start with—are not enough, I decide, to compensate for this indignity.[2]

I lunch at Wendy's, where $4.99 gets you unlimited refills at the Mexican part of the Superbar, a comforting surfeit of refried beans and "cheese sauce." A teenage employee, seeing me studying the want ads, kindly offers me an application form, which I fill out, though here, too, the pay is just $6 and change an hour. Then it's off for a round of the locally owned inns and guesthouses. At "The Palms," let's call it, a bouncy manager actually takes me around to see the rooms and meet the existing housekeepers, who, I note with satisfaction, look pretty much like me—faded ex-hippie types in shorts with long hair pulled back in braids. Mostly, though, no one speaks to me or even looks at me except to proffer an application form. At my last stop, a palatial B&B, I wait twenty minutes to meet "Max," only to be told that there are no jobs now but there should be one soon, since "nobody lasts more than a couple weeks." (Because none of the people I talked to knew I was a reporter, I have changed their names to protect their privacy and, in some cases perhaps, their jobs.)

Three days go by like this, and, to my chagrin, no one out of the approximately twenty places I've applied calls me for an interview. I had been vain enough to worry about coming across as too educated for the jobs I sought, but no one even seems interested in finding out how overqualified I am. Only later will I realize that the want ads are not a reliable measure of the actual jobs available at any particular time. They are, as I should have guessed from Max's comment, the employers' insurance policy against the relentless turnover of the low-wage work-force. Most of the big hotels run ads almost continually, just to build a supply of applicants to replace the current workers as they drift away or are fired, so finding a job is just a matter of being at the right place at the right time and flexible enough to take whatever is being offered that day. This finally happens to me at one of the big discount hotel chains, where I go, as usual, for housekeeping and am sent, instead, to try out as a waitress at the attached "family restaurant," a dismal spot with a counter and about thirty tables that looks out on a parking garage and features such tempting fare as "Pollish [sic] sausage and BBQ sauce" on 95-degree days. Phillip, the dapper young West Indian who introduces himself as the manager, interviews me with about as

---

[2]According to the *Monthly Labor Review* (November 1996), 28 percent of work sites surveyed in the service industry conduct drug tests (corporate workplaces have much higher rates), and the incidence of testing has risen markedly since the Eighties. The rate of testing is highest in the South (56 percent of work sites polled), with the Midwest in second place (50 percent). The drug most likely to be detected—marijuana, which can be detected in urine for weeks—is also the most innocuous, while heroin and cocaine are generally undetectable three days after use. Prospective employees sometimes try to cheat the tests by consuming excessive amounts of liquids and taking diuretics and even masking substances available through the Internet.

much enthusiasm as if he were a clerk processing me for Medicare, the principal questions being what shifts can I work and when can I start. I mutter something about being woefully out of practice as a waitress, but he's already on to the uniform: I'm to show up tomorrow wearing black slacks and black shoes; he'll provide the rust-colored polo shirt with HEARTHSIDE embroidered on it, though I might want to wear my own shirt to get to work, ha ha. At the word "tomorrow," something between fear and indignation rises in my chest. I want to say, "Thank you for your time, sir, but this is just an experiment, you know, not my actual life."

*   *   *

So begins my career at the Hearthside, I shall call it, one small profit center within a global discount hotel chain, where for two weeks I work from 2:00 till 10:00 P.M. for $2.43 an hour plus tips.[3] In some futile bid for gentility, the management has barred employees from using the front door, so my first day I enter through the kitchen, where a red-faced man with shoulder-length blond hair is throwing frozen steaks against the wall and yelling, "Fuck this shit!" "That's just Jack," explains Gail, the wiry middle-aged waitress who is assigned to train me. "He's on the rag again"—a condition occasioned, in this instance, by the fact that the cook on the morning shift had forgotten to thaw out the steaks. For the next eight hours, I run after the agile Gail, absorbing bits of instruction along with fragments of personal tragedy. All food must be trayed, and the reason she's so tired today is that she woke up in a cold sweat thinking of her boyfriend, who killed himself recently in an upstate prison. No refills on lemonade. And the reason he was in prison is that a few DUIs caught up with him, that's all, could have happened to anyone. Carry the creamers to the table in a monkey bowl, never in your hand. And after he was gone she spent several months living in her truck, peeing in a plastic pee bottle and reading by candlelight at night, but you can't live in a truck in the summer, since you need to have the windows down, which means anything can get in, from mosquitoes on up.

At least Gail puts to rest any fears I had of appearing overqualified. From the first day on, I find that of all the things I have left behind, such as home and identity, what I miss the most is competence. Not that I have ever felt utterly competent in the writing business, in which one day's success augurs nothing at all for the next. But in my writing life, I at least have some notion of procedure:

---

[3]According to the Fair Labor Standards Act, employers are not required to pay "tipped employees," such as restaurant servers, more than $2.13 an hour in direct wages. However, if the sum of tips plus $2.13 an hour falls below the minimum wage, or $5.15 an hour, the employer is required to make up the difference. This fact was not mentioned by managers or otherwise publicized at either of the restaurants where I worked.

do the research, make the outline, rough out a draft, etc. As a server, though, I am beset by requests like bees: more iced tea here, ketchup over there, a to-go box for table fourteen, and where are the high chairs, anyway? Of the twenty-seven tables, up to six are usually mine at any time, though on slow afternoons or if Gail is off, I sometimes have the whole place to myself. There is the touch-screen computer-ordering system to master, which is, I suppose, meant to minimize server-cook contact, but in practice requires constant verbal fine-tuning: "That's gravy on the mashed, okay? None on the meatloaf," and so forth—while the cook scowls as if I were inventing these refinements just to torment him. Plus, something I had forgotten in the years since I was eighteen: about a third of a server's job is "side work" that's invisible to customers—sweeping, scrubbing, slicing, refilling, and restocking. If it isn't all done, every little bit of it, you're going to face the 6:00 P.M. dinner rush defenseless and probably go down in flames. I screw up dozens of times at the beginning, sustained in my shame entirely by Gail's support—"It's okay, baby, everyone does that sometime"—because, to my total surprise and despite the scientific detachment I am doing my best to maintain, I care.

The whole thing would be a lot easier if I could just skate through it as Lily Tomlin in one of her waitress skits; but I was raised by the absurd Booker T. Washingtonian precept that says: If you're going to do something, do it well. In fact, "well" isn't good enough by half. Do it better than anyone has ever done it before. Or so said my father, who must have known what he was talking about because he managed to pull himself, and us with him, up from the mile-deep copper mines of Butte to the leafy suburbs of the Northeast, ascending from boilermakers to martinis before booze beat out ambition. As in most endeavors I have encountered in my life, doing it "better than anyone" is not a reasonable goal. Still, when I wake up at 4:00 A.M. in my own cold sweat, I am not thinking about the writing deadlines I'm neglecting; I'm thinking about the table whose order I screwed up so that one of the boys didn't get his kiddie meal until the rest of the family had moved on to their Key Lime pies. That's the other powerful motivation I hadn't expected—the customers, or "patients," as I can't help thinking of them on account of the mysterious vulnerability that seems to have left them temporarily unable to feed themselves. After a few days at the Hearthside, I feel the service ethic kick in like a shot of oxytocin, the nurturance hormone. The plurality of my customers are hard-working locals—truck drivers, construction workers, even housekeepers from the attached hotel—and I want them to have the closest to a "fine dining" experience that the grubby circumstances will allow. No "you guys" for me; everyone over twelve is "sir" or "ma'am." I ply them with iced tea and coffee refills; I return, mid-meal, to inquire how everything is; I doll up their salads with chopped raw mushrooms, summer squash slices, or whatever bits of produce I can find that have survived their sojourn in the cold-storage room mold-free.

There is Benny, for example, a short, tight-muscled sewer repairman, who cannot even think of eating until he has absorbed a half hour of air-conditioning and ice water. We chat about hyperthermia and electrolytes until he is ready to order some finicky combination like soup of the day, garden salad, and a side of grits. There are the German tourists who are so touched by my pidgin "Willkommen" and "Ist alles gut?" that they actually tip. (Europeans, spoiled by their trade-union-ridden, high-wage welfare states, generally do not know that they are supposed to tip. Some restaurants, the Hearthside included, allow servers to "grat" their foreign customers, or add a tip to the bill. Since this amount is added before the customers have a chance to tip or not tip, the practice amounts to an automatic penalty for imperfect English.) There are the two dirt-smudged lesbians, just off their construction shift, who are impressed enough by my suave handling of the fly in the piña colada that they take the time to praise me to Stu, the assistant manager. There's Sam, the kindly retired cop, who has to plug up his tracheotomy hole with one finger in order to force the cigarette smoke into his lungs.

Sometimes I play with the fantasy that I am a princess who, in penance for some tiny transgression, has undertaken to feed each of her subjects by hand. But the non-princesses working with me are just as indulgent, even when this means flouting management rules—concerning, for example, the number of croutons that can go on a salad (six): "Put on all you want," Gail whispers, "as long as Stu isn't looking." She dips into her own tip money to buy biscuits and gravy for an out-of-work mechanic who's used up all his money on dental surgery, inspiring me to pick up the tab for his milk and pie. Maybe the same high levels of agape can be found throughout the "hospitality industry." I remember the poster decorating one of the apartments I looked at, which said "If you seek happiness for yourself you will never find it. Only when you seek happiness for others will it come to you," or words to that effect—an odd sentiment, it seemed to me at the time, to find in the dank one-room basement apartment of a bellhop at the Best Western. At the Hearthside, we utilize whatever bits of autonomy we have to ply our customers with the illicit calories that signal our love. It is our job as servers to assemble the salads and desserts, pouring the dressings and squirting the whipped cream. We also control the number of butter patties our customers get and the amount of sour cream on their baked potatoes. So if you wonder why Americans are so obese, consider the fact that waitresses both express their humanity and earn their tips through the covert distribution of fats.

Ten days into it, this is beginning to look like a livable lifestyle. I like Gail, who is "looking at fifty" but moves so fast she can alight in one place and then another without apparently being anywhere between them. I clown around with

Lionel, the teenage Haitian busboy, and catch a few fragments of conversation with Joan, the svelte fortyish hostess and militant feminist who is the only one of us who dares to tell Jack to shut the fuck up. I even warm up to Jack when, on a slow night and to make up for a particularly unwarranted attack on my abilities, or so I imagine, he tells me about his glory days as a young man at "coronary school"—or do you say "culinary"?—in Brooklyn, where he dated a knock-out Puerto Rican chick and learned everything there is to know about food. I finish up at 10:00 or 10:30, depending on how much side work I've been able to get done during the shift, and cruise home to the tapes I snatched up at random when I left my real home—Marianne Faithfull, Tracy Chapman, Enigma, King Sunny Ade, the Violent Femmes—just drained enough for the music to set my cranium resonating but hardly dead. Midnight snack is Wheat Thins and Monterey Jack, accompanied by cheap white wine on ice and whatever AMC has to offer. To bed by 1:30 or 2:00, up at 9:00 or 10:00, read for an hour while my uniform whirls around in the landlord's washing machine, and then it's another eight hours spent following Mao's central instruction, as laid out in the Little Red Book, which was: Serve the people.

*   *   *

I could drift along like this, in some dreamy proletarian idyll, except for two things. One is management. If I have kept this subject on the margins thus far it is because I still flinch to think that I spent all those weeks under the surveillance of men (and later women) whose job it was to monitor my behavior for signs of sloth, theft, drug abuse, or worse. Not that managers and especially "assistant managers" in low-wage settings like this are exactly the class enemy. In the restaurant business, they are mostly former cooks or servers, still capable of pinch-hitting in the kitchen or on the floor, just as in hotels they are likely to be former clerks, and paid a salary of only about $400 a week. But everyone knows they have crossed over to the other side, which is, crudely put, corporate as opposed to human. Cooks want to prepare tasty meals; servers want to serve them graciously; but managers are there for only one reason—to make sure that money is made for some theoretical entity that exists far away in Chicago or New York, if a corporation can be said to have a physical existence at all. Reflecting on her career, Gail tells me ruefully that she had sworn, years ago, never to work for a corporation again. "They don't cut you no slack. You give and you give, and they take."

Managers can sit—for hours at a time if they want—but it's their job to see that no one else ever does, even when there's nothing to do, and this is why, for servers, slow times can be as exhausting as rushes. You start dragging out each little chore, because if the manager on duty catches you in an idle moment, he will give you something far nastier to do. So I wipe, I clean, I consolidate ketchup bottles and recheck the cheesecake supply, even tour the tables to make sure the customer evaluation forms are all standing perkily in their places—wondering all the time how many calories I burn in these strictly theatrical exercises. When, on a particularly dead afternoon, Stu finds me glancing at a *USA Today* a customer has left behind, he assigns me to vacuum the entire floor with the broken vacuum cleaner that has a handle only two feet long, and the only way to do that without incurring orthopedic damage is to proceed from spot to spot on your knees.

On my first Friday at the Hearthside there is a "mandatory meeting for all restaurant employees," which I attend, eager for insight into our overall marketing strategy and the niche (your basic Ohio cuisine with a tropical twist?) we aim to inhabit. But there is no "we" at this meeting. Phillip, our top manager except for an occasional "consultant" sent out by corporate headquarters, opens it with a sneer: "The break room—it's disgusting. Butts in the ashtrays, newspapers lying around, crumbs." This windowless little room, which also houses the time clock for the entire hotel, is where we stash our bags and civilian clothes and take our half-hour meal breaks. But a break room is not a right, he tells us. It can be taken away. We should also know that the lockers in the break room and whatever is in them can be searched at any time. Then comes gossip; there has been gossip; gossip (which seems to mean employees talking among themselves) must stop. Off-duty employees are henceforth barred from eating at the restaurant, because "other servers gather around them and gossip." When Phillip has exhausted his agenda of rebukes, Joan complains about the condition of the ladies' room and I throw in my two bits about the vacuum cleaner. But I don't see any backup coming from my fellow servers, each of whom has subsided into her own personal funk; Gail, my role model, stares sorrowfully at a point six inches from her nose. The meeting ends when Andy, one of the cooks, gets up, muttering about breaking up his day off for this almighty bullshit.

Just four days later we are suddenly summoned into the kitchen at 3:30 P.M., even though there are live tables on the floor. We all—about ten of us—stand around Phillip, who announces grimly that there has been a report of some "drug activity" on the night shift and that, as a result, we are now to be a "drug-free" workplace, meaning that all new hires will be tested, as will possibly current employees on a random basis. I am glad that this part of the kitchen is so dark, because I find myself blushing as hard as if I had been caught toking up in the ladies' room myself: I haven't been treated this way—lined up in the corridor, threatened with locker searches, peppered with carelessly aimed accusations—since junior high school. Back on the floor, Joan cracks, "Next they'll be telling us we can't have sex on the job." When I ask Stu what happened to inspire the crackdown, he just mutters about "management decisions" and takes the opportunity to upbraid Gail and me for being too generous with the rolls.

From now on there's to be only one per customer, and it goes out with the dinner, not with the salad. He's also been riding the cooks, prompting Andy to come out of the kitchen and observe—with the serenity of a man whose customary implement is a butcher knife—that "Stu has a death wish today."

Later in the evening, the gossip crystallizes around the theory that Stu is himself the drug culprit, that he uses the restaurant phone to order up marijuana and sends one of the late servers out to fetch it for him. The server was caught, and she may have ratted Stu out or at least said enough to cast some suspicion on him, thus accounting for his pissy behavior. Who knows? Lionel, the busboy, entertains us for the rest of the shift by standing just behind Stu's back and sucking deliriously on an imaginary joint.

The other problem, in addition to the less-than-nurturing management style, is that this job shows no sign of being financially viable. You might imagine, from a comfortable distance, that people who live, year in and year out, on $6 to $10 an hour have discovered some survival stratagems unknown to the middle class. But no. It's not hard to get my co-workers to talk about their living situations, because housing, in almost every case, is the principal source of disruption in their lives, the first thing they fill you in on when they arrive for their shifts. After a week, I have compiled the following survey:

- Gail is sharing a room in a well-known downtown flophouse for which she and a roommate pay about $250 a week. Her roommate, a male friend, has begun hitting on her, driving her nuts, but the rent would be impossible alone.
- Claude, the Haitian cook, is desperate to get out of the two-room apartment he shares with his girlfriend and two other, unrelated, people. As far as I can determine, the other Haitian men (most of whom only speak Creole) live in similarly crowded situations.
- Annette, a twenty-year-old server who is six months pregnant and has been abandoned by her boyfriend, lives with her mother, a postal clerk.
- Marianne and her boyfriend are paying $170 a week for a one-person trailer.
- Jack, who is, at $10 an hour, the wealthiest of us, lives in the trailer he owns, paying only the $400-a-month lot fee.
- The other white cook, Andy, lives on his dry-docked boat, which, as far as I can tell from his loving descriptions, can't be more than twenty feet long. He offers to take me out on it, once it's repaired, but the offer comes with inquiries as to my marital status, so I do not follow up on it.
- Tina and her husband are paying $60 a night for a double room in a Days Inn. This is because they have no car and the Days Inn is within walking distance of the Hearthside. When Marianne, one of the breakfast servers, is tossed out of her trailer for subletting (which is against the trailer-park rules), she leaves her boyfriend and moves in with Tina and her husband.

- Joan, who had fooled me with her numerous and tasteful outfits (hostesses wear their own clothes), lives in a van she parks behind a shopping center at night and showers in Tina's motel room. The clothes are from thrift shops.[4]

*   *   *

It strikes me, in my middle-class solipsism, that there is gross improvidence in some of these arrangements. When Gail and I are wrapping silverware in napkins—the only task for which we are permitted to sit—she tells me she is thinking of escaping from her roommate by moving into the Days Inn herself. I am astounded: How can she even think of paying between $40 and $60 a day? But if I was afraid of sounding like a social worker, I come out just sounding like a fool. She squints at me in disbelief. "And where am I supposed to get a month's rent and a month's deposit for an apartment?" I'd been feeling pretty smug about my $500 efficiency, but of course it was made possible only by the $1,300 I had allotted myself for start-up costs when I began my low-wage life: $1,000 for the first month's rent and deposit, $100 for initial groceries and cash in my pocket, $200 stuffed away for emergencies. In poverty, as in certain propositions in physics, starting conditions are everything.

There are no secret economies that nourish the poor; on the contrary, there are a host of special costs. If you can't put up the two months' rent you need to secure an apartment, you end up paying through the nose for a room by the week. If you have only a room, with a hot plate at best, you can't save by cooking up huge lentil stews that can be frozen for the week ahead. You eat fast food or the hot dogs and styrofoam cups of soup that can be microwaved in a convenience store. If you have no money for health insurance—and the Hearthside's niggardly plan kicks in only after three months—you go without routine care or prescription drugs and end up paying the price. Gail, for example, was fine until she ran out of money for estrogen pills. She is supposed to be on the company plan by now, but they claim to have lost her application form and need to begin the paperwork all over again. So she spends $9 per migraine pill to control the headaches she wouldn't have, she insists, if her estrogen supplements were covered. Similarly, Marianne's boyfriend lost his job as a roofer because he missed so much time after getting a cut on his foot for which he couldn't afford the prescribed antibiotic.

My own situation, when I sit down to assess it after two weeks of work, would not be much better if this were my actual life. The seductive thing about wait-

---

[4] I could find no statistics on the number of employed people living in cars or vans, but according to the National Coalition for the Homeless's 1997 report "Myths and Facts About Homelessness," nearly one in five homeless people (in twenty-nine cities across the nation) is employed in a full- or part-time job.

ressing is that you don't have to wait for payday to feel a few bills in your pocket, and my tips usually cover meals and gas, plus something left over to stuff into the kitchen drawer I use as a bank. But as the tourist business slows in the summer heat, I sometimes leave work with only $20 in tips (the gross is higher, but servers share about 15 percent of their tips with the busboys and bartenders). With wages included, this amounts to about the minimum wage of $5.15 an hour. Although the sum in the drawer is piling up, at the present rate of accumulation it will be more than a hundred dollars short of my rent when the end of the month comes around. Nor can I see any expenses to cut. True, I haven't gone the lentil-stew route yet, but that's because I don't have a large cooking pot, pot holders, or a ladle to stir with (which cost about $30 at Kmart, less at thrift stores), not to mention onions, carrots, and the indispensable bay leaf. I do make my lunch almost every day—usually some slow-burning, high-protein combo like frozen chicken patties with melted cheese on top and canned pinto beans on the side. Dinner is at the Hearthside, which offers its employees a choice of BLT, fish sandwich, or hamburger for only $2. The burger lasts longest, especially if it's heaped with gut-puckering jalapeños, but by midnight my stomach is growling again.

So unless I want to start using my car as a residence, I have to find a second, or alternative, job. I call all the hotels where I filled out housekeeping applications weeks ago—the Hyatt, Holiday Inn, Econo Lodge, HoJo's, Best Western, plus a half dozen or so locally run guesthouses. Nothing. Then I start making the rounds again, wasting whole mornings waiting for some assistant manager to show up, even dipping into places so creepy that the front-desk clerk greets you from behind bulletproof glass and sells pints of liquor over the counter. But either someone has exposed my real-life housekeeping habits—which are, shall we say, mellow—or I am at the wrong end of some infallible ethnic equation: most, but by no means all, of the working housekeepers I see on my job searches are African Americans, Spanish-speaking, or immigrants from the Central European post-Communist world, whereas servers are almost invariably white and monolingually English-speaking. When I finally get a positive response, I have been identified once again as server material. Jerry's, which is part of a well-known national family restaurant chain and physically attached here to another budget hotel chain, is ready to use me at once. The prospect is both exciting and terrifying, because, with about the same number of tables and counter seats, Jerry's attracts three or four times the volume of customers as the gloomy old Hearthside.

*   *   *

Picture a fat person's hell, and I don't mean a place with no food. Instead there is everything you might eat if eating had no bodily consequences—cheese fries, chicken-fried steaks, fudge-laden desserts—only here every bite must be paid for, one way or another, in human discomfort. The kitchen is a cavern, a stomach leading to the lower intestine that is the garbage and dishwashing area, from which issue bizarre smells combining the edible and the offal: creamy carrion, pizza barf, and that unique and enigmatic Jerry's scent—citrus fart. The floor is slick with spills, forcing us to walk through the kitchen with tiny steps, like Susan McDougal in leg irons. Sinks everywhere are clogged with scraps of lettuce, decomposing lemon wedges, waterlogged toast crusts. Put your hand down on any counter and you risk being stuck to it by the film of ancient syrup spills, and this is unfortunate, because hands are utensils here, used for scooping up lettuce onto salad plates, lifting out pie slices, and even moving hash browns from one plate to another. The regulation poster in the single unisex restroom admonishes us to wash our hands thoroughly and even offers instructions for doing so, but there is always some vital substance missing—soap, paper towels, toilet paper—and I never find all three at once. You learn to stuff your pockets with napkins before going in there, and too bad about the customers, who must eat, though they don't realize this, almost literally out of our hands.

The break room typifies the whole situation: there is none, became there are no breaks at Jerry's. For six to eight hours in a row, you never sit except to pee. Actually, there are three folding chairs at a table immediately adjacent to the bathroom, but hardly anyone ever sits here, in the very rectum of the gastro-architectural system. Rather, the function of the peritoilet area is to house the ash-trays in which servers and dishwashers leave their cigarettes burning at all times, like votive candles, so that they don't have to waste time lighting up again when they dash back for a puff. Almost everyone smokes as if his or her pulmonary well-being depended on it—the multinational mélange of cooks, the Czech dishwash-ers, the servers, who are all American natives—creating an atmosphere in which oxygen is only an occasional pollutant. My first morning at Jerry's, when the hypo-glycemic shakes set in, I complain to one of my fellow servers that I don't under-stand how she can go so long without food. "Well, I don't understand how you can go so long without a cigarette," she responds in a tone of reproach—because work is what you do for others; smoking is what you do for yourself. I don't know why the antismoking crusaders have never grasped the element of defiant self-nurturance that makes the habit so endearing to its victims—as if, in the American workplace, the only thing people have to call their own is the tumors they are nourishing and the spare moments they devote to feeding them.

Now, the Industrial Revolution is not an easy transition, especially when you have to zip through it in just a couple of days. I have gone from craft work straight into the factory, from the air-conditioned morgue of the Hearthside di-rectly into the flames. Customers arrive in human waves, sometimes disgorged fifty at a time from their tour buses, peckish and whiny. Instead of two "girls" on the floor at once, there can be as many as six of us running around in our brilliant pink-and-orange Hawaiian shirts. Conversations, either with customers or fellow employees, seldom last more than twenty seconds at a time. On my first day, in fact, I am hurt by my sister servers' coldness. My mentor for the day is an emotionally uninflected twenty-three-year-old, and the others, who gossip a little among themselves about the real reason someone is out sick today and the size of the bail bond someone else has had to pay, ignore me completely. On my second day, I find out why. "Well, it's good to see you again," one of them says in greeting. "Hardly anyone comes back after the first day." I feel powerfully vindicated—a survivor—but it would take a long time, probably months, before I could hope to be accepted into this sorority.

I start out with the beautiful, heroic idea of handling the two jobs at once, and for two days I almost do it: the breakfast/lunch shift at Jerry's, which goes till 2:00, arriving at the Hearthside at 2:10, and attempting to hold out until 10:00. In the ten minutes between jobs, I pick up a spicy chicken sandwich at the Wendy's drive-through window, gobble it down in the car, and change from khaki slacks to black, from Hawaiian to rust polo. There is a problem, though. When during the 3:00 to 4:00 P.M. dead time I finally sit down to wrap silver, my flesh seems to bond to the seat. I try to refuel with a purloined cup of soup, as I've seen Gail and Joan do dozens of times, but a manager catches me and hisses "No eating!" though there's not a customer around to be offended by the sight of food making contact with a server's lips. So I tell Gail I'm going to quit, and she hugs me and says she might just follow me to Jerry's herself.

But the chances of this are minuscule. She has left the flophouse and her annoying roommate and is back to living in her beat-up old truck. But guess what? she reports to me excitedly later that evening: Phillip has given her permission to park overnight in the hotel parking lot, as long as she keeps out of sight, and the parking lot should be totally safe, since it's patrolled by a hotel security guard! With the Hearthside offering benefits like that, how could anyone think of leaving?

Gail would have triumphed at Jerry's, I'm sure, but for me it's a crash course in exhaustion management. Years ago, the kindly fry cook who trained me to waitress at a Los Angeles truck stop used to say: Never make an unnecessary trip; if you don't have to walk fast, walk slow; if you don't have to walk, stand. But at Jerry's the effort of distinguishing necessary from unnecessary and urgent from whenever would itself be too much of an energy drain. The only thing to do is to treat each shift as a one-time-only emergency: you've got fifty starving people out there, lying scattered on the battlefield, so get out there and feed them! Forget that you will have to do this again tomorrow, forget that you will have to be alert enough to dodge the drunks on the drive home tonight—just burn, burn, burn! Ideally, at some point you enter what servers call "a rhythm" and psychologists term a "flow state," in which signals pass from the sense organs directly to the muscles, bypassing the cerebral cortex, and a Zen-like emptiness sets in. A male server from the Hearthside's morning shift tells me about the time he "pulled a triple"—three shifts in a row, all the way around the clock—and then got off and had a drink and met this girl, and maybe he shouldn't tell me this, but they had sex right then and there, and it was like, beautiful.

But there's another capacity of the neuromuscular system, which is pain. I start tossing back drugstore-brand ibuprofen pills as if they were vitamin C, four before each shift, because an old mouse-related repetitive-stress injury in my upper back has come back to full-spasm strength, thanks to the tray carrying. In my ordinary life, this level of disability might justify a day of ice packs and stretching. Here I comfort myself with the Aleve commercial in which the cute blue-collar guy asks: If you quit after working four hours, what would your boss say? And the not-so-cute blue-collar guy, who's lugging a metal beam on his back, answers: He'd fire me, that's what. But fortunately, the commercial tells us, we workers can exert the same kind of authority over our painkillers that our bosses exert over us. If Tylenol doesn't want to work for more than four hours, you just fire its ass and switch to Aleve.

True, I take occasional breaks from this life, going home now and then to catch up on e-mail and for conjugal visits (though I am careful to "pay" for anything I eat there), seeing *The Truman Show* with friends and letting them buy my ticket. And I still have those what-am-I-doing-here moments at work, when I get so homesick for the printed word that I obsessively reread the six-page menu. But as the days go by, my old life is beginning to look exceedingly strange. The e-mails and phone messages addressed to my former self come from a distant race of people with exotic concerns and far too much time on their hands. The neighborly market I used to cruise for produce now looks forbiddingly like a Manhattan yuppie emporium. And when I sit down one morning in my real home to pay bills from my past life, I am dazzled at the two- and three-figure sums owed to outfits like Club BodyTech and Amazon.com.

*   *   *

Management at Jerry's is generally calmer and more "professional" than at the Hearthside, with two exceptions. One is Joy, a plump, blowsy woman in her early thirties, who once kindly devoted several minutes to instructing me in the correct one-handed method of carrying trays but whose moods change disconcertingly from shift to shift and even within one. Then there's B.J., a.k.a. B.J.-the-bitch, whose contribution is to stand by the kitchen counter and yell, "Nita, your order's up, move it!" or, "Barbara, didn't you see you've got another table out there? Come on, girl!" Among other things, she is hated for having replaced the whipped-cream squirt cans with big plastic whipped-cream-filled baggies that have to be squeezed with both hands—because, reportedly she saw or thought she saw employees trying to inhale the propellant gas from the squirt cans, in the hope that it might be nitrous oxide. On my third night, she pulls me aside abruptly and brings her face so close that it looks as if she's planning to butt me with her forehead. But instead of saying, "You're fired," she says, "You're doing fine." The only trouble is I'm spending time chatting with customers: "That's how they're getting you." Furthermore I am letting them "run me," which means harassment by sequential demands: you bring the ketchup and they decide they want extra Thousand Island; you bring that and they announce they now need a side of fries; and so on into distraction. Finally, she tells me not to take her wrong. She tries to say things in a nice way, but you get into a mode, you know, because everything has to move so fast.[5]

I mumble thanks for the advice, feeling like I've just been stripped naked by the crazed enforcer of some ancient sumptuary law: No chatting for you, girl. No fancy service ethic allowed for the serfs. Chatting with customers is for the beautiful young college-educated servers in the downtown carpaccio joints, the kids who can make $70 to $100 a night. What had I been thinking? My job is to move orders from tables to kitchen and then trays from kitchen to tables. Customers are, in fact, the major obstacle to the smooth transformation of information into food and food into money—they are, in short, the enemy. And the painful thing is that I'm beginning to see it this way myself. There are the traditional asshole types—frat boys who down multiple Buds and then make a fuss because the steaks are so emaciated and the fries so sparse—as well as the variously impaired—due to age, diabetes, or literacy issues—who require patient nutritional counseling. The worst, for some reason, are the Visible Christians—like the ten-person table, all jolly and sanctified after Sunday-night service, who run me mercilessly and then leave me $1 on a $92 bill. Or the guy with the crucifixion T-shirt (SOMEONE TO LOOK UP TO) who complains that his baked potato is too hard and his iced tea too icy (I cheerfully fix both) and leaves no tip. As a general rule, people wearing crosses or WWJD? (What Would Jesus Do?) buttons look at us disapprovingly no matter what we do, as if they were confusing waitressing with Mary Magdalene's original profession.

I make friends, over time, with the other "girls" who work my shift: Nita, the tattooed twenty-something who taunts us by going around saying brightly, "Have we started making money yet?" Ellen, whose teenage son cooks on the graveyard shift and who once managed a restaurant in Massachusetts but won't try out for management here because she prefers being a "common

---

[5]In *Workers in a Lean World: Unions in the International Economy* (Verso, 1997), Kim Moody cites studies finding an increase in stress-related workplace injuries and illness between the mid-1980s and the early 1990s. He argues that rising stress levels reflect a new system of "management by stress," in which workers in a variety of industries are being squeezed to extract maximum productivity, to the detriment of their health.

worker" and not "ordering people around." Easy-going fiftyish Lucy, with the raucous laugh, who limps toward the end of the shift because of something that has gone wrong with her leg, the exact nature of which cannot be determined without health insurance. We talk about the usual girl things—men, children, and the sinister allure of Jerry's chocolate peanut-butter cream pie—though no one, I notice, ever brings up anything potentially expensive, like shopping or movies. As at the Hearthside, the only recreation ever referred to is partying, which requires little more than some beer, a joint, and a few close friends. Still, no one here is homeless, or cops to it anyway, thanks usually to a working husband or boyfriend. All in all, we form a reliable mutual-support group: If one of us is feeling sick or overwhelmed, another one will "bev" a table or even carry trays for her. If one of us is off sneaking a cigarette or a pee,[6] the others will do their best to conceal her absence from the enforcers of corporate rationality.

But my saving human connection—my oxytocin receptor, as it were—is George, the nineteen-year-old, fresh-off-the-boat Czech dishwasher. We get to talking when he asks me, tortuously, how much cigarettes cost at Jerry's. I do my best to explain that they cost over a dollar more here than at a regular store and suggest that he just take one from the half-filled packs that are always lying around on the break table. But that would be unthinkable. Except for the one tiny earring signaling his allegiance to some vaguely alternative point of view, George is a perfect straight arrow—crew-cut, hardworking, and hungry for eye contact. "Czech Republic," I ask, "or Slovakia?" and he seems delighted that I know the difference. "Václav Havel," I try. "Velvet Revolution, Frank Zappa?" "Yes, yes, 1989," he says, and I realize we are talking about history.

My project is to teach George English. "How are you today, George?" I say at the start of each shift. "I am good, and how are you today, Barbara?" I learn that he is not paid by Jerry's but by the "agent" who shipped him over—$5 an hour, with the agent getting the dollar or so difference between that and what Jerry's pays dishwashers. I learn also that he shares an apartment with a crowd of other

---

[6]Until April 1998, there was no federally mandated right to bathroom breaks. According to Marc Linder and Ingrid Nygaard, authors of *Void Where Prohibited: Rest Breaks and the Right to Urinate on Company Time* (Cornell University Press, 1997), "The right to rest and void at work is not high on the list of social or political causes supported by professional or executive employees, who enjoy personal workplace liberties that millions of factory workers can only daydream about. . . . While we were dismayed to discover that workers lacked an acknowledged legal right to void at work, [the workers] were amazed by outsiders' naive belief that their employers would permit them to perform this basic bodily function when necessary. . . . A factory worker, not allowed a break for six-hour stretches, voided into pads worn inside her uniform; and a kindergarten teacher in a school without aides had to take all twenty children with her to the bathroom and line them up outside the stall door when she voided."

Czech "dishers," as he calls them, and that he cannot sleep until one of them goes off for his shift, leaving a vacant bed. We are having one of our ESL sessions late one afternoon when B.J. catches us at it and orders "Joseph" to take up the rubber mats off the floor near the dishwashing sinks and mop underneath. "I thought your name was George," I say loud enough for B.J. to hear as she strides off back to the counter. Is she embarrassed? Maybe a little, because she greets me back at the counter with "George, Joseph—there are so many of them!" I say nothing, neither nodding nor smiling, and for this I am punished later when I think I am ready to go and she announces that I need to roll fifty more sets of silverware and isn't it time I mixed up a fresh four-gallon batch of blue-cheese dressing? May you grow old in this place, B.J., is the curse I beam out at her when I am finally permitted to leave. May the syrup spills glue your feet to the floor.

I make the decision to move closer to Key West. First, because of the drive. Second and third, also because of the drive: gas is eating up $4 to $5 a day, and although Jerry's is as high-volume as you can get, the tips average only 10 percent, and not just for a newbie like me. Between the base pay of $2.15 an hour and the obligation to share tips with the busboys and dishwashers, we're averaging only about $7.50 an hour. Then there is the $30 I had to spend on the regulation tan slacks worn by Jerry's servers—a setback it could take weeks to absorb. (I had combed the town's two downscale department stores hoping for something cheaper but decided in the end that these marked-down Dockers, originally $49, were more likely to survive a daily washing.) Of my fellow servers, everyone who lacks a working husband or boyfriend seems to have a second job: Nita does something at a computer eight hours a day; another welds. Without the forty-five-minute commute, I can picture myself working two jobs and having the time to shower between them.

So I take the $500 deposit I have coming from my landlord, the $400 I have earned toward the next month's rent, plus the $200 reserved for emergencies, and use the $1,100 to pay the rent and deposit on trailer number 46 in the Overseas Trailer Park, a mile from the cluster of budget hotels that constitute Key West's version of an industrial park. Number 46 is about eight feet in width and shaped like a barbell inside, with a narrow region—because of the sink and the stove—separating the bedroom from what might optimistically be called the "living" area, with its two-person table and half-sized couch. The bathroom is so small my knees rub against the shower stall when I sit on the toilet, and you can't just leap out of the bed, you have to climb down to the foot of it in order to find a patch of floor space to stand on. Outside, I am within a few yards of a liquor store, a bar that advertises "free beer tomorrow," a convenience store, and a Burger King—but no supermarket or, alas, laundromat. By reputation, the Overseas park is a nest of crime and crack, and I am hoping at least for some vibrant, multicultural street life. But desolation rules night and day, except for a thin stream of pedestrian traffic heading for their jobs at the Sheraton or 7-Eleven. There are not exactly people here but what amounts to canned labor, being preserved from the heat between shifts.

*   *   *

In line with my reduced living conditions, a new form of ugliness arises at Jerry's. First we are confronted—via an announcement on the computers through which we input orders—with the new rule that the hotel bar is henceforth off-limits to restaurant employees. The culprit, I learn through the grapevine, is the ultra-efficient gal who trained me—another trailer-home dweller and a mother of three. Something had set her off one morning, so she slipped out for a nip and returned to the floor impaired. This mostly hurts Ellen, whose habit it is to free her hair from its rubber band and drop by the bar for a couple of Zins before heading home at the end of the shift, but all of us feel the chill. Then the next day, when I go for straws, for the first time I find the dry-storage room locked. Ted, the portly assistant manager who opens it for me, explains that he caught one of the dishwashers attempting to steal something, and, unfortunately, the miscreant will be with us until a replacement can be found—hence the locked door. I neglect to ask what he had been trying to steal, but Ted tells me who he is—the kid with the buzz cut and the earring. You know, he's back there right now.

I wish I could say I rushed back and confronted George to get his side of the story. I wish I could say I stood up to Ted and insisted that George be given a translator and allowed to defend himself, or announced that I'd find a lawyer who'd handle the case pro bono. The mystery to me is that there's not much worth stealing in the dry-storage room, at least not in any fenceable quantity: "Is Gyorgi here, and am having 200—maybe 250—ketchup packets. What do you say?" My guess is that he had taken— if he had taken anything at all—some Saltines or a can of cherry-pie mix, and that the motive for taking it was hunger.

So why didn't I intervene? Certainly not because I was held back by the kind of moral paralysis that can pass as journalistic objectivity. On the contrary, something new—something loathsome and servile—had infected me, along with the kitchen odors that I could still sniff on my bra when I finally undressed at night. In real life I am moderately brave, but plenty of brave people shed their courage in concentration camps, and maybe something similar goes on in the infinitely more congenial milieu of the low-wage American workplace. Maybe, in a month or two more at Jerry's, I might have regained my crusading spirit. Then again, in a month or two I might have turned into a different person altogether—say, the kind of person who would have turned George in.

But this is not something I am slated to find out. When my month-long plunge into poverty is almost over, I finally land my dream job—housekeeping. I do this by walking into the personnel office of the only place I figure I might have some credibility, the hotel attached to Jerry's, and confiding urgently that I have to have a second job if I am to pay my rent and, no, it couldn't be front-desk clerk. "All right," the personnel lady fairly spits, "So it's housekeeping," and she marches me back to meet Maria, the housekeeping manager, a tiny, frenetic Hispanic woman who greets me as "babe" and hands me a pamphlet emphasizing the need for a positive attitude. The hours are nine in the morning till whenever, the pay is $6.10 an hour, and there's one week of vacation a year. I don't have to ask about health insurance once I meet Carlotta, the middle-aged African-American woman who will be training me. Carla, as she tells me to call her, is missing all of her top front teeth.

*   *   *

On that first day of housekeeping and last day of my entire project—although I don't yet know it's the last—Carla is in a foul mood. We have been given nineteen rooms to clean, most of them "checkouts," as opposed to "stay-overs," that require the whole enchilada of bedstripping, vacuuming, and bathroom-scrubbing. When one of the rooms that had been listed as a stayover turns out to be a checkout, Carla calls Maria to complain, but of course to no avail. "So make up the motherfucker," Carla orders me, and I do the beds while she sloshes around the bathroom. For four hours without a break I strip and remake beds, taking about four and a half minutes per queen-sized bed, which I could get down to three if there were any reason to. We try to avoid vacuuming by picking up the larger specks by hand, but often there is nothing to do but drag the monstrous vacuum cleaner—it weighs about thirty pounds—off our cart and try to wrestle it around the floor. Sometimes Carla hands me the squirt bottle of "BAM" (an acronym for something that begins, ominously, with "butyric"; the rest has been worn off the label) and lets me do the bathrooms. No service ethic challenges me here to new heights of performance. I just concentrate on removing the pubic hairs from the bathtubs, or at least the dark ones that I can see.

I had looked forward to the breaking-and-entering aspect of cleaning the stay-overs, the chance to examine the secret, physical existence of strangers. But the contents of the rooms are always banal and surprisingly neat—zipped up shaving kits, shoes lined up against the wall (there are no closets), flyers for snorkeling trips, maybe an empty wine bottle or two. It is the TV that keeps us going, from *Jerry* to *Sally* to *Hawaii Five-O* and then on to the soaps. If there's something especially arresting, like "Won't Take No for an Answer" on *Jerry*, we sit down on the edge of a bed and giggle for a moment as if this were a pajama party instead of a terminally dead-end job. The soaps are the best, and Carla turns the volume up full blast so that she won't miss anything from the bathroom or while the vacuum is on. In room 503, Marcia confronts Jeff about Lauren. In 505, Lauren taunts poor cuckolded Marcia. In 511, Helen offers Amanda $10,000 to stop seeing Eric, prompting Carla to emerge from the bathroom to study Amanda's troubled face. "You take it, girl," she advises. "I would for sure."

The tourists' rooms that we clean and, beyond them, the far more expensively appointed interiors in the soaps, begin after a while to merge. We have entered a better world—a world of comfort where every day is a day off, waiting to be filled up with sexual intrigue. We, however, are only gatecrashers in this fantasy, forced to pay for our presence with backaches and perpetual thirst. The mirrors, and there are far too many of them in hotel rooms, contain the kind of person you would normally find pushing a shopping cart down a city street—bedraggled, dressed in a damp hotel polo shirt two sizes too large, and with sweat dribbling down her chin like drool. I am enormously relieved when Carla announces a half-hour meal break, but my appetite fades when I see that the bag of hot-dog rolls she has been carrying around on our cart is not trash salvaged from a checkout but what she has brought for her lunch.

When I request permission to leave at about 3:30, another housekeeper warns me that no one has so far succeeded in combining housekeeping at the hotel with serving at Jerry's: "Some kid did it once for five days, and you're no kid." With that helpful information in mind, I rush back to number 46, down four Advils (the name brand this time), shower, stooping to fit into the stall, and attempt to compose myself for the oncoming shift. So much for what Marx termed the "reproduction of labor power," meaning the things a worker has to do just so she'll be ready to work again. The only unforeseen obstacle to the smooth transition from job to job is that my tan Jerry's slacks, which had looked reasonably clean by 40-watt bulb last night when I handwashed my Hawaiian shirt, prove by daylight to be mottled with ketchup and ranch-dressing stains. I spend most of my hour-long break between jobs attempting to remove the edible portions with a sponge and then drying the slacks over the hood of my car in the sun.

I can do this two-job thing, is my theory, if I can drink enough caffeine and avoid getting distracted by George's ever more obvious suffering.[7] The first few days after being caught he seemed not to understand the trouble he was in, and our chirpy little conversations had continued. But the last couple of shifts he's been listless and unshaven, and tonight he looks like the ghost we all know him to be, with dark half-moons hanging from his eyes. At one point, when I am

---

[7]In 1996, the number of persons holding two or more jobs averaged 7.8 million, or 6.2 percent of the workforce. It was about the same rate for men and for women (6.1 versus 6.2), though the kinds of jobs differ by gender. About two thirds of multiple jobholders work one job full-time and the other part-time. Only a heroic minority—4 percent of men and 2 percent of women—work two full-time jobs simultaneously. (From John F. Stinson Jr., "New Data on Multiple Jobholding Available from the CPS," in the *Monthly Labor Review*, March 1997.)

briefly immobilized by the task of filling little paper cups with sour cream for baked potatoes, he comes over and looks as if he'd like to explore the limits of our shared vocabulary, but I am called to the floor for a table. I resolve to give him all my tips that night and to hell with the experiment in low-wage money management. At eight, Ellen and I grab a snack together standing at the mephitic end of the kitchen counter, but I can only manage two or three mozzarella sticks and lunch had been a mere handful of McNuggets. I am not tired at all, I assure myself, though it may be that there is simply no more "I" left to do the tiredness monitoring. What I would see, if I were more alert to the situation, is that the forces of destruction are already massing against me. There is only one cook on duty, a young man named Jesus ("Hay-Sue," that is) and he is new to the job. And there is Joy, who shows up to take over in the middle of the shift, wearing high heels and a long, clingy white dress and fuming as if she'd just been stood up in some cocktail bar.

Then it comes, the perfect storm. Four of my tables fill up at once. Four tables is nothing for me now, but only so long as they are obligingly staggered. As I bev table 27, tables 25, 28, and 24 are watching enviously. As I bev 25, 24 glowers because their bevs haven't even been ordered. Twenty-eight is four yuppyish types, meaning everything on the side and agonizing instructions as to the chicken Caesars. Twenty-five is a middle-aged black couple, who complain, with some justice, that the iced tea isn't fresh and the tabletop is sticky. But table 24 is the meteorological event of the century: ten British tourists who seem to have made the decision to absorb the American experience entirely by mouth. Here everyone has at least two drinks—iced tea and milk shake, Michelob and water (with lemon slice, please)—and a huge promiscuous orgy of breakfast specials, mozz sticks, chicken strips, quesadillas, burgers with cheese and without, sides of hash browns with cheddar, with onions, with gravy, seasoned fries, plain fries, banana splits. Poor Jesus! Poor me! Because when I arrive with their first tray of food—after three prior trips just to refill bevs—Princess Di refuses to eat her chicken strips with her pancake-and-sausage special, since, as she now reveals, the strips were meant to be an appetizer. Maybe the others would have accepted their meals, but Di, who is deep into her third Michelob, insists that everything else go back while they work on their "starters." Meanwhile, the yuppies are waving me down for more decaf and the black couple looks ready to summon the NAACP.

Much of what happened next is lost in the fog of war. Jesus starts going under. The little printer on the counter in front of him is spewing out orders faster than he can rip them off, much less produce the meals. Even the invincible Ellen is ashen from stress. I bring table 24 their reheated main courses, which they immediately reject as either too cold or fossilized by the microwave. When I return to the kitchen with their trays (three trays in three trips), Joy confronts me with arms akimbo: "What is this?" She means the food—the plates of rejected pancakes, hash browns in assorted flavors, toasts, burgers, sausages, eggs. "Uh, scrambled with cheddar," I try, "and that's . . ." "NO," she screams in my face. "Is it a traditional, a super-scramble, an eye-opener?" I pretend to study my check for a clue, but entropy has been up to its tricks, not only on the plates but in my head, and I have to admit that the original order is beyond reconstruction. "You don't know an eye-opener from a traditional?" she demands in outrage. All I know, in fact, is that my legs have lost interest in the current venture and have announced their intention to fold. I am saved by a yuppie (mercifully not one of mine) who chooses this moment to charge into the kitchen to bellow that his food is twenty-five minutes late. Joy screams at him to get the hell out of her kitchen, please, and then turns on Jesus in a fury, hurling an empty tray across the room for emphasis.

I leave. I don't walk out, I just leave. I don't finish my side work or pick up my credit-card tips, if any, at the cash register or, of course, ask Joy's permission to go. And the surprising thing is that you *can* walk out without permission, that the door opens, that the thick tropical night air parts to let me pass, that my car is still parked where I left it. There is no vindication in this exit, no fuck-you surge of relief, just an overwhelming, dank sense of failure pressing down on me and the entire parking lot. I had gone into this venture in the spirit of science, to test a mathematical proposition, but somewhere along the line, in the tunnel vision imposed by long shifts and relentless concentration, it became a test of myself, and clearly I have failed. Not only had I flamed out as a housekeeper/server, I had even forgotten to give George my tips, and, for reasons perhaps best known to hardworking, generous people like Gail and Ellen, this hurts. I don't cry, but I am in a position to realize, for the first time in many years, that the tear ducts are still there, and still capable of doing their job.

*   *   *

When I moved out of the trailer park, I gave the key to number 46 to Gail and arranged for my deposit to be transferred to her. She told me that Joan is still living in her van and that Stu had been fired from the Hearthside. I never found out what happened to George.

In one month, I had earned approximately $1,040 and spent $517 on food, gas, toiletries, laundry, phone, and utilities. If I had remained in my $500 efficiency, I would have been able pay the rent and have $22 left over (which is $78 less than the cash I had in my pocket at the start of the month). During this time I bought no clothing except for the required slacks and no prescription drugs or medical care (I did finally buy some vitamin B to compensate for the lack of vegetables in my diet). Perhaps I could have saved a little on food if I had gotten to a supermarket more often, instead of convenience stores, but it should be noted that I lost almost four pounds in four weeks, on a diet weighted heavily toward burgers and fries.

How former welfare recipients and single mothers will (and do) survive in the low-wage workforce, I cannot imagine. Maybe they will figure out how to condense their lives—including child-raising, laundry, romance, and meals—into the couple of hours between full-time jobs. Maybe they will take up residence in their vehicles, if they have one. All I know is that I couldn't hold two jobs and I couldn't make enough money to live on with one. And I had advantages unthinkable to many of the long-term poor—health, stamina, a working car, and no children to care for and support. Certainly nothing in my experience contradicts the conclusion of Kathryn Edin and Laura Lein, in their recent book *Making Ends Meet: How Single Mothers Survive Welfare and Low-Wage Work*, that low-wage work actually involves more hardship and deprivation than life at the mercy of the welfare state. In the coming months and years, economic conditions for the working poor are bound to worsen, even without the almost inevitable recession. As mentioned earlier, the influx of former welfare recipients into the low-skilled workforce will have a depressing effect on both wages and the number of jobs available. A general economic downturn will only enhance these effects, and the working poor will of course be facing it without the slight, but nonetheless often saving, protection of welfare as a backup.

The thinking behind welfare reform was that even the humblest jobs are morally uplifting and psychologically buoying. In reality they are likely to be fraught with insult and stress. But I did discover one redeeming feature of the most abject low-wage work—the camaraderie of people who are, in almost all cases, far too smart and funny and caring for the work they do and the wages they're paid. The hope, of course, is that someday these people will come to know what they're worth, and take appropriate action. ∎

Responding to Reading

1. What are your initial comments, reflections, and questions after having read this essay? Did it challenge any of your prior assumptions or beliefs about work, welfare, the minimum wage, or economic mobility?

2. Describe Ehrenreich's writing style, citing examples from the text to illustrate your points.

3. Ehrenreich employs some statistics in the body of her essay and some in the footnotes. Why might she have opted for this arrangement?

4. Revisit Ehrenreich's accounts of low-wage people struggling to find and maintain housing and health care. What are some possible solutions to those problems?

5. Reread the final paragraph of the essay. What might Ehrenreich mean when she ends with "take appropriate action"? To which possible kind (or kinds) of action is she referring?

6. Articulate connections and comparisons between Ehrenreich's essay and Bambara's "The Lesson." In what ways do they participate in a similar kind of "social imagination"? Where do they depart?

Short Story: Lesléa Newman, A *Letter to Harvey Milk*

Lesléa Newman is the author of more than 30 books for adults and children, including Heather Has Two Mommies, Writing from the Heart, In Every Laugh a Tear, *and* Still Life with Buddy. *The following short story is from the collection* A Letter to Harvey Milk and Other Stories. *The story has also been made into a film and adapted for the stage.*

I.

The teacher says we should write about our life, everything that happened today. So *nu*, what's there to tell? Why should today be different than any other day? May 5, 1986. I get up, I have myself a coffee, a little cottage cheese, half an English muffin. I get dressed. I straighten up the house a little, nobody should drop by and see I'm such a slob. I go down to the Senior Center and see what's doing. I play a little cards, I have some lunch, a bagel with cheese. I read a sign in the cafeteria, Writing Class 2:00. I think to myself, why not, something to pass the time. So at two o'clock I go in. The teacher says we should write about our life.

Listen, I want to say to this teacher, I. B. Singer I'm not. You think anybody cares what I did all day? Even my own children, may they live and be well, don't call. You think the whole world is waiting to see what Harry Weinberg had for breakfast?

The teacher is young and nice. She says everybody has something important to say. Yeah, sure, when you're young you believe things like that. She has short brown hair and big eyes, a nice figure, *zaftig* like my poor Fannie, may she rest in peace. She's wearing a Star of David around her neck, hanging from a purple string, that's nice. She gave us all notebooks and told us we're gonna write something every day, and if we want we can even write at home. Who'd a thunk it, me—Harry Weinberg, seventy-seven years old—scribbling in a notebook like a schoolgirl. Why not, it passes the time.

So after the class I go to the store, I pick myself up a little orange juice, a few bagels, a nice piece of chicken, I shouldn't starve to death. I go up, I put on my slippers, I eat the chicken, I watch a little TV, I write in this notebook, I get ready for bed. *Nu*, for this somebody should give me a Pulitzer Prize?

II.

Today the teacher tells us something about herself. She's a Jew, this we know from the *Mogen David* she wears around her neck. She tells us she wants to collect stories from old Jewish people, to preserve our history. *Oy*, such stories that I could tell her, shouldn't be preserved by nobody. She tells us she's learning Yiddish. For what, I wonder. I can't figure this teacher out. She's young, she's pretty, she shouldn't be with the old people so much. I wonder is she married. She doesn't wear a ring. Her grandparents won't tell her stories, she says, and she's worried that the Jews her age won't know nothing about the culture, about life in the *shtetls*. Believe me, life in the *shtetl* is nothing worth knowing about. Hunger and more hunger. Better off we're here in America, the past is past.

Then she gives us our homework, the homework we write in the class, it's a little *meshugeh*, but alright. She wants us to write a letter to somebody from our past, somebody who's no longer with us. She reads us a letter a child wrote to Abraham Lincoln, like an example. Right away I see everybody's getting nervous. So I raise my hand. "Teacher," I say, "you can tell me maybe how to address such a letter? There's a few things I've wanted to ask my wife for a long time." Everybody laughs. Then they start to write.

I sit for a few minutes, thinking about Fannie, thinking about my sister Frieda, my mother, my father, may they all rest in peace. But it's the strangest thing, the one I really want to write to is Harvey.

Dear Harvey:

You had to go get yourself killed for being a *faygeleh*? You couldn't let somebody else have such a great honor? Alright, alright, so you liked the boys, I wasn't wild about the idea. But I got used to it. I never said you wasn't welcome in my house, did I?

Nu, Harvey, you couldn't leave well enough alone? You had your own camera store, your own business, what's bad? You couldn't keep still about the boys, you weren't satisfied until the whole world knew? Harvey Milk, with the big ears and the big ideas, had to go make himself something, a big politician. I know, I know, I said, "Harvey, make something of yourself, don't be an old *shmegeggle* like me, Harry the butcher." So now I'm eating my words, and they stick like a chicken bone in my old throat.

It's a rotten world, Harvey, and rottener still without you in it. You know what happened to that *momzer*, Dan White? They let him out of jail, and he goes and kills himself so nobody else should have the pleasure. Now you know me, Harvey, I'm not a violent man. But this was too much, even for me. In the old country, I saw things you shouldn't know from, things you couldn't imagine one person could do to another. But here in America, a man climbs through the window, kills the Mayor of San Francisco, kills Harvey Milk, and a couple years later he's walking around on the street? This I never thought I'd see in my whole life. But from a country that kills the Rosenbergs, I should expect something different?

Harvey, you should be glad you weren't around for the trial. I read about it in the papers. The lawyer, that son of a bitch, said Dan White ate too many Twinkies the night before he killed you, so his brain wasn't working right. Twinkies, *nu*, I ask you. My kids ate Twinkies when they were little, did they grow up to be murderers, God forbid? And now, do they take the Twinkies down from the shelf, somebody else shouldn't go a little crazy, climb through a window, and shoot somebody? No, they leave them right there next to the cupcakes and the donuts, to torture me every time I go to the store to pick up a few things, I shouldn't starve to death.

Harvey, I think I'm losing my mind. You know what I do every week? Every week I go to the store, I buy a bag of jellybeans for you, you should have something to *nosh* on, I remember what a sweet tooth you have. I put them in a jar on the table, in case you should come in with another crazy petition for me to sign. Sometimes I think you're gonna just walk through my door and tell me it was another *meshugeh* publicity stunt.

Harvey, now I'm gonna tell you something. The night you died the whole city of San Francisco cried for you. Thirty thousand people marched in the street, I saw it on TV. Me, I didn't go down. I'm an old man, I don't walk so good, they said there might be riots. But no, there were no riots. Just people walking in the street, quiet, each one with a candle, until the street looked like the sky all lit up with a million stars. Old people, young people, Black people, white people, Chinese people. You name it, they were there. I remember thinking, Harvey must be so proud, and then I remembered you were dead and such a lump rose in my throat, like a grapefruit it was, and then the tears ran down my face like rain. Can you imagine, Harvey, an old man like me, sitting alone in his apartment, crying and carrying on like a baby? But it's the God's truth. Never did I carry on so in all my life.

And then all of a sudden I got mad. I yelled at the people on TV: for getting shot you made him into such a hero? You couldn't march for him when he was alive, he couldn't *shep* a little *naches*?

But *nu*, what good does getting mad do, it only makes my pressure go up. So I took myself a pill, calmed myself down.

Then they made speeches for you, Harvey. The same people who called you a *schmuck* when you were alive, now you were dead, they were calling you a *mensh.* You were a *mensh,* Harvey, a *mensh* with a heart of gold. You were too good for this rotten world. They just weren't ready for you.

Oy Harveleh, alav ha-sholom,
Harry

III.

Today the teacher asks me to stay for a minute after class. *Oy,* what did I do wrong now, I wonder. Maybe she didn't like my letter to Harvey? Who knows?

After the class she comes and sits down next to me. She's wearing purple pants and a white T-shirt. *"Feh,"* I can just hear Fannie say. "God forbid she should wear a skirt? Show off her figure a little? The girls today dressing like boys and the boys dressing like girls—this I don't understand."

"Mr. Weinberg," the teacher says.

"Call me Harry," I says.

"O.K., Harry," she says. "I really liked the letter you wrote to Harvey Milk. It was terrific, really. It meant a lot to me. It even made me cry."

I can't even believe my own ears. My letter to Harvey Milk made the teacher cry?

"You see, Harry," she says, "I'm gay, too. And there aren't many Jewish people your age that are so open-minded. At least that I know. So your letter gave me lots of hope. In fact, I was wondering if you'd consider publishing it."

Publishing my letter? Again I couldn't believe my own ears. Who would want to read a letter from Harry Weinberg to Harvey Milk? No, I tell her. I'm too old for fame and glory. I like the writing class, it passes the time. But what I write is my own business. The teacher looks sad for a moment, like a cloud passes over her eyes. Then she says, "Tell me about Harvey Milk. How did you meet him? What was he like?" *Nu,* Harvey, you were a pain in the ass when you were alive, you're still a pain in the ass now that you're dead. Everybody wants to hear about Harvey.

So I tell her. I tell her how I came into the camera shop one day with a roll of film from when I went to visit the grandchildren. How we started talking, and I said, "Milk, that's not such a common name. Are you related to the Milks in Woodmere?" And so we found out we were practically neighbors forty years ago, when the children were young, before we moved out here. Gracie was almost the same age as Harvey, a couple years older, maybe, but they went to different schools. Still, Harvey leans across the counter and gives me such a hug, like I'm his own father.

I tell her more about Harvey, how he didn't believe there was a good *kosher* butcher in San Francisco, how he came to my store just to see. But all the time I'm talking I'm thinking to myself, no, it can't be true. Such a gorgeous girl like this goes with the girls, not with the boys? Such a *shanda*. Didn't God in His wisdom make a girl a girl and a boy a boy—boom they should meet, boom they should get married, boom they should have babies, and that's the way it is? Harvey I loved like my own son, but this I never could understand. And *nu*, why was the teacher telling me this, it's my business who she sleeps with? She has some sadness in her eyes, this teacher. Believe me I've known such sadness in my life. I can recognize it a hundred miles away. Maybe she's lonely. Maybe after class one day I'll take her out for a coffee, we'll talk a little bit, I'll find out.

IV.

It's 3:00 in the morning, I can't sleep. So *nu*, here I am with this crazy notebook. Who am I kidding, maybe I think I'm Yitzhak Peretz? What would the children think, to see their old father sitting up in his bathrobe with a cup of tea, scribbling in his notebook? *Oy, meyn kinder*, they should only live and be well and call their old father once in a while.

Fannie used to keep up with them. She could be such a *nudge*, my Fannie. "What's the matter, you're too good to call your old mother once in a while?" she'd yell into the phone. Then there'd be a pause. "Busy-shmusy," she'd yell even louder. "Was I too busy to change your diapers? Was I too busy to put food into your mouth?" *Oy*, I haven't got the strength, but Fannie could she yell and carry on.

You know sometimes, in the middle of the night, I'll reach across the bed for Fannie's hand. Without even thinking, like my hand got a mind of its own, it creeps across the bed, looking for Fannie's hand. After all this time, fourteen years she's been dead, but still, a man gets used to a few things. Forty-two years, the body doesn't forget. And my little *Faigl* had such hands, little *hentelehs*, tiny like a child's. But strong. Strong from kneading *challah*, from scrubbing clothes, from rubbing the children's backs to put them to sleep. My Fannie, she was so ashamed from those hands. After thirty-five years of marriage when finally, I could afford to buy her a diamond ring, she said no. She said it was too late already, she'd be ashamed. A girl needs nice hands to show off a diamond, her hands were already ruined, better yet buy a new stove.

Ruined? *Feh*. To me her hands were beautiful. Small, with veins running through them like rivers, and cracks in the skin like the desert. A hundred times I've kicked myself for not buying Fannie that ring.

V.

Today in the writing class the teacher read my notebook. Then she says I should make a poem about Fannie. "A poem," I says to her, "now Shakespeare you want I should be?" She says I have a good eye for detail. I says to her, "Excuse me Teacher, you live with a woman for forty-two years, you start to notice a few things."

She helps me. We do it together, we write a poem called "Fannie's Hands":

> Fannie's hands are two little birds
> that fly into her lap.
> Her veins are like rivers.
> Her skin is cracked like the desert.
> Her strong little hands
> baked *challah*, scrubbed clothes,
> rubbed the children's backs.
> Her strong little hands
> and my big clumsy hands
> fit together in the night
> like pieces of a jigsaw puzzle
> made in Heaven, by God.

So *nu*, who says you can't teach an old dog new tricks? I read it to the class and such a fuss they made. "A regular Romeo," one of them says. "If only my husband, may he live and be well, would write such a poem for me," says another. I wish Fannie was still alive. I could read it to her. Even the teacher was happy, I could tell, but still, there was a ring of sadness around her eyes.

After the class I waited till everybody left, they shouldn't get the wrong idea, and I asked the teacher would she like to go get a coffee. "*Nu*, it's enough writing already," I said. "Come, let's have a little treat."

So we take a walk, it's a nice day. We find a diner, nothing fancy, but clean and quiet. I try to buy her a piece of cake, a sandwich maybe, but no, all she wants is coffee.

So we sit and talk a little. She wants to know about my childhood in the old country, she wants to know about the boat ride to America, she wants to know did my parents speak Yiddish to me when I was growing up. "Harry," she says to me, "when I hear old people talking Yiddish, it's like a love letter blowing in the wind. I try to run after them, and sometimes I catch a phrase that makes me cry or a word that makes me laugh. Even if I don't understand, it always touches my heart."

Oy, this teacher has some strange ideas. "Why do you want to speak Jewish?" I ask her. "Here in America, everybody speaks English. You don't need it. What's done is done, what's past is past. You shouldn't go with the old people so much. You should go out, make friends, have a good time. You got some troubles you want to talk about? Maybe I shouldn't pry," I say, "but you shouldn't look so sad, a young girl like you. When you're old you got plenty to be sad. You shouldn't think about the old days so much, let the dead rest in peace. What's done is done."

I took a swallow of my coffee, to calm down my nerves. I was getting a little too excited.

"Harry, listen to me," the teacher says. "I'm thirty years old and no one in my family will talk to me because I'm gay. It's all Harvey Milk's fault. He made such an impression on me. You know, when he died, what he said, 'If a bullet enters my brain, let that bullet destroy every closet door.' So when he died, I came out to everyone—the people at work, my parents. I felt it was my duty, so the Dan Whites of the world wouldn't be able to get away with it. I mean, if every single gay person came out—just think of it!—everyone would see they had a gay friend or a gay brother or a gay cousin or a gay teacher. Then they couldn't say things like 'Those gays should be shot.' Because they'd be saying you should shoot my neighbor or my sister or my daughter's best friend."

I never saw the teacher get so excited before. Maybe a politician she should be. She reminded me a little bit of Harvey.

"So *nu*, what's the problem?" I ask.

"The problem is my parents," she says with a sigh, and such a sigh I never heard from a young person before. "My parents haven't spoken to me since I told them I was gay. 'How could you do this to us?' they said. I wasn't doing anything to them. I tried to explain I couldn't help being gay, like I couldn't help being a Jew, but that they didn't want to hear. So I haven't spoken to them in eight years."

"Eight years, *Gottenyu*," I say to her. This I never heard in my whole life. A father and a mother cut off their own daughter like that. Better they should cut off their own hand. I thought about Gracie, a perfect daughter she's not, but your child is your child. When she married the *Goy*, Fannie threatened to put her head in the oven, but she got over it. Not to see your own daughter for eight years, and such a smart, gorgeous girl, such a good teacher, what a *shanda*.

So what can I do, I ask. Does she want me to talk to them, a letter maybe I could write. Does she want I should adopt her, the hell with them, I make a little joke. She smiles. "Just talking to you makes me feel better," she says. So *nu*, now I'm Harry the social worker. She says that's why she wants the old people's stories so much, she doesn't know nothing from her own family history. She wants to know about her own people, maybe write a book. But it's hard to get the people to talk to her, she says, she doesn't understand.

"Listen, Teacher," I tell her. "These old people have stories you shouldn't know from. What's there to tell? Hunger and more hunger. Suffering and more suffering. I buried my sister over twenty years ago, my mother, my father—all dead. You think I could just start talking about them like I just saw them yesterday? You think I don't think about them every day? Right here I keep them," I say, pointing to my heart. "I try to forget them, I should live in peace, the dead are gone. Talking about them won't bring them back. You want stories, go talk to somebody else. I ain't got no stories."

I sat down then. I didn't even know I was standing up, I got so excited. Everybody in the diner was looking at me, a crazy man shouting at a young girl.

Oy, and now the teacher was crying. "I'm sorry," I says to her. "You want another coffee?"

"No thanks, Harry," she says. "I'm sorry, too."

"Forget it. We can just pretend it never happened," I say, and then we go.

VI.

All this crazy writing has shaken me up inside a little bit. Yesterday I was walking home from the diner, I thought I saw Harvey walking in front of me. No, it can't be, I says to myself, and my heart started to pound so, I got afraid I shouldn't drop dead in the street from a heart attack. But then the man turned around and it wasn't Harvey. It didn't even look like him at all.

I got myself upstairs and took myself a pill, I could feel my pressure was going up. All this talk about the past—Fannie, Harvey, Frieda, my mother, my father—what good does it do? This teacher and her crazy ideas. Did I ever ask my mother, my father, what their childhood was like? What nonsense. Better I shouldn't know.

So today is Saturday, no writing class, but still I'm writing in this crazy notebook. I ask myself, Harry, what can I do to make you feel a little better? And I answer myself, make me a nice chicken soup.

You think an old man like me can't make chicken soup? Let me tell you, on all the holidays it was Harry that made the soup. Every *Pesach* it was Harry skimming the *shmaltz* from the top of the pot, it was Harry making the *kreplach*. I ask you, where is it written that a man shouldn't know from chicken soup?

So I take myself down to the store, I buy myself a nice chicken, some carrots, some celery, some parsley—onions I already got, parsnips I can do without. I'm afraid I shouldn't have a heart attack *shlepping* all that food up the steps, but thank God, I make it alright.

I put up the pot with water, throw everything in one-two-three, and soon the whole house smells from chicken soup.

I remember the time Harvey came to visit and there I was with my apron on, skimming the *shmaltz* from the soup. Did he kid me about that! The only way I could get him to keep still was to invite him to dinner. "Listen, Harvey," I says to him. "Whether you're a man or a woman, it doesn't matter. You gotta learn to cook. When you're old, nobody cares. Nobody will do for you. You gotta learn to do for yourself."

"I won't live past fifty, Har," he says, smearing a piece of rye bread with *shmaltz.*

"Nobody wants to grow old, believe me, I know," I says to him. "But listen, it's not so terrible. What's the alternative? Nobody wants to die young, either." I take off my apron and sit down with him.

"No, I mean it Harry," he says to me with his mouth full. "I won't make it to fifty. I've always known it. I'm a politician. A gay politician. Someone's gonna take a pot shot at me. It's a risk you gotta take."

The way he said it, I tell you, a chill ran down my back like I never felt before. He was forty-seven at the time, just a year before he died.

VII.

Today after the writing class, the teacher tells us she's going away for two days. Everyone makes a big fuss, the class they like so much already. She tells us she's sorry, something came up she has to do. She says we can come have class without her, the room will be open, we can read to each other what we write in our notebooks. Someone asks her what we should write about.

"Write me a letter," she says, "Write a story called 'What I Never Told Anyone.'"

So, after everyone leaves, I ask her does she want to go out, have a coffee, but she says no, she has to go home and pack.

I tell her wherever she's going she should have a good time.

"Thanks, Harry," she says. "You'll be here when I get back?"

"Sure," I tell her. "I like this crazy writing. It passes the time."

She swings a big black bookbag onto her shoulder, a regular Hercules this teacher is, and she smiles at me. "I gotta run, Harry. Have a good week." She turns and walks away and something on her bookbag catches my eye. A big shiny pin that spells out her name all fancy-shmancy in rhinestones: Barbara. And under that, right away I see sewn onto her bookbag an upside-down pink triangle.

I stop in my tracks, stunned. No, it can't be, I says to myself. Maybe it's just a design? Maybe she doesn't know from this? My heart is beating fast now, I know I should go home, take myself a pill, my pressure, I can feel it going up.

But I just stand there. And then I get mad. What, she thinks maybe I'm blind as well as old, I can't see what's right in front of my nose? Or maybe we don't remember such things? What right does she have to walk in here with that, that thing on her bag, to remind us of what we been through? Haven't we seen enough?

Stories she wants. She wants we should cut our hearts open and give her stories so she could write a book. Well, alright, now I'll tell her a story.

This is what I never told anyone. One day, maybe seven, eight years ago—no, maybe longer, I think Harvey was still alive—one day Izzie comes knocking on my door. I open the door and there's Izzie, standing there, his face white as a sheet. I bring him inside, I make him a coffee. "Izzie, what is it," I says to him. "Something happened to the children, to the grandchildren, God forbid?"

He sits down, he doesn't drink his coffee. He looks through me like I'm not even there. Then he says, "Harry, I'm walking down the street, you know I had a little lunch at the Center, and then I come outside, I see a young man, maybe twenty-five, a good-looking guy, walking toward me. He's wearing black pants, a white shirt, and on his shirt he's got a pink triangle."

"So," I says. "A pink triangle, a purple triangle, they wear all kinds of crazy things these days."

"*Heshel*," he tells me, "don't you understand? The gays are wearing pink triangles just like the war, just like in the camps."

No, this I can't believe. Why would they do a thing like that? But if Izzie says it, it must be true. Who would make up such a thing?

"He looked a little bit like *Yussl*," Izzie says, and then he begins to cry, and such a cry like I never heard. Like a baby he was, with the tears streaming down his cheeks and his shoulders shaking with great big sobs. Such moans and groans I never heard from a grown man in all my life. I thought maybe he was gonna have a heart attack the way he was carrying on. I didn't know what to do. I was afraid the neighbors would hear, they shouldn't call the police, such sounds he was making. Fifty-eight years old he was, but he looked like a little boy sitting there, sniffling. And who was *Yussl*? Thirty years we'd been friends, and I never heard from *Yussl*.

So finally, I put my arms around him, and I held him, I didn't know what else to do. His body was shaking so, I thought his bones would crack from knocking against each other. Soon his body got quiet, but then all of a sudden his mouth got noisy.

"Listen, *Heshel*, I got to tell you something, something I never told nobody in my whole life. I was young in the camps, nineteen, maybe twenty when they took us away." The words poured from his mouth like a flood. "*Yussl* was my best friend in the camps. Already I saw my mother, my father, my Hannah marched off to the ovens. *Yussl* was the only one I had to hold on to.

"One morning, during the selection, they pointed me to the right, *Yussl* to the left. I went a little crazy, I ran after him. 'No, he stays with me, they made a mistake,' I said, and I grabbed him by the hand and dragged him back in line. Why the guard didn't kill us right then, I couldn't tell you. Nothing made sense in that place.

Yussl and I slept together on a wooden bench. That night I couldn't sleep. It happened pretty often in that place. I would close my eyes and see such things that would make me scream in the night, and for that I could get shot. I don't know what was worse, asleep or awake. All I saw was suffering.

"On this night, *Yussl* was awake, too. He didn't move a muscle, but I could tell. Finally he said my name, just a whisper, but something broke in me and I began to cry. He put his arms around me and we cried together, such a close call we'd had.

"And then he began to kiss me. 'You saved my life,' he whispered, and he kissed my eyes, my cheeks, my lips. And Harry, I kissed him back. Harry, I never told nobody this before. I, we . . . we, you know, that was such a place that hell, I couldn't help it. The warmth of his body was just too much for me and Hannah was dead already and we would soon be dead too, probably, so what did it matter?"

He looked up at me then, the tears streaming from his eyes. "It's O.K., Izzie," I said. "Maybe I would have done the same."

"There's more, Harry," he says, and I got him a tissue, he should blow his nose. What more could there be?

"This went on for a couple of months maybe, just every once in a while when we couldn't sleep. He'd whisper my name and I'd answer with his, and then we'd, you know, we'd touch each other. We were very, very quiet, but who knows, maybe some other boys in the barracks were doing the same.

"To this day I don't know how it happened, but somehow someone found out. One day *Yussl* didn't come back to the barracks at night. I went almost crazy, you can imagine, all the things that went through my mind, the things they might have done to him, those lousy Nazis. I looked everywhere, I asked everyone, three days he was gone. And then on the third day, they lined us up after supper and there they had *Yussl*. I almost collapsed on the ground when I saw him. They had him on his knees with his hands tied behind his back. His face was swollen so, you couldn't even see his eyes. His clothes were stained with blood. And on his uniform they had sewn a pink triangle, big, twice the size of our yellow stars.

"*Oy*, did they beat him but good. 'Who's your friend?' they yelled at him. 'Tell us and we'll let you live.' But no, he wouldn't tell. He knew they were lying, he knew they'd kill us both. They asked him again and again, 'Who's your friend? Tell us which one he is.' And every time he said no, they'd crack him with a whip until the blood ran from him like a river. Such a sight he was, like I've never seen. How he remained conscious I'll never know.

"Everything inside me was broken after that. I wanted to run to his side, but I didn't dare, so afraid I was. At one point he looked at me, right in the eye, as though he was saying, *Izzie, save yourself. Me, I'm finished, but you, you got a chance to live through this and tell the world our story.*

"Right after he looked at me, he collapsed, and they shot him, Harry, right there in front of us. Even after he was dead they kicked him in the head a little bit. They left his body out there for two days, as a warning to us. They whipped us all that night, and from then on we had to sleep with all the lights on and with our hands on top of the blankets. Anyone caught with their hands under the blankets would be shot.

"He died for me, Harry, they killed him for that, was it such a terrible thing? *Oy*, I haven't thought about *Yussl* for twenty-five years maybe, but when I saw that kid on the street today, it was too much." And then he started crying again, and he clung to me like a child.

So what could I do? I was afraid he shouldn't have a heart attack, maybe he was having a nervous breakdown, maybe I should get the doctor. *Vay iss mir,* I never saw anybody so upset in my whole life. And such a story, *Gottenyu.*

"Izzie, come lie down," I says, and I took him by the hand to the bed. I laid him down, I took off his shoes, and still he was crying. So what could I do? I lay down with him, I held him tight. I told him he was safe, he was in America. I don't know what else I said, I don't think he heard me, still he kept crying.

I stroked his head, I held him tight. "Izzie, it's alright," I said. "Izzie, Izzie, *Izzaleh.*" I said his name over and over, like a lullaby, until his crying got quiet. He said my name once softly, *Heshel,* or maybe he said *Yussl,* I don't remember, but thank God he finally fell asleep. I tried to get up from the bed, but Izzie held onto me tight. So what could I do? Izzie was my friend for thirty years, for him I would do anything. So I held him all night long, and he slept like a baby.

And this is what I never told nobody, not even Harvey. That there in that bed, where Fannie and I slept together for forty-two years, me and Izzie spent the night. Me, I didn't sleep a wink, such a lump in my throat I had, like the night Harvey died.

Izzie passed on a couple months after that. I saw him a few more times, and he seemed different somehow. How, I couldn't say. We never talked about that night. But now that he had told someone his deepest secret, he was ready to go, he could die in peace. Maybe now that I told, I can die in peace, too?

VIII.

Dear Teacher:

You said write what you never told nobody, and write you a letter. I always did all my homework, such a student I was. So *nu,* I got to tell you something. I can't write in this notebook no more, I can't come no more to the class. I don't want you should take offense, you're a good teacher and a nice girl. But me, I'm an old man, I don't sleep so good at night, these stories are like a knife in my heart. Harvey, Fannie, Izzie, *Yussl,* my father, my mother, let them all rest in peace. The dead are gone. Better to live for today. What good does remembering do, it doesn't bring back the dead. Let them rest in peace.

But Teacher, I want you should have my notebook. It doesn't have nice stories in it, no love letters, no happy endings for a nice girl like you. A bestseller it ain't, I guarantee. Maybe you'll put it in a book someday, the world shouldn't forget.

Meanwhile, good luck to you, Teacher. May you live and be well and not get shot in the head like poor Harvey, may he rest in peace. Maybe someday we'll go out, have a coffee again, who knows? But me, I'm too old for this crazy writing. I remember too much, the pen is like a knife twisting in my heart.

One more thing, Teacher. Between parents and children, it's not so easy. Believe me, I know. Don't give up on them. One father, one mother, it's all you got. If you were my *tochter*, I'd be proud of you.

Harry   ■

Responding to Reading

1. Do some research on the real-life Harvey Milk. Why would Newman choose to feature him in her title?

2. Harry has a distinctive narrative voice. Describe it. Why does Newman include Yiddish words and phrases in Harry's thoughts and dialogue?

3. Locate two or three turning points in the story. How and why do characters change at these pivotal moments?

4. Analyze one of the recurring themes or motifs of the story. Themes and motifs you might consider include memory, trauma, oppression, writing, intergenerational conflict/connection, and cultural/religious/sexual identity.

5. Examine the relationships of parents and children, older and younger generations. How do different generations conflict, connect, and interact in the narrative?

6. Consider the role of memory—both personal memory and collective memory. How do the teacher and Harry seek to remember and/or forget memories? How do they deal with memories and with trauma? What might the story be suggesting about the roles of memory and history for us?

7. Attempt to create a psychological interpretation of the story. Consider the traumas that both Harry and the teacher have experienced. What psychological processes do they go through in dealing with them? Research Freud's notion of "the return of the repressed" and apply it. You might also consider the role that writing, in particular, plays in the process of healing and reconciliation for Harry and the teacher.

8. List the various ways that characters employ writing in the story. Include the kinds of writing, the purposes for the writing, and the effects of the writing (for both the writer and the receiver).

9. Consider the different kinds of oppression and violence that surface. How are they different? How might they be related? How might this story inform our understanding of oppression and violence?

10. Han Suyin, a Chinese physician and writer, said, "Truth, like surgery, may hurt, but it cures." Consider this quotation in relationship to Newman's story.

WRITING TO DISCOVER

Both "The Lesson" and "A Letter to Harvey Milk" center on characters that enter new communities as teachers, and both are narrated by learners. Write down at least three characteristics of the teachers and learners in each of these two stories. Then compare and analyze the teacher/learner dynamics that are evident in the stories.

If you are preparing to enter a community as a tutor or teacher, how might these narratives inform your experience?

Rhetorical Strategies for Writing about Literature and Culture

Most successful essays that respond to literature adopt a claim-support structure. Neither restating the plot to prove that you've done the reading nor sharing your gut response is enough. You need to stretch beyond reading to the levels of *interpretation* or *criticism*, both of which demand that you engage in *analysis* and construct an *argument*. Engaging in analysis doesn't mean that you need to be dispassionate, for good literature activates both our minds and emotions. And constructing an argument doesn't mean that you need to be argumentative, but rather that you must risk advancing a claim (some call it a thesis) and use both solid reasoning and textual evidence to demonstrate the merits of the claim. Your aim is to provide the reader with a fresh and insightful interpretation of the text.

Claims

You can make several kinds of claims in literary essays. The following 10 issues—6 related to interpretation, 4 to criticism—can serve to frame your claim. These are certainly not the only kinds of workable claims, but they are potential starting points.

Interpretation

- *Theme.* What ideas, questions, concerns, or general topics unify the text? How is a theme developed? What specific strategies, details, symbols, and conflicts reveal the theme? Does the story encourage a particular view on the theme?
- *Tension/conflict/contraries.* What tensions, conflicts, and/or contraries propel the narrative? How are they developed and how are they resolved (if at all)?
- *Cause and effect.* What are the specific causes for corresponding happenings in the narrative? What events or insights trigger character development, shifts in perspective, changes in understanding, reversals in plot, resolutions of conflict, and so on?
- *Pattern.* Where is there repetition, and what effect does it have? What oppositions and ironies are evident and how are they reconciled, if at all? How are the parts connected to the whole?
- *Symbolism.* What symbols operate in the text? How do they relate to themes and patterns? How do the symbols inform and/or complicate the meaning(s) of the text?
- *Character development.* How and why do main characters change? Can psychoanalysis inform our understanding of characters and their actions?

Criticism

- *Evaluation.* What are your criteria for evaluating the quality of literature or some particular aspect of the work? How does a chosen text match or not match those criteria? How can the tenets of an established theory (e.g., formalism, feminism, Marxism) be used to evaluate a particular work of literature?
- *Comparison.* How does this text relate to other texts of its kind? What texts, ideas, or cultural movements might have influenced the work? Can you articulate convincing or insightful affinities, comparisons, or contrasts between the literary text and other texts? You can consider your own experience as a text that can be put in conversation with the literary work; this approach is especially appropriate for the "connecting literature to service" essays.
- *Historical and cultural context.* How do history and culture inform, explain, or influence the literary work (and vice versa)?
- *Social, political, and ethical import.* How does the text raise awareness of, or prompt action in response to, particular social, political, or ethical issues? How does the text contribute to debates about pressing social concerns? How do the views expressed in the text relate to your own social concerns?

Even though the kinds of claims listed above are rather conventional, your particular claim should strive for originality, recalling the advice from Chapter 1 that essays move readers from the *known* to the *new*.

Keep in mind the difference between a topic and a claim. Choosing a topic (such as "Trauma in 'A Letter to Harvey Milk'") is different from making a claim (such as "Writing is one mechanism by which Harry revisits, and to some extent heals, traumas that he has long repressed."). A topic circumscribes a general subject area; a claim (often called a thesis) articulates a specific, debatable assertion that is developed through logical reasoning and supported by evidence. The best claims are intellectually adventuresome.

Support

After you settle on a claim, you need to develop it, and developing a claim requires not only sound reasoning but also supporting evidence. Depending on the kind of claim you explore, several kinds of evidence can be used, including

- Details and passages from the literary text
- Logical explanations of cause–effect relationships, patterns, textual features, and so on
- Discussions of common literary terms as they relate to the text (character, setting, theme, irony, conflict, symbols, motifs, etc.)
- Information on the historical, cultural, or biographical contexts for the piece
- Scholarship recounting how experienced literary critics have interpreted the text
- Comparisons to other literary and nonliterary texts that inform your interpretation
- Personal experiences that relate to and enrich your reading of the text

Most literary analysis essays employ several kinds of supporting evidence, but the most important kind is noted in the first bullet above—passages culled from the literary text itself.

Integrating a claim and support for that claim in a coherent line of argument demands attention to structure and organization. Some literary essays place their claims right at the beginning and then march through the subclaims and evidence, following the skeletal structure of a traditional outline. Other literary essays delay the thesis, adopting rhetorical features more akin to those of the personal essays described in Chapter 2. Ultimately, any essay you write in response to literature is to some degree persuasive, in that you are convincing the audience that your argument has merit. By persuading your reader to at least consider (and perhaps even adopt) your interpretation or your response, you not only prove your mettle as a critical reader but also, through active reading, participate fully in the creative process that was begun when the author of the literary work sat down and put pen to paper.

Student Essay: Jennifer May, *One Star, Two Triangles*

When she wrote this essay, Jennifer May was a first-year student planning to major in business marketing and psychology.

ONE STAR, TWO TRIANGLES

Everyone can identify the sign of the cross. To some it is a sign of Christianity, to others it is a symbol of a closed-minded religion. Still others know it as a sign of life, resurrection, and salvation. All these are correct symbolic representations, because symbols, like time, are dynamic. They stand still only in recollection. However, to truly understand a symbol, it has to be understood in its historical and cultural context. For instance, historically the cross was not a symbol of life. Quite the opposite, it was a symbol of death, and not only death, a criminal's death. The Roman Empire used the cross as a way to impose punishment on those who disagreed with it, those that violated their often discriminatory laws. Many Christians were crucified for their beliefs, and more importantly Jesus, their God incarnate, was martyred on the cross. Because of the vivid emotions and trauma that the cross caused, it made a very vivid symbol, and Christians took that symbol of death, used the potency it had, and formed it into a symbol of life. The Romans still used the cross as a method of oppression, but the more they threatened with the cross, the stronger Christians united. The cross was no longer a threat to them; it was no longer a formidable sign of punishment. It now stood for something entirely different. It unified them; it gave them strength and purpose, because quite simply, for them, the symbol had changed.

The cross is just one of many symbols that hold a deep historic meaning. In Lesléa Newman's story "A Letter to Harvey Milk," there are several symbols that add depth to the story when viewed in their historical context. While "A Letter to Harvey Milk" can be read with no knowledge of its background, the symbols and figures in the story will take on a much deeper meaning if their history is understood. Consequently, Newman may have chosen Harvey Milk as a key figure in her story because of his well-known historical role. Harvey Milk was the first gay politician elected to office, but it was his assassination that made him such an icon. Harvey Milk and George Moscone, the mayor of San Francisco, were killed by Dan White in 1977 for openly supporting gay civil rights (Cloud). The gay population of San Francisco was appalled, and they showed their distress at Harvey's death by holding a candlelight ceremony for him, which Harry describes in his letter to Harvey Milk: ". . . people walking in the street, quiet, each one with a candle, until the street looked like the sky all lit up with a million stars" (Newman 35).

While most people who read "A Letter to Harvey Milk" wonder who Harvey Milk was, few stop to ponder what exactly the other symbols in the story were, such as the Star of David and the pink triangle. The Star of David is first encountered in the story when Harry sees his writing teacher wearing it "around her neck, hanging from a purple string" (Newman 32). The Star of David is a relatively modern Jewish symbol of two interlocking triangles pointed in opposite directions. While the symbol has few ancient references, scholars of this century have attached a very theological significance to it. Franz Rosenzweig relates the triangle that points up to God, and the triangle pointed down to the Jewish people, symbolically showing that God and the Jewish people are inseparable (Rich). Yet the Star of David has more significance to it than just the theological. It, like the cross, was a symbol that had dual meanings of both life and death. The Nazi regime used the yellow star to mark Jews as a separate, inferior people, and by the 1940s, most Jews had learned to fear what the yellow Star of David had come to represent. But this was not the end of the yellow star's symbolism either. By the time Harry had reached his old age, the Star of David had metamorphasized again, much like the cross had. German powers had used it to dehumanize the Jewish people, and the Jews in turn took the star and turned it into a symbol of pride. Harry shows this view of the star after he sees the teacher wearing it and thinks, "that's nice."

The pink triangle, like the Star of David, also has historic symbolism, one that Harry experienced firsthand by living through the Holocaust. While the Star of David was forced on all Jewish people under Nazi domain, the pink triangle was an even worse symbol to have stitched across your garments. Most guards took great care to set gays apart as despicable, like the ones in "A Letter to Harvey Milk" do in this excerpt:

> They had him on his knees with his hands tied behind his back. His face was swollen so, you couldn't even see his eyes. His clothes were stained with blood. And on his uniform they had sewn a pink triangle, big, twice the size of our yellow stars. "Oy, did they beat him but good." (Newman 45)

Because of the trauma associated with the Holocaust, symbols from the past mean a lot to Harry. This is shown by his casual approval of the star that the teacher wears around her neck and his incredible reaction to the pink triangle stitched on her book bag. In fact, the pink triangles caused intense reactions in the story twice. The first sight triggered Harry's emotions as follows:

> . . . then I get mad. What, she thinks maybe I'm blind as well as old, I can't see what's right in front of my nose? Or maybe we don't remember such things? What right does she have to walk in here with that, that thing on her bag, to remind us of what we been through? Haven't we seen enough? (Newman 42)

After his emotions calmed, his memories took over and he remembered other pink triangles, ones that brought the same negative feelings. Pink triangles do not symbolize gay pride to Harry. For him they are forever tied to concentration camps, as Izzie relates when he tells Harry of the shock he felt at encountering a gay man on the street:

> I come outside, I see a young man, maybe twenty-five, a good-looking guy, walking toward me. He's wearing black pants, a white shirt, and on his shirt he's got a pink triangle. . . . The gays are wearing pink triangles just like the war, just like in the camps. (Newman 43)

Harry discussed the pink triangle with friends his own age, people that already understood the stigma attached to the symbol, but he never talked to his teacher about it even though he knew she was gay. Discussion is a way of communication between generations, and a lot of discussion between Harry and the teacher came about because of a letter he wrote to a gay man. Yet there was no discussion of the pink triangle or what it symbolized to either one of them. Harry still held it in his mind as it was in the past, a symbol of oppression and dehumanization. He did not see that it had changed like the cross and the Star of David had. Young homosexuals, like his teacher, had taken the old symbol of hatred and turned it into something they could use, something they had pride in and something that unified them, but Harry still saw it as a form of torture and degradation, a part of his past that he would never be proud of.

Throughout the whole story, there is a conflict of generations, a war between past and the present. Harry desperately wants the past to be behind him, and in different ways throughout the story he keeps reiterating "What's done is done, what's past is past" (Newman 39). Yet in every aspect of his life the past keeps resurfacing to haunt him. As he writes he thinks of his dead wife, friends, and relatives. He talks to the teacher and she asks him for stories from the old days and tries to learn Yiddish. His friends walk down the street and are confronted by pink triangles, signs that were the ultimate disgrace a mere forty years ago. Harry cannot fathom why young people would blatantly display any sign of homosexuality; he does not understand that the meaning of the pink triangle has changed. Jews wore the Star of David before the war, as a sign of their nationality. After the war it was a sign of pride that they had survived, still Jewish. They were forced to wear stars because of the culture they were born into; they were forced to wear triangles because, in the Nazi's eyes, they chose to be despicable. No matter how harsh the concentration camps were, they could not change the fact that Jews were obviously Jews, but they could change the fact that gays were openly gay. Harry lived through the Holocaust and was still proud to be Jewish, but he would not associate with the pink triangle again, no matter what views he held on homosexuality.

In the traditional Jewish religion, homosexuality is not condoned. The teacher's parents expressed this by their reaction to her coming out of the closet. "My parents haven't spoken to me since I told them I was gay. 'How could you do this to us?' they said" (Newman 39), and the teacher herself said so in one of her conversations with Harry. "I'm gay, too. And there aren't many Jewish people your age that are so open-minded" (Newman 36). Like the teacher said, Harry was unique. He did not hold the traditional Jewish views of his generation. Time and time again he accepted gay people as any others. He talked to the teacher, treated her as a daughter, befriended Harvey Milk, and held Izzie as he admitted his previous homosexual activities. It is clear that homosexuality did not offend Harry, despite his age and the common views of his generation and culture. It was the pink triangles that upset him, people branding themselves of their own free will with no respect for those that had been forced to wear them.

One of the themes in "A Letter to Harvey Milk" is change, from the past to the present, from one generation to the next. Time seems to be much more adaptable than people, especially when it comes to traumatic events. Every twenty years there is an entirely new generation with few of the stigmas the previous generation had. Each new generation sees the symbols of the past, but when people like Harry are unable to discuss what the symbols meant in the past, it is easy to see how symbols change so quickly. Just like the cross changed from a symbol of excruciating death to one of resurrected life, the pink triangle changed from one of degradation to one of pride. Harry hated the symbol because it stood for the past, it stood for a time worse than the present, a present where his loved ones were all gone and he had to cook for himself. Harry could not tell the teacher what the pink triangle was all about, because the story was "like a knife, twisting" (Newman 47) in his heart. But he did write to her. He did more than tell her what the pink triangle was historically. He showed her what it was to him. He did this because he did not hate homosexuals; he saw them as people, as much a part of the downward triangle in the Star of David as everyone else. After all, for Jews, half a star is a triangle.

WORKS CITED

Cloud, John. *Time 100*. Time Magazine. 20 Sept. 2001. http://www.time.com/time/time100/heroes/profile/milk01.html.

Newman, Leslea. "A Letter to Harvey Milk." *A Letter to Harvey Milk: Short Stories*. Ithaca, NY: Firebrand, 1988. 32–47.

Rich, Tracey. *Star of David*. 16 Sept. 2001. Jewish Virtual Library. 20 Sept. 2001. http://www.us-israel.org/jsource/Judaism/star.html.   ∎

Peer Review Questions

The following questions are intended to help you respond productively to the drafts of others:

1. Which parts of the draft seem particularly promising?

2. Where do you get confused?

3. Does the writer present a claim (and not just a topic)? Is that claim debatable? Does it engage in interpretation and/or criticism? How might the writer sharpen his or her claim?

4. Does the writer include direct quotations from the literary text to support claims and points? Where is this done well? Where might more passages from the story/poem prove helpful?

5. What other kinds of support does the writer use to develop his or her line of argument?

6. What do you want to hear more about?

ENDNOTE

Like other modes of art, such as music and photography, literature offers a window on a culture and, at times, invites us to see social issues in a new way. By inviting us to identify imaginatively with the perspectives of others, literature can help us to better understand our shared culture, and even to better understand ourselves.

6

Preparing for Outreach: Respect and Reciprocity

How can we involve ourselves with communities respectfully and responsibly? When can community service actually be unethical or counterproductive? When you are involved in community action, what ethical questions and concerns are especially important to keep in mind? This chapter introduces key issues that often surface when people do service in local communities. The readings in this chapter will help you reflect on the larger social context of outreach work, the motives of service, the dynamics of reciprocity, and the process of building respectful partnerships.

True generosity consists precisely in fighting to destroy the causes which nourish false charity. False charity constrains the fearful and subdued, the "rejects of life," to extend their trembling hands. True generosity lies in striving so that these hands— whether of individuals or entire peoples—need be extended less and less in supplication, so that more and more they become human hands which work and, working, transform the world.

—Paulo Freire, *Pedagogy of the Oppressed*

Our first impulse when approaching outreach work might be "just get out there and do it." A central theme of this book is *action*, so indeed we should act. Yet responsible action demands reflection. According to Brazilian literacy educator Paulo Freire, action without reflection is activism—that is, unthinking action for its own sake. Freire further says that reflection without action is verbalism— empty words. Responsible community action is a fragile but generative process that involves both grounded action and critical reflection.

We can think of action and reflection as stages in a continuous cycle—act then reflect, then act with new understanding, then reflect as that new understanding is tested by experience, and so on—but the ultimate goal is to fully integrate action and reflection, folding each into the other. This process has many permutations. For example, scholar Donald Schön speaks of the "reflective practitioner"; Jesuit theology speaks of the "contemplative in action"; Freire speaks of "praxis."

One essential time for reflection should be in advance of engaging in service; and one essential topic for reflection should be the relationships among those involved in, and affected by, community action. This chapter both grapples with problems that have traditionally been associated with community service and offers some frameworks for thinking through the ethical complexities of outreach work. It also invites you to participate in several modes of reflection—reading, discussing, and writing—to arrive at your own understanding of the ethics of service.

WRITING TO DISCOVER

As you prepare to engage in outreach work, what do you anticipate will be most appealing about it? List what you are most eager or excited about. If you are currently doing outreach work, write a list of your favorite things about it. Also, list your greatest concerns, anxieties, and fears.

Respect and *reciprocity* are two pivotal themes in this chapter. Before you engage in outreach work, you should examine default notions of community service as "doing charity" or "helping the less fortunate" or "serving a client," for such phrases suggest unequal, vertical relationships in which servers give from above and recipients accept from below. Rather than adopt a mindset of paternalistic charity or consumerist service, ethical social action seeks to recognize the human dignity of all participants. The prevailing spirit should be that of *partnership*. Sound partnerships are premised on reciprocity; all sides give and receive, all open themselves to learning and growth. Mature social action is built on such presumptions of equality and exchange.

ASSIGNMENT OPTIONS:
Ethical Dimensions of Outreach

CHARITY, PROJECT, AND SOCIAL CHANGE: ESSAY ON THE NATURE OF A COMMUNITY ORGANIZATION AND ITS WORK

Select a community organization or a community action effort on which to focus (ideally, it would be an organization you are working with or hope to work with). Using Keith Morton's categories of charity, project, and social change (explained below), discern how that organization and its work relates to the three categories. Does it fit neatly into one category? Does it defy easy categorization? Support your claim with specific evidence, which may include the organization's own publications, observations of the organization's work, interviews, and your experience with the organization. Also reflect on how other organizations approach the same social issue addressed by your chosen organization, and share which approach you prefer and why.

ESSAY ON AN ETHICAL CONCERN

Using the reading selections in the chapter to develop and support your claims, compose an essay centering on a complex ethical question. Be sure to pose a question that is debatable, on which intelligent people can disagree. Such questions might include (but are not limited to):

1. In your view, which ethical concerns should be foremost in the minds of those doing service in a community? How do those concerns apply to your particular community work?
2. Discuss an ethical issue that has emerged from your own community work. What is its nature, what are its implications, and how does it relate to the readings?
3. How do matters of power, wealth, and privilege affect service work in communities? Why do some emphasize the danger of *noblesse oblige* and certain forms of "charity"?
4. Of the three kinds of service—charity, project, and social change—is one more ethical or desirable than the others? How? Why?
5. In what ways can community service work be counterproductive and even unethical?
6. What constitutes an ethical relationship between a teacher/tutor and a learner? How do the readings by Coles and McKnight depict the ideal learning relationship? Also relevant to this question are readings by Freire and Fishman in the special section "What Is Literacy?".

Whatever question you choose to explore, think about how you can integrate your own experience, specific examples, sound reasoning, and the chapter readings as you build an essay.

Charity, Project, and Social Change

Community service takes many forms. It can involve serving dinner at a soup kitchen, tutoring youth, acting as a mentor, participating in a one-day cleanup project, volunteering with Habitat for Humanity, founding a peer antiviolence program, raising funds for cancer research, doing an alternative spring break, writing letters for Amnesty International, helping with a neighborhood arts program, garnering support for an environmental campaign, and countless other initiatives.

Individual motives for engaging in service are likewise diverse. Some want to alleviate the immediate suffering of others. Some do service because it makes them feel good about themselves. Some act on deeply held religious convictions. Some aspire to reform economic, cultural, or governmental structures. Some hope to raise awareness about a key issue. Some enjoy the camaraderie of collective efforts. Some are driven to solve problems. Some want to give something back to society. Some act on social justice ideals.

WRITING TO DISCOVER

For each of the three questions below, rank your responses from 1 (most preferred) to 3 (least preferred).

1. Which of the following is most important to you?
   _____ A. Helping someone solve a problem or fulfill a need
   _____ B. Participating in a worthwhile service organization or community project
   _____ C. Raising people's awareness about a social issue or community problem

2. Which of the following activities do you consider the most meaningful?
   _____ A. Helping another individual
   _____ B. Building a program or organization to help others
   _____ C. Participating in a public protest or working to change a public policy

3. How do you know when community action has been successful?
   _____ A. When a particular person's problems have been solved
   _____ B. When many people have volunteered time or money to a project
   _____ C. When public awareness of injustice widens and systems change

Now reflect on your choices. Opting for "A" suggests a more individual-based approach to service, "B" a more project-based approach, and "C" a more systems-based approach. Did your choices cluster around one kind of approach? Were they varied? Write a few sentences explaining what your choices might reveal about your attitude toward community action. Then compare your reflections with those of classmates.

Reflecting on how one's individual community work or service-learning fits into a broader social context is essential to informed social action. Keith Morton, who teaches courses in American Studies and Public Service at Providence College, has written extensively on service-learning, and in one article he outlines "three distinct but related paradigms of service"—charity, project, and social change. Morton claims that "each paradigm is based upon distinctive worldviews, ways of identifying and addressing problems, and long term visions of individual and community transformation."[1] The following chart summarizes each approach.

Charity	Project	Social Change
Charity involves delivering direct service to individuals, often for a limited time. Decisions about service and control of service remains with the provider.	Project models define problems and solutions and implement well-conceived plans and programs for achieving those solutions.	Sometimes called advocacy, social change initiatives address root or structural causes of social injustice. People affected by the change participate in the work, and the aim is to change a whole system.
Examples: Donating food to a community pantry; serving meals for a day at a soup kitchen; handing out blankets to the homeless on cold nights.	Examples: Building homes for low-income residents; providing tutoring program to help students with homework and reading skills; implementing a needle-exchange program to prevent the spread of AIDS.	Examples: Working with low-income parents to start a child care cooperative in their neighborhood; helping a national women's group advocate for federal policies that support women's health and equal rights; helping youth in a school start a peer AIDS awareness, education, and prevention program.

Many people see *social change* as the most developed and preferred kind of service because it gets at root causes of injustice and challenges normative ways of thinking. Morton, however, argues that each kind of service—if done well and responsibly—has merits. "Each paradigm," he argues, "contains a world view, a problem statement, and an agenda for change" (p. 24).

---

[1]Morton, Keith. "The Irony of Service: Charity, Project, and Social Change in Service-Learning," *Michigan Journal of Community Service Learning* 2 (1995), p. 21.

WRITING TO DISCOVER

As a class, list several local nonprofit organizations and community action efforts. Then discern how each fits (or doesn't fit) one of Morton's categories. Do certain kinds of community action fit into more than one category?

It might be helpful to look at how several different community organizations address one particular social issue. Take, for example, mental health. Some local organizations may hold occasional special events or provide emergency services for mentally ill residents (charity category); other organizations may host a job training program (project category); and still other organizations may work to change people's embedded attitudes toward mental illness or may lobby for laws that support mental health concerns (social change).

Now consider your own work: Into which category does the community service (or prospective service) that you do best fit. How? Why?

Are there alternative ways that community organizations, or you personally, could approach this same social concern? For example, if you work with a food pantry (charity category), consider alternatives to how hunger, as a social concern, can be addressed from project and social change perspectives.

Essay: Robert Coles, *Community Service Work*

Robert Coles is a professor of medical humanities at Harvard University and the author of acclaimed books on child psychiatry, contemporary social problems, and literary criticism. In his essay "Community Service Work," Coles considers the roles of community service and critical reflection in his life as a college student and then later as a teacher.

When I was a college student I did "volunteer work," as we then called it. I tutored some boys and girls who were having trouble with reading, writing, arithmetic. I left one part of Cambridge, Massachusetts, for another—often on foot, so that I could enjoy what my father had taught me to call a good hike. When I came back to "school," certain scenes I had witnessed and certain statements I had heard would stay with me—come to mind now and then as I pursued various courses, lived a certain late-adolescent life.

Often, when I went home to visit my parents, they inquired after my extracurricular teaching life. My mother was inclined to be religiously sentimental: it was good that I was helping out some youngsters in trouble. For her the sin of pride was around any corner; hence our need to escape that constant pull of egoism—to work with others on behalf of their lives, with our own, for a change, taking a back seat. My father, a probing scientist, commonly took a different tack and asked me many times the same question, "What did you learn?"

I was never quite sure how to answer my father, and often I had no need to do so. My mother was quick to reply, emphasizing her notion of the education such tutoring can afford a college student: "the lesson of humility," a favorite phrase of hers. If any amplification was necessary, she could be forthcoming with another well-worn piety: "There but for the grace of God. . . ."

My father's question often came back to haunt me, no matter my mother's hasty, biblical interventions. What *did* I learn? What was I *supposed* to learn? I was, after all, the teacher, not the student. Anyway, these were elementary school children, and there was nothing new in the ground I was covering with them every week. But I had listened to my father too often, on long walks through various cities, to let the matter rest there. He was born and grew up in Yorkshire, England, and was a great walker, a great observer as he kept his legs moving fast. He was also an admirer of George Orwell long before *Animal Farm* and *1984* were published—the early Orwell who wrote *Down and Out in London and Paris*, *The Road to Wigan Pier*, and *Homage to Catalonia*; the Orwell, that is, who explored relentlessly the world around him and described carefully yet with dramatic intensity the nature of that world.

My father had introduced me to those books before I went to college, and they returned to me as I did volunteer work—a scene, some words, or, more generally, Orwell's social and moral inquiry as both are conveyed in his several narrative efforts. I was beginning to realize that Orwell was a "big brother" for me in a manner far at variance to the already widespread meaning of that phrase. He was helping me make sense of a continuing experience I was having—sharing his wisdom with me, giving me pause, prompting in me scrutiny not only of others (the children I met, and occasionally their parents) but my own mind as it came up with its various opinions, conclusions, attitudes.

Later, at college, I would read the poetry and prose of William Carlos Williams—his long poem *Paterson,* his Stecher trilogy, *White Mule, In the Money, The Buildup.* Williams tried hard to evoke the rhythms of working-class life in America—the struggle of ordinary people to make their way in the world, to find a satisfactory manner of living, of regarding themselves. He knew how hard it is for people like himself (well-educated, well-to-do) to make contact in any substantial way with others, who work in factories or stores or on farms, or, indeed, who do not work at all or are lucky to be intermittently employed.

When he emphasized his search for an American "language," Williams was getting at the fractured nature of our nation's life—the divisions by race, class, region, culture which keep so many of us unaware of one another, unable to comprehend one another. Often as I went to do my tutoring, and heard words I never before knew—or heard words used in new and arresting ways—and as I learned about the memories and hopes and habits and interests of people in a neighborhood rather unlike the one where I lived, I thought of Williams' poems and stories and realized how much he owed to the humble people of northern, industrial New Jersey. As he once put it to me, years after I graduated from college, "Those house calls [to attend his patients] are giving me an education. Every day I learn something new—a sight, a phrase—and I'm made to stop and think about my world, the world I've left behind." He was reminding both of us that the "education" he had in mind was no one-way affair.

From French, **noblesse oblige** literally means "nobility obliges" and refers to the moral obligation of those of high birth, social position, or wealth to act with generosity toward those of lower status or economic means.

I fear it took some of us doing our volunteer work a good deal of time to learn the lesson Williams was putting to word. At my worst, I must admit, a sense of noblesse oblige was at work—a conviction that I would share certain (intellectual) riches with "them." Only when I went with Williams on some of his house calls—observed him paying close heed to various men, women, and children—did I begin to realize how much his mind grew in response to the everyday experiences he was having.

Now, many years later, I find myself a teacher at a university, offering courses for undergraduates and for students in professional schools (law, medicine, business, education). I work with many young people who are anxious to do community service of one kind or another—teach in urban schools, offer medical or legal assistance to needy families. At times I stand in awe of some of those youths—their determination, their decency, their good-heartedness, their savvy. I also notice in many of them a need for discussion and reflection: a time to stop and consider what they would like to be doing, what they are doing, what they are having difficulty doing. A college senior put the matter to me this way one afternoon: "I started this work [volunteer work in a school near a large urban low-rent housing project] as something apart from my courses, my life here as a student. I wanted to be of use to someone other than myself—and in a really honest moment, I'd probably add that I was also being selfish: It would beef up my brag sheet when I apply to a graduate school. But hell, I'd been doing this kind of [volunteer] work since high school—a part of our church's activities, so I shouldn't be too cynical about my motives! But the last thing I expected was that I'd come back here [to his dormitory] and want to read books to help me figure out what's happening [in the neighborhood where he does volunteer work]. I've designed my own private course—and it helps; I can anticipate certain troubles, because I've learned from the reading I do, and I get less discouraged, because I've seen a bigger view, courtesy of those writers."

He said much more, but the gist of his remarks made me realize that there are social scientists and novelists and poets and essayists who have offered that student so very much—their knowledge, their experience, their sense of what matters, and not least, their companionship—as fellow human beings whose concerns are similar to those of the youths now sweating things out in various student volunteer programs. Put differently, those writers (or film makers or photographers) are teachers, and their subject matter is an important one for many of our country's students, engaged as they are in acts of public service.

Our institutions of higher learning might certainly take heed—not only encourage students to do such service, but help them stop and mull over what they have heard and seen by means of books to be read, discussions to be had. This is the very purpose, after all, of colleges and universities—to help one generation after another grow intellectually and morally through study and the self-scrutiny such study can sometimes prompt.　■

Responding to Reading

1. Detail what, in particular, Coles learns from various people: his mother, his father, and William Carlos Williams. How does he meld these views into his own understanding?

2. Who has influenced your thinking about public service? How? Do any of Coles's thoughts resonate with your own?

3. When reflecting on his experiences both tutoring and with Williams, he writes, "At my worst, I must admit, a sense of noblesse oblige was at work." Working from the context of the passage and from the definition in the marginal note, what is *noblesse oblige*? Why does Coles find it problematic? What are alternatives to it?

4. Why, for Coles, is reflection a necessary component of community service work? What specific kinds of reflection does he recommend?

Principles of Good Practice for Combining Service and Learning

As with all pursuits, service-learning can be done well or poorly, done with critical awareness or in blissful ignorance. In an effort to encourage responsible service and rigorous learning, a group of more than 70 organizations drafted ten principles that should serve as a guide for community-based learning initiatives. The ten principles, articulated in 1989 by that group, are listed below; as you review the list, consider how your own service-learning experience relates to each of the principles:

1. An effective program engages people in responsible and challenging actions for the common good.
2. An effective program provides structured opportunities for people to reflect critically on their service experience.
3. An effective program articulates clear service and learning goals for everyone involved.
4. An effective program allows for those with needs to define those needs.
5. An effective program clarifies the responsibilities of each person and organization involved.
6. An effective program matches service providers and service needs through a process that recognizes changing circumstances.
7. An effective program expects genuine, active, and sustained organizational commitment.
8. An effective program includes training, supervision, monitoring, support, recognition, and evaluation to meet service and learning goals.
9. An effective program insures that the time commitment for service and learning is flexible, appropriate, and in the best interests of all involved.
10. An effective program is committed to program participation by and with diverse populations.

Source: Principles of Good Practice for Combining Service and Learning, by Ellen Porter Honnet and Susan J. Poulsen. A Wingspread Special Report. Racine, WI: The Johnson Foundation, 1989.

WRITING TO DISCOVER

These 10 principles were primarily written for organizers of service-learning initiatives. Write down at least five principles of good practice that *students* should keep in mind when working with community organizations or otherwise involved in community action efforts.

Share your principles with others and, through discussion, arrive at the 10 most important principles.

Responding to Reading

1. Given the essay by Robert Coles, which of the principles for good practice are evident in his experience and recommendations?

2. How does your own service-learning experience relate to the 10 principles listed above? Are there any areas that could be improved? If so, how could

program designers better carry out their work? How could students better carry out their responsibilities?

3. As a student, which of the principles can you influence, and which are beyond your influence? Given those you can affect, how, in particular, can you help apply them to the community work you are (or will be) doing?

4. Imagine that you are in a position to design a community program related to one of your own interests. What would it be and how might you go about it? Do your plans reflect awareness of the principles of good practice? If not, how could you incorporate them into your plan?

Behind these principles for practice are enduring values of community and communication, respect, and reciprocity. The reading selection below, by John McKnight, also addresses these themes.

Also Consider

Three earlier readings—"Becoming Literate: A Lesson from the Amish" by Andrea Fishman; "The Banking Concept of Education" by Paulo Freire; and "Conversational Ballgames" by Nancy Sakamoto—raise important questions for those engaged in community service. Fishman, Freire, and Sakamoto explore the dynamics of intercultural communication and the importance of reciprocity.

Essay: John McKnight,
John Deere and the Bereavement Counselor

John McKnight is the Director of the Community Studies Program at the Center for Urban Affairs and Policy Research at Northwestern University in Evanston, Illinois, and has authored many works, including a guide for community development titled Community Building from the Inside Out. *The following essay is from his book* Community and Its Counterfeits.

McKnight is concerned about power relationships in communities and is suspicious of many governmental and social services programs. McKnight argues for an organic and grassroots approach to community development, where instead of having outside agencies or "experts" define needs and implement programs to address them, community members themselves assess problems, set goals, and work together toward solutions.

In 1973, E. F. Schumacher startled Western societies with a revolutionary economic analysis that found that small is beautiful. His book of the same name concluded with these words: "The guidance we need . . . cannot be found in science or technology, the value of which utterly depends on the ends they serve; but it can still be found in the traditional wisdom of mankind."

Because traditional wisdom is passed on through stories rather than studies, it seems appropriate that this chapter should start with a story.

The story begins as the European pioneers crossed the Alleghenies and started to settle the Midwest. The land they found was covered with forests. With great effort they felled the trees, pulled up the stumps, and planted their crops in the rich, loamy soil.

When they finally reached the western edge of the place we now call Indiana, the forest stopped and ahead lay a thousand miles of the great grass prairie. The Europeans were puzzled by this new environment. Some even called it the Great Desert. It seemed untillable. The earth was often very wet and it was covered with centuries of tangled and matted grasses.

The settlers found that the prairie sod could not be cut with their cast-iron plows, and that the wet earth stuck to their plowshares. Even a team of the best oxen bogged down after a few yards of tugging. The iron plow was a useless tool to farm the prairie soil. The pioneers were stymied for nearly two decades. Their western march was halted and they filled in the eastern regions of the Midwest.

In 1837, a blacksmith in the town of Grand Detour, Illinois, invented a new tool. His name was John Deere, and the tool was a plow made of steel. It was sharp enough to cut through matted grasses and smooth enough to cast off the mud. It was a simple tool, the "sodbuster," that opened the great prairies to agricultural development.

Sauk County, Wisconsin, is the part of that prairie where I have a home. It is named after the Sauk Indians. In 1673, Father Marquette was the first European to lay his eyes upon their land. He found a village laid out in regular patterns on a plain beside the Wisconsin River. He called the place Prairie du Sac. The village was surrounded by fields that had provided maize, beans, and squash for the Sauk people for generations reaching back into unrecorded time.

When the European settlers arrived at the Sauk Prairie in 1837, the government forced the native Sauk people west of the Mississippi River. The settlers came with John Deere's new invention and used the tool to open the area to a new kind of agriculture. They ignored the traditional ways of the Sauk Indians and used their sodbusting tool for planting wheat.

Initially, the soil was generous and the farmers thrived. However, each year the soil lost more of its nurturing power. It was only thirty years after the Europeans arrived with their new technology that the land was depleted. Wheat farming became uneconomical and tens of thousands of farmers left Wisconsin seeking new land with sod to bust.

It took the Europeans and their new technology just one generation to make their homeland into a desert. The Sauk Indians, who knew how to sustain themselves on the Sauk Prairie, were banished to another kind of desert called a reservation. And even they forgot about the techniques and tools that had sustained them on the prairie for generations.

And that is how it was that three deserts were created: Wisconsin, the reservation, and the memories of a people.

A century and a half later, the land of the Sauks is now populated by the children of a second wave of European farmers who learned to replenish the soil through the regenerative powers of dairying, ground-cover crops, and animal manures. These third- and fourth-generation farmers and townspeople do not realize, however, that a new settler is coming soon with an invention as powerful as John Deere's plow.

The new technology is called "bereavement counseling." It is a tool forged at the great state university, an innovative technique to meet the needs of those experiencing the death of a loved one, a tool that can "process" the grief of the people who now live on the Prairie of the Sauk.

As one can imagine the final days of the village of the Sauk Indians before the arrival of the settlers with John Deere's plow, one can also imagine these final days before the arrival of the first bereavement counselor at Prairie du Sac. In these final days, the farmers and the townspeople mourn the death of a mother, brother, son, or friend. The bereaved are joined by neighbors and kin. They meet grief together in lamentation, prayer, and song. They call upon the words of the clergy and surround themselves with community.

It is in these ways that they grieve and then go on with life. Through their mourning they are assured of the bonds between them and renewed in the knowledge that this death is a part of the past and the future of the people on the Prairie of the Sauk. Their grief is common property, an anguish from which the community draws strength and which gives it the courage to move ahead.

Into this prairie community the bereavement counselor arrives with the new grief technology. The counselor calls the invention a service and assures the prairie folk of its effectiveness and superiority by invoking the name of the great university while displaying a diploma and license.

At first, we can imagine that the local people will be puzzled by the bereavement counselor's claims. However, the counselor will tell a few of them that the new technique is merely to *assist* the bereaved's community at the time of death. To some other prairie folk who are isolated or forgotten, the counselor will offer help in grief processing. These lonely souls will accept the intervention, mistaking the counselor for a friend.

For those who are penniless, the counselor will approach the County Board and advocate the "right to treatment" for these unfortunate souls. This right will be guaranteed by the Board's decision to reimburse those too poor to pay for counseling services.

There will be others, schooled to believe in the innovative new tools certified by universities and medical centers, who will seek out the bereavement counselor by force of habit. And one of these people will tell a bereaved neighbor who is unschooled that unless his grief is processed by a counselor, he will probably have major psychological problems in later life.

Several people will begin to contact the bereavement counselor because, since the County Board now taxes them to *ensure* access to the technology, they will feel that to fail to be counseled is to waste their money and to be denied a benefit, or even a right.

Finally, one day the aged father of a local woman will die. And the next-door neighbor will not drop by because he doesn't want to interrupt the bereavement counselor. The woman's kin will stay home because they will have learned that only the bereavement counselor knows how to process grief in the proper way. The local clergy will seek technical assistance from the bereavement counselor to learn the correct form of service to deal with guilt and grief. And the grieving daughter will know that it is the bereavement counselor who *really* cares for her, because only the bereavement counselor appears when death visits this family on the Prairie of the Sauk.

It will be only one generation between the time the bereavement counselor arrives and the disappearance of the community of mourners. The counselor's new tool will cut through the social fabric, throwing aside kinship, care, neighborly obligations, and community ways of coming together and going on. Like John Deere's plow, the tools of bereavement counseling will create a desert where a community once flourished.

And finally, even the bereavement counselor will see the impossibility of restoring hope in clients once they are genuinely alone, with nothing but a service for consolation. In the inevitable failure of the service, the bereavement counselor will find the desert even in herself.

There are those who would say that neither John Deere nor the bereavement counselor has created a desert. Rather, they would argue that these new tools have great benefits and that we have focused unduly upon a few negative side effects. Indeed, they might agree with Eli Lilly, founder of the famous drug company, whose motto was "A drug without side effects is no drug at all."

To those with this perspective, the critical issue is the amelioration or correction of the negative effects. In Lilly's idiom, they can conceive of a new drowsiness-creating pill designed to overcome the nausea created by an anticancer drug. They envision a prairie scattered with pyramids of new technologies and techniques, each designed to correct the error of its predecessor, but none without its own error to be corrected. In building these pyramids, they will also recognize the unlimited opportunities for research, development, and badly needed employment. Indeed, many will name this pyramiding process "progress" and note its positive effect upon the gross national product.

The countervailing view holds that these pyramiding service technologies are now counterproductive constructions, essentially impediments rather than monuments.

E. F. Schumacher helped clarify for many of us the nature of those physical tools that are so counterproductive that they become impediments. There is an increasing recognition of the waste and devastation created by these new physical tools, from nuclear generators to supersonic transports. They are the sons and daughters of the sodbuster.

It is much less obvious that the bereavement counselor is also the sodbuster's heir. It is more difficult for us to see how service technology creates deserts. Indeed, there are even those who argue that a good society should scrap its nuclear generators in order to recast them into plowshares of service. They would replace the counterproductive *goods* technology with the *service* technology of modern medical centers, universities, correctional systems, and nursing homes. It is essential, therefore, that we have new measures of service technologies that will allow us to distinguish those that are impediments from those that are monuments.

We can assess the degree of impediment incorporated in modern service technologies by weighing four basic elements. The first is the monetary cost. At what point do the economics of a service technology consume enough of the commonwealth that all of society becomes eccentric and distorted?

Schumacher helped us recognize the radical social, political, and environmental distortions created by huge investments in covering our land with concrete in the name of transportation. Similarly, we are now investing 12 percent of our national wealth in "health care technology" that blankets most of our communities with a medicalized understanding of well-being. As a result, we now imagine that there are mutant human beings called health consumers. We create costly "health-making" environments that are usually large, windowless rooms filled with immobile adult bicycles and dreadfully heavy objects purported to benefit one if they are lifted.

The second element to be weighed was identified by Ivan Illich as "specific counterproductivity." Beyond the negative side effect is the possibility that a service technology can produce the specific inverse of its stated purpose. Thus, one can imagine sickening medicine, stupidifying schools, and crime-making corrections systems.

The evidence grows that some service technologies are now so counterproductive that their abolition is the most productive means to achieve the goal for which they were initially established. Take, for example, the experiment in Massachusetts where, under the leadership of Dr. Jerome Miller, the juvenile correction institutions were closed. As the most recent evaluation studies indicate, the Massachusetts recidivism rate has declined while comparable states with increasing institutionalized populations see an increase in youthful criminality.

There is also the discomforting fact that during doctor strikes in Israel, Canada, and the United States, the death rate took an unprecedented plunge.

Perhaps the most telling example of specifically counterproductive service technologies is demonstrated by the Medicaid program, which provides "health care for the poor." In most states, the amount expended for medical care for the poor is now greater than the cash welfare income provided for that same poor population. Thus, a low-income mother is given $1.00 in income and $1.50 in medical care. It is perfectly clear that the single greatest cause of her ill health is her low income. Nonetheless, the response to her sickening poverty is an ever-growing investment in medical technology—an investment that now consumes her income.

The third element to be weighed is the loss of knowledge. Many of the settlers who came to Wisconsin with John Deere's sodbuster had been peasant farmers in Europe. There, they had tilled the land for centuries using methods that replenished its nourishing capacity. However, once the land seemed unlimited and John Deere's technology came to dominate, they forgot the tools and methods that had sustained them for centuries in the old land and created a new desert.

The same process is at work with the modern service technologies and the professions that use them. One of the most vivid examples involves the methods of a new breed of technologists called pediatricians and obstetricians. During the first half of the twentieth century, these technocrats came, quite naturally, to believe that the preferred method of feeding babies was with a manufactured formula rather than breast milk. Acting as agents for the new lactation technology, these professionals persuaded a generation of women to abjure breastfeeding in favor of their more "healthful" way.

In the fifties in a Chicago suburb, there was a woman named Marion Thompson who still remembered that babies could be fed by breast as well as by can. However, she could find no professional to advise her. She searched for someone who might still remember something about the process of breastfeeding. Fortunately, she found one woman whose memory included the information necessary to begin the flow of milk. From that faint memory, breastfeeding began its long struggle toward restoration in our society. She and six friends started a club that multiplied itself into thousands of small communities and became an international association of women dedicated to breastfeeding: La Leche League. This popular movement reversed the technological imperative in only one generation and has established breastfeeding as a norm in spite of the countervailing views of the service technologists.

Indeed, the American Academy of Pediatrics finally took the official position that breastfeeding is preferable to nurturing infants from canned products. It was as though the Sauk Indians had recovered the Wisconsin prairie and allowed it once again to nourish a people with popular tools.

The fourth element to be weighed is the "hidden curriculum" of the service technologies. As they are implemented through professional techniques, the invisible message of the interaction between professional and client is, "You will be better because I know better." As these professional techniques proliferate across the social landscape, they represent a new praxis, an ever-growing pedagogy that teaches this basic message of the service technologies. Through the propagation of belief in authoritative expertise, professionals cut through the social fabric of community and sow clienthood where citizenship once grew.

It is clear, therefore, that to assess the purported benefits of service technologies, they must be weighed against the sum of the socially distorting monetary costs to the commonwealth; the inverse effects of the interventions; the loss of knowledge, tools, and skills regarding other ways; and the antidemocratic consciousness created by a nation of clients. When the benefits are weighed in this balance, we can begin to recognize how often the tools of professionalized service make social deserts where communities once bloomed.

Unfortunately, the bereavement counselor is but one of many new professionalized servicers that plow over our communities like John Deere's sodbusting settlers. These new technologists have now occupied much of the community's space and represent a powerful force for colonizing the remaining social relations. Nonetheless, resistance against this invasion can still be seen in local community struggles against the designs of planners, parents' unions demanding control over their children's learning, women's groups struggling to reclaim their medicalized bodies, and community efforts to settle disputes and conflicts by stealing the property claimed by lawyers.

Frequently, as in the case of La Leche League, this decolonization effort is successful. Often, however, the resistance fails and the new service technologies transform citizens and their communities into social deserts grown over with a scrub brush of clients and consumers.

This process is reminiscent of the final English conquest of Scotland after the Battle of Culloden. The English were convinced by a history of repeated uprisings that the Scottish tribes would never be subdued. Therefore, after the battle, the English killed many of the clansmen and forced the rest from their small crofts into the coastal towns, where there was little work and no choice but to emigrate. Great Britain was freed of the tribal threat. The clans were decimated and their lands given to the English lords, who grazed sheep where communities once flourished. My Scots ancestors said of this final solution of the Anglo-Saxon, "They created a desert and called it freedom."

One can hear echoes of this understanding in today's social deserts, where modern "Anglo-Saxons" declare the advantages of exiled clienthood, describing it as self-fulfillment, individual development, self-realization, and other mirages of autonomy.

Our modern experience with service technologies tells us that it is difficult to recapture professionally occupied space. We have also learned that whenever that space is liberated, it is even more difficult to construct a new social order that will not be quickly co-opted again.

A vivid current example is the unfortunate trend developing within the hospice movement. In the United States, those who created the movement were attempting to detechnologize dying—to wrest death from the hospital and allow it to occur within the family.

Since the movement began in the 1970s, we have seen the rapid growth of "hospital-based hospices" and new legislation reimbursing those hospices that will formally tie themselves to hospitals and employ physicians as central "caregivers."

The professional co-optation of community efforts to invent appropriate techniques for citizens to care in the community has been pervasive. We need to identify the characteristics of those social forms that are resistant to colonization by service technologies while enabling communities to cultivate care. These authentic social forms are characterized by three basic dimensions: They tend to be *uncommodified*, *unmanaged*, and *uncurricularized*.

The tools of the bereavement counselor have made grief into a *commodity* rather than an opportunity for community. Service technologies convert conditions into commodities, and care into service.

The tools of the *manager* convert communality into hierarchy, replacing consent with control. Where once there was a commons, the manager creates a corporation.

The tools of the *pedagogue* create monopolies in place of cultures. By making a school of everyday life, community definitions and citizen action are degraded and finally expelled.

It is this hardworking team—the service professional, the manager, and the pedagogue—that pulls the tools of "community-busting" through the modern social landscape. Therefore, if we are to recultivate community, we will need to return this team to the stable, abjuring their use.

How will we learn again to cultivate community? Schumacher concluded that "the guidance we need ... can still be found in the traditional wisdom." Therefore, we can return to those who understand how to allow the Sauk Prairie to bloom and sustain a people.

One of their leaders, a chief of the Sauk, was named Blackhawk. After his people were exiled to the land west of the Mississippi and their resistance movement was broken at the Battle of Bad Axe, Blackhawk said of the prairie:

There, we always had plenty; our children never cried from hunger, neither were our people in want. The rapids of our river furnished us with an abundance of excellent fish and the land, being very fertile, never failed to produce good crops of corn, beans, pumpkins, and squash. Here our village stood for more than a hundred years. Our village was healthy and there was no place in the country possessing such advantages, nor hunting grounds better than ours. If a prophet had come to our village in those days and told us that the things were to take place which have since come to pass, none of our people would have believed the prophecy.

But the settlers came with their new tools and the prophecy was fulfilled. One of Blackhawk's Wintu sisters described the result:

The white people never cared for land or deer or bear. When we kill meat, we eat it all. When we dig roots, we make little holes. When we build houses, we make little holes. When we burn grass for grasshoppers, we don't ruin things. We shake down acorns and pinenuts. We don't chop down trees. We only use dead weed. But the whites plow up the ground, pull down the trees, kill everything.

The tree says, "Don't. I am sore. Don't hurt me!" But they chop it down and cut it up.

The spirit of the land hates them. They blast out trees and stir it up to its depths. They saw up the trees. That hurts them. . . . They blast rocks and scatter them on the ground. The rock says, "Don't. You are hurting me!" But the white people pay no attention. When [we] use rocks, we take only little round ones for cooking. . . .

How can the spirit of the earth like the white man? Everywhere they have touched the earth, it is sore.

Blackhawk and his Wintu sister tell us that the land has a Spirit. Their community on the prairie, their ecology, was a people guided by that Spirit.

When John Deere's people came to the Sauk Prairie, they exorcised the Prairie Spirit in the name of a new god, Technology. Because it was a god of their making, they believed they were gods.

And they made a desert.

There are incredible possibilities if we are willing to fail to be gods.

*   *   *

This chapter, imagining the advent of bereavement counselors in the Sauk Prairie, was written in October 1984. On September 18, 1986, the following article appeared in the *Sauk-Prairie Star*, the newspaper for the citizens of Sauk Prairie.

Grieving Will Be Seminar Topic

Sauk Prairie High School guidance staff will present a seminar on grieving for freshmen and seniors at Sauk Prairie High School during the week of September 22–26. The seminar is being presented due to the recent losses of classmates for students in the classes of 1990 and 1987.

Freshmen will attend the seminar in conjunction with required health classes. Students who have no health classes first semester will be assigned a presentation during study halls.

Seniors will attend the seminar in conjunction with family living classes. Students who do not have a family living class will be assigned a presentation.

Parents are welcome to call the Guidance Center to discuss any concerns they may have. Parents must authorize students not attending the seminars. ∎

Responding to Reading

1. Have you ever been the recipient of "help" or "service" that you found uncomfortable, inappropriate, or counterproductive? How might that experience relate to McKnight's notion of "disabling help"?

2. McKnight draws a parallel between plowing practices and bereavement counseling. What is the common issue or lesson that links these two examples? What point is he making?

3. According to McKnight, how do modern social services systems commodify needs and undermine communities? What do you think about McKnight's theories?

4. If we take McKnight's critique seriously, how *should* we best go about community work? Provide a few examples.

Peer Review Questions

The following questions can help guide responses to essay drafts.

1. Which parts of the draft seem particularly promising?

2. Where do you get confused?

3. Does the writer present a claim that is debatable?

4. Consider the logic of the argument. Where is it sound? Where does it break down?

5. What kinds of support does the writer use to develop his or her line of argument? How are the readings used?

6. Take a few moments to play devil's advocate to the writer's position. What is the best case against the position? How could the writer anticipate and address your objections?

ENDNOTE

This chapter's readings selections by Coles and McKnight grapple with complex ethical matters that merit continued attention by those engaged in service work. For Coles and McKnight—as it should be for you—reflection on service, relationships, and hopeful action is not a one-time event but rather an ongoing activity.

7

Writing about the Community

This chapter focuses on writing and research that is directly connected to community life. What does that kind of research look like? How does one go about doing it? Two assignment options are explained: the community-based research essay and the agency profile report. These two assignments demand similar research methods—such as interviewing, doing fieldwork, evaluating sources, and synthesizing various strands of inquiry—but use different formats.

Traditionally, writing tasks for school are rather self-contained affairs—the writer sits down alone to craft an essay. Or perhaps the assignments involve finding sources in the library or on the Web. Such approaches to writing can certainly be valuable; but often they result in a disembodied or distanced treatment of a topic. In contrast, the writing-about-the-community assignments presented in this chapter insist that writers get out into local communities to observe, listen, interview, inquire, and act. This community-based approach usually lends vitality, complexity, and currency to writing because the work is rooted in the blood and bone of community life.

This chapter's assignment options—the community-based research essay and the agency profile report—invite you to blend inquiry with experience, to combine study with community engagement.

WRITING TO DISCOVER

Think back to research papers or projects you have completed, both in school and out of school (e.g., researching college options or a personal interest). Which experiences were negative, and what made them so? Which experiences were rewarding, and why?

As a class, pool your observations and compile a list of at least six characteristics that mark fruitful research. Include not just characteristics of good research papers but also factors that motivate most people in the research process.

Every community is a complex ecosystem of people, places, institutions, and social forces that is ripe for reflection. The primary means of reflection described in this chapter is *community-based research.* Such research can be a *prelude to community service,* a means by which to help newcomers understand social issues and engage in community work more knowingly, more responsibly, and more effectively. For example, if you were tutoring youth in a diverse population, you could research a number of issues related to tutoring—child development, the impact of race and ethnicity on learning, second language acquisition, schooling practices, concerns such as tracking in schools, and so on. Also, working with a partner community organization, such as a tutoring program or a nonprofit agency, brings with it a responsibility to know and understand that organization—its history, aims, values, practices, and problems—and this presents another opportunity for inquiry.

Community-based research can also be *a companion to community service*—a way to process experience, explore complex problems, prompt awareness, and spur critical reflection. Such writing about the community can be achieved through personal essays that focus on service experiences, investigations of problems that arise in the course of service, and analyses of social concerns that form the context for service. For example, if you were working at a homeless shelter, research questions could emerge from personal experience (How do I make sense of what I saw today?), from specific local problems (What options for job training are available in the area?), or from analysis of the social context for service (Which local, national, and global economic forces create and/or shape the problem of homelessness?).

Community-based research can also be *a form of social action in its own right.* The research process can open lines of communication between students and community members about shared concerns; research findings can prompt individuals to deeper critical knowledge of pressing social problems; and the text you produce can help social change organizations do their work.

ASSIGNMENT OPTIONS:
Writing about the Community

THE COMMUNITY-BASED RESEARCH ESSAY: EXPLORING A SOCIAL CONCERN OR LOCAL PROBLEM

This project combines some practices that have traditionally been associated with the research paper with community-based strategies. The aim is to engage you in a process of inquiry into a social concern or local problem and to help your audience arrive at a deeper understanding of that particular social matter.

The essay should be built around a specific research question. If you are currently engaged in community outreach, you should choose a research question that emerges from that experience; if you are not engaged in community outreach, you should choose a research question of interest that also holds relevance for the local community.

The essay should draw on several kinds of sources, including

- Personal experience (if it is relevant to the topic)
- At least one interview with a campus or community member who has experience related to your research question
- Observations, field notes, and/or journal notes
- A variety of library and Web sources (a minimum of three reliable sources)

Two sample community-based research essays are included in this chapter.

THE AGENCY PROFILE REPORT

This project involves researching a local community organization and its context. The report can be particularly useful if you plan to work with the organization in the near future. But even if you are not anticipating such work, investigating a local nonprofit or social change organization serves to widen your awareness of community issues and resources.

Your goal in this assignment is to explain the mission, history, values, habits, and activities of a particular community organization. Furthermore, you should devote special attention to the organization's internal and external communication practices—to how the agency functions as a *discourse community* (see Chapter 4 for an explanation of this concept).

The report should follow the empirical research report format and involve several kinds of research, including

- At least one interview with contact persons at the agency
- Some of the agency's own documents and publications
- Library and Web research on the agency and its context

With instructor permission, the report can be undertaken as a collaborative project. Two sample agency profile reports are included in this chapter.

Ethical Concerns in Community-Based Research

Before beginning the community-based components of projects, researchers should attend to a number of ethical considerations. They should ask: What is the purpose of this research project? Who might benefit from it, and how? Who might it hurt, and how? Can I foresee any potentially problematic consequences of the research process or unintended uses for the research results? Does the research process respect the rights and dignity of all involved?

Community-based research brings with it special ethical responsibilities. Most importantly, researchers and community members should aspire to create reciprocal relationships that are based on respectful exchanges of goodwill, knowledge, time, and material benefits. University researchers have a troubling history of using communities as a site to gather data (a tangible benefit for them), with too little thought applied to both how the community members are represented and what benefits should accrue to them. Service-learning implies a two way street: learners learn and also provide service; community members likewise learn, even as they, too, provide the service of assisting students in academic pursuits.

These concerns are addressed at length in Chapter 6, but a few practical considerations deserve to be repeated here:

- *Approach potential contributors with graciousness and respect.* If local or campus community members opt to participate in your research, consider that a gift, and express appreciation.

- *Consider, in advance, the perspectives of community partners.* Know, for example, that many nonprofit agencies are busy places, often overworked and underfunded. Be flexible in scheduling meetings and respect the time limitations of staff by being well prepared for those meetings.

- *Attend to differences of culture, language, and privilege.* Assuming that your outlook, culture, values, or language are normative reveals a rather dangerous egoism. You should work to understand your own social position and to value the perspectives of others.

- *Keep all parties informed and updated.* Before you start a project, community members must be informed about its purpose, the research procedures, what exactly you expect from the organization (such as the number and duration of anticipated interviews), and the ways the final project will be used and distributed. Regular progress reports, to both community partners and the instructor, are also vital.

- *Create formal and informal opportunities for dialogue and feedback.* Share your work in process and invite response to it. This is particularly important to verifying the accuracy and integrity of your written representations of individuals and/or organizations.

- *Find ways that your research can benefit community members and organizations.* Although your research might be motivated by a school assignment, you should inquire about ways that it could be of use or interest to participating organizations. You should offer to share copies of the final product.

When in doubt about the ethics of your research practices, consult with your instructor.

The following several sections are each keyed to one of the two assignment options: the community-based research essay or the agency profile report. The "Methods of Research" section that follows those sections applies to both assignments.

Community-Based Research Essay: Exploring Options

If you are writing a community-based research essay, you can start by identifying broad areas of interest. Which kinds of issues are most important to you— those related to children? the elderly? education? women's health? the environment? the arts? poverty? homelessness? something else?

WRITING TO DISCOVER

Initial Survey of Interests and Options

Based on your interests, list several possible topic areas:

- Which social issues are of most interest to you?
- If you are currently engaged in community service, how might that work serve as a source for topics?
- Which community issues are related to your academic major?
- Which issues of interest to you have been in the national, local, or campus news lately?

Share the potential topic(s) with your instructor and fellow writers for feedback.

To further narrow potential topics, you should ask the following:

- How do these social concerns manifest themselves in the local community and/or on campus?
- Are any local organizations or individuals addressing the concerns?
- Who might I be able to interview to learn more about them?

If a potential topic area has little or no application to the local area, you will want to reconsider the topic.

Before you even start the research process, it can be worthwhile to write down your reasons for choosing a particular topic as well as your relevant experiences with and opinions about the issue. Some call this a "crash-through draft," in which you informally (and rather quickly) write what you know now, why it is significant, and where you suspect that your inquiry will take you. This draft can serve as a starting place, helping to preserve a sense of your own particular perspective, which can sometimes get lost during the research process.

Community-Based Research Essay: Finding a Focus

Recall from earlier chapters the difference between a topic and a claim. A *topic* circumscribes a general subject area; a *claim* (often called a *thesis*) articulates a specific, debatable assertion that is developed through logical reasoning and supported by evidence. Another way to think about a claim, especially in the beginning stages of the writing and research process, is to frame it as a *research question*.

Narrowing from a topic to a research question can be a useful strategy because many researchers discover a main claim only after having the opportunity to spend some time researching a topic. Furthermore, many researchers revise initial claims (or even initial research questions) after happening upon unexpected discoveries or insights along the way. Most importantly, then, a research question propels inquiry and provides a focus to the writing process.

It might be helpful to think of narrowing in stages. A topic can be narrowed to a more specific issue, and the issue can be further focused and reframed as a question. Note the following example:

Topic	Tutoring in multicultural settings
Issue	Effectiveness of different tutoring strategies
Research question	Which strategies have proven effective for tutoring youth in multicultural settings?
Community-oriented research question	How might such findings inform the practices of the local youth tutoring program? And, just as importantly, how might the experiences of the local program inform available research?

Some research questions are better than others. Take, for example, the sample essay "Who Deserves a Head Start?" (see p. 321). The author, Erin Collins, was clearly interested in children and education, so the choice of researching Head Start made sense. However, although a question such as What is Head Start? might yield some interesting defining information for those who know nothing about the program, it would be a weak research question because it would invite little analysis and contribute little to current debates about early childhood education or public policy. Instead, the author opts for a sharper, more purpose-driven, and ultimately more compelling research question: Given the promising results of Head Start, why isn't the program funded enough to serve all eligible children? This leads the author to make and support the claim that the U.S. government should, in fact, expand funding for the program. This is the kind of research question and claim that can leverage social action.

In the student essay that follows, the writer takes on a broad topic, bilingual education, but then narrows it to a more specific question and ultimately to a community-oriented research question:

Topic	Bilingual education
Issue	English immersion versus ESL programs
Research question	What are the advantages and disadvantages of differing approaches to bilingual education?
Community-oriented research question	Given the available research, as well as the particular circumstances of the local school system, which bilingual education policies might best serve students in our city?

What follows is a sample community-based research essay written by a student, Erin Elmore. Notice that Elmore selects a debatable research question that is relevant to both herself and her local community. She also draws on several kinds of sources: periodicals, books, Web sites, an interview, and her own experience. Later sections of this chapter detail how you should use similar methods of gathering information, as well as ways that you can synthesize such information and structure your argument.

Student Research Essay: Erin Elmore, *Pursuing an Educated Mind*

When she wrote this essay, Erin Elmore was a first-year student planning to major in English.

PURSUING AN EDUCATED MIND: THE DEBATE OVER THE
EFFECTIVENESS OF ELEMENTARY BILINGUAL EDUCATION

As a child, I was fortunate to have never struggled with classroom basics. I could understand my teacher and what she was teaching, never having to struggle daily. Maria, however, was not quite as lucky. When she was only 8 years old, Maria immigrated to the United States with her family. Having never been previously exposed to English, she was unable to comprehend anything that was said to her. All she knew was Spanish, her native tongue. I remember the day when Maria joined my third grade class. She looked nervous. Mrs. Miller, my teacher, had no idea how to help her. She would stand over Maria, towering like a giant and repeating herself, in English, over and over again, growing louder each time. Mrs. Miller's actions struck me as odd—Maria wasn't deaf, she just couldn't understand English. Even as a third grader, I understood that yelling at her wasn't going to make Maria understand. Why couldn't Mrs. Miller understand as well?

During that year, Maria spent a lot of time outside of class. While we were busy with our TAAS readers and math worksheets, Maria was whisked away to her ESL classes and her tutoring programs. Over the course of the year, Maria did learn some English. She was able to comprehend more of what was being said to her. Yet she still did not gain a complete understanding. Maria still struggled in class. She still had problems with basic comprehension.

In elementary schools across America, thousands of students face the same problem as Maria did. Nationwide, over 2.8 million public school students are not fluent in English, and the numbers continue to rise 100% each decade ("Double Talk?"). Having little control of the English language, these students are often put in special classes and programs to help them learn the basics of the language. Although these programs attempt to help these students adjust to their new environment and overcome the language barrier, it seems as if certain programs seldom do so. Some students do achieve success in these programs; however, many children enter the programs, become trapped in them, and never escape to reach levels of equality in the regular classroom. As one of my teachers, vehemently opposed to the ESL system, always argued, "In the end, they graduate with barely half of a high school education." My own observations throughout elementary and secondary schooling led me to wonder about the efficiency of these programs. What are the opportunities for assistance available to non-English speaking elementary age students, and how effective are these programs in teaching children English and other basic skills?

HISTORY OF BILINGUAL EDUCATION

Bilingual education has been in use since the mid-1800s. In fact, early reports state that about 4% of American children were instructed at least part of the time in a non-English language, in most cases, German. In the earlier part of the 20th century, due to the situation with the First World War, "fears about the loyalty of non-English speakers . . . prompted a majority of states to enact English-only instruction laws designed to 'Americanize' these groups" ("History of Bilingual Education"). This lasted until the passing of the Bilingual Education Act in 1968, which provided federal funding of bilingual education programs with the non-English speakers' native languages. Soon afterward, the *Lau v. Nichols* Supreme Court ruling stated that "English only classrooms made a mockery of public education by providing unequal education to the Limited English Proficiency (LEP) students . . . [and] required schools to take affirmative steps to overcome the language barriers" ("History of Bilingual Education"). On this principle, the Equal Educational Opportunity Act was passed in 1974 to further develop the resources available for the LEP students.

In addition to federal mandates concerning bilingual education, many states, including Kansas, have passed legislation "explicitly permitting bilingual instruction," while other states, such as Texas, have passed legislation that "mandates" bilingual instruction for LEP students, mainly in those states with high immigrant minority numbers (Ovando and Collier 31). The debate over the necessity of bilingual programs for adequate education for LEP students arises not only on the national level, but on the state level as well, and continues to develop through the years as more LEP students arrive in America and the need for effective programs increases.

TYPES OF PROGRAMS AVAILABLE

There are many types and variations of programs available for non-English speaking students. As stated by researchers Miramontes, Nadeau, and Commins, these programs can be divided into four basic categories

> that are distinguished by their variability in the students' primary language for instruction. . . . Category I: Full primary language foundation; Category II: Primary language support—literacy only; Category III: Primary language content reinforcement—no literacy; and Category IV: all English. (71)

To explain, Category I focuses on larger bilingual goals, usually taking 6–7 years to complete. However, there are some shorter programs in this category, including the early exit programs in which the students are placed under a time schedule and ushered through the program at a faster speed. In the second program, students are taught the fundamentals of reading and writing in their native languages so that a better understanding can be reached as these fundamentals are then transferred to English. These programs require a more lengthy daily commitment to be effective. Category III is similar to Category II, but focuses on content areas rather than literacy in the basic language. Students are taught basic content of the material in their native tongue and then re-taught in English (Miramontes, Nadeau, and Commins 72–75).

The last category is much different than the previous three. Only English is used during teaching—the student's native language is never used. As a result, chances for miscommunication and difficulties understanding frequently arise and these programs, often called immersion or ESL (English as a Second Language) classes, tend to take much longer (three years as opposed to one in an immersion program) to work sufficiently. These English-only programs are often compared with being thrown suddenly into a pool: the student is completely immersed in the new language and will either sink or swim based on his success or failure to grasp the language on his or her own.

SPECIFIC PROGRAMS IN THE MANHATTAN AREA

In Manhattan, Kansas, special classes for non-English speaking students are a relatively new offering. According to Nancy Kole, Principal at Lee School and Coordinator for the district's ESL program, "The need for such programs in Manhattan has always been present—the students have always been there—but formal entrance and exit tests and ESL evaluations did not start until last year, the 2000–2001 school year." Manhattan has never had actual bilingual classes, only the ESL pull-out programs. Part of the reason for the absence of bilingual programs is the diversity of the non-English speaking students. Among the LEP students in the district, there are eleven to twelve different languages spoken, so it would be difficult to have a bilingual program that focuses on only one language (Kole). It would not be economical for the teachers or the children. Rather, the ESL classes are used with an emphasis on English rather than the child's native tongue, and as a result, children speaking a wide variety of languages can be grouped together.

EFFECTIVENESS OF IMPLEMENTED PROGRAMS

The debate over bilingual education is lengthy and complicated. Supporters of the bilingual programs "call it necessary; forty percent of students across the country who have difficulty speaking English never complete high school" while those against the programs call it "expensive and potentially isolating for students" ("Double Talk?").

There is much data to support both sides of the bilingual argument. Some sources claim that the bilingual child has advantages over one who speaks only English. According to Alejandro Brice, "It is generally agreed that proficient children, who are balanced in both languages, show some cognitive advantage over proficient monolinguals" (Brice and McKibbin 10). By strengthening their comprehension of both languages, bilingual students tend to score higher on their aptitude and comprehension tests. While this may be true, there are also documented cases of immersion techniques yielding more effective results than bilingual ones. At English-immersion elementary schools in California, reading scores of second graders went from the 10th percentile to the 24th and math scores jumped from the 18th to 32nd percentile ("English First" 2).

Part of the reason that data can be found to support both sides of the debate is that many outside influences affect the instruction, not only the type of program used. The proficiency of the teacher in both languages, the student's level of comprehension entering the program, and the amount of time spent using the native and English languages at home all have a great effect on the success of each student in the program.

Yet the fact remains that bilingual programs offer students an opportunity not available through English-only immersion methods. In these programs, students are taught at least some of the material in two languages—first in their native languages, and then in English. Basic skills and understanding must be mastered in the primary language before any understanding in English can take place. In support of bilingual programs, Principal Kole argues

> What you're after is an educated mind. Language shouldn't matter if the teaching can expand the student's knowledge easier or more fully. Use the language that helps the student gain knowledge. Why try to dig through a rock when you can just walk around it?

If students can first understand a concept—such as the idea of writing as putting words down on paper to tell a story and the premise of reading—then they are more likely to catch on more quickly to the concept when applied through English instruction.

One main consideration in the argument is the geographic location of the program. In larger cities with a greater population of LEP students of the same language background, bilingual programs can be effective. In smaller cities where the LEP population is more diverse, as is the case in Manhattan, Kansas, such programs are not always feasible.

SUGGESTIONS FOR INCREASED EFFECTIVENESS

In our growing multicultural world, fluency in more than one language is an enormous benefit, and in many professions, is even required. Learning a second language is not an easy task—it takes years of study, practice, and immersion to master. Bilingual adults are valued in today's business world and in society. Although the process may be long and daunting, many people are willing to go through it in order to achieve some degree of bilingualism. Bilingualism is a trait that we as a society praise and value, but we are not as quick to foster it in non-English speaking youth. LEP students have "great bilingual potential," but with the use of immersion English-only programs, this potential is "thrown away because it is not pursued" (Kole). Students are forced into an English mold and their own language is usually not developed. Are the current methods of instruction effective for the non-English speaking students of Manhattan? It is possible that the methods work wonderfully for some. But it is more likely that the programs are not meeting the needs of all LEP students. Should Manhattan implement a bilingual program? I believe the answer to be yes. Such a program would help not only individuals but also the community to grow in knowledge by preparing students for life in a multi-literate world.

It is possible that if Maria had been exposed to bilingual programs, she might not have struggled so often in her schoolwork. She would have learned the concepts in Spanish and then understood what she was being taught in English. The language in which she learned is not what would have been important. What mattered would have been that she was learning—that she was developing an educated mind.

WORKS CITED

Brice, Alejandro and Celeste Roseberry McKibbin. "Choice of Languages in Instruction: One Language or Two?" *Teaching Exceptional Children.* 33.4 (March/April 2001): 10–16.

Crawford, James. *Bilingual Education: History, Politics, Theory and Practice.* Trenton: Crane Publishing: 1989.

"Double Talk?" *Online Newshour.* PBS. 21 September 1997. Transcript. 12 October 2001. http://www.pbs.org/newshour/bb/education/july–dec97/bilingual_9–2/

"English First." *The American Enterprise.* 11.2 (March 2000): 9.

Kole, Nancy. Personal Interview. 15 October 2001.

"History of Bilingual Education." *Rethinking Schools Online.* Vol. 12, No. 3. Spring 1998. 12 October 2001. http://www.rethinkingschools.org/Archives/12_03/langst.htm

Miramontes, Ofelia B., Adel Nadeau, and Nancy L. Commins. *Restructuring Schools for Linguistic Diversity: Linking Decision Making to Effective Programs.* New York: Teachers College Press, 1997.

Ovando, Carlos J. and Virginia P. Collier. *Bilingual and ESL Classrooms: Teaching in Multicultural Contexts.* New York: McGraw-Hill, 1985.

Porter, Rosalie Pedalino. "The Benefits of English Immersion." *Educational Leadership.* 57.4 (Dec 1999/Jan 2000): 52–56.   ■

Responding to Reading

1. What do you find effective about this essay? What could be improved?

2. Why does Elmore begin her essay with a personal anecdote (which she returns to in her conclusion)? How else might one begin essays? What are the advantages and disadvantages of each approach?

3. What kinds of evidence does the essay present? Are some kinds of evidence more persuasive than others?

4. Notice Elmore's section headings. What purpose do they serve?

Community-Based Research Essay: Writing a Proposal

A proposal can help to define and sharpen a writer's conception of a project. Moreover, writing a proposal opens an opportunity for feedback early in the writing process, and this often saves time and effort down the line. A proposal should be two to three double-spaced pages.

The proposal should answer the following questions:

- What is your research question?
- What are your reasons for pursuing that particular question?
- What are potential ethical problems you might encounter in the research process? How do you anticipate dealing with them?
- What are the aims of the project?
- How do you anticipate going about the project?
- What questions and concerns do you have at this point?

Your instructor may also ask you to include a preliminary list of sources.

Agency Profile Report: Exploring Options and Selecting an Organization

If you are writing an agency profile report, you might or might not have a choice about the organization you will investigate. Instructors may have sound reasons for selecting community organizations in advance (such as prior experience with those organizations or plans to work more closely with those organizations later in the course).

If the choice of which agency you will investigate is open, the first step is clear: You need to find an appropriate community organization. As with the research essay, your interests should help to narrow the possibilities. You should also consider your history (Have you been personally involved with any local nonprofit or service organizations?) and your future (Are there local community organizations related to your career goals?). If the agency profile is a prelude to a service-learning project, that might predetermine your choice.

After listing a few areas of interest, you can survey local and campus options by consulting your instructor, a campus volunteer/community service office, a local chapter of the United Way, campus volunteer fairs, and the telephone book. After identifying a few possibilities, you need to make an initial inquiry. Doing so involves locating the appropriate contact person, explaining the purpose of your project, and clarifying what you would expect of the staff (at least one site visit and one interview). Generally agencies welcome such projects and even take your interest as a compliment; but some may have sound reasons to decline (such as the inability to spare time, confidentiality concerns for their clients, or discouraging experiences with previous student projects).

Initial Survey of Interests and Options

List five or six broad social and/or local community issues in which you are interested (children? literacy? health? poverty? the environment? and so on). Mark the two topics that you currently find most engaging. Find out which nonprofit, social service, and social change organizations in the local community address those issues.

The following is a sample agency profile report. In order to create a successful report, the authors needed to conduct interviews, consult Web sites, and analyze agency documents. Then they had to synthesize those sources and use the empirical research report genre.

Student Agency Profile Report: Amanda Hoyt, Leta Reppert, and Adam Taylor, *The Boys and Girls Clubs of Manhattan*:

When they composed this report, Amanda Hoyt, Leta Reppert, and Adam Taylor were first-year students at Kansas State University. After writing this report, they went on to complete a service-learning project with the Boys and Girls Clubs that involved writing and designing three newsletters that announced club news and events.

THE BOYS AND GIRLS CLUBS OF MANHATTAN: HOW WRITING
CAN SERVE UNDERPRIVILEGED CHILDREN
To inspire and enable all young people, especially those from disadvantaged circumstances, to realize their full potential as productive, responsible and caring citizens.
—Mission Statement of the Boys and Girls Clubs of America

Boys and Girls Clubs of America began to provide a place for boys to play in the mid-eighteenth century. Since then, it has expanded its services to include girls, as well (*Official*). Boys and Girls Clubs offer programs in the areas of character and leadership development: education and career development; health and life skills; the arts; and sports, fitness, and recreation (Allen). Its alumni include Michael Jordan, Denzel Washington, and Bill Clinton (*Official*). The Boys and Girls Clubs of Manhattan became a charter member of Boys and Girls Clubs of America in 1994 (Allen).

Our group wanted to write about the Boys and Girls Clubs (BGC) because we wanted to work with an organization that helps children, and these clubs do that not only locally, but also nationally. The BGC uses writing in many ways to help it to serve children. While researching, we learned that the BGC of Manhattan uses writing both to find resources and to communicate with children, their parents, and the community.

OBJECTIVES

In this report, we examine how writing is used by the Boys and Girls Clubs of Manhattan, but to do that we must also investigate the organization itself. The information we have gathered will help us to understand how writing is used in a non-academic setting and will also help us to understand the Boys and Girls Clubs better, which will be useful when we do further work with their organization. For this project, we needed to learn what kinds of writing the Boys and Girls Clubs use and how they use writing to accomplish their goal of helping children.

METHOD

We relied on interviews, brochures, and Internet web pages to prepare this project. Additionally, Amanda works as a volunteer with the Boys and Girls Clubs and was able to provide first-hand information.

We first interviewed Barb Allen, the Executive Director of the Boys and Girls Clubs of Manhattan. Adam, Amanda, and Leta all attended this interview and took notes. Additionally, we brought a tape-recorder to insure that we did not miss anything. Allen was able to provide us with useful information about how the Boys and Girls Clubs work and the types of writing they use.

Our next interview was with Regina Banks, the Director of Program Development at the Manhattan branch. She provided us with much insight about the program as well as about its writing needs. We also tape-recorded this interview.

The brochures we used were published by the BGC of Manhattan. It uses these brochures to inform the community about itself and its programs. These brochures helped us to understand the BGC and the programs it offers.

The websites of the Boys and Girls Clubs of America and of the Boys and Girls Clubs of Manhattan both provided us with much valuable information. The national website provided more detailed information about the organization as a whole, while the local website provided us with information pertaining specifically to the Manhattan area.

Amanda's volunteering experience allowed us to see the organization from the inside and helped us to see the ways that the Boys and Girls Clubs of Manhattan works to help children. Amanda was able to see first-hand how much the children enjoyed being there and how the staff served as positive role models for them.

FACTS AND RESULTS

Although the Manhattan branch of the Boys and Girls Clubs did not become a member of Boys and Girls Clubs of America until 1994, it had been at work in the Manhattan community long before that. It originated in 1973 as a program called Teen Outreach. Although originally directed at teens, the Manhattan branch now serves children between the ages of six and eighteen years old. In 2001, the Boys and Girls Clubs of Manhattan have a record membership of 1029 children, to which they offer programs ranging from tutoring and guitar lessons to sports activities (Allen).

The Boys and Girls Clubs of Manhattan employ two full-time workers and several part-time workers. At present, they also have 426 volunteers. The reason they have so many employees is that the national organization requires them to maintain a worker to child ratio of at least one to fifteen (Allen).

Allen told us that the Boys and Girls Clubs of Manhattan are located at five sites in and around Manhattan, all of which provide before or after school programs or both. There are sites at Eisenhower and Anthony middle schools, Northview School, and 305 S. Fourth Street, in addition to one in Junction City. The Fourth Street location also offers activities specifically for teenagers and a Wednesday night program for the whole family. At the after-school programs, the workers divide the children into groups according to their ages and rotate them through several activities. The children are offered tutoring, arts and crafts, and games every day. Additionally, the Boys and Girls Clubs provide the children with after-school snacks to enable them to concentrate better and to keep them from being disruptive.

The Spot is the BGC's Friday and Saturday night program for teens. At The Spot, teens can dance, watch movies, talk with friends, and learn skills that will help them throughout their lives (*The Spot*). All of these activities take place in a safe environment that lets parents feel at ease about what their children are doing. Within the last year, The Spot has grown from one teen per night to approximately thirty (Banks). The Spot offers many different programs for teens and even gives them the opportunity to compete for scholarships (*The Spot*).

The Boys and Girls Clubs try to give the children that they serve a sense of competence, a sense of usefulness, a sense of belonging, and a sense of power or influence (*Boys*). They hope to be able to instill in the children feelings of self-worth that might not be reinforced anywhere else in their lives. "[W]e want to make sure that every child that walks in that door—that we find something that they can do and they can do well," Allen told us.

Children enjoy the programs that the BGC offers, but the main reason they come is because of the care that the staff shows for them. According to Banks, "The reason they come—one of the big reasons—they don't care that we have two pool tables, they don't care that we have . . . kind of a cool gym, they come because there's a staff here that really cares about them."

Allen said that the Boys and Girls Clubs of Manhattan do little publicizing. They are almost at full capacity now, and they worry that advertising would interest more children in the program than they currently have the money or facilities to serve. Children pay a membership fee of five dollars a year, as well as additional fees for some activities, but this is not nearly enough to pay for all of the services provided. Banks told us that membership fees were enough to pay for the organization's liability insurance five years ago, but now they may not even cover that.

Because of the discrepancy between the membership fees and the actual cost of running the program, the Boys and Girls Clubs of Manhattan must seek funding from other sources. It currently receives funding from the United Way, the City of Manhattan, Riley County, federal and corporate grants, and individual donors. In Allen's words: "[W]e get funding from anybody that'll give us money."

DISCUSSION AND CONCLUSIONS

Allen writes many grants to try to find funding so that the BGC will continue to be able to provide services. She learns about available grants from many sources, including the *Kansas Directory of Foundations,* the Boys and Girls Clubs of America, and individuals. According to Allen, community grants are not as difficult to write as federal grants because their requirements are not as specific.

The Boys and Girls Clubs use writing not only to gain funding, but also to inform children, their parents, and the community about available programs and about the organization's needs (Allen). Each of the sites in the Manhattan area has its own newsletter to inform children and parents about information specific to that site. For example, if one of the sites were having a special activity or had a special need, that information would go out in these newsletters. Regina Banks does most of the writing for the newsletters (Banks).

Allen would like the Manhattan branch to start a community newsletter, but writing a newsletter would only take more time out of her already overfull schedule. This newsletter would be helpful to the BGC because it would provide information about the Clubs' needs and perhaps inspire people to donate more of their time and money to helping these children.

The Boys and Girls Clubs distributes its brochures and fliers around Manhattan. In this way, they are able to provide information about programs to children, as well as inform the public about the BGC.

The website of the Boys and Girls Clubs of Manhattan, www. bgclubmanhattan.com, also provides the community with information. By clicking on different links, a visitor to the BGC's website can find information about programs, membership, and events at the Boys and Girls Clubs. The Vanyon company originally designed the website, but Boys and Girls Club staff now maintain it (Allen). By posting their information on the web, the Boys and Girls Clubs have made it accessible to many people, including potential members, volunteers, and donors.

RECOMMENDATIONS

According to Banks, one of the most important things to keep in mind when writing for the BGC's newsletters is the need to make them both kid and parent friendly. Inserting pictures can help to catch kids' attention and make them more likely to read the letter. When writing for parents, it is important to write concisely, since they will be more likely to read something that is short and will not take much time.

When writing grants, it is important to answer the required questions completely and honestly (Allen). The writer must accurately show why the organization needs the money and how it will be used. It is necessary to tell what the club already does in the area the grant is designed to help and why this money will improve the BGC's services (Banks).

The Boys and Girls Clubs can use any assistance that people are willing to offer, whether donations of time or of money. Even though the Boys and Girls Clubs do not do much advertising, the writing still takes up much of the staff's valuable time. Additionally, if there were more volunteers, it might be possible to start a community newsletter, which would help them to improve and enlarge their services. Most of the volunteers for the Boys and Girls Clubs work with the children, but the job of writing is equally important because without writing, the Boys and Girls Clubs would not be able to function. Even a small contribution of time can help; in 2000, the 426 volunteers worked for a total of nearly 10,000 hours. Many of these volunteers were college students and probably only volunteered a few hours a week. On the other hand, one seventy-two year old woman has volunteered nearly every day for the past few years. Whether the volunteers are able to donate two or twenty hours a week, and whether they write or supervise children, they all play an important role in fulfilling the Boys and Girls Clubs' mission of helping children to "realize their full potential."

WORKS CITED

Allen, Barb. Personal interview. 30 Oct. 2001.

Banks, Regina. Personal interview. 5 Nov. 2001.

Boys and Girls Clubs of Manhattan, Inc.: The Positive Place for Kids. Manhattan, KS: The Boys and Girls Clubs of Manhattan.

The Official Site of Boys and Girls Clubs of America. The Boys and Girls Clubs of America. 6 Nov. 2001 *http://www. bgca.org/.*

The Spot: For Teens Only. Manhattan, KS: The Boys and Girls Clubs of Manhattan.

Vanyon, Inc. *Boys and Girls Clubs of Manhattan, Inc.* The Boys and Girls Clubs of Manhattan. 7 Nov. 2001 *http://www.bgclubmanhattan.com/.* ■

Methods for Research (for Both the Community-Based Research Essay and the Agency Profile Report)

One of the keys to writing about the community is finding a way to translate the ephemeral quality of lived experience into the linearity of written text—in other words, how to capture life in writing. Anyone who has written a personal essay has already grappled with this problem and addressed it by employing such strategies as narrative and description. With writing-about-the-community assignments, you should also employ those strategies, but in addition you will need to develop other approaches to rendering and interpreting experience other than your own. There are several tools for doing this, including

- Keeping a journal
- Taking field notes
- Interviewing
- Using sources

Because human memory is notoriously unreliable, these methods help to record events and ideas that might otherwise be lost in the rush of experience. But they do even more than that. They help you notice what might otherwise get overlooked, hear perspectives that differ from your own, allow a certain critical distance that invites analysis, and understand more fully both yourself and your community. Synthesizing these various sources—and melding them with your own personal experience and perspective—propels fruitful writing about the community.

Keeping a Journal

Keeping a journal is a tried-and-true practice for writers of all kinds. Many people use journals to record events, play with language, express private thoughts, and work through emotional tangles. While writing about the community, your journaling should also involve logging events, making observations, recording fragments of thought, questioning, brainstorming, speculating, posing problems, solving problems, doing informal analysis, responding to readings, connecting readings to experience, and testing ideas. In the context of a group project, journals can also help to document each individual's experience within the collaborative venture.

There is no one right way to keep a journal, but some basic principles should be followed:

- *Write regularly.* Be sure to contribute entries after each visit to a community site or with a community partner, after doing reading that spurs thinking, and when you feel stuck or confused. Write at least weekly, and don't get behind—you don't want to have to backdate entries and re-create reflection.

- *Venture beyond recording.* It is important to record events; but a journal is also a place to speculate about what those events *mean.* This entails reflection, inquiry, and interpretation. You should explore connections, organize your thoughts, consider context, try out hypotheses, engage in analysis, and list things that you need to inquire about further.

- *Take risks.* A journal is a place to be adventuresome. You should record your honest reactions to events and your emerging suppositions. Rather than devote energy to writing what you believe teachers want to hear, be true to your own thinking process, even if it means playing with contradictory thoughts or muddling through incomplete ideas. (Albert Einstein once remarked, "If at first an idea does not seem absurd, there is no hope for it.")

Journal writing is one means by which to spark ideas and sort thoughts. A journal can also be a means of dialogue (if you share the entries with your instructor and/or classmates, inviting response). As a repository of observations and emerging ideas, a journal can prove useful in developing and supporting claims for essays or reports.

WRITING TO DISCOVER

To help contextualize your chosen research question or community organization, try the particle–wave–field strategy for generating ideas. Richard Young, Alton Becker, and Kenneth Pike developed this approach to rhetorical invention as a method for exploring issues in a way that emphasizes context and connections:

Particle	*	A particular event, idea, topic, or issue serves as the particle.
Wave	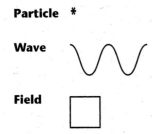	By situating that particle in time and history, it becomes part of a continuous wave. Time stretches before and after, providing a linear context.
Field		Thinking of the particle in a field of social relationships highlights its connections to broader economic, political, and cultural forces.

The following is an example of how to apply the particle–wave–field approach to a potential essay or report topic.

Let's say that you hope to do an agency profile report on the local chapter of Big Brothers/Big Sisters (BB/BS) or a research essay on youth mentoring. That would be your particle.

Now think of the BB/BS chapter as part of a wave, as situated in the stream of time. When was this chapter founded, and in response to what social circumstances was it founded? Before this organization was founded, how did the community approach the activity of mentoring youth? How has this chapter of BB/BS developed and changed over the years?

Now consider this chapter of BB/BS as in a field, in a web of social forces. Is this chapter part of a national organization? How is it funded? In response to what social circumstances was that broad network started? How is it related to other organizations of its kind? Is it related to federal, state, and local government social service programs or to faith-based initiatives?

Further, consider an even wider field: Why does the community need such a mentoring program in the first place? What social forces, such as changes in family or economic structures, create the need for such programs? Are there other ways that the community could (or does) respond to those needs and circumstances?

Heed novelist E. M. Forster's maxim, "Only connect," and flesh out as many relationships as you can.

Taking Field Notes

Whereas journals are often associated with expressing personal thoughts, feelings, and ideas, field notes record observations concretely and systematically. A simple fact of human memory is that most of what we experience is quickly forgotten—and even if we remember key events in broad strokes, many of the details get lost. Field notes preserve experience; also, by prompting us to pay closer attention to surroundings, they can help us see more clearly.

As with a journal, regular field notes entries are essential. Occasions for taking notes can be rather ordinary—for example, a visit to a neighborhood during which you take field notes on the character and layout of public spaces and the activity around you. You might also (after receiving the appropriate permissions) take field notes at special events: during a tutoring session at a community center (if you are writing a research essay related to tutoring) or at a staff meeting of a non-profit agency (if you are writing an agency profile report about that organization).

You should record field notes while an event is happening or immediately after. Sitting down to write notes even a few hours later can result in too many details being forgotten.

Field notes should be concrete and specific. You should avoid vague or abstract descriptions of behavior and instead use detailed sensory descriptions (what you actually see and hear). Anthropologist Clifford Geertz calls this "thick description." For example, when observing at a tutoring center, you might write, "The kids were happy." But this is much too vague. Instead, you should record what the kids were doing that indicated to you that they were happy. How many children and tutors were there? What were their specific activities? Who was interacting with whom, and how? What were they saying (record quotations, if possible), and how were they saying it? Also make observations about the context: What time is it? What does the room look like? What books and materials are being used? and so on.

As you gather notes, you might also start to organize them under subject headings, which can speed the retrieval process when you're consulting notes during the writing of an essay or report.

You should also realize that media other than writing—sketches, diagrams, photos, video, recordings, artifacts, and so on—can be part of field notes. *But remember that before photographing or recording, you should always get explicit permission from both the partner organization and the individuals involved (and, if children are present, from their parents or guardians).*

A Checklist for Field Notes

- Were notes taken during or immediately after observation?
- Are entries dated?
- Are observations concrete and specific?
- Have you included particular quotations?
- Are you using any subject headings?
- Have you included separate personal reflections and conclusions in a journal, in the margins, or in brackets?

If you opt to combine your field notes and your journal, it would be helpful to create a system that distinguishes between your factual observations and your personal reactions. One method is to draw a line down the middle of the page, using one side for field notes and the other for personal musings; another method is to write field notes as regular text but place [brackets] around personal reflections.

Interviewing

Interviews are one of the most important sources for a project, and productive interviews demand skill and preparation. The "Gathering Data: Interviewing" section of Chapter 4 (p. 168–171) lists several tips for conducting successful interviews, such as using open-ended questions, adopting appropriate body language, and taking notes. You should review that section as you prepare to do interviews for your community projects. You should keep in mind that the interview is not only an occasion for you to extract information that you can use for school writing; it is also an opportunity to exchange views, open lines of communication around a shared interest, and initiate a relationship.

Your first task is to determine the appropriate person to interview. In the case of a research essay, you might need to confer with your instructor or use informal networks to determine potential interviewees. For an agency profile report, the executive director, public relations director, and coordinator of volunteers for your chosen agency are often the most appropriate interviewees.

In any case, when you find the right contact person, you need to explain your project succinctly and communicate how long the interview should take (often about 30 minutes). You should also find out as much as you can about your interviewee and/or organization *before* the interview. You would not, for example, want to ask for information that is readily available on an agency's Web site or in its publications. It would be better to devote interview time to gathering and discussing information that is unavailable through any other means.

As you prepare, you should come up with about 20 potential questions, and you should share them with your classmates and instructor for feedback. You don't want to be saying to yourself a few days after the interview, "I should have asked about . . ."

Although one interview is required for either assignment in this chapter, you might want to consider doing two or three. Including a variety of viewpoints generally enriches research projects.

Interview Preparation

BEFORE THE INTERVIEW

- Find out as much as possible about the interviewee and organization.
- Plan interview questions.
- If you are collaborating, have a team plan.
- When setting up an interview, be clear about its purpose and how long you expect it to take.

ESTABLISHING RAPPORT

- Greet the interviewee warmly and express appreciation for the meeting.
- Introduce yourself.
- Remind the interviewee about the purpose of the interview.
- If you want to tape the interview, ask for permission.
- Give your interviewee an invitation to talk about himself/herself by asking a question such as "How did you come to work for _____?"

MAIN QUESTIONS

- Be prepared with at least 15 questions that are tailored to the needs of your project.

CLOSING STRATEGIES

- Ask, "Is there any way that the essay/report that I'm writing could be of interest or use to you or your organization? Would you like to see it in draft form? Would you like a copy of the final draft?"
- Invite a final thought, by saying something such as: "Can you think of anything we haven't covered?"
- Ask for documents that could help you (agency brochures, newsletters, etc.).
- Ask about other potential people to interview (other staff, program participants, etc.).
- Ask whether (and how) you can follow up later if you have more questions.
- Let the interviewee know how helpful he or she has been.
- Thank the interviewee for his or her time and generosity.

Using Sources

Finding, selecting, and using print and digital sources are essential to both the research essay and the agency profile. Good researchers build on and respond to the findings and insights of others.

For the projects in this chapter, several kinds of sources are likely to prove useful, including

- *Specialized academic books and articles, such as scholarly journal articles.* These supply information and insight on a given topic. The expert perspective of such research can lend authority, support, context, and/or contrast to your own claims.

- *Popular press sources, such as magazine articles.* More accessible to nonspecialists than scholarly or technical works, popular press articles, books, and Web sites often provide local, regional, or national news; overviews and investigations of issues; distillations of key questions; and opinions, editorials, and commentary.

- *Reference works, such as encyclopedias and dictionary entries.* Both general and specialized reference works (whether in print, CD-ROM, or online formats) provide basic factual information that can be used to support claims and supply context.

- *Government documents, such as U.S. Census data.* Federal and state governments sponsor credible data collection and analysis on a range of issues, particularly concerning demographics and economics.

- *World Wide Web sites, such as institutional, commercial, and personal pages.* The variety of materials available on the Web is enormous, ranging from the idiosyncratic to the mainstream and from the deceptive to the reliable.

- *Online and CD-ROM databases, such as the Expanded Academic Index or particular disciplinary databases and bibliographies.* These are efficient ways to locate general and specialized sources, and in some cases they speed the retrieval process by including full digital texts.

- *Documents from your community partner, such as brochures or public relations materials.* These materials can prove essential in understanding the specific characteristics and local flavor of an organization.

Exactly what sources you use depends, of course, on the nature and scope of the project. In general, you should draw on several different kinds of sources be-

cause doing so enriches the number of perspectives represented in your research, and this in turn builds credibility with your audience.

Finding sources that are appropriate to your topic or research question can
sometimes be as simple as searching a library catalog or an online database by
subject or key word. But be aware that such searches do not always immediately point you to the most appropriate sources, which means you might need
to do a good deal of digging in order to find information that is really useful
to your project. In most cases, consulting with a reference librarian is a wise
move.

Evaluating Sources.   There is no shortage of available information—in
fact, we live in an age of information overload. Accessing information has become relatively easy, but *assessing* it remains a challenge. This means that
evaluating and *selecting* information with a critical eye has become a vital skill in
contemporary culture. Finding information on a general topic usually is not
difficult, but finding the *right* information and putting it to responsible use is a
formidable task.

Evaluating sources is a skill that comes with experience, but both novice and
seasoned researchers can start with three key principles for discernment:

- *Relevance.* One simple (even if disheartening) fact of the research process
  is that much of what one finds, especially in the preliminary stages, may
  not be used in the final product. Just as it takes lots of mining to discover
  a few gold nuggets, it might take hours of searching and scanning to find
  the few articles that speak to your particular research question.

- *Bias.* Not all sources are created equal: Some are credible, some reveal obvious sympathies, some hide biases, and some are downright manipula-
  tive. Part of being a good researcher involves adopting a critical eye on
  matters of perspective and bias. For example, publications of the politically conservative Heritage Foundation will be shaped by its values, just as
  publications of the politically liberal American Civil Liberties Union will
  be shaped by its values. Although pure objectivity is ever-elusive, several
  questions can flesh out the reliability of a source: Where does the document come from? Why would that author and/or organization print it? In
  other words, *cui bono* (who benefits)? What is the history of the organization publishing the work, and what are the qualifications of the writer?
  Has the work been through an editorial or review process? Is there open
  disclosure? When making these determinations, you might need to consult with someone who is knowledgeable in the field. Finally, detecting
  sympathies or biases in a source does not automatically disqualify it from
  use, but you are obligated to make readers aware of the bias.

- *Currency.* You should think of research not as a static, isolated pursuit but rather as part of dynamic, ongoing social conversation. Facts and data can change over time; attitudes and ways of thinking evolve; some findings become outdated; and some findings might be refuted, revised, qualified, or confirmed by later thinkers. This does not mean that newer is always better; sometimes newness can be trendiness. But it does mean that you should at least investigate the latest findings related to your research question and include sources that reflect contemporary thinking in that field.

Questions for Evaluating Sources

RELEVANCE

- Is this source directly related to my research question or topic of inquiry?
- Does the source provide support, contrast, or context to my particular focus?

BIAS

- Where does the source come from?
- *Cui bono?*
- What kind of review or editorial process has the publication been through?
- Is there open disclosure? (That is, does the document clearly indicate who has written it, where the information in the document comes from, and whether the writer is associated with any particular organization or political affiliation?)

CURRENCY

- Am I using the most recent factual information?
- Do some of my sources reflect current thinking in the field?
- Are any of the publication dates in the past three years?

Special Considerations for Web Sources.   The World Wide Web and online databases are often the first places people turn to when searching for information. The ease and efficiency with which online information can be accessed has made the Internet a favorite research tool; but the avalanche of information on the Web can be overwhelming, and the quality and credibility of Web sources varies enormously. Typing key words into a search engine is only the start of the online research process.

Some Web documents and online databases simply duplicate print sources (online versions of journal articles, for example), and in those cases the questions of relevance, bias, and currency listed earlier apply as is. But you should take special care with sources posted exclusively on the Web. Anyone can create and post a Web page. The up side of this is the democratizing effect that the Web can have on personal expression, dialogue, and the dissemination of information; the down side is that open access increases opportunities for deception and manipulation. Someone with a narrow personal agenda or with limited knowledge can masquerade as an expert; partisan political groups can spin their views as objective and benevolent; commercial interests can hide their financial motives behind altruistic rhetoric; a site can look polished and professional yet still be a front for a hate group. One should be particularly cautious of Web pages that are devoid of any identifiable author or sponsoring organization. The Web is a wide-open, exciting network of voices and possibilities, but you must approach it with healthy skepticism.

One way to quickly assess one characteristic of a site is to look at the tag at the end of the Web address (e.g., .com, .edu, .org, .gov). Each of these tags signals a broad category to which the page belongs: *.com* signals the commercial, for-profit arena; *.edu* signals educational institutions; *.org* signals the nonprofit sphere; and *.gov* signals government. There remains significant variance in credibility within any single category, but the Web address ending can at least serve as a starting point for evaluation. Other questions for evaluating Web sources are listed in the following box.

Questions for Evaluating Web Sources

In addition to questions of relevance, bias, and currency, you should ask

- Who created the Web site and why?
- What does the Web address ending (e.g., .com, .edu, .org, .gov) suggest about the site?
- How does this site compare and contrast to similar sites? Can you locate differing perspectives?
- Is there open disclosure about the author and/or sponsoring organization, the sources of funding, and the purpose of the site? Is there contact information such as a mailing address and phone number?
- If this is a personal Web site, what do you know about the person who created it, and how does that affect the credibility of the material?

As with print sources, using a variety of digital sources can improve your credibility with readers. Rather than rely exclusively on the Web for research, gather a mix of print and electronic sources.

Summary, Paraphrase, and Direct Quotation of Sources. There are three basic ways to insert source material into a text: summary, paraphrase, and direct quotation. Each has advantages, and researchers should be familiar with all three methods:

	Summary	Paraphrase	Direct Quotation
What is it?	Represents the general ideas and conclusions from a source in one's own words.	Translates the content of a specific passage from a source into one's own words and syntax.	Reproduces the exact wording and syntax of a source.
Why choose it?	To introduce large blocks of source material efficiently.	To include a specific part of source material, representing it faithfully but recrafting the prose to fit the purpose and style of the argument.	To let the source speak for itself, especially when the exact wording aptly supports, illustrates, or exemplifies a claim or subclaim.
How to do it?	Summarize the source in one's own words. Signal phrases are sometimes used.	Rewrite the passage, adjusting wording and syntax to fit smoothly with the sentences before and after it. Signal phrases are usually used.	Introduce the passage with a signal phrase and reproduce the exact wording of the source, housing it in quotation marks. Use an ellipsis (. . .) to indicate where text is omitted, and employ indented block quote format if the passage runs over three lines.
How to document it?	(1) In-text citation (2) Source listed in Works Cited list	(1) In-text citation (2) Source listed in Works Cited list	(1) In-text citation (2) Source listed in Works Cited list

Good research papers usually demonstrate a mix of the three approaches. Relying too heavily on only one method suggests that the advantages of the other methods are being overlooked. Moreover, it can become stylistically tiresome.

Signal Phrases

Source material should not just be dropped into a text—that can be jarring for the reader. Rather, the writer should introduce sources to the reader and telegraph how they should be received. One effective way to do this is by using signal phrases.

Signal phrases, also called *tag phrases,* are short passages that help prepare the reader for source material. They often reveal the name of the author, sometimes adding information that contributes to his or her authority (e.g., "Historian Christopher Parker argues that . . . ", "According to data posted on the Economics Institute Web site, . . . "). Signal phrases can also do the important work of suggesting how the reader should receive the source (e.g., "The following passage from Mike Rose's *Lives on the Boundary* illustrates how tracking systems in schools can hurt working-class children: . . . "). Although signal phrases are usually placed at the beginning of sentences, they can be placed elsewhere (e.g., "The primary causes of poverty, Louise Robinson explains, are . . . "). Remember that the use of signal phrases is not limited to introducing print and electronic sources. Signal phrases are also helpful when integrating passages from interviews, journals, and field notes.

Documentation Conventions.   Whether a source is summarized, paraphrased, or directly quoted, it must be documented. Inserting in-text citations and compiling Works Cited lists can be tedious, but these functions are important because the underlying principles governing documentation are honesty, disclosure, and respect. At heart, research is a collaborative process: Each new researcher stands on the shoulders of those who have come before. Those researchers deserve respect and credit, which makes explicit acknowledgment of their intellectual work essential. Rather than view your research and writing as an isolated assignment, you should see it as part of an ongoing conversation—a conversation in which all participants honestly acknowledge when they are drawing on the insights and findings of others.

Documentation should give readers a clear pathway back to source material. In most documentation systems, this is a two-part process: An in-text citation uses a shorthand notation (usually the author's last name and the page number, but sometimes also a title or publication date) to signal the specific source, and the Works Cited or References list provides full bibliographic information on each source, allowing the reader to locate all the works consulted.

There is nothing magical or transcendent about the rules of documentation in any given system. Essentially, different communities of researchers have settled on particular conventions and agreed to use them consistently. For example, scholars in English studies usually use Modern Language Association (MLA) format, and researchers in the social sciences usually use American Psychological Association (APA) format. Other disciplines have their own systems, as do many professions. To determine exactly how to document different kinds of sources in a particular system, you should consult an up-to-date reference work or writing handbook. MLA and APA are the systems most commonly included in writing handbooks.

Although they are generally stable, documentation systems, like language itself, change with the times. In the past few decades, for example, new formats have evolved to document Web and other electronic sources.

Methods for Synthesizing and Organizing (for Both the Community-Based Research Essay and the Agency Profile Report)

The word *text* derives from the same root as *textile*; the terms share an origin in the verb *to weave*. Accordingly, you might think of research texts as weaving several major ideas, voices, subpoints, and sources into one cloth.

Keep in mind that you, the weaver, should guide the work deliberately and leave a distinctive personal mark on your text. Rather than dump data on readers, your task is to synthesize various strands of inquiry.

In the early stages of synthesizing, questions of *purpose* are critical:

- What is this text supposed to *do*?
- Is the piece primarily informative or persuasive? Or is there some other purpose?

The intent of the agency profile report is primarily informative. And although research essays are often likewise informative, many adopt a persuasive posture (such as the essay "Who Deserves a Head Start?" on pp. 321–328, which argues for a particular public policy). Keeping the purpose of your essay in mind will be helpful in selecting which ideas and sources to emphasize as well as in choosing an organizational structure.

Synthesizing is also about identifying and articulating *connections*. You need to review all your sources (experience, interviews, print sources, Web pages, etc.) and ask

- How do particular ideas, sources, issues, or questions connect to one another?
- What is the nature of those relationships? For example, do two sources highlight a contrast? Do several of the voices reinforce or amplify each other? Do they clarify, refute, illuminate, or contradict each other?

Questions of *hierarchy* are also important:

- Which ideas are most important?
- Which connections are most meaningful?
- Where is the real intellectual excitement? Where am I saying something new and original?
- Which ideas are tangential or expendable? Which ideas are so obvious that they can be taken for granted by your audience and therefore cut? Which are interesting but don't really contribute to the argument being developed?

Ethos, Logos, and Pathos

The ancient Greek philosopher and rhetorician Aristotle proposed that when composing and delivering a persuasive speech, three concerns—ethos, logos, and pathos—need to be properly addressed. What Aristotle theorized about ancient oratory many now find applicable to writing.

Ethos concerns the writer, particularly the writer's credibility. If an audience finds the writer's ethos, or persona, trustworthy, that audience will be more open to persuasion.

Logos concerns the content of the argument itself, particularly the soundness of reasoning and the quantity and quality of evidence presented. The more logical and well supported the argument, the more likely the audience is to accept it.

Pathos concerns the audience, particularly emotional appeals that will move the audience. By understanding the characteristics, concerns, and inclinations of an audience, the writer can appeal to the audience strategically.

The challenge is to properly weave and balance ethos, logos, and pathos, and different circumstances call for different proportions. A lab report, for example, might leverage logos (facts, results, analysis) over ethos or pathos. Alternately, a letter appealing for disaster relief donations might emphasize pathos (sympathy for victims) over the others.

A community-based research essay should address all three factors. Consider Aristotle's theory in relation to the following essay by Peter Marin, "Helping and Hating the Homeless." Marin establishes his ethos by presenting himself not only as a serious journalist who has researched his topic but also as an insider who has experienced homelessness himself. He develops the logos of his argument by marshaling several kinds of evidence—statistics, history, expert opinions, social analysis—and organizing it in a sensible arrangement. Marin also appeals to pathos, particularly the reader's compassion for those who have experienced tragedy, by weaving in stories about individuals who give a human face to a broad social problem.

Essay: Peter Marin, *Helping and Hating the Homeless*: *The Struggle at the Margins of America*

Peter Marin is a writer who regularly contributes to Harper's Magazine, *in which the following essay was published.*

When I was a child, I had a recurring vision of how I would end as an old man: alone, in a sparsely furnished second-story room I could picture quite precisely, in a walk-up on Fourth Avenue in New York, where the second-hand bookstores then were. It was not a picture which frightened me. I liked it. The idea of anonymity and solitude and marginality must have seemed to me, back then, for reasons I do not care to remember, both inviting and inevitable. Later, out of college, I took to the road, hitchhiking and traveling on freights, doing odd jobs here and there, crisscrossing the country. I liked that too: the anonymity and the absence of constraint and the rough community I sometimes found. I felt at home on the road, perhaps because I felt at home nowhere else, and periodically, for years, I would return to that world, always with a sense of relief and release.

I have been thinking a lot about that these days, now that transience and homelessness have made their way into the national consciousness, and especially since the town I live in, Santa Barbara, has become well known because of the recent successful campaign to do away with the meanest aspects of its "sleeping ordinances"—a set of foolish laws making it illegal for the homeless to sleep at night in public places. During that campaign I got to know many of the homeless men and women in Santa Barbara, who tend to gather, night and day, in a small park at the lower end of town, not far from the tracks and the harbor, under the rooflike, overarching branches of a gigantic fig tree, said to be the oldest on the continent. There one enters much the same world I thought, as a child, I would die in, and the one in which I traveled as a young man: a "marginal" world inhabited by all those unable to find a place in "our" world. Sometimes, standing on the tracks close to the park, you can sense in the wind, or in the smell of tar and ties, the presence and age of that marginal world: the way it stretches backward and inevitably forward in time, parallel to our own world, always present, always close, and yet separated from us—at least in the mind—by a gulf few of us are interested in crossing.

Late last summer, at a city council meeting here in Santa Barbara, I saw, close up, the consequences of that strange combination of proximity and distance. The council was meeting to vote on the repeal of the sleeping ordinances, though not out of any sudden sense of compassion or justice. Council members had been pressured into it by the threat of massive demonstrations—"The Selma of the Eighties" was the slogan one heard among the homeless. But this threat that frightened the council enraged the town's citizens. Hundreds of them turned out for the meeting. One by one they filed to the microphone to curse the council and castigate the homeless. Drinking, doping, loitering, panhandling, defecating, urinating, molesting, stealing—the litany went on and on, was repeated over and over, accompanied by fantasies of disaster: the barbarian hordes at the gates, civilization ended.

What astonished me about the meeting was not what was said; one could have predicted that. It was the power and depth of the emotion revealed: the mindlessness of the fear, the vengefulness of the fury. Also, almost none of what was said had anything to do with the homeless people I know—not the ones I traveled with, not the ones in town. They, the actual homeless men and women, might not have existed at all.

If I write about Santa Barbara, it is not because I think the attitudes at work here are unique. They are not. You find them everywhere in America. In the last few months I have visited several cities around the country, and in each of them I have found the same thing: more and more people in the streets, more and more suffering. (There are at least 350,000 homeless people in the country, perhaps as many as 3 million.) And, in talking to the good citizens of these cities, I found, almost always, the same thing: confusion and ignorance, or simple indifference, but anger too, and fear.

What follows here is an attempt to explain at least some of that anger and fear, to clear up some of the confusion, to chip away at the indifference. It is not meant to be definitive; how could it be? The point is to try to illuminate some of the darker corners of homelessness, those we ordinarily ignore, and those in which the keys to much that is now going on may be hidden.

*   *   *

The trouble begins with the word "homeless." It has become such an abstraction, and is applied to so many different kinds of people, with so many different histories and problems, that it is almost meaningless.

Homelessness, in itself, is nothing more than a condition visited upon men and women (and, increasingly, children) as the final stage of a variety of problems about which the word "homelessness" tells us almost nothing. Or, to put it another way, it is a catch basin into which pour all of the people disenfranchised or marginalized or scared off by processes beyond their control, those which lie close to the heart of American life. Here are the groups packed into the single category of "the homeless":

- Veterans, mainly from the war in Vietnam. In many American cities, vets make up close to 50 percent of all homeless males.
- The mentally ill. In some parts of the country, roughly a quarter of the homeless would, a couple of decades ago, have been institutionalized.

- The physically disabled or chronically ill, who do not receive any benefits or whose benefits do not enable them to afford permanent shelter.
- The elderly on fixed incomes whose funds are no longer sufficient for their needs.
- Men, women, and whole families pauperized by the loss of a job.
- Single parents, usually women, without the resources or skills to establish new lives.
- Runaway children, many of whom have been abused.
- Alcoholics and those in trouble with drugs (whose troubles often begin with one of the other conditions listed here).
- Immigrants, both legal and illegal, who often are not counted among the homeless because they constitute a "problem" in their own right.
- Traditional tramps, hobos, and transients, who have taken to the road or the streets for a variety of reasons and who prefer to be there.

You can quickly learn two things about the homeless from this list. First, you can learn that many of the homeless, before they were homeless, were people more or less like ourselves: members of the working or middle class. And you can learn that the world of the homeless has its roots in various policies, events, and ways of life for which some of us are responsible and from which some of us actually prosper.

We decide, as a people, to go to war, we ask our children to kill and to die, and the result, years later, is grown men homeless on the street.

We change, with the best intentions, the laws pertaining to the mentally ill, and then, without intention, neglect to provide them with services; and the result, in our streets, drives some of us crazy with rage.

We cut taxes and prune budgets, we modernize industry and shift the balance of trade, and the result of all these actions and errors can be read, sleeping form by sleeping form, on our city streets.

The liberals cannot blame the conservatives. The conservatives cannot blame the liberals. Homelessness is the *sum total* of our dreams, policies, intentions, errors, omissions, cruelties, kindnesses, all of it recorded, in flesh, in the life of the streets.

You can also learn from this list one of the most important things there is to know about the homeless—that they can be roughly divided into two groups: those who have had homelessness forced upon them and want nothing more than to escape it; and those who have at least in part chosen it for themselves, and now accept, or in some cases, embrace it.

I understand how dangerous it is to introduce the idea of choice into a discussion of homelessness. It can all too easily be used to justify indifference or brutality toward the homeless, or to argue that they are only getting what they "deserve." And yet it seems to me that it is only by taking choice into account, in all of the intricacies of its various forms and expressions, that one can really understand certain kinds of homelessness.

The fact is, many of the homeless are not only hapless victims but voluntary exiles, "domestic refugees," people who have turned not against life itself but against *us*, our life, American life. Look for a moment at the vets. The price of returning to America was to forget what they had seen or learned in Vietnam, to "put it behind them." But some could not do that, and the stress of trying showed up as alcoholism, broken marriages, drug addiction, crime. And it showed up too as life on the street, which was for some vets a desperate choice made in the name of life—the best they could manage. It was a way of avoiding what might have occurred had they stayed where they were: suicide, or violence done to others.

We must learn to accept that there may indeed be people, and not only vets, who have seen so much of our world, or seen it so clearly, that to live in it becomes impossible. Here, for example, is the story of Alice, a homeless middle-aged woman in Los Angeles, where there are, perhaps, 50,000 homeless people. It was set down a few months ago by one of my students at the University of California, Santa Barbara, where I taught for a semester. I had encouraged them to go find the homeless and listen to their stories. And so, one day, when this student saw Alice foraging in a dumpster outside a McDonald's, he stopped and talked to her:

> She told me she had led a pretty normal life as she grew up and eventually went to college. From there she went on to Chicago to teach school. She was single and lived in a small apartment.
>
> One night, after she got off the train after school, a man began to follow her to her apartment building. When she got to her door she saw a knife and the man hovering behind her. She had no choice but to let him in. The man raped her.
>
> After that, things got steadily worse. She had a nervous breakdown. She went to a mental institution for three months, and when she went back to her apartment she found her belongings gone. The landlord had sold them to cover the rent she hadn't paid.
>
> She had no place to go and no job because the school had terminated her employment. She slipped into depression. She lived with friends until she could muster enough money for a ticket to Los Angeles. She said she no longer wanted to burden her friends, and that if she had to live outside, at least Los Angeles was warmer than Chicago.
>
> It is as if she began back then to take on the mentality of a street person. She resolved herself to homelessness. She's been out West since 1980, without a home or job. She seems happy, with her best friend being her cat. But the scars of memories still haunt her, and she is running from them, or should I say *him*.

This is, in essence, the same story one hears over and over again on the street. You begin with an ordinary life; then an event occurs—traumatic, catastrophic; smaller events follow, each one deepening the original wound; finally, homelessness becomes inevitable, or begins to *seem* inevitable to the person involved—the only way out of an intolerable situation. You are struck continually, hearing these stories, by something seemingly unique in American life, the absolute isolation involved. In what other culture would there be such an absence or failure of support from familial, social, or institutional sources? Even more disturbing is the fact that it is often our supposed sources of support—family, friends, government organizations—that have caused the problem in the first place.

Everything that happened to Alice—the rape, the loss of job and apartment, the breakdown—was part and parcel of a world gone radically wrong, a world, for Alice, no longer to be counted on, no longer worth living in. Her homelessness can be seen as flight, as failure of will or nerve, even, perhaps, as *disease.* But it can also be seen as a mute, furious refusal, a self-imposed exile far less appealing to the rest of us than ordinary life, but *better,* in Alice's terms.

We like to think, in America, that everything is redeemable, that everything broken can be magically made whole again, and that what has been "dirtied" can be cleansed. Recently I saw on television that one of the soaps had introduced the character of a homeless old woman. A woman in her thirties discovers that her long-lost mother has appeared in town, on the streets. After much searching, the mother is located and identified and embraced; and then she is scrubbed and dressed in style, restored in a matter of days to her former upper-class habits and role.

A triumph—but one more likely to occur on television than in real life. Yes, many of those on the streets could be transformed, rehabilitated. But there are others whose lives have been irrevocably changed, damaged beyond repair, and who no longer want help, who no longer recognize the *need* for help, and whose experience in our world has made them want only to be left alone. How, for instance, would one restore Alice's life, or reshape it in a way that would satisfy *our* notion of what a life should be? What would it take to return her to the fold? How to erase the four years of homelessness, which have become familiar to her, and as much a home, as her "normal" life once was? Whatever we think of the way in which she has resolved her difficulties, it constitutes a sad peace made with the world. Intruding ourselves upon it in the name of redemption is by no means as simple a task—or as justifiable a task—as one might think.

It is important to understand too that however disorderly and dirty and unmanageable the world of homeless men and women like Alice appears to us, it is not without its significance, and its rules and rituals. The homeless in our cities mark out for themselves particular neighborhoods, blocks, buildings, doorways. They impose on themselves often obsessively strict routines. They reduce their world to a small area, and thereby protect themselves from a world that might otherwise be too much to bear.

Pavlov, the Russian psychologist, once theorized that the two most fundamental reflexes in all animals, including humans, are those involving freedom
and orientation. Grab any animal, he said, and it will immediately struggle to accomplish two things: to break free and to orient itself. And this is what one sees
in so many of the homeless. Having been stripped of all other forms of connection, and of most kinds of social identity, they are left only with this: the raw stuff
of nature, something encoded in the cells—the desire to be free, the need for familiar space. Perhaps this is why so many of them struggle so vehemently
against us when we offer them aid. They are clinging to their freedom and their
space, and they do not believe that this is what we, with our programs and our
shelters, mean to allow them.

*   *   *

Years ago, when I first came to California, bumming my way west, the marginal world, and the lives of those in it, were very different from what they are
now. In those days I spent much of my time in hobo jungles or on the skid rows
of various cities, and just as it was easier back then to "get by" in the easygoing
beach towns on the California coast, or in the bohemian and artistic worlds in
San Francisco or Los Angeles or New York, it was also far easier than it is now to
survive in the marginal world.

It is important to remember this—important to recognize the immensity of
the changes that have occurred in the marginal world in the past twenty years.
Whole sections of many cities—the Bowery in New York, the Tenderloin in San
Francisco—were once ceded to the transient. In every skid-row area in America
you could find what you needed to survive: hash houses, saloons offering free
lunches, pawnshops, surplus-clothing stores, and, most important of all, cheap
hotels and flophouses and two-bit employment agencies specializing in the
kinds of labor (seasonal, shape-up) transients have always done.

It was by no means a wonderful world. But it *was* a world. Its rituals were
spelled out in ways most of the participants understood. In hobo jungles up and
down the tracks, whatever there was to eat went into a common pot and was
divided equally. Late at night, in empties crisscrossing the country, men would
speak with a certain anonymous openness, as if the shared condition of transience created among them a kind of civility.

What most people in that world wanted was simply to be left alone. Some of
them had been on the road for years, itinerant workers. Others were recuperat-
ing from wounds they could never quite explain. There were young men and a
few women with nothing better to do, and older men who had no families or
had lost their jobs or wives, or for whom the rigor and pressure of life had
proved too demanding. The marginal world offered them a respite from the
other world, a world grown too much for them.

But things have changed. There began to pour into the marginal world—slowly in the sixties, a bit faster in the seventies, and then faster still in the eighties—more and more people who neither belonged nor knew how to survive there. The sixties brought the counterculture and drugs; the streets filled with young dropouts. Changes in the law loosed upon the streets mentally ill men and women. Inflation took its toll, then recession. Working-class and even middle-class men and women—entire families—began to fall into a world they did not understand.

At the same time the transient world was being inundated by new inhabitants, its landscape, its economy, was shrinking radically. Jobs became harder to find. Modernization had something to do with it; machines took the place of men and women. And the influx of workers from Mexico and points farther south created a class of semipermanent workers who took the place of casual transient labor. More important, perhaps, was the fact that the forgotten parts of many cities began to attract attention. Downtown areas were redeveloped, reclaimed. The skid-row sections of smaller cities were turned into "old townes." The old hotels that once catered to transients were upgraded or torn down or became warehouses for welfare families—an arrangement far more profitable to the owners. The price of housing increased; evictions increased. The mentally ill, who once could afford to house themselves in cheap rooms, the alcoholics, who once would drink themselves to sleep at night in their cheap hotels, were out on the street—exposed to the weather and to danger, and also in plain and public view: "problems" to be dealt with.

Nor was it only cheap shelter that disappeared. It was also those "open" spaces that had once been available to those without other shelter . . . property rose in value, the nooks and crannies in which the homeless had been able to hide became more visible. Doorways, alleys, abandoned buildings, vacant lots—these "holes" in the cityscape, these gaps in public consciousness, became *real estate*. The homeless, who had been there all the time, were overtaken by economic progress, and they became intruders.

You cannot help thinking, as you watch this process, of what happened in parts of Europe in the eighteenth and nineteenth centuries: the effects of the enclosure laws, which eliminated the "commons" in the countryside and drove the rural poor, now homeless, into the cities. The centuries-old tradition of common access and usage was swept away by the beginnings of industrialism; land became *privatized*, a commodity. At the same time something occurred in the cultural psyche. The world itself, space itself, was subtly altered. It was no longer merely to be lived in; it was now to be owned. What was enclosed was not only the land. It was also *the flesh itself* it was cut off from, denied access to, the physical world.

And one thinks too, when thinking of the homeless, of the America past, the settlement of the "new" world which occurred at precisely the same time that the commons disappeared. The dream of freedom and equality that brought men and women here had something to do with *space,* as if the wilderness itself conferred upon those arriving here a new beginning: the Eden that had been lost. Once God had sent Christ to redeem men; now he provided a new world. Men discovered, or believed that this world, and perhaps time itself, had no edge, no limit. Space was a sign of God's magnanimity. It was a kind of grace.

Somehow, it is all this that is folded into the sad shapes of the homeless. In their mute presence one can sense, however faintly, the dreams of a world gone aglimmering, and the presence of our failed hopes. A kind of claim is made, silently, an ethic is proffered, or, if you will, a whole cosmology, one older than our own ideas of privilege and property. It is as if flesh itself were seeking, this one last time, the home in the world it has been denied.

*   *   *

Daily the city eddies around the homeless. The crowds flowing past leave a few feet, a gap. We do not touch the homeless world. Perhaps we cannot touch it. It remains separate even as the city surrounds it.

The homeless, simply because they are homeless, are strangers, alien—and therefore a threat. Their presence, in itself, comes to constitute a kind of violence; it deprives us of our sense of safety. Let me use myself as an example. I know, and respect, many of those now homeless on the streets of Santa Barbara. Twenty years ago, some of them would have been my companions and friends. And yet, these days, if I walk through the park near my home and see strangers bedding down for the night, my first reaction, if not fear, is a sense of annoyance and intrusion, of worry and alarm. I think of my teenage daughter, who often walks through the park, and then of my house, a hundred yards away, and I am tempted—only tempted, but tempted, still—to call the "proper" authorities to have the strangers moved on. Out of sight, out of mind.

Notice: I do not bring them food. I do not offer them shelter or a shower in the morning. I do not even stop to talk. Instead, I think: my daughter, my house, my privacy. What moves me is not the threat of *danger*—nothing as animal as that. Instead there pops up inside of me, neatly in a row, a set of anxieties, ones you might arrange in a dollhouse living room and label: Family of bourgeois fears. The point is this: our response to the homeless is fed by a complex set of cultural attitudes, habits of thought, and fantasies and fears so familiar to us, so common, that they have become *second* nature and might as well be instinctive, for all the control we have over them. And it is by no means easy to untangle this snarl of responses. What does seem clear is that the homeless embody all that bourgeois culture has for centuries tried to eradicate and destroy.

If you look to the history of Europe you find that homelessness first appears (or is first acknowledged) at the very same moment that bourgeois culture begins to appear. The same processes produced them both: the breakup of feudalism, the rise of commerce and cities, the combined triumphs of capitalism, industrialism, and individualism. The historian Fernand Braudel, in *The Wheels of Commerce,* describes, for instance, the armies of impoverished men and women who began to haunt Europe as far back as the eleventh century. And the makeup of these masses? Essentially the same then as it is now: the unfortunates, the throwaways, the misfits, the deviants.

> In the eighteenth century, all sorts and conditions were to be found in this human dross . . . widows, orphans, cripples . . . journeymen who had broken their contracts, out-of-work labourers, homeless priests with no living, old men, fire victims . . . war victims, deserters, discharged soldiers, would-be vendors of useless articles, vagrant preachers with or without licenses, "pregnant servant-girls and unmarried mothers driven from home," children sent out "to find bread or to maraud."

Then, as now, distinctions were made between the "homeless" and the supposedly "deserving" poor, those who knew their place and willingly sustained, with their labors, the emergent bourgeois world.

> The good paupers were accepted, lined up and registered on the official list; they had a right to public charity and were sometimes allowed to solicit it outside churches in prosperous districts, when the congregation came out, or in market places. . . .
> When it comes to beggars and vagrants, it is a very different story, and different pictures meet the eye: crowds, mobs, processions, sometimes mass emigrations, "along the country highways or the streets of the Towns and Villages," by beggars "whom hunger and nakedness has driven from home.". . . The towns dreaded these alarming visitors and drove them out as soon as they appeared on the horizon.

And just as the distinctions made about these masses were the same then as they are now, so too was the way society saw them. They seemed to bourgeois eyes (as they still do) the one segment of society that remained resistant to progress, unassimilable and incorrigible, inimical to all order.

It is in the nineteenth century, in the Victorian era, that you can find the beginnings of our modern strategies for dealing with the homeless: the notion that they should be controlled and perhaps eliminated through "help." With the Victorians we begin to see the entangling of self-protection with social obligation, the strategy of masking self-interest and the urge to control as *moral duty.* Michel Foucault has spelled this out in his books on madness and punishment: the zeal with which the overseers of early bourgeois culture tried to purge, improve, and purify all of urban civilization—whether through schools and prisons, or quite literally, with public baths and massive new water and sewage systems. Order, ordure—this is, in essence, the tension at the heart of bourgeois culture, and it was the singular genius of the Victorians to make it the main component of their medical, aesthetic, *and* moral systems. It was not a sense of justice or even empathy which called for charity or new attitudes toward the poor; it was *hygiene.* The very same attitudes appear in nineteenth-century America. Charles

Loring Brace, in an essay on homeless and vagrant children written in 1876, described the treatment of delinquents in this way: "Many of their vices drop from them like the old and verminous clothing they left behind. . . . The entire change of circumstances seems to cleanse them of bad habits." Here you have it all: *vices, verminous clothing, cleansing them of bad habits*—the triple association of poverty with vice with dirt, an equation in which each term comes to stand for all of them.

These attitudes are with us still; that is the point. In our own century the person who has written most revealingly about such things is George Orwell, who tried to analyze his own middle-class attitudes toward the poor. In 1933, in *Down and Out in Paris and London,* he wrote about tramps:

> In childhood we are taught that tramps are blackguards . . . a repulsive, rather dangerous creature, who would rather die than work or wash, and wants nothing but to beg, drink or rob hen-houses. The tramp monster is no truer to life than the sinister Chinaman of the magazines, but he is very hard to get rid of. The very word "tramp" evokes his image.

All of this is still true in America, though now it is not the word "tramp" but the word "homeless" that evokes the images we fear. It is the homeless who smell. Here, for instance, is part of a paper a student of mine wrote about her first visit to a Rescue Mission on skid row.

> The sermon began. The room was stuffy and smelly. The mixture of body odors and cooking was nauseating. I remember thinking: how can these people share this facility? They must be repulsed by each other. They had strange habits and dispositions. They were a group of dirty, dishonored, weird people to me.
>
> When it was over I ran to my car, went home, and took a shower. I felt extremely dirty. Through the day I would get flashes of that disgusting smell.

To put it as bluntly as I can, for many of us the homeless are *shit.* And our policies toward them, our spontaneous sense of disgust and horror, our wish to be rid of them—all of this has hidden in it, close to its heart, our feelings about excrement. Even Marx, that most bourgeois of revolutionaries, described the deviant *lumpen* in *The Eighteenth Brumaire of Louis Bonaparte* as "scum, offal, refuse of all classes." These days, in puritanical Marxist nations, they are called "parasites"—a word, perhaps not incidentally, one also associates with human waste.

What I am getting at here is the *nature* of the desire to help the homeless—what is hidden behind it and why it so often does harm. Every government program, almost every private project, is geared as much to the needs of those giving help as it is to the needs of the homeless. Go to any government agency, or, for that matter, to most private charities, and you will find yourself enmeshed, at once, in a bureaucracy so tangled and oppressive, or confronted with so much moral arrogance and contempt, that you will be driven back out into the streets for relief.

Santa Barbara, where I live, is as good an example as any. There are three main shelters in the city—all of them private. Between them they provide fewer than a hundred beds a night for the homeless. Two of the three shelters are religious in nature: the Rescue Mission and the Salvation Army. In the mission, as in most places in the country, there are elaborate and stringent rules. Beds go first to those who have not been there for two months, and you can stay for only two nights in any two-month period. No shelter is given to those who are not sober. Even if you go to the mission only for a meal, you are required to listen to sermons and participate in prayer, and you are regularly proselytized—sometimes overtly, sometimes subtly. There are obligatory, regimented showers. You go to bed precisely at ten: lights out, no reading, no talking. After the lights go out you will find fifteen men in a room with double-decker bunks. As the night progresses the room grows stuffier and hotter. Men toss, turn, cough, and moan. In the morning you are awakened precisely at five forty-five. Then breakfast. At seven-thirty you are back on the street.

The town's newest shelter was opened almost a year ago by a consortium of local churches. Families and those who are employed have first call on the beds—a policy which excludes the congenitally homeless. Alcohol is not simply forbidden in the shelter; those with a history of alcoholism must sign a "contract" pledging to remain sober and chemical-free. Finally, in a paroxysm of therapeutic bullying, the shelter has added a new wrinkle: If you stay more than two days you are required to fill out and discuss with a social worker a complex form listing what you perceive as your personal failings, goals, and strategies—all of this for men and women who simply want a place to lie down out of the rain!

It is these attitudes, in various forms and permutations, that you find repeated endlessly in America. We are moved either to "redeem" the homeless or to punish them. Perhaps there is nothing consciously hostile about it. Perhaps it is simply that as the machinery of bureaucracy cranks itself up to deal with these problems, attitudes assert themselves automatically. But whatever the case, the fact remains that almost every one of our strategies for helping the homeless is simply an attempt to rearrange the world *cosmetically*, in terms of how it looks and smells to *us*. Compassion is little more than the passion for control.

*   *   *

The central question emerging from all this is, What does a society owe to its members in trouble, and *how* is that debt to be paid? It is a question which must be answered in two parts: first, in relation to the men and women who have been marginalized against their will, and then, in a slightly different way, in relation to those who have chosen (or accept or even prize) their marginality.

As for those who have been marginalized against their wills, I think the general answer is obvious: A society owes its members whatever it takes for them

to regain their places in the social order. And when it comes to specific remedies, one need only read backward the various processes which have created
homelessness and then figure out where help is likely to do the most good.
But the real point here is not the specific remedies required—affordable housing, say—but the basis upon which they must be offered, the necessary underlying ethical notion we seem in this nation unable to grasp: that those who are
the inevitable casualties of modern industrial capitalism and the free-market
system are entitled, *by right,* and by the simple virtue of their participation in
that system, to whatever help they need. They are entitled to help to find and
hold their places in the society whose social contract they have, in effect,
signed and observed.

Look at that for just a moment: the notion of a contract. The majority of
homeless Americans have kept, insofar as they could, to the terms of that contract. In any shelter these days you can find men and women who have worked
ten, twenty, forty years, and whose lives have nonetheless come to nothing.
These are people who cannot afford a place in the world they helped create.
And in return? Is it life on the street they have earned? Or the cruel charity we so
grudgingly grant them?

But those marginalized against their will are only half the problem. There remains, still, the question of whether we owe anything to those who are volun-
tarily marginal. What about them: the street people, the rebels, and the recalci-
trants, those who have torn up their social contracts or returned them
unsigned?

I was in Las Vegas last fall, and I went out to the Rescue Mission at the lower
end of town, on the edge of the black ghetto, where I first stayed years ago on
my way west. It was twilight, still hot; in the vacant lot next-door to the mission
200 men were lining up for supper. A warm wind blew along the street lined
with small houses and salvage yards, and in the distance I could see the desert's
edge and the smudge of low hills in the fading light. There were elderly alcoholics in line, and derelicts, but mainly the men were the same sort I had seen
here years ago: youngish, out of work, restless and talkative, the drifters and
wanderers for whom the word "wanderlust" was invented.

At supper—long communal tables, thin gruel, stale sweet rolls, ice water—a
huge black man in his twenties, fierce and muscular, sat across from me. "I'm
from the Coast, man," he said. "Never been away from home before. Ain't sure
I like it. Sure don't like *this* place. But I lost my job back home a couple of weeks
ago and figured, why wait around for another. I thought I'd come out here, see
me something of the world."

After supper, a squat Portuguese man in his mid-thirties, hunkered down
against the mission wall, offered me a smoke and told me: "Been sleeping in my
car, up the street, for a week. Had my own business back in Omaha. But I got

bored, man. Sold everything, got a little dough, came out here. Thought I'd work construction. Let me tell you, this is one tough town."

In a world better than ours, I suppose, men (or women) like this might not exist. Conservatives seem to have no trouble imagining a society so well disciplined and moral that deviance of this kind would disappear. And leftists envision a world so just, so generous, that deviance would vanish along with inequity. But I suspect that there will always be something at work in some men and women to make them restless with the systems others devise for them, and to move them outward toward the edges of the world, where life is always riskier, less organized, and easier going.

Do we owe anything to these men and women, who reject our company and what we offer and yet nonetheless seem to demand *something* from us?

We owe them, I think, at least a place to exist, a way to exist. That may not be a *moral* obligation, in the sense that our obligation to the involuntarily marginal is clearly a moral one, but it is an obligation nevertheless, one you might call an existential obligation.

Of course, it may be that I think we owe these men something because I have liked men like them, and because I want their world to be there always, as a place to hide or rest. But there is more to it than that. I think we as a society need men like these. A society needs its margins as much as it needs art and literature. It needs holes and gaps, *breathing spaces,* let us say, into which men and women can escape and live, when necessary, in ways otherwise denied them. Margins guarantee to society a flexibility, an elasticity, and allow it to accommodate itself to the natures and needs of its members. When margins vanish, society becomes too rigid, too oppressive by far, and therefore inimical to life.

It is for such reasons that, in cultures like our own, marginal men and women take on a special significance. They are all we have left to remind us of the narrowness of the received truths we take for granted. "Beyond the pale," they somehow redefine the pale, or remind us, at least, that *something* is still out there, beyond the pale. They preserve, perhaps unconsciously, a dream that would otherwise cease to exist, the dream of having a place in the world, and of being *left alone.*

Quixotic? Infantile? Perhaps. But remember Pavlov and his reflexes coded in the flesh: animal, and therefore as if given by God. What we are talking about here is *freedom,* and with it, perhaps, an echo of the dream men brought long ago, to wilderness America. I use the word "freedom" gingerly, in relation to lives like these: skewed, crippled, emptied of everything we associate with a full, or realized, freedom. But perhaps this is the condition into which freedom has fallen among us. Art has been "appreciated" out of existence; literature has become an extension of the university, replete with tenure and pensions; and as for politics, the ideologies which ring us round seem too silly or shrill by far to speak for life. What is left, then, is this mute and intransigent independence, this "waste" of life which refuses even interpretation and which cannot be assimilated to any ideology, and which therefore can be put to no one's use. In its crippled innocence and the perfection of its superfluity it amounts, almost, to a rebellion against history, and that is no small thing.

Let me put it as simply as I can: what we see on the streets of our cities are two dramas, both of which cut to the troubled heart of the culture and demand from us a response we may not be able to make. There is the drama of those struggling to survive by regaining their place in the social order. And there is the drama of those struggling to survive outside of it.

The resolution of both struggles depends on a third drama occurring at the heart of the culture: the tension and contention between the magnanimity we owe to life and the darker tending of the human psyche: our fear of strangeness, our hatred of deviance, our love of order and control. How we mediate by default or design between those contrary forces will determine not only the destinies of the homeless but also something crucial about the nation, and perhaps—let me say it—about our own souls.   ■

Responding to Reading

1. Locate specific passages where Marin builds his credibility—his *ethos*—with readers.

2. What different kinds of evidence does Marin use in exploring homelessness? What parts of the essay do you find most convincing or insightful, and why?

3. Consider the structure of this essay. How does each section connect to the one before and after it? How does Marin's structure compare to that of the other two research essays in this chapter, "Pursuing an Educated Mind" (pp. 279–284) and "Who Deserves a Head Start?"(pp. 321–329). What are the advantages of each organizational pattern?

Organizing the Community-Based Research Essay

The structure of the community-based research essay is open. Each writer needs to decide what organizing principle will best serve the purpose of his or her essay. However, conventional structural patterns can prove useful. Take, for example, the five-part schema for oratory proposed centuries ago by the Roman rhetorician Quintilan, which can be readily translated to fit the needs of a contemporary research essay:

Introduction (*exordium*)   →   Introduction to topic and research question (and often justification of its significance)

Narration (*narratio*)   →   History/context of problem or issue

Argument (*confirmatio*)   →   Your main line of argument/claims and support

Refutation (*refutatio*)   →   Refutation of critics to your position as well as responses to anticipated objections

Conclusion (*peroratio*)   →   Conclusions and recommendations

This pattern of organizing is particularly appropriate for essays that adopt a persuasive posture. It is, for example, evident in the essay by Erin Collins, "Who Deserves a Head Start?" (pp. 321–329). The first section introduces the research question; the next three subtitled sections provide history and context ("History of Head Start," "Head Start Structure," "Current Government Involvement"); the next section argues the author's main claim ("All Children Should Be Served"); the next section answers critics ("Why Should Children Not Be Served?"); and the final section asserts an ethical plea and a policy recommendation ("What Needs to Be Done?").

You may also consider other ways of organizing. The following are a few common organizational patterns:

- *Narrative.* Storytelling—autobiographical or otherwise—is fundamental to human consciousness, making it a powerful organizing principle, one that can work not only in personal essays but also in research essays. Sometimes personal narrative serves primarily to introduce the topic; sometimes the narrative reemerges at the very end of the essay, functioning as a framing device; sometimes the narrative runs throughout.

- *Cause and effect.* Helping readers to comprehend causal relationships is important to understanding many social problems.

- *Compare/contrast and synthesis.* Showcasing similarities and differences among two or more ideas, entities, or perspectives often serves to clarify a topic or research question. By the end of the essay, however, you should be sure to have articulated the significance and/or implications of the comparison.

- *Hybrid.* Challenging conventional structures reflects a creative and often refreshing approach to research. For example, in his essay "Helping and

Hating the Homeless: The Struggle at the Margins of America," Marin combines narrative, definition, history, statistical evidence, opinion, and analysis to explore the complexities of homelessness. His hybrid structure helps readers see the subject from multiple angles, which in turn animates and enriches the piece.

Many other patterns for organizing can work: classification, definition, argument by example or analogy, and so on. There are no absolute rules for synthesizing and organizing essays and reports. The writer must judiciously balance his or her intent, the conventions of the genre, and the needs of the audience. Each must decide which structure works best in his or her particular case. Most fundamentally, the writer is responsible for guiding the audience, for shepherding readers through the essay.

Forecasting and Signposting

If the structure of a document is visible, it gives the reader a map to follow, and this, in turn, improves reader comprehension. Two typical strategies for doing this are forecasting and signposting:

- *Forecasting.* Books usually include a table of contents to forecast the topics covered. Similarly, in essays, a forecasting statement, which usually appears near the beginning of the essay, can inform readers of what is covered and how the essay is organized (e.g., "After explaining the four primary sources of groundwater contamination, I propose a plan for reducing water pollution."). Forecasting the content of sections can also be an effective strategy. Sometimes a writer has good reason to withhold advance information (if, for example, he or she wants to build up to the main claim); and sometimes forecasting the organization is unnecessary because the structure is self-evident (as, for example, with an empirical research report). Most of the time, however, forecasting statements improve reader comprehension.

- *Signposting.* Signposts help readers avoid getting lost along the way. They can be as simple as introductory phrases for paragraphs (e.g., "The second reason tracking in schools is problematic is . . . ") or extra spacing to signal a break between main sections. For longer essays and reports, headings are effective signposts, helping the reader to organize the essay into sensible chunks and providing for efficient scanning and navigation. Notice how Erin Collins's essay "Who Deserves a Head Start?" uses six subheadings to guide the reader.

Student Research Essay: Erin Collins, *Who Deserves a Head Start?*

When she wrote this essay, Erin Collins was a first-year student at Bentley College in Waltham, Massachusetts, planning to major in accounting.

WHO DESERVES A HEAD START?

Four-year-old Joey (not his real name), a lovable, intelligent little boy from the South Bronx, N.Y., will be ready for kindergarten this fall, thanks to the La Peninsula Head Start program. But one year ago, Joey's success in the classroom would not have seemed possible.

When Joey was 3, his mother had a second baby. Shortly thereafter, Joey's grandmother, who cared for him during the day, passed away. To make ends meet, Joey's mother, who is raising her children alone, had to give up college and go to work. Joey became very moody, was confused at times, and had fits of anger.

'I often wonder what would have happened to Joey if he weren't in Head Start,' says Martha Watford, who directs La Peninsula's five Head Start programs in the South Bronx. 'I know he would have been suspended as soon as he got into kindergarten, and possibly would have been placed in special education. I'm not sure anyone would have had the time to see what his potentials are.'

Instead, Watford says, Head Start has helped give Joey a sense of self-worth and 'the feeling that someone cares for him and that he is not alone,' which has brought out his natural creativity and inquisitiveness (Head Start Works, CDF).

Early education in a child's life is of vital importance. The unfortunate truth is that not all children receive an education that provides them with the knowledge that is needed to thrive in the world. Many children live in an environment that does not provide or encourage receiving a solid education. These children, many from lower class families, usually begin their schooling at a disadvantage. The government established a program designed for children of low-income families to prepare them for success in schools: Head Start. As the name suggests, the program intends to provide disadvantaged children with a "head start." Head Start is a free comprehensive program designed for low-income children. The program is designed to help with the child's development of their emotional, physical, mental and social welfare. The program teaches children a number of different helpful things. Other than academics, the program teaches the children how to take care of their bodies. Some Head Start programs teach students simple tasks like how to correctly brush their teeth. Others provide children with health care screenings. The Head Start programs provide health and dental services to children and families who might otherwise not have them (Research and Evaluation, NHSA).

There are so many children in America like Joey whose lives could be improved if only they could get Head Start's early education, health and social services, nutrition, and support for their parents. Yet, amazingly only 40% of eligible children are being served! The program has had thirty-five years "of strong bipartisan support and proven track record of helping children learn and stay in school, be safe and healthy, and ultimately become productive, taxpaying citizens" (Head Start Works, CDF). Given the program's successful track record, how come the program is not funded to serve all eligible children?

Being involved in this cluster [of courses at Bentley College] has exposed me to problems of early education. I had no idea that so many factors contributed to this problem and the degree of the problems affiliated with the education that a lower-class child receives. The first time I visited the Hamilton school I began to see what I had only heard and read about. I believe that in order to improve a child's education it must start early in their schooling.

HISTORY OF HEAD START

In 1964, President Lyndon Johnson signed the Economic Opportunity Act that established Head Start (History of Education, Britannica Online). Head Start began in the summer of 1965 with an enrollment of 561,000 children. Throughout the years the number fluctuated from 333,000 in 1977 to 835,000 in 1999 (Head Start Statistics Fact Sheet). When the program first began, the government appropriated $96,400,000 towards the Head Start program. Now the estimated congressional appropriation for the fiscal year 2000 is totaling $5.267 billion. Since the program's start in 1965, Head Start has helped more than 15 million children to become productive citizens in the United States (Children Deserve A Fair Share).

In 1973 in Kansas City, Missouri, a national conference was held for the directors of numerous community action associations. A handful of Head Start program directors attending the conference discussed the need for a private, national association that could advocate specifically for the Head Start community in Congress. This need to advocate was because the Nixon administration was threatening to eliminate community action agencies, which sponsored the majority of Head Start programs. The administration believed that the community action agencies were not effectively accomplishing what they were intended to do. Then in the later part of 1973, the National Directors Association was formed, which was the forerunner of the National Head Start Association (NHSA). Eventually on June 7, 1990, this association merged with three others, the Head Start Parents Association, Head Start Staff Association, and Head Start Friends Association, to form what is known today as the NHSA.

In 1994 the Head Start Reauthorization Act established the Early Head Start program (FAQ, NHSA). During the years before age three, a critical period of brain development is occurring. So, this program was established to serve low-income pregnant women and families with infants and toddlers under the age of 3. Currently there are 142 Early Head Start programs serving over 10,000 children and families.

HEAD START STRUCTURE

The structure of Head Start is an important factor that contributes to its success. The program allows for flexibility within the different communities, while at the same time is regulated by the national Head Start model (Reauthorization, NHSA).

Children between the ages of three and five are eligible for the Head Start program. Priority is usually given to children of four years of age. Their families also must meet the Federal poverty guidelines. Christine Gnadt, a director at the Chelsea Head Start Program, explained that one person in a four-member family working at "Stop and Shop" would bring in enough money to disqualify them for the program. The chart below from the Federal Register gives the 1999 Federal poverty guidelines:

1999 HHS Poverty Guidelines

Size of Family Unit	48 Contiguous States and D.C.	Alaska	Hawaii
1	$ 8,240	$10,320	$ 9,490
2	11,060	13,840	12,730
3	13,880	17,360	15,970
4	16,700	20,880	19,210
5	19,520	24,400	22,450
6	22,340	27,920	25,690
7	25,160	31,440	28,930
8	27,980	34,960	32,170
For each additional person, add	2,820	3,520	3,240

(Federal Register, pp. 13428–13430).

Different programs throughout the country establish priorities for enrolling children based on community needs and available funds. In every program in the United States, ten percent of enrollment is set aside for children in families that exceed the poverty guidelines and another additional ten percent of enrollment is set aside for children with disabilities. Head Start programs can be located at numerous different buildings or centers. Some programs are fortunate enough to have their own buildings while others operate out of basements of churches.

At the program, teachers and volunteers help and teach the children. Every person there is a critical asset. The volunteers are "an effective way of mobilizing community resources to strengthen Head Start Services" (Research and Evaluation, NHSA). The Head Start programs are required to develop quality volunteer programs as a part of their programs. Volunteers at a Head Start program can be "professionals and nonprofessionals, parents, local residents, and members of the larger community, board members and those who serve on policy and advisory groups, those who work in classrooms, offices, or kitchens, and those who provide necessary health education, medical and dental examinations, and other health services" (FAQ, NHSA). These volunteers can do numerous tasks from assisting with classroom activities to transporting children to playground supervision.

There are certain requirements for people interested in teaching at a Head Start program. The recommended credential is the Child Development Associate (CDA) credential. A person must complete a CDA assessment and be awarded the CDA credential. Someone who wants to complete an assessment must provide proof of training in early childhood care and they need experience (FAQ, NHSA).

CURRENT GOVERNMENT INVOLVEMENT

In 1998, NHSA lobbied to have the federal government increase appropriations by an amount of not less than $575 million (Head Start Appropriations, NHSA). According to the NHSA, if the government did not increase appropriations then the goal of servicing one million children by the year 2002 will be unachievable. Fortunately, on January 26, 1999 Vice President Gore requested that the federal funding for the Head Start program increase by $607 million in the fiscal year 2000. An increase of $607 million would be the largest increase in history (President Clinton's FY 2000 Budget, CDF). If this were to pass then the total funding for Head Start would total $5.267 billion (Government Affairs, NHSA). With this additional funding, it is estimated that 877,000 children and their families will be able to participate in the Head Start program in the year 2000. This would increase the percentage of children being served from 40% to 44%. This gives the government two years to reach the goal of servicing one million children by the year 2002. If the government is able to reach their goal, then only 50% of eligible children will have the opportunity to participate in the Head Start program. Why is the goal only to service one million disadvantaged children, when that still leaves an *additional* one million children who are not being served?

In the President's fiscal year budget for the year 2000, he proposes to increase funds for the Early Head Start program to $420 million. Since the cost of serving an infant or toddler is greater than the associated cost of serving a three-, four- or five-year old, this increase will allow an additional 7,000 children and families to be served.

ALL CHILDREN SHOULD BE SERVED

Since 1965, Head Start has helped more than 15 million children to develop the vital skills needed to become productive citizens of the United States. Yet, what about the other millions of children not able to attend Head Start because the government does not fund every child eligible for the program? To service one million children is the goal for the year 2002. However, why only one million and not *everyone?*

Over the next decade the Congressional Budget Office estimates that the nation will have a surplus of over $2.7 trillion. The government needs to think of the country's future and invest a small fraction of that surplus into child education. The Children's Defense Fund estimates that an additional $7.37 billion a year could fully fund Head Start! That's a small amount to invest into the country's future when one thinks of the long-run return (Children Deserve A Fair Share, CDF).

The short and long term effects that Head Start has upon the children that have the privilege of attending are overwhelming. One has to remember that the majority of children enrolled in Head Start come from disadvantaged homes and are considered "at risk." When children from disadvantaged homes are provided with the numerous experiences that the program offers "the benefits are significant, both in terms of improved quality of life for these children when they become adults and in terms of lower costs to society for welfare, grade retention, special education, social services, and crime costs" (Resource Paper, Government Affairs).

If the government was now to spend an additional $7.37 billion a year to fully fund and serve all eligible children, the money they would receive in the long run would exceed their investment. Unemployment rates for high school graduates are seventy-five percent lower than non-graduates. In 1998, 2,756 children dropped out of high school every school day (1998 U.S. Profile, CDF). The National Head Start Association states, "One third more at risk children who attend a quality early childhood program graduate high school than those who do not attend. If the program were fully funded, dropout rates would decrease so the government would receive more money back in taxes. This is because children who attend preschool programs like Head Start and graduate are likely to earn 25 percent more than non-graduates are" (Government Affairs, NHSA). This additional money that these people are being paid reflects the additional money that the government will receive in taxes.

Although the average cost of public education differs from state-to-state, its average is around $5,200 per student, per year. Children who attend early education programs are 25 percent less likely to be held back. Taxpayers pay for public education so the money saved could be put towards improving public education as a whole. In addition, it is estimated (varies from state to state) that for special education programs, it is an additional $1,800 per student, per year. Children who attend preschool spend 1.3 years less in special education programs. Again, this additional money could be used to improve other areas of education (Government Affairs, NHSA).

The 1998 U.S. profile displays that 5,753 children are arrested everyday in America. Of those 5,753 children, 280 of them are arrested for violent crimes. At risk children are five times more likely to be arrested repeatedly than those who attend early childhood programs. Jerry Walsh, head of the education program at Suffolk County jail, stated that "it costs approximately $30,000 overall per inmate a year." This price includes the cost of education that some inmates receive. He also said that he believes in programs like Head Start because children need to begin on the "right track" so they do not end up in jails. In addition, he states that "the government needs to put money into Head Start because society ends up saving in the long-run." Other than saving money because the crime rate should decrease, people are saved from being victims of crimes.

Former students of early education programs are three times more likely to own a home. With an increase of students into these programs, more houses will be bought and owned. The government receives property taxes from homeowners, so the more homeowners, the more money the government receives. The economy also benefits from the increase in real-estate sales.

Given that the government is expected to accumulate a $2.7 trillion surplus over the next decade one should conclude that a small fraction of this, less than 3%, should be invested into the Head Start program so that all children are being served. In both the long and short term, the government would receive a larger amount of money through taxes than is invested into Head Start. In addition, the benefits that society will receive far outweigh the small price the government will pay. These benefits include crime reduction, less teen-age pregnancies, economic gains, and a larger amount of educated Americans. So instead of only being partially funded and only serving 40% of eligible children, Head Start should be fully funded and serve all eligible children.

WHY SHOULD CHILDREN NOT BE SERVED?

Some critics believe that Head Start should be eliminated and funding stopped even for the small percentages that are served. The criticism centers on evidence suggesting that the initial boost given by Head Start does not last. "Experts such as Edward Zigler of Yale University and Fred Hechinger, former education editor of the *New York Times,* maintain that the gains initially achieved after short-term compensatory early education do not last and that by the eighth grade (and certainly high school) the performance of children who completed one-year Head Start programs is not much better than that of children who did not" (Petty, 677). One important point to point out is that these *disadvantaged* children are not doing any worse. In addition, critics here are not referring to the nutritional, mental, physical and social boost. Children who attend Head Start are never going to forget the valuable skills that they have learned. Children are taught the proper way to brush their teeth, receive health care screenings, are able to interact with other children, and their parents become involved with their educational careers.

Another 15-year longitudinal study conducted by the Chicago board of education compared 3,000 graduates of one- and two-year preschool program to a control group consisting of 1,700 children.

> Ultimately, the eighth-grade reading and math scores of the children from the preschool group were found to be somewhat lower than those of the control group— an artifact, apparently, of the slightly higher socioeconomic status of the control-group children. However, when the results were adjusted to account for that factor, the reading and math scores of the preschool group were no better than those of the control group. Similarly, the graduation rates of the children with one or two years of preschool training were no better than those of the children without it. These findings were essentially the same as those reported in earlier studies of Head Start conducted by Abt Associations in 1977 and by Westinghouse in 1969 (Petty 677).

Critics use studies such as this one to conclude that Head Start is just another federal program that does not work. Yet, this is an incorrect conclusion. Again, this study only measures scholastic achievements. Concluding that one year of Head Start programs does not accomplish scholastic achievement does not imply that the program does not work—rather that children should be in the program for more than one year. More importantly, when this study states that the scores were "somewhat lower" this means that the scores were almost the same. After the scores were adjusted, the scores were "no better," yet this means that they were no worse. Given that these children come from disadvantaged backgrounds, these results are impressive. In addition, this study proves that Head Start is accomplishing its goals.

A number of different studies confirm that an extended exposure to early childhood education does produce long-term improvements. "A recent study by J.S. and Dorothy Fuerst found that inner-city children, particularly girls, who had been exposed to four to six years of early childhood education demonstrated lasting improvements. For boys, an even longer exposure seemed necessary before the approach 'took.' But this extended exposure definitely did make a substantial impact: 75% to 80% of the girls graduated from high school, while among boys who were exposed to the extended program, 70% graduated from high school" (Petty 677).

Nevertheless, the argument in favor of fully funding Head Start outweighs the opposition's argument. For the critics who argue that Head Start is an ineffective program, they need to take a closer look at data, while remembering that Head Start is designed to give disadvantaged children a boost that allows Head Start children to compete with children from more fortunate homes.

WHAT NEEDS TO BE DONE?

What would happen if the government adopts the critic's suggestion of eliminating Head Start all together? Thousands of disadvantaged babies and young children will not be able to attend preschool. Some may argue that preschool had no lasting effects, yet numerous studies disprove this. In addition, many of these critics that are arguing for the elimination of Head Start are the parents who are sending their own children to preschool. Why should only the privileged be able to benefit from preschool?

Privileged children should not be the only ones to go to preschool and that is why Head Start is so beneficial to society. Head Start is well worth the cost in terms of future social costs, considering the government might make money in the long run. At-risk children who attend preschool are one-third more likely to graduate from high school, spend 1.3 years less in special education, one-third less likely to have out-of-wedlock births, 25% less likely to be retained in grade, five times less likely to be arrested repeatedly by age 27, and three times more likely to be homeowners by age 27, than those at-risk children who do not attend preschool programs like Head Start.

Given these numerous statistics that show the government could end up making money and benefit society if they fully funded Head Start, the only question that remains is: Why is Head Start not already fully funded? With the upcoming budget surplus of $2.7 trillion, the government needs to increase money appropriations for Head Start by $7.37 billion so that instead of only serving 40% of eligible children they can serve all the disadvantaged babies and children eligible for Head Start. Just think of how many other children's future could be saved like Joey's, the young boy from the South Bronx, N.Y.

WORKS CITED
Children's Defense Fund. "Children deserve a fair share of the federal budget surplus." http://www.childrensdefense.org/clintonsurplus.html
Children's Defense Fund. "Children In The States."http://www.childrensdefense.org/states/data_us.html
Children's Defense Fund. "President Clinton's FY2000 Budget: What's in it for children?" http://www.childrensdefense.org/clintonbudget2000.html
Children's Defense Fund. "Head Start *Works.*" http://www.childrensdefense.org/voice0497.html
Cristine Gnadt, personal interview, 16 March. 1999.
Department of Health and Human Services, "FAQ." http://www.2.acf.dhhs.gov/programs/hsb/text_only_html/faq.htm
Department of Health and Human Services, "Head Start Statistic Fact Sheet." http://www.2.acf.dhhs.gov/programs/hsb/text_only_hml/_1998_fs.html
Department of Health and Human Services, "Federal Register." 18 March 1999: 13428–13430.
"Diplomas and diapers: schooling for young street mothers and their babies." *Children Today* Winter–Spring. 1994: 28–34.
"Former Head Start parents' characteristics, perceptions of school climate, and their involvement in their children's education." *The Elementary School Journal* Mar. 1998: 339–350

"History of Education: Education in the 20th century: WESTERN PATTERNS OF EDUCATION: The United States.: Federal involvement in local education." *Britannica Online.* http://www.eb.com.180/cgi-bin/g?Doc=macro/5002/2/201.html

National Head Start Association, "Research and Evaluation." http://www.nhsa.org/research/bites.htm

NHSA Government affairs, "Head Start appropriations." http://www.nhsa.org/govaff/appropr.htm

NHSA Government Affairs, "Reauthorization of the Head Start Program." http://www.nhsa.org/govaff/reauthor.htm

NHSA Legislative update, "Government Affairs." http://www.nhsa.org/govaff/Legislative/legislative020199.htm1 Feb. 1999.

"Perspectives of former Head Start children and their parents on school and the transition to school." *The Elementary School Journal* 98 (1998): 311–317

Petty, Roy. "The best use of federal funds for early childhood education." *Phi Delta Kappa* 77 (1996): 676–683.

"President signs measures on Head Start, savings." *The Boston Globe* 28 October 1998: A21.

Walsh, Jerry. Interview. Nicole Grossi. Feb. 1999.

ADDITIONAL BIBLIOGRAPHY

Begley, Sharon. "Your Child's Brain." *Newsweek* 19 Feb. 1996: 54–57.

Mills, Kay. *Something better for my children: the history and people of Head Start.* New York: Dutton, 1998.

"Statement on signing the Human Services Amendments of 1994." *Weekly Compilation of Presidential Documents* 23 May 1994: 1112–1121. ∎

Responding to Reading

1. Compare this research essay to the one presented earlier in the chapter, "Pursuing an Educated Mind: The Debate Over the Effectiveness of Bilingual Education" (pp. 279–284). Which specific parts of each essay do you find more or less effective? Support your responses with examples from the texts.

2. How many different *kinds* of sources does Collins use? How does she weave in those sources and document them?

3. What particular suggestions might you make to improve this essay?

Peer Review Questions

The Community-Based Research Essay Drafts

The following questions can assist you in evaluating drafts of your own essay and those of classmates.

1. What parts of the draft are particularly strong?

2. What parts of the draft are confusing or deserve to be better developed?

3. Does the essay have an engaging title and opening section? What are some ways they could be improved?

4. Does the introduction make clear the purpose of the essay, the research question, and the significance of the research question?

5. What organizational structure is evident in the draft? Can readers follow it easily? How are forecasting and signposting used?

6. Does the writer use at least three reliable print and/or digital sources? Are interview, journal, and/or field notes excerpts woven in? What additional sources might help improve the essay?

7. Where does the writer do a good job of weaving in sources? Where could this be improved? Is a mix of summary, paraphrase, and quotation used? Where could signal phrases help introduce source material?

8. Is there an in-text citation and a Works Cited listing for each source?

9. Comment on the quality of the prose. Where does it seem particularly engaging or animated? Where might it be improved?

10. What do you want to hear more about?

Organizing the Agency Profile Report

When you are choosing an essay structure, conventional genres and patterns can serve as a guide. The most basic of these is the introduction/body/conclusion schema, but this schema is so general as to be of little practical use. For the agency profile report assignment in this chapter, the structure is prescribed: you must use the empirical report format, which is commonly used in the sciences and social sciences.

Agency Profile Report: Empirical Research Report Structure

Introduction and objectives	What are you trying to discover? Why is the research important? What background does the reader need?
Method	How did you gather data? Are the research methods sound?
Results/facts	What are your results?
Discussion and conclusions	How do you interpret the results? What is the significance of the results?
Recommendations (sometimes combined with discussion and conclusions)	What are the implications of the findings? How should one act on them?

Chapter 4 introduces the empirical research report genre in more detail. If you are not familiar with that chapter, reading it is recommended. When you use the empirical report format, the established structure guides synthesis.

The following sample agency profile report, "RSVP with Grant Money, Please: An Investigation into a Non-Profit Organization's Writing Needs," illustrates how a collaborative team of student writers uses the empirical report format to present research.

Student Agency Profile Report: Paul Creekmore, Karen Smith, and Evan Tritsch, *RSVP with Grant Money, Please: An Investigation into a Non-Profit Organization's Writing Needs*

Paul Creekmore, Karen Smith, and Evan Tritsch were first-year students at Kansas State University when they wrote this report. Doing so helped them prepare for a later service-learning project with the Retired and Senior Volunteer Program (RSVP) that involved doing research on potential grant-funding charitable foundations to determine whether the grant criteria and deadlines for each foundation matched RSVP's own grant-seeking criteria.

RSVP WITH GRANT MONEY, PLEASE: AN INVESTIGATION
INTO A NON-PROFIT ORGANIZATION'S WRITING NEEDS

As students in college, we are exposed to writing all the time. Whether it be in the form of essays on exams or epic reports, every college student must do some form of writing before graduating. However, the writing done within a college classroom is very different from that done by professionals. As students, we have the luxury of knowing exactly what our professors want to see in the papers we write. In many cases, we are even able to obtain feedback from our professors before turning the paper in for a final grade. But in the "real world" things do not work the same way. Missing the deadline for a report will not simply result in a bad grade, or, at worst, academic probation; instead, it can result in far more severe consequences, such as the loss of a job. For this reason we must understand the importance that writing plays outside of the realm of academia.

OBJECTIVES

Having completed research on the role that writing plays in an academic discourse community, our goal is to expand on that research and move it into the realm of nonacademic discourse communities. Our specific task was to research a local community organization to find out as much about it as possible, including its history and mission as well as its past and current projects. Furthermore, we were interested in the rules and methods of writing that people within the organization used. Specifically, we were put into contact with a grant writer at the local chapter of the Retired and Senior Volunteer Program (RSVP).

METHODS

For this project, two groups were set up to do separate projects with RSVP. However, while doing the research, we collaborated and shared information. Our group—consisting of Paul Creekmore, Karen Smith, and Evan Tritsch—worked together with the second RSVP group whose members included Scott Cronin, Anna Finkelson, and Richard O'Konski. With so many people researching the same topic, we were able to search through several different sources.

Our primary source of information was our contact person at RSVP, Scott Brinkman. Scott completed his Masters studies at New Mexico University and graduated with a Masters degree in Physical Science. While doing research at New Mexico University, Scott contributed to the writing of three successful grants. After completing his studies, Scott decided to pursue grant writing as employment. Since August 2000 Scott has worked full time as the grant writer for RSVP.

Scott provided us with information in several ways. The first came in the form of a lecture he gave to our Expository Writing class. This lecture provided some basic insight into the type of writing that Scott does, as well as the programs that RSVP runs. To get more in-depth information, Paul and Richard conducted an extended interview with Scott at his office. They both took notes and recorded the interview for later review to ensure accurate presentation of the data. During the interview, Scott gave them samples of his writings as well as fliers that described some of his other efforts to fund RSVP's projects.

To supplement the lecture and interview, our group underwent additional research to find information on RSVP. Karen's search of the library found the RSVP Operations Handbook that contains all of the guidelines that RSVP chapters must follow. By scouring the Internet, Scott and Evan were able to find web pages of other RSVP chapters around the United States. Anna did an extensive search of newspaper databases and came up with several relevant articles.

RESULTS

In order to understand the role that writing plays within this organization, it was first necessary to understand the background of the program. Started in 1971, RSVP is one of the largest national volunteer organizations in the country (Corporation 4). As part of the National Senior Service Corps, RSVP taps the knowledge, talents, and experiences of over half a million older Americans through any of the more than 760 results-driven projects (Baber 1).

The national organization is broken up into local chapters across the United States. For this report, we were interested specifically in the Manhattan chapter of RSVP. Its mission is to accomplish the "dual purpose of engaging persons 55 and older in volunteer service to meet critical community needs; and to provide a high quality experience that will enrich the lives of the volunteers" (Corporation 11). Scott Brinkman also provided us with a more personal view of the Manhattan mission. He emphasized their goal "to provide senior and retired community members in Manhattan with the opportunity to make the most of their golden years" by giving them "the opportunity to volunteer their time to benefit the community."

Although RSVP is a volunteer program, several people work full-time to en-sure that the organization meets its day-to-day needs. At the head of RSVP is an Executive Director who oversees all the separate departments. Each of these de-partments focuses on a different aspect of the organization and takes care of op-erational needs. Within the departments, people are hired to take care of some very specific needs of each department head. For example, Scott is a grant writer, so his job is to find funding for the Leadership in Literacy program. Scott considers this hierarchy of RSVP "fairly structured, but kind of loose." All the people who, like Scott, work in the day-to-day activities of RSVP are known as "paid volunteers" due to the small amount of pay that they receive while work-ing for the volunteer organization. Because RSVP is nationally based, it has con-tacts with other nonprofit organizations. One of these is Americorps, through which RSVP obtains its paid volunteers (Brinkman).

In addition to the paid volunteers, RSVP enlists the help of unpaid volunteers. These volunteers are older community members, ages 55 and over, who donate their time to the many programs offered by RSVP. As a national program, RSVP gives almost half a million retired and senior citizens the opportunity to better their communities through service projects. The level of participation is com-pletely up to the volunteer. Some may volunteer just a few hours a week while others volunteer on an almost full-time basis. The average number of hours per volunteer is just four per week (Corporation 4).

The current project of the volunteers in the Manhattan chapter is called Leadership in Literacy. According to Scott, the goal of this program is "to tackle the problem of low literacy rates and underdeveloped reading capabilities of kindergarten students." He noted that studies have shown poverty as the single greatest factor for low performance in school. As a result, Bluemont Elementary School was chosen for the project because it was found to have the highest per-centage of low-income families. However, students are not placed into the pro-gram simply for having low income. Instead, they are tested and then referred to the program by their teachers. The parents of a student are allowed to decide whether or not they wish to have their child participate in the program. Those who do enter the program are provided with an extended day kindergarten where students can receive the valuable one-on-one interaction that they may be lacking at home or in school (Brinkman). In previous years, this program has raised students' scores on one test by an average of 12 percent, and on another by as much as 24 percent (Retired 2).

As a nonprofit organization, RSVP has no means of generating revenue to pay for staff and projects such as this. Consequently, it must rely on outside sources to provide funding. Scott is the person in charge of finding this money. He looks for money primarily through grants. Grants are sums of money provided by private corporations or the federal government to fund nonprofit organizations such as RSVP. Although many grants exist, they have restrictions placed on them that limit the organizations that can apply for them. Scott described the grant process as "feast or famine, with a lot of famine" (Brinkman).

Because of the difficulty of obtaining grants, Scott has come up with other ways to fund RSVP projects. He is currently working on a fundraiser called the One Thin Dime Drive. The goal of the program is to persuade corporate sponsors to donate ten cents for every book that children read through the Leadership in Literacy Program. However, businesses that do not want to participate in the program but still wish to help fund RSVP may give donations (Retired). Unfortunately, and even though last year the children read 15,000 books, Scott has been unsuccessful in finding sponsors.

Since Scott has been unable to acquire sponsorship for his One Thin Dime Drive, he is forced to continue his grant writing. The process starts by looking for possible grants. Hundreds of grants are available, but Scott must sort through them to find the few for which RSVP meets the criteria. After finding a potential grant, Scott must begin to do the research that will support his plea for money. Much of his research is done to find information about the effects of poverty. He searches libraries as well as the Internet. To get a first hand perspective, Scott also volunteers at the school. This gives him the chance to interact with the children involved in the program and better understand their situation. The final place Scott finds information is from other grants written on the same subject. Scott noted a peculiarity of grant writing when he said, "grant writers are willing to let you cut and paste anything you want" (Brinkman).

Once the research is complete, Scott can transition into writing. Scott goes through all his information and takes notes about statistics, general information, and thoughts he had while reading. Sometimes this process fills up several notebooks. After he has finished taking notes, he looks back through his notes and marks the information he feels is most important. He then categorizes and structures the information. Before long, he is able to begin putting his ideas on paper. After finishing a draft, Scott will let it sit, only to come back to it and find numerous flaws. He will then redo the proposal. He may repeat this several times before finally producing a paper with which he is satisfied.

Each grant proposal has specific guidelines that must be met. Usually the length is severely limited. For this reason, Scott has to "cut the pork." Grant writing requires a straightforward approach to writing. This is sometimes difficult for Scott because he has so much information available and does not know what to cut. However, if the guidelines for a grant are not met, the grant can be sent back immediately with no indication of what was wrong with it.

DISCUSSION AND CONCLUSIONS

Writing is absolutely crucial to the functioning of RSVP. In fact, it falls into one of Frank Smith's ten uses of language—to get material needs met (12). Without the writing that Scott does, RSVP would have no way of funding its projects and would, therefore, be forced to stop providing excellent services to the community. Although the process of grant writing can be long and, more often than not, fruitless, it is still very important in helping not only RSVP, but also the community as a whole. In addition, Scott's other projects, such as the One Thin Dime Drive, offer members of the community the opportunity to make a difference through their contributions when they might not otherwise volunteer.

Within the Leadership in Literacy program, communication plays a very different role than it does within the organization as a whole. Instead of simply being a means of achieving a goal, writing and communication skills *are* the goals of this program. Even though the program focuses directly on reading skills, overall literacy is the primary goal. Therefore, by teaching children to read, one is invariably teaching them to write at the same time. The Leadership in Literacy program is doing more than it has planned without even knowing it.

As an organization, RSVP is very effective in meeting its goal of promoting "the engagement of older persons as community resources" (Corporation 11). The programs provided by RSVP give retired people the chance to still be important. However, the programs do not benefit just the volunteers. Statistics show that Leadership in Literacy is a very effective tool for overcoming the problem of illiteracy (Retired). The senior volunteers are the ones who make that possible. As Jan Czech wrote in an article about RSVP programs, "Seniors are no longer these little old people you put on a shelf and lock away" (Czech 4).

This report shows that the use of writing transcends the world of academics and extends into the "real world." This project has not only helped us to gain a better understanding of the role that writing plays within RSVP, but it has also given us insight into the workings of RSVP. The knowledge we gained about this organization will be beneficial when we move into the second phase of the project and begin our own work for RSVP.

WORKS CITED

Baber, Bonnie. "Senior Volunteers Honored for Service; Thanks, Recognition Highlight RSVP Luau." *The Times Picayune* 19 Oct 2000: 1. Online. Lexis-Nexis. 30 Oct. 2000.

Brinkman, Scott. Personal interview. 31 Oct. 2000

Corporation for National Service. *RSVP: Retired and Senior Volunteer Program Operations Handbook.* Washington: GPO, April 2000.

Czech, Jan. "'RSVP' Program Responds to the Needs of Seniors." *The Buffalo News* 21 Nov. 1999: 4NC. Online. Lexis-Nexis. 30 Oct. 2000

Retired and Senior Volunteer Program. *One Thin Dime Drive.* Manhattan. 2000.

Smith, Frank. *Writing and the Writer.* Hillsdale, NJ: Erlbaum, 1982. ∎

Responding to Reading

1. Compare this agency profile report to the one presented earlier in the chapter (pp. 286–291). Which report—or which specific parts of either report—do you find more effective, and why?

2. In what specific ways do each of the reports weave in material from interviews? Which does so more effectively?

3. Locate places in both reports where the writers use each the following strategies: forecasting; signposting; summarizing, paraphrasing, and directly quoting sources; and using signal phrases.

Peer Review Questions
Agency Profile Report Drafts

The following questions can assist you in evaluating drafts of your own report and those of others.

1. Does the draft follow the empirical report structure? Which sections seem underdeveloped? Which seem strong?

2. Does the introductory section articulate the purpose and significance of the report?

3. Are the methods clearly described? How do the writers build (or not build) the credibility of those methods?

4. Does the "Results" section include paraphrases and direct quotations from the interview(s)? How are other sources woven into the text?

5. Does the "Discussion and Conclusions" section follow logically from the "Results" section? Which parts of this section do you find particularly insightful? Which parts deserve more explanation and/or support?

6. In what ways are the particular writing and communication practices of the agency discussed?

7. What are the three most significant things that you learned about the organization? What do you want to hear more about?

8. In the final section, do the writers make specific conclusions and helpful recommendations?

9. Comment on the quality of the prose. Where does it seem particularly crisp or animated? Where does it seem unclear or lifeless?

10. Is there an in-text citation and a Works Cited listing for each source?

ENDNOTE

At its best, research is a process of discovery, one that results in documents that are meaningful to both the writer and the audience. One of the special benefits of writing about the community is that it prepares you to embark on community action with more knowledge and awareness than you had before. This is particularly important if you intend to participate in any of the writing-for-the-community or writing-with-the-community projects outlined in the next two chapters.

8

Writing for the Community

In what ways can writing help the work of nonprofit agencies? How is writing for community organizations different from writing for academic courses? What are some key strategies for being a successful writer on a collaborative team and in a workplace? This chapter answers these questions as it guides you through a writing-for-the-community project with a nonprofit organization.

Every community has organizations that serve citizens and work for social justice, and nearly all those organizations use writing to help get their work done. This chapter describes and supports partnerships between emerging writers and community organizations, especially ways that students can write *for* local nonprofits.

In their day-to-day working operations, nonprofit agencies, government offices, advocacy groups, and community organizations rarely need the kinds of writing generated in school, such as essays or tests. But they do need newsletter articles, reports, grant research, manuals, brochures, press releases, and other such documents that fall under the headings "workplace writing," "technical writing," and "professional writing." Some call this "real-world writing"; but in fact, academic discourse is just as "real" and valuable as workplace discourse. However, while these types of discourse are equally important, they are quite different, as will become clear in this chapter and in the course of your project.

Creating professional documents for local organizations is neither quick nor easy, but it is rewarding. Beyond simply drafting and revising a document, such writing involves getting to know an organization, creating a relationship with a community partner, understanding the conventions of workplace discourse, and learning to work and write collaboratively.

You need to be aware that writing-for-the-community projects tend to be complex and unpredictable, which can be both exciting and disquieting. Community writing projects demand an ability to cope with uncertainty. Such projects also require personal commitment, patience, creativity, open communication, problem-solving skills, and hard work. Moreover, because agency-based projects often hinge on the quality of the student/community partnership, it is especially important that you read Chapter 6 before moving on to this one.

What students find particularly rewarding about writing for community agencies is the sense that their work—and, in particular, their writing—is making an immediate and visible contribution to an organization that serves the public good. The writing done is for more than a grade; it will be put to use to help the organization do its work, and it might, in fact, be read by a wide audience.

Understanding Workplace Writing

Good academic and workplace writing both demand critical thinking, attention to audience, knowledge of writing conventions, and practice. Yet there are differences between the two. For example, the purpose of most school writing is to show what you know, to demonstrate your mastery of a subject. In contrast, the purpose of most professional writing is to get something done, to meet an immediate and practical organizational need. Thus, the two kinds of writing perform different kinds of social action. As you anticipate working with a community organization, you need to be less concerned about proving your merit as a student and more concerned about how you, as a writer, can help the organization meet its goals.

Differences Between Academic and Workplace Writing

Academic Writing	Workplace Writing
Purpose is to show what you know, demonstrate mastery of subject	Purpose is to meet an organizational need, serve a practical end
Most writing is solo	Most writing is collaborative
Highly structured, teacher-defined process	Loosely structured or negotiated process
Audience is teacher and peers	Audience is the organization and its constituency (and sometimes the general public)
All that will showcase your intelligence, creativity, and expertise is included	Only what the intended readers will need and use is included
Few texts include visuals or emphasize document design	Most texts demand visuals and emphasize document design
Use of sources and documentation follows academic conventions	Sources and documentation, if needed at all, follow the organization's conventions
Measure of success is a good grade	Measure of success is whether the document works in practice and serves its intended purpose

Student Perspective: Audrey,
Stepping Out of My Comfort Zone

What follows is an essay by Audrey, a student who worked with a team of three other first-year students to complete a writing-for-the-community project as part of an English course. Pay attention to how Audrey's expectations about writing were challenged by her service-learning experience.

STEPPING OUT OF MY COMFORT ZONE:
MY EXPERIENCE WITH THE COMMUNITY PROJECT

A project without rules, without structure . . . also known as my personal hell. I like to do things "by the book." Give me a list of instructions: I'll follow them. Tell me what to do, when to do it, how to do it . . . I'll get it done. So how does someone like me handle a writing project in which there aren't rules or a list of expectations or even a basic outline on how to create the paper? It was difficult. It was extremely difficult. But I survived, and I learned the value of flexibility in both writing and in my life while gaining an appreciation for how writing can be used in a practical setting to help others.

The group writing project assigned in my English course required us to work with a non-profit organization within the community in order to produce a piece of writing that could be employed by that organization. It had no specific instructions. At first, we weren't even told exactly what we would be writing. We knew that we were to speak with the people at the organization we would be helping. We knew that we were to write a paper about the organization. That seemed like all we knew. I was not looking forward to this project at all.

The assignment broke all boundaries for me. Prior to this project, I always knew exactly what to expect when it came to completing work for English classes. From the time I began to write, I had been given a formula—a specific format in which to place my thoughts. My essays were to be five paragraphs long—one for introduction, three for the body, and one for a conclusion. I learned to manipulate my words and thoughts to create something that I knew would earn me an "A" and the approval of my current teacher. But when it came to this project, I had no clue. That scared me.

However, I definitely began feeling better about the whole project when I learned that I had been assigned to help produce a press release for the Regional AIDS Project (RAP).

Piece of cake! I thought. I was on my high school newspaper staff for three years. I was editor my senior year. This was going to be so easy! We'd get together as a group, talk to the people at the Regional AIDS Project, then we'd turn it in and be done! How difficult was that?

It started out fairly simple. Another group member and I went to visit with some people who work for the Regional AIDS Project. They gave us a lot of information about the AIDS Quilt display, the event for which we were to write the press release. We decided as a group that each of us would write a press release, then we would combine them. This is where the project began to get difficult. Fitting the ideas of four people all into one short paper was a struggle. Though we didn't have any major conflicts, it was imperative that each of us be willing to compromise. One group meeting and numerous e-mails later, our group had a great press release to which we each made contributions. It even followed the inverted pyramid style of writing I had been taught in my high school journalism classes—the most important facts were placed right at the beginning while the less important details were placed closer to the end. It was beautifully written and it was done exactly the way I had been taught since my sophomore year of high school.

Just one day after writing the press release, we held our second meeting with the people at RAP. I really believed that meeting with them would be the last because I thought we had created a great press release for the organization. However, just seconds after we handed the paper to the director of the Regional AIDS Project, I saw a look of dissatisfaction on her face.

"Well, for starters, I'd really like the first paragraph not to include any of these dates and times."

What? Who, what, when, where, why, and how . . . You always put that information in the first paragraph. Always! I thought to myself.

"I would also like to have this quote in the second paragraph rather than at the end. That way, people will become more interested and read further."

Oh, no. You have got to be kidding me! Quotations belong at the end. They are a final, opinionated thought. They are not important information. Quotations are always the very last thing. ALWAYS! I know this!

As she continued correcting the press release and rearranging the inverted pyramid structure that we had carefully formed, I was overcome with disappointment. Where had we gone wrong? The paper followed the format exactly. I knew it did. Why didn't the structure work? I thought that all journalistic writing was supposed to be formulated. I began to question all the formats I had learned in my years as a writer.

Before the group met again to correct the press release, I spent some serious time thinking about the meeting with RAP. What exactly did this organization need? Well, it needed a way to present information to the public about the quilt display—an event that would hopefully educate people and in turn save a few lives. How could this press release do that? Well, first it needed to be interesting—it needed to make the reader want to find out more. Because we were dealing with a sensitive issue, it needed to appeal to the reader's emotions. I began to realize that the style of writing I had learned in my high school journalism classes didn't allow for this. The organization needed a different sort of writing . . . one that abandoned some of the standards I had learned for producing journalistic writing.

The group got together and we worked hard to change the press release. We kept in mind the purpose of the event and followed the instructions that the director of RAP had given us. And it worked. The people from RAP really liked our second press release; it was work they felt could help them reach a lot of people.

This project was a lesson in flexibility. I learned that there is not a set format for writing. There are guidelines for writing. And these guidelines are not set in stone; they can be changed to fit the situation. I also learned that writers must be able to adapt to each individual setting. We must work to understand the purpose of our writing so we can communicate that to our audience.

I am sure that I will be in many different situations in regards to writing throughout my life, and each will have a different set of standards. I must be open to learning these different styles and I must adapt to them in order to be successful.

The term "successful" means something different to me now than it did before this project. Prior to my work with RAP, a successful assignment was one that earned me an "A," one that made my parents proud, one that made my teacher think of me as an exemplary student. Now, I believe that in order for something to be successful, it must serve its purpose. The assignment for RAP was very successful because it fulfilled two purposes. The first purpose was to give the Regional AIDS Project a piece of writing that could be used to draw people's attention to an event it was sponsoring. The second was to make me step out of my comfort zone and learn a new skill—flexibility.   ■

In this reflective essay, Audrey recounts her ups and downs, which many people encounter during service-learning projects. In fact, when researchers Chris Anson and L. Lee Forsberg studied a group of college students entering professional organizations as writers, they noticed that most students moved through three stages: *high hopes,* then *disorientation* and a crisis of confidence, and ultimately *resolution* as the document began to take shape.[1] You are likely to have a similar experience when writing for community organizations, so when the process seems disorienting, know that you're not alone.

---

[1] Anson, Chris M., and L. Lee Forsberg. "Moving Beyond the Academic Community: Transitional Stages in Professional Writing," *Written Communication* 7 (1990), pp. 200–231.

A Proven Process

Community writing initiatives vary in size, scope, and purpose, but most successful projects build on a foundation of careful planning and extensive consultation. The following sections describe a process that has proven successful for such projects.

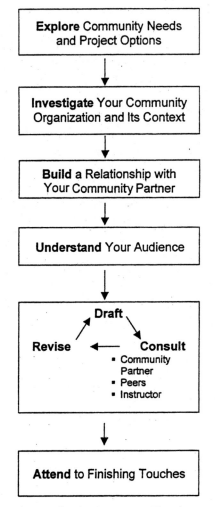

Writing for the Community Flowchart

Later in this chapter, a section is devoted to each of the steps in the flowchart, and each includes pragmatic advice for undertaking successful writing-for-the-community projects. But before we launch into the project, two critical concerns must first be addressed: collaboration and reflection.

Collaborative Writing

Most workplace writing is a collaborative enterprise, and you might therefore be teamed with classmates to complete your service-learning project. Collaborative work, and collaborative writing in particular, is not easy; it takes planning, communication, skill, and effort. Some attention to collaboration early in the process can save you serious problems and frustrations later.

WRITING TO DISCOVER

Think about times when you have worked on collaborative or team projects, whether for school, job, family, church, clubs, or sports. List at least four such occasions.

Consider times when group dynamics went wrong. What happened? What were the particular reasons for the breakdowns?

Now consider occasions when the group dynamics went well. What happened? Which specific factors made the team efforts successes?

Share your experiences and findings with a classmate.

Although there is no magic solution to making collaborative work effortless, several strategies can improve productivity and stave off disaster:

- *Emphasize communication.* Communication needs to work in several directions: among team members, between the team and the community partner, and between the team and the instructor. Some communication matters are practical, such as setting regular meeting times and responding to email messages. Others are more slippery (but just as important), such as ensuring that all team members are listened to, speaking up as concerns surface, and keeping team members, community partners, and instructors continually informed of both progress and problems.

- *Set regular meeting times and firm deadlines.* Everyone has a busy life. By setting a regular meeting time, you ensure that all know when to meet and for how long. Also, by creating a time line with firm draft deadlines in advance, you keep the project moving.

- *Assign roles.* It makes sense to both divide labor and leverage individual strengths. One team member might be good at maintaining contact with the community partner, another might be a good editor, and another might be great at layout and desktop publishing. However, remember that even though team members may have primary responsibility for one aspect of the project, each person is not an individual operator. You can't just divide up a project, go your separate ways, and then expect to plug the pieces together. The whole team is responsible for the whole project, which means that everyone needs to communicate, review the work of others, and negotiate final drafts.

- *Ask for help if things go astray.* If group dynamics start to sour, whether due to personal conflicts, slacking, or some other factor, you should let your instructor know. This is not whining; rather, it is a wise move. Avoiding the problem won't make it go away, and often things just get progressively worse, putting the entire project in jeopardy. Be proactive; ask for assistance.

Collaborative writing does not come naturally. It takes planning and effort. One way to formalize this planning is to write a *group contract.* Such a contract can spell out

- Team goals
- Contact information for each individual
- Days/times when all team members are available to meet
- Regularly scheduled days/times for team meetings
- Preferred methods for communicating with each other
- Specific individual roles and responsibilities
- Consequences that will follow when individuals miss meetings or fail to uphold their responsibilities

Because each community project is different, each contract should be adjusted to fit its context.

Another way to raise awareness of group dynamics is to have team members do a personality or learning style assessment, such as the Meyers-Briggs Type Indicator or the Kolb Learning Styles Inventory. These tools can help make collaborative teams more aware of each individual's inclinations, learning preferences, strengths, and weaknesses, which, in turn, can help the group anticipate problems and leverage strengths. While many test services charge fees, several are free. Two free Web-based tools are the VARK and the Keirsey Temperament Sorter. The VARK (www.vark-learn.com) assesses whether one's primary learning style is visual, aural, read/write, or kinesthetic (hands-on). The Keirsey Temperament Sorter (www.keirsey.com) focuses on personality types more than on learning styles. After taking the online questionnaires, compare your results with those of others on your team.

Keep in mind that many psychologists dispute the legitimacy of such personality and learning tests. Results should not be taken as absolute judgments of one's character or capabilities. Rather, they should be starting points for discussion. For the purposes of group writing projects, such assessments should be used to the degree that they help team members understand each other better and work together more efficiently.

Reflection

Rather than simply race through the steps in the collaborative writing process, you should strive to be a *reflective practitioner*. Engaging in reflection will not only ensure a better final product but also lead to more substantial learning and personal satisfaction. Reflection can take many different forms, each of which has value:

- *Reflection on community needs and social justice.* Why does your community partner organization exist and who does it serve? What community needs or issues does the organization address? What larger social, political, and economic forces shape those needs? What are the root causes of these forces? What are alternative ways of addressing those needs or issues? Who defines "need"? What historical and cultural knowledge helps contextualize the work of your community partner organization?

- *Reflection on your relationship with the community partner.* Do you understand the values, history, and goals of your community partner organization? Are you accommodating your community partner's work schedule and needs? What are you doing to build and maintain a healthy working relationship?

- *Reflection on the rhetorical situation.* What is the purpose of your document? Who are the primary and "hidden" audiences for your project? What are the characteristics of those readers? How will your document meet your readers' needs? Can you anticipate and address future uses for your document in the organization?

- *Reflection on project process and progress.* Is your project progressing according to plan? What problems are emerging and how are you dealing with them? Are you regularly keeping both your community partner and instructor updated? What are your biggest surprises, challenges, and rewards? If you are working as a team, what group dynamics are in play?

- *Reflection on your own learning.* What are the most important things you are learning? Have your prior beliefs or attitudes been challenged? What have you discovered about writing and about working in a professional situation? How does your project experience relate to your academic life, personal life, and/or future plans?

The Project Journal

To facilitate reflection, your instructor might ask you to keep a project journal, whether on paper or in the form of email messages to your instructor. Such journals can take many approaches. One format is detailed in the following box.

Project Log/Dialogic Journal

Starting with the exploratory stages of a project, you should keep a project log/dialogic journal and update it regularly (at least once a week). As suggested by its name, the log/journal serves two purposes:

1. You can use it to log your project progress so that the instructor can stay apprised of how the group (and each individual) is making headway. Be sure to log all group meetings, community partner meetings, due dates for drafts, and your particular responsibilities; also briefly comment on these entries (How did the meeting go? Why did you get assigned particular duties within the group? How much time and effort did you commit to the project this week?).

2. In the dialogic journal you are invited to reflect both on the project and on the issues it raises for you. This can be informal and free-flowing, but should involve serious thinking, too. The instructor is concerned with the degree of your inquiry—how ardently you grapple with problems and pursue ideas that surface during the course of the project. Review the five categories of reflection described earlier in this chapter and use them to guide your writing. Also consider the issues raised in earlier chapters of this book.

Depending on your instructor's preferences, keep your log and journal entries in a notebook or send entries as email messages.

Exploring Community Needs and Project Options

Your instructor may already have established community writing projects, in which case you can skip this section. But if you are charged with finding your own project, you should read this section.

First, take an inventory of your interests. Which social issues do you find important? Which relate to your career goals? Which do you want to learn more about? The range of possibilities is wide: the environment, education, youth, the elderly, women's health, poverty, mentoring, literacy, homelessness, mental illness, the arts, and so on. Then investigate which organizations in your area address your interests: use the phonebook; consult an outreach office on campus, if there is one; contact The United Way; and ask around.

Possible writing-for-the-community projects can include the following types of writing:

- Research reports for an organization
- Articles for newsletters
- Brochures, fact sheets, or other public relations materials
- Revisions, updates, and redesigns of existing brochures or other in-house publications
- Press releases
- Publicity materials for programs and events
- Volunteer recruitment materials
- Volunteer or other in-house manuals
- Reports on potential sources for grant funding
- Research assistance that contributes to a grant proposal
- Surveys and reports on student or client attitudes toward particular issues of interest to the organization
- Web sites

This list is not comprehensive. There may be other kinds of writing that local organizations could use—and you can't find out what is *really* needed until you inquire directly. Remember to use the organization's needs, rather than your own preferences, as a starting place. The sections below should guide you in making contact with such organizations.

Sample Projects

The following are writing-for-the-community projects completed by teams of students at Kansas State University in 2001–2002:

- A local food distribution center asked students to survey clients on how well the organization was meeting community and client needs. With the center's director, the team created a survey. Then, on two separate days, they visited the pantry and invited walk-in clients to complete the survey. After compiling the data, the team submitted it and a one-page summary/analysis to the director. She will use that report in shaping future policy. Another group did a similar kind of survey and report for the campus Women's Center, to assess the impact of the Campaign for Nonviolence that it had organized.

- Speak United, a grassroots advocacy group that is active in local politics on low-income housing, living wage, and related issues, asked for assistance in writing the preapplication for a grant. After studying several other grant proposals that the organization had written and working through several drafts with the staff, a student team completed the preapplication.
- The local zoo publishes a newsletter for its volunteers and the community. One team researched and wrote an article about the arrival of a new species of wolf.
- The Wellness Project on campus sponsored two projects: a report (for internal use) that researched how other colleges were implementing the social norms theory of substance abuse prevention and a brochure (for students on campus) explaining how and why the university was implementing a social norms media campaign on campus.
- The local arts center asked students to write a press release for an upcoming play. This involved reading the script for the play, interviewing the director, and pitching the event in a way that would attract ticket sales.
- A local day-care center that serves low-income families needed its brochure updated, revised, and redesigned. The team revised the text and visuals of the brochure to both serve the practical needs of its audience (parents considering the day-care center) and promote the center's values (i.e., care, professionalism, education).

A crucial issue in selecting a project is assessing whether it is the right "fit" for you, your team, and your college course. You don't want a project that is too clerical and doesn't draw on your skills as a writer. So, for example, simply posting prewritten material on the Web or filing at an office would be inappropriate. You also don't want to take on a project that is too large and complex in scope or that requires too much insider knowledge. So, for example, writing a grant proposal or writing the organization's annual report would be out of bounds. You want a project that challenges you as a writer but that can also be completed in a reasonably short time.

Investigating Your Community Organization and Its Context

Before working with an organization, you need to know something about that organization. As detailed in Chapter 4, researchers who study writing have discovered that learning to write is not just about applying the right grammar and usage skills; instead, it is akin to entering a community and picking up the habits and insider knowledge of that community. In order to be a successful writer for or within an organization, you need to learn and adopt the values and conventions of that particular discourse community. The more you know, the more successful your service-learning project is likely to be.

For example, consider one project students did for a local zoo. Before starting the project—which involved researching soon-to-arrive animals and adding entries on them to an existing volunteer manual—the group did an agency profile report of the sort described in Chapter 7. The group interviewed the community partner and did research on the zoo. By doing so, it learned critical information that affected its writing, information that the group would otherwise have discovered only through trial and error. For example, one thing the group learned was that while many people thought of the zoo as a venue for entertainment, the zoo staff saw it as a place committed primarily to education and research. That is how the zoo staff wanted to be perceived, and they wanted those values reflected, whether directly or indirectly, in all their documents. Therefore, when the students composed entries for the manual, it kept the educational and research goals and image of the zoo in mind.

Writing an agency profile can be a helpful first step in preparing for a community project. But even if you are not writing a profile, you should devote some of the first meeting with your community partner to learning about the fundamental features of that organization. Among the topics to cover are the organization's

- Mission
- History
- Values
- Organizational structure
- Writing conventions

While you may be anxious to immediately get started on the writing, learning about these things first can save you from serious mistakes and frustrations later.

Building a Relationship with Your Community Partner

A community partner is not someone who simply assigns you a project and then collects it several weeks later. Rather than think in terms of a transaction, you should think in terms of a *relationship*. Healthy relationships require time, thought, and effort.

With your first agency phone call and meeting, you set the tone for a working relationship. You will want to make the right first impression and then build a deeper and stronger partnership with each subsequent communication. Experience shows that if the student–community partner relationship falters, then so will the writing project. Before your first contact with an organization, review Chapter 6, which outlines several key principles that govern healthy and ethical partnerships.

The First Meeting: Making a First Impression

Consider the importance of first impressions. When you meet someone new, you quickly develop opinions, feelings, and assessments. Fair or not, such first impressions tend to stick (or take a good deal of time to change). Therefore, you and your team need to devote significant planning and effort to your first contacts with your community partner. Ask yourselves what you want the community partner to think of you after that initial meeting.

First, of course, you need to set a meeting. In some cases your instructor will have already spoken to the community agency; in other cases you will make a "cold call." Making a phone call might seem like simple business, but you should still write a script for it. You will want to communicate who you are and why you are calling, explain concisely the purpose of the meeting you're proposing, and have several possible meeting times at your fingertips.

The purpose of your first meeting might be to investigate project options, it might be to determine expectations for a preestablished project, or it might be to gather information for writing an agency profile report.

Community Partner Perspective

Advice I'd give to a group of writers working for a place like ours is that they should be sensitive that the organization is a *working* organization.

Some students don't realize that we can't work on *their* time. For example, they may call in the morning and want to meet 2 P.M. that day, because their project is due. In the real world they need to be especially sensitive to the organization's schedule.

Shirley Bramhall, Executive Director
The Flint Hills Breadbasket

Chapter 7 provides basic advice for conducting meetings and interviews with community partners (review pages 295–296). As noted there, before the meeting you should brainstorm a substantial list of questions, and rank the questions in order of importance.

Outline for a First Meeting

ESTABLISH RAPPORT

- Arrive on time and prepared
- Introduce yourself
- Express your interest in the organization

EXPLAIN YOUR PURPOSE

- Do this in two or three sentences

ASK QUESTIONS AND TAKE NOTES

- Content of questions depends on purpose (have at least 10 questions ready)
- If you are gathering information for an agency profile, see Chapter 7
- If discussing a project, ask about goals, time lines, audience, format, process, sample documents (as models), budget, technology issues, special concerns, etc.
- Be prepared with follow-up questions to clarify points and to explain your capabilities and limitations

EMPLOY CLOSING STRATEGIES

- Invite a final thought (e.g., "Is there anything else we should keep in mind as we prepare to start this project?")
- Briefly confirm key expectations to ensure that you grasp them correctly, and clear up anything that is still confusing
- Schedule your next meeting (or establish a regular meeting time) as well as the best method for future communications (phone? email? best times to contact?)
- Thank the community partner and express enthusiasm about working together.

Shared Expectations: Letter of Understanding

Meetings with your community partner present opportunities to discuss and establish project expectations. Detailing those expectations in writing is wise. This can be done with a letter of understanding, which should be written within a week of the meeting at which you first discuss your project. This letter should include the following information:

- A brief explanation of the purpose of the letter
- A statement of project objectives and how you propose to meet them

- A request for anything you need from the community partner
- A time line for drafts and meetings
- Methods for communicating
- A closing that invites response and expresses both professionalism and warmth

Writing this letter is part of building your relationship with the community partner, and the tone should be serious but upbeat. The letter also serves as a record and as a contract for you, your partner, and your instructor. The following is an example of a letter of understanding.

Sample Letter of Understanding

October 20, 2001

Cheryl Jackson, Volunteer Coordinator
4th Street Shelter
1832 4th Street
City, ST 12345

Dear Ms. Jackson:

This letter is to follow up on our October 18 meeting, at which we discussed the writing project we will be doing in the coming weeks. As we understand it, we will create a three-fold brochure that will be used to help recruit more student volunteers for the shelter. Our group is excited about the prospect of helping 4th Street Shelter in its work with the homeless.

PROJECT OBJECTIVES

The brochure will aim to recruit college student volunteers, especially at volunteer fairs such as the one held on our campus. We think that in order for the brochure to work, it needs to not only include basic information but also make volunteering at the shelter appealing to students. Therefore, the brochure will probably do things like feature a current volunteer, include photos, include facts about possible work-study pay, emphasize the flexible hours, and let the potential volunteers know what they would do and why it is important work.

Because of the limited budget, we understand that the brochure will need to be in black and white. Still, we hope to make it visually appealing in a way that college students will respond to.

WHAT WE NEED FROM YOU

In order to create the brochure, we will need a few things from you, including

- Basic information on hours of operation, volunteer guidelines, etc.
- The name of at least one current college volunteer who we might contact to feature in the brochure
- The shelter logo, in digital format, if you have it
- Photos, if you have them
- Your preferred software format, if any, so that you can revise the brochure in the future
- Your constructive feedback on drafts

Hopefully, we can get most of these things at our October 29 meeting.

TIME LINE

As we discussed, it makes sense for each of us to volunteer at the shelter for at least a week so that we can understand how 4th Street Shelter works. (Some of us plan a longer commitment.) During that time, we can also start gathering information. Here is our current project schedule:

Oct 21–29	Volunteer at shelter/gather information
October 29 (3:30pm)	Meet at your office to pick up information and plan
Nov. 7	Have rough draft ready for review and feedback
Nov. 8–15	Revise the draft and resubmit another draft, if needed
Nov. 16–25	Share the draft with other students for feedback and finalize the draft
Nov. 25	Submit a final draft on paper and disk

In order to keep in touch, we have included our phone numbers and email addresses below. Tim will serve as the main contact with you for the project.

This is our understanding of the project. Please share with us your thoughts on our plans, especially if they don't match your intentions. We look forward to working with you on this project and to seeing you at our October 29 meeting.

Sincerely,

Tim Mitchell	Ariana Warr	Tyson Hilton
555-4378	555-1776	555-2238
tmit@college.edu	warr@college.edu	thilton@college.edu

Understanding Your Audience

One of the commandments of writing is "Know your audience." After project expectations are confirmed, a detailed audience analysis is essential.

The most fundamental question is *Who, in particular, will read the document, and for what purpose?* One of the key distinctions for nonprofit agency documents is whether they will be used internally (read only by the agency staff; for example, a report) or externally (published for the public; for example, a newsletter or brochure).

Knowing demographic factors such as the gender, age, and education level of the audience is essential. Moreover, knowing the attitudes of audience members is important. For example, that the audience for a school newsletter will be parents is crucial to the newsletter writers, who will correspondingly pick topics that parents are likely to find interesting and write in a style appropriate to adults. But it is also important to acknowledge that parents of school-age children tend to be very busy. These audience characteristics should guide the writer's decisions about content, style, and document design.

Be sure to consider audiences besides the main audience. For example, writing for the school newsletter will likely involve a *gatekeeper audience*. This audience would be those—often editors or administrators—who arbitrate what goes into the newsletter and how it is generated. There might also be *hidden audiences*. Who, for example, might see the newsletter in its draft stages? And who beyond parents—perhaps school board members or the public at large—might also read the published newsletter?

The worksheet in the following box can help guide audience analysis. You should take notes in response to each of the questions on the worksheet. If you cannot answer some of them, you need to gather more information from your community partner or directly from the prospective audience members.

Audience Analysis Worksheet

MAIN AUDIENCE

- Who is your primary reader/audience?
- What is your reader's relationship to you?
- What are the demographic characteristics of your audience, such as age, gender, education level, cultural background, political leanings, and special affiliations?
- How familiar is your reader with your subject?
- Does your reader have communication preferences (e.g., expects visuals, uses particular media or technologies)?

- What is your reader's attitude toward the subject?
- Does your reader need to be informed or persuaded?
- How will your audience read the document (start to finish? jump around?)?
- How will the reader use the information you provide?

OTHER READERS AND STAKEHOLDERS

- Who else is likely to read your document?
- Are there any gatekeeper audiences?
- Are there any hidden audiences?
- Who else could be affected by your document?

CONTEXT

- What situational events, circumstances, or factors might influence what you write and how it is received?
- How will the document be circulated throughout its life cycle?

In addition to analyzing audience characteristics that should shape writing choices, you should also consider what attitudes you want to encourage your audience to adopt. For example, if you are writing a coaching manual for a youth recreational league that values sportsmanship over competition, the content and style of the manual should reflect and promote this spirit. Even if the audience is not predisposed to thinking about sportsmanship, the manual should invoke that characteristic in readers.

Drafting, Consulting, and Revising

At some point you need to simply sit down and write. But you should not expect to be able to hammer out a project in one sitting. Even the very best writers work through multiple drafts, and this is particularly true in cases in which the document requires consultation with others (in this case, your community partner). In fact, most writing-for-the-community projects cycle through several drafts (sometimes 3 or 4, sometimes 10 or 15). The process involves *drafting, consulting* (with peers, the instructor, and the community partner), and *revising*. Every project is unique, so there is no universal formula for drafting and revising. But at the very least you will want to have one consultation meeting with your community partner to share a draft and receive feedback, and you will want to have a few meetings with your instructor, as well. Most projects require many such meetings.

As you work, you will want to return again and again to the questions in the Audience Analysis Worksheet. Your document needs to be reader-centered; that is, your composing should be guided more by your readers' needs than by your own preferences.

Genre/Format

In workplace writing, genres, or general formats, tend to be fairly established. When writing for a community organization, you might need to learn a new genre rather quickly, which is challenging but possible. For example, if you are asked to write a news release but have never written such a thing before, you will first need to learn how most news releases are structured; otherwise, yours will look like an oddity. You will also need to consult with your community partner to see if the "standard" news release genre is appropriate for your particular case. (Recall Audrey's reflections on format at the beginning of this chapter.)

One way to understand a genre is to examine several models of its type. If you are writing a news release, you could, for example, read and analyze several news releases by businesses and nonprofit organizations (some are available on the Web). Better yet, you could ask your community partner for news releases that the organization has written in the past. When you review samples, you should identify common rhetorical features: Are they all roughly the same length? Do they follow a similar pattern of organization? Do they all use a particular tone? Do they have a similar visual layout? As scholar Carolyn Miller suggests, we should think of genres not as rigid formats but as forms of social action.[2] That is, genres establish and fulfill readers' expectations, and thus they help readers act on the information in the text. Genres are more like tools than empty vessels.

It is helpful to review a range of documents published by your community partner organization because publications often form a family of documents that share visual features, project common values, or employ established terminology. Even relatively small things such as featuring common colors or a particular logo, or including certain legal language, can prove important. Thus, if you are writing a brochure for an organization, you should first review other brochures and publicity materials produced by that organization and ask your contact person whether the new brochure should share visual and textual cues with the others. You should also ask your community partner about the availability of a "style sheet," a form that details the organization's preferred conventions of style and usage.

---

[2]Miller, Carolyn. "Genre as Social Action," *Quarterly Journal of Speech* 70 (1984): pp. 151–167.

ASSIGNMENT
Genre Analysis Worksheet

Gather several (a minimum of three) examples of the kind of document your community partner agency is asking you to write. Take notes on the features and conventions that are common to those models. Account for the organizational pattern, visual layout, physical features (length, size, paper type, binding, etc.), tone/voice, vocabulary, style, graphics, headings, transitions, and so on. Also do the following:

- After listing the features/conventions, sort them according to relative importance, using the categories "absolutely essential," "common to most," and "optional/variable."
- Consider how your anticipated audience is likely to read documents of this genre. Will readers scan it? read it carefully from start to finish? skip around? How will some generic features (such as headings) help your readers navigate the document? What are the motives people have for reading the document?
- Anticipate how readers might respond if you departed from the conventions of the genre. Which conventions/features, in particular, could be modified? How might the audience respond to such variations? Which variations might confuse or alienate the audience?

Document Design

Whereas most academic writing requires little in the way of graphics and design, most professional writing demands appropriate verbal/visual integration. For example, a brochure needs to *look* like a brochure, not just include blocks of dense text (no matter how well written the text is). In most cases, document design and written text must work in concert to achieve the rhetorical purpose of the communication.

Learning all about design in a few weeks is impossible. But you can quickly grasp some basics that will save you from visual blunders. First, follow the advice given earlier in this chapter about reviewing other documents produced by your organization and similar organizations. Are there common design features? You need not slavishly follow samples—after all, bringing a fresh design perspective may be among your greatest contributions. But you should be aware of common visual features.

Understanding some fundamental principles and practical techniques of page design can be particularly helpful in completing successful writing-for-the-community projects. While reading the following article, consider how the design advice presented might apply to your own project.

Article: Christine Sevilla,
Page Design: Directing the Reader's Eye

Christine Sevilla is president of lumin guild, an organization that works with businesses on design and research matters. She leads seminars on information design, creates instructional systems, and serves as an adjunct professor for Rochester Institute of Technology. This article is based on her book Information Design Desk Reference.

Effective page design maps a viewer's route through information. When designing information, your objective is to lead the viewer's eye directly to your message. Readers of English read from left to right and from the top of the page to the bottom. (The typical page-scanning pattern actually forms a Z.) This habit of left-to-right eye movement dominates most design decisions in the West and is the basis for most conventional graphic design of print publications.

A few important principles—emphasis, flow, alignment, repetition, and unity—and a couple of techniques—styles and grids—can make your layout work for you. Use and place graphics and copy well (with feedback from representatives of your audience), develop clear, understandable content, and your message will come through loud and clear.

A FEW DESIGN PRINCIPLES

Design principles offer guidelines for presenting information clearly. Sure, the rules are made to be broken, but they are best broken by the experts.

Emphasis

Without emphasis, nothing stands out. In any document, you undoubtedly want to stress something. Generally the top of the page is the most eye-catching location, but readers also tend to focus on the brightest, most contrasting, and heaviest elements. Your focal point should dominate the layout; to be safe, you can locate it at the top, where a reader's eyes naturally begin to scan the page. Use color, placement, and size judiciously to amplify the meaning of your text. Color, for instance, is not absolutely necessary for readability—and if used without restraint, it can be distracting. If a page has more than one dominant element or focal point, your reader has to guess where to start.

Flow

The elements in your design should flow, directing the reader's eye from element to element. For example, look at the two report covers in Figure 1. Which one leads your eye better along the page?

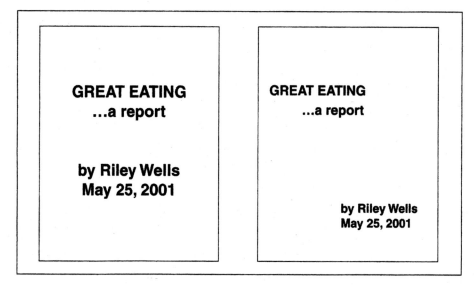

Figure 1. Two examples of a report cover.

The example on the right makes better use of the space on the page and aligns the elements along an implied line from the end of the word "report" to the beginning of the word "by." The reader's eye follows the path.

Simple lines can pull the reader's eye toward the most important information, or toward elements that follow in a sequence. A line used this way, called a *leading line* in art or photography, guides viewers in the direction you set. Often the line is implied: Think of a news photo in which several people are looking intently at one person in the corner—the line of this gaze directs the reader's attention toward this person.

Alignment

Alignment assists the flow of a document. The document on the top in Figure 2 contains many random elements. Readers are not directed to any particular place as a starting point, nor are they provided a clear path to follow as they scan the page. Aligning the textual elements, removing unnecessary elements, sizing the needed graphics, and creating a large banner to signal a starting point give readers a path to follow in the bottom document in Figure 2.

Repetition

Graphic elements cannot do all the work in the variety of documents and Web sites we create. Consistent repetition is a key to navigation. If your text is arranged in regular, repeating patterns, your readers can easily learn the rhythms in your document and predict where information will be located.

Figure 2. *The document on the bottom illustrates how proper alignment directs the reader's eye.*

Unity

Unity refers to how well the layout hangs together. What would you think if your grocery store stocked dog food, candy, and beer on the same aisle? How would you know where to find these items? Fortunately, most stores are organized more coherently, but even if disparate items were on the same aisle, consistent signage and different shelving styles could signal their location. Unity establishes a relationship among parts, even if the parts are quite different. Repetition of headings throughout this magazine, for example, establishes a unifying visual guide, connecting a variety of content types.

A FEW TECHNIQUES

Two significant ways to ensure consistency and unity in document layout are setting styles and using a grid.

Styles

Spend much time writing on a computer and you'll want to establish a design style—a consistent visual hierarchy. The main benefit of establishing a style before creating a document, presentation, or Web site is enhancing the user's ease of navigation. Word processing packages have default styles that you can modify, or you can develop your own style. The beauty of automated style setting is its uniformity, which allows you to do less thinking about structure and more thinking about content. This advantage is especially critical for large documents.

To get an idea of how styles can work for you, create a short document like the one on the left in Figure 3 and modify it until you see exactly the look you want. The original document is very "flat" and undifferentiated, while the document on the right has a certain "texture" that draws the eye to specific items.

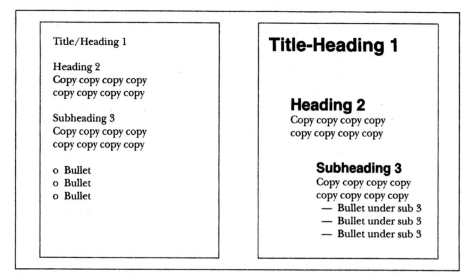

Figure 3. A document without a design style (left) and a document with a design style (right).

In the example on the right in Figure 3, formatting items such as outdenting, indenting, alignment, and font styles and sizes organize the copy for readability.

Grids

Page design layout grids, like those in Figure 4, are most often depicted as gray blocks (the copy) against a white background (the page). For a text-heavy document, a good layout is critical to the reader's comfort and ability to navigate. You create patterns that will familiarize the reader with the organization of elements on the page.

The first thing your reader sees is not the title or other details of the page, but its overall pattern and contrast. Repetition is a key to navigation. If your text is organized into regular, repeating patterns, you will make it easy for the reader to learn the structure and rhythm of your document and to predict where information is likely to be found.

A grid is a basis for decisions, like a visual procedure. Establish a layout grid for handling your text and graphics and use it to build consistency and unity within a longer document. (If you're creating a poster or an ad, you don't need to use a grid since repetition isn't a factor.) Repetition provides a coherent graphic identity that reinforces a distinct sense of "place," making your document more memorable. A clear and consistent visual hierarchy allows readers to find information quickly.

Page through a few books and sketch out the grids you observe. Look at an encyclopedia, a cookbook, and other books full of illustrations, and then look at some newsletters or magazines. The grid provides the structure for the layout and items that cross columns, like headlines, photos, illustrations, or captions, which add liveliness and visual variety. The modified version of Grid C in Figure 5 shows a graphic, represented as a box with an X, and body text that spans two columns. The eye accepts the merger of the two right columns, and the document is enhanced by controlled variety.

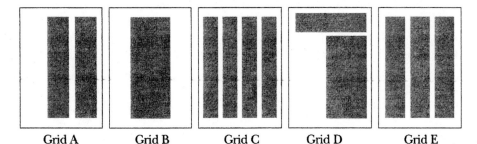

| Grid A | Grid B | Grid C | Grid D | Grid E |

Figure 4. Examples of layout grids.

Figure 5. Modified Grid C from Figure 4.

Almost any grid can be made to work, but there are some clear choices. Newspapers use the multi-column grid for two reasons: Several stories need to appear on one page, and articles can be read more quickly if the column is narrower. A narrative report or book would employ Grids B or D, which contain a scanning column (the white space beside the text) for inclusion of graphics or headings. A dictionary or encyclopedia might use a variation on Grid A, which allows for illustrations in the scanning column while permitting quick reading of the text areas. Newsletters often use formats like Grid E. Considerations such as font and space between lines affect grid decisions, too: Smaller fonts and tighter spacing lend themselves to grids with narrower columns.

It isn't necessary to limit yourself to one grid within a document. But each grid should have a purpose; don't confuse the reader by using different grids carelessly. You'll notice the use of several grids in a magazine, for example, but they will all appear in a logical format that is suited to the material. Letters to the editor will appear in two or three narrow columns, while a main article may have one large column with a scanning column of white space. Letters are usually short and readers appreciate a format that allows quick scanning, while a main article commands a larger dedicated space, with headlines or illustrations in the scanning column. The grid you choose depends on what you're building. There is no "one-size-fits-all" for the variety of documents out there. Fitting the formatting to the content can make the information more understandable.

HANDLING GRAPHICS

Graphic Markers

People often skim a document to find something worth reading. The markers they see should be integral to the content. Decorative graphics, such as icons and other visual markers, have their uses, but they can cause confusion if used without a clear purpose. Ask yourself or a potential audience member whether an element adds clarity or helps the reader navigate. If the reader can manage just as well without the graphic element, leave it out. Clarity is enhanced by restraint. Give your readers only what they need to understand the message.

I recall a book that was intended to be a reference for a computer system. Unfortunately, the book employed an elaborate set of graphic symbols that required as much effort to decode as it took to read the text they labeled! A good example of the use of graphic symbols is a guide to flowering plants that includes simple symbols for shade or sun, perennial or annual, and wet or dry conditions. In this case, the symbols are functioning as shorthand, freeing the reader from poring over text to find out specific details.

Placing Graphics

It is best to use flush left or flush right placement for headings and graphics. Think of these positions as having a hinge upon which things can hang and flip one way or the other: The hinge provides an anchor in space so that elements do not appear to be free floating. (Free-floating text can be used effectively, but it requires some know-how.) Centering elements within a column is less effective because white space is broken; it is better to combine white space into one larger unit. Also, centering breaks the reader's rhythm of returning to the beginning of the line.

A very useful guideline, offered by the out-of-print *Xerox Publishing Standards: A Manual of Style and Design* (Watson-Guptill Publications, 1988), is to maintain the integrity of the vertical scanning area and the right margin. Xerox defines the following rules for placing graphics (numbers correspond to the blocks in Figure 6):

1. Place a *small* graphic flush right with the column of text. Positioning the graphic close to the text indicates the connection between them.
2. Place a graphic that is *the same width as the text column* flush right and left justified.
3. If the graphic is *narrower than the text column,* place it flush left within the text column.
4. Limit the *area of an illustration* to the width of the margins of the document.
5. If the graphic is *wider than the text column,* place it flush right within the text column and let it extend into the white space, which is called the scanning column.

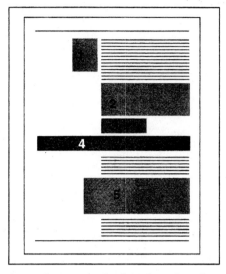

***Figure 6. An example of graphics aligned
with column edges.***

THE TEST

When you think your work is complete, ask at least one member of your target audience to look at it and tell you what message is initially conveyed. Find out if he or she has reviewed it in the way you had expected, and if any elements were inappropriate—perhaps too jarring, too large, too small, or difficult to read. Your reviewer's feedback can help you fine-tune your message beyond the design basics.

Enjoy your next layout project! ■

In addition to the principles and techniques outlined by Sevilla, several other design elements merit consideration.

You should avoid *clutter.* Is there any verbal or visual material that doesn't serve a function? If so, remove it.

White space on a page gives the reader's eye a chance to rest. It can be used to signal separations between different sections or elements. A page saturated with text from top to bottom, margin to margin, can be taxing.

Because many workplace documents are read referentially (i.e., readers jump around from section to section) rather than sequentially (i.e., from start to finish), *headings and lists* are important. They improve scanability; they give readers signposts that help them locate information quickly. Both numbered lists and bulleted lists are popular. With any type of list, be sure that the list points are parallel in structure.

NOT PARALLEL:

- Exercise daily
- Healthy eating
- Find ways to reduce your stress levels

PARALLEL:

- Exercise daily
- Eat well
- Reduce stress levels

Finally, *fonts* can significantly affect the tone of a document:

Some fonts convey a whimsical tone,
Others speak more seriously.

Be strategic in your choices of fonts, and resist the impulse to include too many different fonts. You might also consider the common design choice of using serif fonts for large blocks of text (because the horizontal finishing strokes on the ends of the letters help guide the reader's eye across the page) and sans serif fonts for headings (because they stand out). You should also consider font choice in relation to different media. For example, sans serif fonts such as Arial are generally more readable on computer screens, and thus they are fitting for Web sites.

Resources For Document Design

Books and Web sites on visual communication abound. Here are a few places to start:

BOOKS

- Robin Williams, *The Non-Designer's Design Book* (Peachpit, 1994)
- Karen A. Schriver, *Dynamics in Document Design* (Wiley, 1997)
- Charles Kostelnick and David D. Roberts, *Designing Visual Language* (Allyn & Bacon, 1998)

WEB SITES

- Kelly's Design Tips for Effective Visual Communication, http://itech.fgcu.edu/tips/intro.html
- Graphic Design at About.com, http://graphicdesign.about.com

Progress Reports

Ensuring quality and monitoring progress are key concerns for both instructors and community partners, and they are mainly handled through meetings, conferences, and email messages. But for projects that run longer than four weeks, using progress report memos can be an important step in maintaining a healthy relationship with your community partner and keeping your instructor informed. Components of a progress report include:

Introduction	What work does your report cover?
Results of past work	What have you done to date?
Plans for future work	What will you do and when?
Conclusions and recommendations	How do things stand overall?

Sample Progress Report Letter

March 25, 2002

Shannon Anders
Education Director, City Zoo
Animal Way
Your City, FL XXXXX

Dear Ms. Anders:

This letter reports our progress on the newsletter writing project. Since our meeting on March 15, we have been doing research for the white-naped crane article we promised for the volunteer newsletter.

RESULTS FROM THE PAST TWO WEEKS

Through library sources, Web sites, and interviews with zoo staff, we have gathered all the information we need. In sitting down to write the article, we have had a difficult time condensing all the information into a short newsletter article, but we expect to have it done by this Monday, March 29.

PLANS FOR THE NEXT TWO WEEKS

On March 29 we will drop off the draft for your review. After you have had time to read it, we would like to schedule a meeting to discuss your advice for revision. Then we can move on to proofreading.

We are a few days behind our original schedule, but we still expect to meet the deadline for the May newsletter.

Sincerely,
Angel Rios   Bob Cutler

cc: Edward Nelson, Instructor
Enclosure

Anticipating Issues

Students have been doing agency-based and service-learning writing projects for over a decade, and several key concerns surface again and again. You can benefit from the accumulated experience of others by becoming aware of the following potential problems and how to deal with them:

- *Recalibrate to serve your community partner.* For over 15 years you have written for teachers, to get traditional grades, and suddenly you are asked to favor your community partner's perspective over that of your instructor. Many students find this counterintuitive and difficult; it is hard to shake the teacher-centered habit. To help address this concern, try thinking of your instructor as a coach or project manager rather than as a judge and jury. After all, the primary evaluation of your project lies with the community partner and its intended audience.

- *Expect to feel overwhelmed and disoriented.* At some point in the process, often in the second and third weeks, students get frustrated and often doubt themselves and the prospect of project success. Recall the feelings that Audrey expressed in her reflections on her community project. Share your anxieties with your instructor, seek clarification from your community partner, keep working, and be patient. Things will come together. And when they do, the rewards are great.

- *Plan for delays and scheduling mishaps.* School schedules are contained and predictable; real life is messy and unpredictable. Moreover, nonprofit agencies are generally understaffed and underfunded, which means the employees are especially busy. Your community partner might not be able to meet when you want to meet; or meetings might be canceled due to unforeseen circumstances. You might even experience a staff change midway through your project. Therefore, you need to be flexible and build a reasonable cushion (at least a week or two) into your schedule. Projects almost always take longer to complete than initially expected.

- *Expect technology challenges.* Desktop publishing programs are getting increasingly user-friendly, but generating and formatting documents tends to gobble up many hours. Plan for that time, and likewise plan for unexpected technology problems such as crashes, lost disks, and software bugs. Back up everything.

Community Partner Perspective

Student writers need to trust their abilities, trust themselves. We can give them critical feedback, but they need to take some initiative and have confidence in their own ideas.

Melanie Brockington, Director
Court Appointed Special Advocates (CASA) of Manhattan, KS

Advance planning can help you avoid many problems. But even with the best planning, unexpected issues often surface. Problem solving, communication, and consultation are the only good solutions when these such concerns arise. Ask your teammates for help; ask your instructor for help. Community projects demand that you be a creative problem solver rather than a passive rule follower.

Attending to Finishing Touches

After you have cycled several times through drafting, consulting, and revising, your project will be moving toward completion. In the final stages, you should address the following issues.

Copyediting

Documents for public consumption usually need to be crafted in standard edited English—that is, they need to meet general conventions for usage and grammar. Most readers are unforgiving; they notice even little mistakes. As one student has said in referring to editing, "In this kind of writing, there is no room for error. It has to be perfect." This means that you and/or your team need to comb through your final draft carefully. You should also recruit several outside readers to review your document.

Community Partner Perspective

Student writers need to be aware of the importance of correct grammar and usage. It really affects the way the public views them.

Adene Winter, Executive Director
Manhattan Day Care and Learning Center

User Testing

User testing means performing a "test run" of your project to see if it does its job. If possible, you should test your document with its intended audience. For example, if you are creating materials to help a tutoring program recruit more male tutors, you should test your recruitment documents with a few male friends and a few male strangers. Do they respond as you would expect them to?

Planning for the Document's Future

Often the documents you create will be revised or updated in the future. To ease that revision process, be sure to

- Give your community partner both hard copies and digital/disk copies of your final draft
- Anticipate potential software compatibility problems by including information on the applications that you used and the formats in which the documents are saved

Letter of Transmittal

When submitting a major writing project, you should consider including a letter of transmittal that includes the following parts:

Introduction	Mention the accompanying communication.
Body	Describe the contents and special features of the document. Include information on how you have planned for the document's future use.
Closing	End with a short paragraph that conveys a positive sense of your working relationship and that invites the reader to contact you, if needed.

The following is a sample letter of transmittal.

Sample Letter of Transmittal

7 May 2001

Judy Davis
Executive Director
The Crisis Center, Inc.
P.O. Box 1526
Manhattan, KS 66502

Subject: Volunteer Training Manual

Dear Judy:

We are pleased to submit the attached Volunteer Training Manual, along with a copy of it on disk.

We revised the manual to be used by trainees attending your semiannual Volunteer Training Workshop both to educate them on the dynamics of domestic violence and sexual assault and to prepare them to volunteer in a variety of capacities for CCI. It is divided into seven sections, to coincide with the chronological organization of the Volunteer Training Workshop.

Because this manual and the information it contains will continually evolve, we have a few recommendations for how to continue its development:

- We suggest a user test at the June workshop so you can continue to adapt the manual to the volunteers' needs. The Manual Evaluation Form for all trainees to fill out is located on page 135. You might find that the other three workshop evaluation forms will suffice for trainee feedback at future workshops.
- We recommend that you show the manual to other CCI staff members, especially Hope, the Hotline Coordinator, Debi, the Police-Response Advocate Coordinator, and Karen, the Sexual Assault Services Coordinator, to accommodate their specialized knowledge in these areas of the manual.
- We recommend that you continue to produce the manual in its looseleaf-binder format to streamline the addition and deletion of information for future workshops. Enclosed is a copy of the manual on disk so you can make these changes as necessary.

We have enjoyed revising the Volunteer Training Manual for CCI and feel confident that our work will help increase the effectiveness of your Volunteer Training Workshop. If you have any questions about the manual, please feel free to contact us by phone or email, using the information below. Please be advised that Andrea and Marisa will be leaving Manhattan by May 12, but Dee Anne will reside in Manhattan until spring 2002.

Sincerely,

Andrea J. Erman	Marisa K. Proctor	Dee Anne Anderson
555-9549	555-4337	555-5898
princesalandrea@college.edu	mkproctor@college.edu	dee_anne@college.edu

Enclosure: Manual, disk

Not all letters of transmittal will be as detailed and involved as the preceding example. Many will be shorter and, if agreeable to the community partner, delivered via email. See, for example, the following letter of transmittal.

Sample Letter of Transmittal

December 7, 2001

Michael Anderson, Development Director
Pax Center
2333 Oak Street
Your Town, ST 12345

Dear Mr. Anderson:

Attached to this email message is the final draft of the research report on local demographics that we've been working on with you for the past several weeks. It includes the revisions you suggested at our last meeting. We hope that the information will be helpful to you as you write the Fisher Foundation grant.

Thank you for contributing to our positive learning experience. Please feel free to let us know if there is anything more that we can do to help. Our contact information is included below.

Sincerely,

Ed Rattle	Kelly Dosik
er@college.edu	dosik@college.edu

Reflecting on a Completed Project

When all the hard work of a community writing project is done, you can feel gratified in having contributed—as both a writer and a citizen—to your local community. This is also an opportune time to reflect on the whole writing and service-learning process.

ASSIGNMENT OPTIONS
Reflecting on Workplace Writing

COMPARE–CONTRAST ESSAY

Draw on your experience to compare academic writing and workplace writing.

REFLECTIVE ESSAY

Examine your project log/journal for critical experiences. Do you see any recurrent themes? patterns? How has your thinking about writing and/or service changed since the outset of your project?

SELF-ASSESSMENT LETTER TO INSTRUCTOR

In this letter you assess both the quality of the final project and your particular contributions.

- Quality of Project: How well does the document meet the needs of the organization? What has been the assessment of your community partner? Given more time and/or resources, how would you improve the document?

- Your Contributions: What parts of the project bear your individual stamp? What role(s) did you play in group dynamics? What is your overall assessment of your team's process? Are there any ways that you could have better performed your duties? What are the most significant things that you learned through doing the project?

Sample Self-Assessment Letter

What follows is a letter written by a student in response to the "Self-Assessment Letter to Instructor" assignment detailed above.

Assistant Professor Thomas Deans
Department of English
Kansas State University
Manhattan, KS 66506

Dear Dr. Deans:

I am writing you in order to personally assess the project my group recently completed for the Flint Hills Breadbasket, and to assess my contribution to that project.

ASSESSMENT OF PRODUCT QUALITY

Overall, I think we did a wonderful job in revising the volunteer guide in order to meet the needs identified by Shirley Bramhall, Executive Director of the Breadbasket. The previous document wasn't quite appropriately developed, accessible, or visually appealing. Shirley identified that she wanted the document revised so that it included more specific information for volenteers to use, however, we improved the manual in so many more ways than this. I believe that the final product is:

- More accessible to the reader, as it has more headings and better organization
- More informational, as we have added more details about specific volunteer work and volunteer concerns
- More persuasive, as we have revised the manual to really make volunteers feel good about their job, which will hopefully increase their desire to continue volunteering for the Breadbasket
- More visually appealing, as the new design and added pictures/clip art make the guide more aesthetically pleasing

I believe our document quality should be determined by how well we have met Shirley's requirements, how well we have incorporated lessons learned in class, and how usable the product is. Shirley's response has been very positive, and after having another staff member at the Breadbasket read the manual, it appears to be usable. If we had more time, I'm sure we could have produced a better document. I believe that the layout could have been improved more with time, and the manual could have benefited from color printing, spiral binding, and inserted tabs to separate the sections.

ASSESSMENT OF MY CONTRIBUTIONS

I believe I made a valid contribution to the group project. While I did help write and format the agency profile report and the other smaller memos and assignments, and help to rewrite/format/organize sections of the manual, my major contribution was in redesigning the volunteer guide, and inserting and formatting the textual changes made by members of my group. As I was identified as the member of the group with the strongest design/computer skills, and as I was the only one with the appropriate software, I was able to use these strengths to conceptualize a new layout and to create this new layout through use of Adobe PageMaker. The rest of the group made valuable contributions in giving me wonderfully revised/new text, and photographs to insert; and by helping me edit the final product.

While I felt confident in my ability to complete this project, I did have some struggles along the way. First, as I helped re-write some of the sections, I found that I struggled much with being concise. Second, I found working with a group to be at times very stressful. Third, as I previously had limited knowledge of Adobe PageMaker, the project really pushed me to learn how to use the program. After struggling with these three issues, I can see now how these struggles created wonderful learning experiences for me. My technical writing has improved in its conciseness and will be beneficial in future projects, my increased ability to work and find compromise with a group has better prepared me for future group work, and my increased skills in using PageMaker will also come in very handy in the future.

As for group dynamics, I think I played a role as conceptualizer and computer technician. During the beginning of the project, our process for working together was not very pleasant or efficient. Tension ran high as we tried to do everything at once, and as we had very different ideas about writing style and writing processes. However, as time went on, we assessed and assigned our individual roles, and developed an appropriate process for completing work. The process that got us safely through the project is as follows:

- Conceptualize
- Plan/Organize
- Write/Compile
- Edit

As for work distribution, I don't really think that it was as balanced as it could be. While most members of the group volunteered to take on duties and make significant contributions to the group project, another member didn't ever seem to volunteer for anything, and didn't seem to make many significant contributions. As the only designer for the project, I often wished that the design work could have been distributed more equally. However, I understand that this could not be helped—as I was the only group member with the software and knowledge of how to use it.

Overall, I really enjoyed working with my group. Though we had a rough start, I believe we have created a very healthy and productive working relationship. I am very excited about the new volunteer guide that we have produced, and am very glad that I had this service learning experience.

Sincerely,

Mary VanLeeuwen   ■

Community Writing Project Samples

The four service-learning projects that follow were done by small teams of college students working for nonprofit agencies. All but one of the documents—the three-fold brochure—were completed by students in first-year writing courses.

AIDS Quilt Event Publicity

The following press release and radio announcement were written to publicize an event sponsored by a community organization. This project is the one that Audrey discusses in her essay "Stepping Out of My Comfort Zone," which can be found earlier in this chapter.

AIDS QUILT TO COME TO MANHATTAN

The AIDS Memorial Quilt will be displayed at the Ecumenical Campus Ministries Building (ECM), 1021 Denison, from November 30 through December 2 in recognition of World AIDS Day. The event is sponsored by the Regional AIDS Project (RAP) and the NAMES Project.

"No one can remain unaffected when you look at the panels, each depicting the person's life in words, pictures and memorabilia. These art works, for that in fact is what they are, touch the heart in ways that mere words can not," says Eunice Dorst, Project Director. Each section of the Quilt is made up of panels in memory of a loved one who has died from AIDS. Five sections of the Quilt will contain panels in memory of local residents.

Eight of the sections of the Quilt will be available for public viewing at the ECM Building on November 30 from 9am to 9pm, December 1 from 9am to 4pm, and December 2 from 12pm to 7pm.

There will also be a Candlelight Walk beginning in Triangle Park and concluding at the ECM Building, where a short memorial service will take place. The walk will start at 5:30pm on November 30. Other activities include a video titled "Living with AIDS," which was produced by KSU and features a local person talking about his life since being infected with HIV, a Memory Bell, and Memory Square.

Moore Hall will also host the Quilt during the week of December 4 through December 8. For more information about the Quilt, please call the Regional AIDS Project at 555-####.

*   *   *

RADIO PUBLIC SERVICE ANNOUNCEMENT

AIDS isn't over. You can see it in the statistics and in the news. Now, see it in the faces of the men, women, and children who have lost their lives to this disease. The AIDS Memorial Quilt will be on display on November 30 from 9am to 9pm, December 1 from 9am to 4pm, and December 2 from 12pm to 7pm at the Ecumenical Campus Ministries Building, located at 1021 Denison. For more information, please call the Regional AIDS Project at 555-####.   ∎

Zoo Newsletter Article

The following article was written for the volunteer newsletter of a local zoo. The writers included a photo of the maned wolf to accompany the text.

MANED WOLF: NEW ADDITION TO ZOO

What looks like a fox, is called a wolf, and is really neither? It's the newest attraction to Sunset Zoo—the maned wolf. Sunset Zoo has been lucky enough to acquire two of these endangered animals.

Characterized by long stilt-like legs and large ears, these peculiar looking animals are often confused with foxes because of their coloring and body structure. However, the name "maned wolf" is also misleading, because it is not a "true wolf"; it is in the same family as wolves, but in a separate genus, making it a unique addition to the zoo.

Standing at 3 feet tall and weighing approximately 50 pounds, maned wolves are native to South America, and predominately Brazil. With only 2,200–2,300 remaining, they have been put on the endangered species list by the Brazilian government and the U.S. Fish and Wildlife Service. The declining population is due to agricultural development, which has led to the destruction of their food supply and territory.

Their food supply consists of both plants and animals, making them omnivores. They prefer to eat lobeira—a tomato-like fruit—and small animals such as rodents and chickens. Their habit of killing chickens has reduced the maned wolf population even more, due to trouble with the farmers.

Brazilian folklore teaches that the maned wolf has both supernatural and medicinal powers. For instance, some believe that

---

DID YOU KNOW?

- Maned wolves dig for rodents with their teeth, not their feet.
- They use their ears both as sound detectors and heat radiators.
- Pups are born blind.
- Their back legs are taller than their front legs.
- They are taller than they are long.
- The Brazilian name for maned wolves is Aguar Gua'za, which means giant fox.

maned wolves can kill a chicken with a stare, that the right eye brings good luck in gambling, that children who wear the tooth of a maned wolf will have good dental health for the rest of their lives, and that the maned wolf's bark can forecast rain.

The maned wolf is an interesting animal and a valuable addition to Sunset Zoo. The zoo is lucky to have these animals because of their endangered status. Hopefully, their rareness will attract more visitors to the zoo. They are located on the lower trail, and are most active in the morning.   ■

Survey and Report

For this project, the director of a local food pantry asked students to gather information from clients so that she could better assess the organization's performance. The students worked with the director to write the survey (which went through several drafts), then conducted the survey on two separate days, and then wrote a short report summarizing and analyzing the results.

December 6, 2001

Shirley Bramhall, Executive Director
Flint Hills Breadbasket
905 Yuma Street
Manhattan, KS 66502

Dear Shirley,

We are pleased to enclose the results from the survey we conducted, and hope it is of benefit to you. We included the completed surveys, along with several blank copies. In case you wish to conduct the survey again, we have included a disc with the same information for easy editing.

Thank you for being so flexible while working with us. We hope these results are just preliminary and the survey can be used again in the future.

Should you need to reach us, our contact information is included below.

Sincerely,

Tamara Bowles	Ashley DeForest	Cook Jones
943 Moore Hall	526 West Hall	230 Marlatt Hall
Manhattan, KS 66506	Manhattan, KS 66506	Manhattan, KS 66506
(785) 555-2376	(785) 555-3883	(785) 555-3970
tb@college.edu	ald@college.edu	cj@college.edu
enclosure		

FLINT HILLS BREADBASKET REPORT OF SURVEY

On November 27th and 28th, 2001, a survey consisting of twelve questions was administered to 28 persons to gather responses about the work of the Flint Hills Breadbasket. Of the 28 completed questionnaires, responses were received from 17 males and 11 females. The questions ranged from how often the person used the Breadbasket to opinions on how the Breadbasket could improve. The following is a summary of the respondents' views and answers on the Flint Hills Breadbasket.

The questionnaire first asked the respondents if they used the Breadbasket only during the holidays or if throughout the year. Twenty-three respondents said they use the Breadbasket throughout the year, while three said only during the holidays, and one person said it was his first time.

Next, we asked for the respondents to check which blank classifies how often they use the Breadbasket. Twelve said they use it one to five times a year; five people said monthly; four people said weekly; two people said a few times a week; zero people said daily; and, two said for the first time.

We asked the respondents to rank four different areas concerning Breadbasket on a scale from one to five, with one being poor, three being average, and five being exceeds.

- For the accessibility of Breadbasket, all but one of the respondents ranked this question between average and exceeds.
- Transportation to the Breadbasket was ranked the lowest of the four areas, with five selecting poor.
- Regarding the application procedure, over half of the respondents ranked this question between average and exceeds.
- For staff and volunteer friendliness, an overwhelming majority of people said the Breadbasket exceeds in this area.

The last close-ended question asked how well the community was meeting individuals' needs. Most responses were in the middle, with twelve responding "for the most part," and nine responding "somewhat."

To conclude this survey, the respondents were asked three open-ended questions.

- Most responded to the question "Do you have any suggestions on how the process could be made easier and more user-friendly?" with "no."
- For the question "Is there an area of service the Breadbasket could improve," a few respondents commented on having more employees to speed up the process, while others mentioned specific things that could help them.
- The last question, "If you could ask the community to change something, what would it be?" brought forth comments about a free legal service, an accessible rental assistance program, and a transportation system. There were other various comments, along with the statement of "no." ∎

Informational Brochure

This brochure was created by two students in a technical writing course. They were asked by a mental health center to condense for general readers a twenty-page Surgeon General's report on mental health.

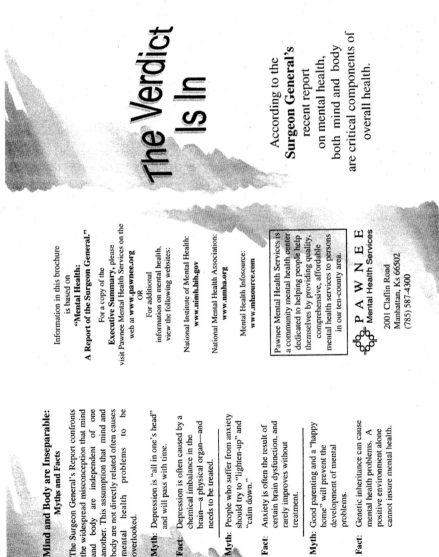

The Verdict Is In

According to the **Surgeon General's** recent report on mental health, both mind and body are critical components of overall health.

Information in this brochure is based on
**"Mental Health:
A Report of the Surgeon General."**

For a copy of the
Executive Summary, please visit Pawnee Mental Health Services on the web at **www.pawnee.org**
OR
For additional information on mental health, view the following websites:

National Institute of Mental Health:
www.nimh.nih.gov

National Mental Health Association:
www.nmha.org

Mental Health Infosource:
www.mhsource.com

Pawnee Mental Health Services is a community mental health center dedicated to helping people help themselves by providing quality, comprehensive, affordable mental health services to persons in our ten-county area.

PAWNEE
Mental Health Services

2001 Claflin Road
Manhattan, Ks 66502
(785) 587-4300

Mind and Body are Inseparable:
Myths and Facts

The Surgeon General's Report confronts the widespread misconception that mind and body are independent of one another. This assumption that mind and body are not directly related often causes mental health problems to be overlooked.

Myth: Depression is "all in one's head" and will pass with time.

Fact: Depression is often caused by a chemical imbalance in the brain—a physical organ—and needs to be treated.

Myth: People who suffer from anxiety should try to "lighten-up" and "calm down."

Fact: Anxiety is often the result of certain brain dysfunction, and rarely improves without treatment.

Myth: Good parenting and a "happy home" will prevent the development of mental problems.

Fact: Genetic inheritance can cause mental health problems. A positive environment alone cannot insure mental health.

The Verdict Is In

On the Subject of Health . . .

Which health issues are the people you know talking about?

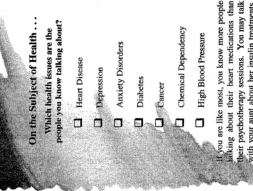

- ☐ Heart Disease
- ☐ Depression
- ☐ Anxiety Disorders
- ☐ Diabetes
- ☐ Cancer
- ☐ Chemical Dependency
- ☐ High Blood Pressure

If you are like most, you know more people talking about their heart medications than their psychotherapy sessions. You may talk with your aunt about her insulin treatments, but how many of your co-workers openly discuss their anxiety disorders?

Why is this the case?

While all of these health problems are common in our society, it is often considered inappropriate to discuss mental health issues. Because of the taboo nature of the subject, many who need mental health care will not seek it for fear of shame or embarrassment. The unfortunate result is that minor problems can escalate into severe conditions that are more difficult to treat.

The Surgeon General's Report

This report is a landmark document in which the federal government is taking an official stance on mental health problems and their debilitating effects. The main purpose of the Surgeon General's report is to encourage individuals to "seek help if [they] have a mental health problem or think [they] have symptoms of a mental disorder." The report asserts steadfast opposition to the "cruel and unfair stigma" our society has imposed upon mental health issues.

Mental Health Facts

- 1 in 5 children have a diagnosable mental disorder. Only 1/3 receive treatment.
- Severe mental illnesses are more common than cancer, diabetes, or heart disease.
- 51 million Americans suffer from a mental disorder in any given year. Only 8 million will receive treatment.
- 6 million older adults suffer from late life depression. Only 10% get treatment.
- Depression is the 2nd leading cause of disability worldwide.
- People with depression are 4 times more likely to develop heart disease.
- With treatment, nearly 80% of those suffering from depression and/or anxiety begin to improve within a few weeks.
- Almost 1/2 of all primary care visits are due to conditions either caused or worsened by mental problems.

Mental Health Throughout Life

Mental health issues present themselves in different ways throughout one's lifespan.

◆ Childhood

Although the period of childhood and adolescence is typically characterized by the "ups and downs" associated with growing up, it is crucial to assess mental health at all stages of childhood. Risk factors include: physical problems, family addiction, low birth weight, intellectual disabilities, poverty, and abuse or neglect. Early detection is necessary to ensure healthy development.

◆ Adulthood

Mental health problems can result from trauma, divorce, financial difficulty, and other stressful life events. If problems are not treated, they can develop into serious conditions and jeopardize the mental health of those with whom they are intimately involved.

◆ Older Adulthood

While stressful life events increase with age, "persistent bereavement or depression" is not normal. Problems can result from declining health, death of loved ones, or feeling useless. Addressing mental health issues in older adults benefits mental state and physical health as well.

On the Subject of Health . . .

ENDNOTE

Because they are put to use by community partners, writing-for-the-community projects can be particularly gratifying. After completing such a project, be sure to keep a copy for yourself. When applying for a job or an internship, such projects demonstrate not only your ability to write for nonacademic audiences but also your capacity for working collaboratively to meet an organization's needs.

9

Writing with the Community

In addition to projects with nonprofit agencies, what are some ways that writing can be a means of community action? How can two particular kinds of community writing—proposals and oral histories—be done effectively? This chapter describes those two approaches to social change, both of which hinge on writing and emerge from direct collaboration between students and community members.

At its most basic—and often most effective—social action is about community members getting together to solve a problem, address a need, work together. As demonstrated in Chapter 8, existing nonprofit, government, and religious organizations can be helpful in addressing community needs, and one valuable kind of service involves writing for such organizations to help them deliver their services. However, you might be interested in a community or campus issue that no local organizations are addressing. In that case, you need to work outside established social service networks. Indeed, for some, creating a project from scratch is the most gratifying kind of community action. Grassroots efforts can take countless forms, many of which hinge on writing, and this chapter illustrates two main ways to write *with* the community: crafting proposals and composing oral histories.

These are two very different ways of using writing as social action. *Proposals* are calls to action, persuasive documents that can lead to both immediate and long-term changes in communities and on campuses. *Oral histories*, on the other hand, work toward justice by giving voice to those who often go unheard or who have little access to the literacy skills needed to write their stories.

The service-learning initiatives featured in this chapter are premised on developing respectful and reciprocal partnerships between novice writers and community members, so it is especially important that you read Chapter Six before moving on to this one.

384

ASSIGNMENT OPTIONS
Proposals and Oral Histories

PROPOSAL

Compose a proposal in the form of a letter that describes a campus or community problem and argues for a specific solution. Involve key community members in both defining the problem and proposing a solution.

ORAL HISTORY

Using the guidelines discussed in this chapter, compose an oral history. When submitting the oral history, also include a one- to two-page companion paper that reflects on what you were trying to accomplish in the piece and on the rhetorical choices you made with respect to theme, structure, style, symbolic elements, perspective, voice, and so on.

Proposals to Address Community Problems and Injustices

A proposal is a call to action. Perhaps at times you have thought to yourself, "X should be done differently," or "I wish I could change X," or "A good way to solve this problem would be . . . " Proposals are a means of moving a particular audience to act. And when they are done well, proposals can lead to concrete social change. Even when proposals are not successful in motivating audiences to take specific actions, they can still raise awareness.

Proposals are among the most common kinds of written arguments. For example, employees often write proposal reports to suggest more efficient ways of going about business. Nonprofit organization staff, academic researchers, and others compose grant proposals to request funding from charitable foundations or government agencies. Engineers, architects, and builders write project proposals to win contracts. Politicians write public policy proposals to push broad plans of action on social or economic matters. Even forms of writing that might not include the term *proposal*—such as a scholarship application essay that argues why a candidate is worthy of an award, or a newspaper editorial that suggests and justifies a public policy—are, in fact, kinds of proposals. All these types of writing adopt persuasive postures and call on the audience to act.

This section focuses on crafting proposals as brief but informed letters that respond to campus or local community concerns and that involve collaborating with various constituencies.

Identifying Issues and Problems

Proposals respond to local, specific circumstances. Therefore, each campus and community presents its own problems and calls for its own unique solutions.

For this assignment, consider campus and community problems that create injustices or that affect the quality of public life. Ask *Is this a real community or campus concern, or is it just my own pet peeve?* A broken dryer in the dorm is certainly an irritant, but it is hardly a significant community or justice concern. If, on the other hand, campus police are perceived as engaging in racial profiling, this is a matter of social justice. You should look for proposal-writing situations that will serve the public good.

WRITING TO DISCOVER

List at least three campus concerns or problems that you think deserve attention. List at least three local community or hometown issues that deserve attention. Share your possibilities with others.

Identifying Stakeholders

Writing with the community demands that you listen for and respond to the many voices that make up a community. Every campus or community problem is housed in a web of relationships. Responsible and effective community work involves consulting the people in that web—the stakeholders—and involving them in every stage of the process, from identifying the nature of a problem, to proposing a solution, to implementing it.

The proposal-writing process suggested here is less about asserting your will on others than it is about working together to propose a solution that serves the public good. Accounting for the interests of stakeholders does not mean trying to please everyone. That simply isn't possible—and it often isn't even desirable. But it does entail at least *listening* to everyone involved, granting each a voice in the process.

You can easily identify some stakeholders in a process. For example, if you are concerned about increasing recycling on campus, the most obvious stakeholders might be students and the university administration. Other people already are, or potentially could be, important players in this issue: the trash removal staff members who would be responsible for much of the work, the budget officials who would worry about costs, local and national environmental groups that might be willing to share expertise, academic departments (especially those with an environmental studies bent) that could contribute their insights, alumni who still care about their alma mater, parents and prospective students, and so on.

Furthermore, it is important to explore the predispositions of these various stakeholders. Which stakeholders are likely to be committed to the status quo, and why? Which are likely to be indifferent? Which are likely to be immediate allies? Which might need some convincing?

Identifying stakeholders should be one of the first tasks you undertake when approaching a community issue and considering a proposal. You should also remain open to the addition of stakeholders who were not at first evident or who later adopt an interest in the issue.

WRITING TO DISCOVER
Write-Around

In any community, there will be many (often conflicting) perspectives on any particular issue. This exercise is intended to help flesh out multiple perspectives on a social concern. Acknowledging and understanding multiple perspectives is a pathway to deeper understanding and more effective problem solving.

Try this:

1. As a class, select a pressing community issue; campus or local policies and problems often work well.
2. Brainstorm a list of all the people who have a stake in the issue (list the roles on the board or have someone take notes). This list should probably include at least 10 people, ranging from those creating the policy, to those affected by it, to those of varying political opinions who comment on it, to ordinary citizens, and so on.
3. Gather in a circle and assign each member of the class to play the role of one of the stakeholders. Use your imagination to put yourself in the shoes of that community member and to adopt both the attitude and the voice of that person. (For example, if the issue is a recently imposed ban on homeless people sleeping in local parks, the stakeholders would include the homeless people themselves, police, advocates for the homeless, a civil rights attorney, local business owners, parents of kids who play in the park, officials from the city government, conservative and progressive political commentators, and so on.)

4. On a blank sheet of paper, write a role name from the list of stakeholders and then freewrite from your adopted perspective, giving voice to that persona. Do this quickly: Get down two to three sentences in three or four minutes. Write from *within* each role. Don't be afraid to be contentious, if that is in character for the stakeholder. The point is to get as many different viewpoints as possible on the page.

5. Pass your paper to the right. Upon receiving a new paper, quickly adopt another role (of your choice) and respond in that role to the passage that was passed to you. Put yourself in dialogue with (or perhaps against) that passage.

6. After three or four minutes, pass again to the right. Keep adopting different roles and keep responding in writing.

After each person has played the role of at least 4 stakeholders, retrieve your original paper and see how the written dialogue unfolded. Use this as a basis for class discussion.

This exercise asks you to imaginatively identify with several different perspectives. Of course, an even better option would be to invite the actual stakeholders to represent themselves. This can be achieved by inviting several stakeholders to class or by circulating within the community, listening to multiple perspectives.

Another key question to ask when exploring stakeholders is *Who has the power to act?* Sometimes this question is easily answered. In a proposal on improving sexual education in local high schools (included later in the chapter), the state school board, because it oversees curriculum requirements, is the logical addressee for a proposal that suggests curricular and policy changes. Sometimes more than one constituency has the power to act. For example, in the following sample, the obvious power broker is the university administration, but the proposal author realizes that appealing to alumni, who could pressure the administration, might be an effective approach.

Sample Proposal: Letter to Alumni

Some proposals are written in report format, but many are written as letters, as in the following example.

April 10, 2001

Dear Alumni,

Hello. My name is Maeg Yosef. I am currently an undergraduate student at your Alma Mater, the University of Massachusetts-Amherst. I am writing to you on the behalf of a coalition of students called S.C.A.R.C.E. (Student Coalition Against Racist and Classist Education). It is my hope that this letter will move you to learn more about the present state of education at the University, and to exert your power as a graduate of UMass to help those who are presently working to graduate.

As someone who has worked to enter and succeed in the University, you know that it's no simple task. I am sure that you would agree that UMass, as a public institution, has a responsibility to provide adequate support and resources to all of its students during their stay, and to make the University equally accessible to all potential students through enthusiastic recruitment efforts and equitable admissions policies.

UMass agrees, too—at least in writing. It is part of the UMass-Amherst mission statement to provide educational access and support to *all* students of the Commonwealth, especially to historically disadvantaged groups, namely students of color and low-income students. Unfortunately, UMass-Amherst is not living up to its own words:

- The numbers of ALANA (African-, Latin-, Asian-, Native-American) students in entering classes has decreased 19% since 1997.
- The number of students from families making less than $60,000/yr has declined 60% since 1985.
- African American freshman enrollment has declined 45% since 1997.
- Latino freshman enrollment has declined 41% since 1996.

You may be skeptical of these numbers. I would be too, if I had not researched them, along with other students, in the UMass Factbooks, a compilation of student statistics put out each year by the University. These declining enrollment figures can be attributed to a lack of recruitment in ALANA and low-income communities, as well as a lack of adequate financial aid and recruitment and admission practices.

In addition to declining numbers, support programs for students of color and low-income students at UMass, such as English as a Second Language and the Women of Color Leadership Network, are facing serious cutbacks. In fact, the entire university is preparing for a round of cuts, possibly as high as ten percent, at the same time that the University is pouring millions of dollars into investments such as distance learning. These cuts will hurt the education of every student on campus and make it even more difficult, if not impossible, for ALANA and low-income students to get the support they need.

How can this situation possibly be changed? SCARCE is demanding that the University implement admissions practices that will succeed in bringing a diverse student body to this campus, by effective recruitment and programs for "at-risk" high-school students. We are also demanding increased budgets for ALANA and low-income support programs. UMass has already written plans for these initiatives, but not put them into action.

From your standpoint as an alum, you still have a powerful say in what happens for the students at this University. I welcome you to find out for yourself the situation at UMass—by contacting us at the addresses below or by contacting UMass. If you are angered by what I've shared with you or by what you discover, tell the UMass administration what you think. Your input matters. Write a letter, make a phone call. Tell the University that you are demanding something very simple: that UMass-Amherst follow its own mission by supporting ALL of its students and students-to-be, regardless of their race or class.

Sincerely,

Maeg Yosef   ■

Responding to Reading

1. What do you find convincing—or not convincing—about this letter? Point to specific passages.

2. How does the letter appeal to its audience's specific interests?

3. How does the letter anticipate potential objections of the audience?

4. What specific changes might you suggest to make this letter more effective?

Proposal Structure

A proposal can be framed as a formal proposal report (often submitted with a letter of transmittal [see Chapter 8]), as a letter to an individual or to an organization, or as a letter to the general public (a newspaper editorial, for example). Sometimes other genres, such as essays suggesting a solution to a problem, adopt the core features of the proposal.

Skeleton for a Proposal

TRADITIONAL SEQUENCE	QUESTIONS TO GUIDE WRITING
Problem and justification	What is the nature of the problem? Is it a legitimate problem? What is the background (including previous attempts to solve the problem)? How is the problem affecting/hurting people? Why should the reader care?
Presentation of solution	What is the most fitting solution? How will the solution solve the problem? What benefits will it bring?
Summary and refutation of opposing views	Why should other ways of solving the problem be rejected?
Justification of proposed solution	What reasons are there for enacting the proposal? What are the specific methods, stages, and costs of the proposed solution? How can it realistically be implemented?
Exhortation to act	What should readers *do*?

Crafting a successful proposal is challenging because it must motivate people to depart from the status quo. The natural inclination of most people is to leave things as they are. Moreover, it's not enough to convince people that your idea is good; moving the audience to *action* is the goal, and it demands an argument not only with strong intellectual force but also with compelling emotional appeal. Recall from Chapter 7 that persuasive arguments balance logos (a well-supported line of argument), pathos (a fitting use of emotional appeals), and ethos (a sense of trust in the credibility of the writer).

Often the greatest challenge in writing a proposal is convincing the audience that the problem in question really is a problem. Just because *you* see something as a significant problem doesn't mean that *others* do. Your first job is to awaken the audience to a sense of a problem and its implications. Both sample proposals included in this chapter do this, in part, by citing statistics. But often statistics are not enough. You need to show how the problem affects real people.

Often this involves including specific examples and illustrations of how the problem is creating injustice, telling stories of how the problem is creating suffering for individuals, explaining how the problem is impeding efficiency, and/or describing how potential is being squandered. You also need to employ rhetorician Kenneth Burke's strategy of "identification." To be persuasive, you must find a way to make the reader identify with the problem, see that it affects him or her in a meaningful way, and recognize that the solution will actually benefit him or her.

Presentation of the solution demands similar care. You need to provide compelling enough justifications and enough supporting detail so that readers see the solution as not just credible but highly desirable. The audience is likely to ask several skeptical questions while reading about a proposed solution: Is the proposed solution really practical? Is it cost-effective? Are there any unintended consequences? It is your job to anticipate and respond to such questions. Needless to say, in both the presentation of the problem and in the justification for the solution, proposals often demand extensive research, as is evident in the following sample.

After presenting your solution—or just before presenting it—you should also anticipate and reject other possible solutions. This helps convince readers that your solution is indeed the best option.

Proposals often end with exhortations to action. A proposal should tell readers what to do; if the proposal is persuasive enough, readers will do it.

Sample Proposal: Letter to Board of Education

The following proposal was written by students who started out being concerned about the high rates of teen pregnancy that they noticed in many rural schools. One student wrote her community-based research essay on this problem and on the need for better sexual education in the high school curriculum. During that research she also discovered that public high schools in her state were, in fact, required by law to offer some form of sex education, although the law was very loosely written and enforced. No local community organizations or nonprofit agencies were working on sex education issues. Therefore, the students decided to write a proposal to the body that has authority over setting school policy: the state school board.

In order to write a persuasive proposal, the students realized that they needed the support of more than just anecdotal evidence. They needed sound data that would help them describe the problem and convince the audience that the problem was real. Therefore, in consultation with a psychology professor, they created a survey and asked several school administrators in the region whether they could conduct the survey in health classes. Some schools agreed; some balked. The students also distributed some surveys on their own, outside school.

Sarah _____, Chad _____, Kelly _____
Kansas State University
_____ West Hall
Manhattan, KS 66506

December 1, 1998

The Kansas Department of Education
120 SE 10th
Topeka, KS 66612

Dear Kansas Board of Education:

In 1988 the Kansas Board of Education mandated sexual education in all high schools, which in our opinion was an important and courageous decision. We, three students attending Kansas State University, admire the fact that because of this mandate, many school systems throughout the state of Kansas realize the importance of sexual education. However, through research, we have discovered that improvements are still needed. Our project focuses on creating a form of accountability for sexual education courses in Kansas high schools. Our main goal is to suggest that a standardized survey could solve the problem of inconsistent, and in some cases non-existent, sexual education instruction in our public schools.

Through our research, which consisted of surveying approximately 150 Kansas high school freshmen and sophomores, we discovered a lack of accountability for sexual education in our public schools. The mandate makes each high school responsible for creating its own curriculum for sexual education; however, nothing guarantees that the high school teaches that curriculum. Therefore, as a possible solution to the problem, we have created a sexual education survey. Our survey determines whether developing a standardized survey for sexual education solves the accountability problem.

The survey contains three sections (see attachment). The first part analyzes how the course was taught; the second tests students on subjects that should have been covered in each course; and the final part gathers information on each student's perception of the sexual education they received. We feel that the test would be most effective if it were distributed, once a year, to sophomores in every Kansas high school. The survey not only evaluates sexual education, but also solicits student input.

The best way to determine whether a standardized sexual education test is necessary would be to do a study with the survey. Therefore, we contacted high schools throughout the state of Kansas. We chose nine schools, ranging from size 1A-6A, in which to implement our survey. However, we discovered some problems during this process. Only four of the nine high schools allowed us to distribute the surveys. Why wouldn't the high schools allow us to survey their students? One reason given by administrators was that they wanted to protect their students. What are they trying to protect them from? The students should be receiving sexual education in high school and therefore need no protection from this subject.

Furthermore, since the mandate allows each high school to create its own curriculum, we discovered difficulty in creating one test for every school. Each school had something different that it wanted eliminated from the survey. For example, one school eliminated questions referring to sexual lifestyles (homosexuality/heterosexuality); another school would not allow us to include questions concerning forms of contraception.

Even though we ran into problems, we gathered some interesting results from the schools that did participate:

- 35% of students stated that they have not received any form of sexual education thus far.
- 20–30% of students, when asked to rate the areas of sexual education taught (such as forms of contraception, sexually transmitted diseases, and abstinence), rated all areas as "bad" or "not at all."
- 49% of students surveyed could not name 4 forms of contraception.
- 36% of students, when asked what they would change about their sexual education, said that either sexual education courses should be offered or increased.

These statistics suggest that high school students want and need sexual education, and that even among those who received information, many feel that they could benefit from additional courses.

The conflicts we experienced prove that sexual education is a very sensitive topic. However, it is a mandated course and often not taught efficiently. Our results prove that approximately 30% of the high school students surveyed report either not being offered a sexual education course, or not feeling that they receive adequate sexual education.

We realize that our sample size was rather small; however, we think it is important to not only note what results we gathered from this survey, but also ask ourselves why we were not allowed to survey more schools. How are we to know the effectiveness of a curriculum if we are not allowed to evaluate the course? Any course—whether math, science, English or sexual education—

needs evaluation to guarantee success. Therefore, we ask you to conduct a larger scale survey across the state of Kansas.

Our project suggests needed improvements in Kansas high school sexual education courses. We feel the need to bring these results to your attention. We have enclosed the survey we created with the assistance of faculty at Kansas State University. We simply used this survey for our research, but we received positive feedback from the teachers and students to whom it was administered. Therefore, if you do choose to implement a similar survey, we foresee cooperation between Kansas public high schools and the Kansas Board of Education because it addresses the needs of students. Due to our shared interests in the well-being of Kansas high school students, we ask you to consider our proposal.

Sincerely,

Chad_____   Sarah_____   Kelly_____   ■

Peer Review Questions for Proposal Draft

No proposal should go public without extensive review. The following questions can help assess a draft and provide feedback that is helpful to the revision process.

1. Which are the strongest parts of the draft?
2. Does the problem strike you as a legitimate problem? Is it presented as a significant enough concern to merit acting on it?
3. Does the draft appeal *both* to the audience's intellect and emotions? How could it improve on those appeals?
4. What is the tone of the proposal?
5. Adopt a skeptical position in response to the proposal. What are your key objections? On what points is the proposal vulnerable? How might the writer be able to anticipate and address those potential objections?
6. Does the proposal provide the reader with a clear and realistic plan of action? Is it readily apparent what the reader should do? Is there anything that could impede that action?

Composing Oral Histories

Whereas official histories and the mainstream media record and celebrate the lives of people whom culture has deemed important, oral histories account for and celebrate the lives of ordinary folks—indeed, people who are often over-looked or marginalized.

The recording of oral history can be particularly rewarding for the individuals whose experiences end up being written down. It can serve not only as an act of validation but also as a means of preserving personal, family, and community history.

Oral histories can function as social action in public ways, too, by awakening a wider audience to people and stories that might otherwise be lost to time. Oral histories render visible experiences that can serve to build community identity and pride. Moreover, they can help readers develop an appreciation for the participation of non-elite groups in a community's history.

> Ultimately, in researching and writing public history our purpose is to help people look at their past again and learn something valuable to them in the present. As ethnographers, we seek an understanding of how individuals participate in, live, and change a community culture. And for us, as researchers and human beings, we learn the answers to some of our questions about our collective past and present.
>
> *Valerie Raleigh Yow*
> From Recording Oral History: A Practical Guide for Social Scientists, *Sage Publications*

Oral histories attempt to capture the texture and detail of the lives of real people. Among the most widely known examples of oral histories are books by Studs Terkel, such as *Working* and *The Good War: An Oral History of World War II*.

In the following essay, Professor Susie Lan Cassel describes how writing down oral histories was an important personal and community writing experience for her students.

Essay: Susie Lan Cassel, *Writing from Another's Memory: In Quest of Oral History*

Susie Lan Cassel is associate chair of the Literature and Writing Department as well as Coordinator of the Ethnic Studies Program at California State University–San Marcos.

My father is older. Growing up, I was excruciatingly aware that he was older than my friends' fathers, older than my teachers, older than my mother and, in fact, older than my grandmother. While my friends' parents told stories about the radical 60's and the Vietnam war, my father told stories about living on a farm during World War I and being drafted for World War II and the Korean

War. His stories were different from the others, and they covered such long periods of (unfamiliar) time that I could never keep them straight.

Although I took my father's stories for granted when I was young, even resenting their repetition sometimes, I missed my father's stories when I went away to college because I feared, at times, that I might never hear them again. And I felt badly that I never had them quite right. Did he work as a wrestling coach before or after World War II? Did he start a dairy business when he was on the farm or sometime later? On breaks between semesters, I went home and asked him to talk about his boyhood on the farm and his role on a ship in World War II, but I still couldn't keep things straight—there were too many events, too many important details, too many different places. So I began to write things down. I returned to college after each break with a new story—or a familiar story that was now fleshed out and chronologically clear—and, eventually, I had on my computer the outline of my father's long life and his many experiences.

Learning to know my father better, and being able to build upon our relationship through the process of writing the tales he would tell, was so satisfying and meaningful to me as a daughter and as a writer that when I became a college instructor, I was excited to learn about a field in interdisciplinary studies that was developing in new directions called "oral history recovery." Growing out of the work of historians and anthropologists, "oral history" often refers to the story of someone's life that has been written down or "recovered" by an interviewer. Typically, the "subjects" selected for interviews do not write down their own life stories for a number of different reasons, including the lack of time, interest, or language skills, or out of a belief that few people will be interested in the events or experiences that these subjects have encountered. However, historians and anthropologists, among a growing number of scholars in other fields, are increasingly looking to recovered oral histories for unique information that can help us to understand a variety of different issues, ranging from the experience of immigration, to the implementation of cultural or religious beliefs, to the psychological effects of growing old. While the recovered oral history of one person may be insightful and mesmerizing in itself (or maybe not), a cross section of histories recovered from people of similar age or region or experience gives us a snapshot of lived experience unlike that found in other sources. In this sense, oral history provides an immensely valuable record of human life that uniquely informs our answers to the questions of our time and of our regions.

It was with these new insights about the value of oral history recovery that I decided to include an oral history assignment in a thematically based class that I was teaching on "Immigrant Testimonials." As readers and writers, our class would spend part of the semester analyzing selections of published works written by immigrants about the experience of crossing from one geographical and cultural region to another. Since we live in a city on the border between Mexico and the United States where there also happens to be an influx of immigrants from all over the world, we would spend the latter part of the class writing the oral history of a willing immigrant.[1] What better way to make real the lessons of hardship, transition, and adaptation, I thought, than to have students become recoverers rather than consumers of the text?

From the first class, students seemed excited (if a little intimidated) about the project. The students (rightly) wondered what it meant to be an "immigrant" and they wondered how they could cover decades of life history in the course of a few short pages and even fewer weeks. For the purposes of the assignment, "immigrant" was defined in the broadest of possible terms to include anyone who was significantly affected by a move from one cultural or regional sphere to another. To help ease the stress they felt about covering a person's whole life, I made it clear that oral histories (and auto/biographies, for that matter) are always selective. No one can ever write down everything that happens in one's own life or in another's life. The more important question is *how* students focus their writings and their interviews to produce a meaningful text. To ease some of the shyness and fear about meeting new people, I allowed students to work in pairs for the interviews as long as they wrote separate narratives. In this way, we could compare the different interpretations of their research as captured in their oral histories. If relevant, students could write about their own experiences or those of willing friends, relatives, or classmates.

In preparation for the first interviews, we devoted a class to developing questions and discussing various approaches to oral history recovery, including a "scripted approach" where interviewers use a standard set of questions from which straying is not allowed; a "prompt approach" where questions are introduced to encourage interviewees to speak freely about their interests; and a "directed approach" where interviewers have in mind certain issues for which they would like responses. They develop relevant questions beforehand and then pursue leads in a more direct manner in search of in-depth knowledge about a particular topic. Due to time constraints, we implemented the latter. Students were required to conduct a two-hour interview every two weeks (for a total of three interviews or about six hours) and to turn in a journal of their notes from each interview session.

Generally speaking, students learned basic information about their subjects during the first interview—the who, what, when, why, and how of immigrating. The second interview was used to hone in on more specific themes or issues around which the narrative could be focused. By the third interview, students shared with

---

[1] The local Community Service-Learning office was instrumental in providing the names of organizations and individuals who were willing to be interviewed as part of this project. For instance, they contacted familiar community partners, such as the local Chinese Historical Society, and sought new members, like Jewish community organizations and international "houses" located within our city. On my campus, the committee in charge of work involving human subjects also had to approve of all aspects of the assignment and required from me a long application prior to the beginning of the course, including permission slips and release forms signed by all students and subjects involved in interviews.

their subjects a draft of the essay. This served as an opportunity to clarify misunderstandings, fill in gaps, and gain tacit approval. Some students required additional interview sessions, but three meetings seemed adequate time for most.

The course required two very different types of writing. This was an important point to make clear. In the first part of the course, students wrote two short thesis-bound papers that analyzed specific readings. For the final, the oral history narrative, students were told that a simple recounting of the facts of the interviews, however accurate and interesting, would not satisfy the requirements of the assignment. A simple chronology of an immigrant's life would not draw the readers' attention in the most meaningful way to the subject's feelings and analysis about the immigration experience. The best papers, then, would have as their focus a specific theme or issue regarding immigration which would serve as the organizing motif for the paper.

One of the biggest challenges students faced was how, as writers, to focus and organize the information gathered from hours of discussions into a compelling and unified ten-page text. Students deliberated over what form or genre their prose would take—which style of presentation would best capture the intimacies of thought, the thrill of adventure, the profound insight of experience? Would they use the most intimate and reflective of forms, the diary, or the more deliberate and audience-focused epistle? Would they record the stories from the third person voice as a biography or attempt to speak in the first person voice of an autobiography or memoir? Given the information they had acquired, what would they gain and lose from each form, from each decision? What criteria could they use to decide?

The issue of voice was perhaps the most difficult (and eventually the most rewarding) choice they had to make. Students were so respectful of their subjects that most hesitated to write in the first person "I" for fear that they could not adequately capture the voice that they had now been listening to for several weeks. Towards the end of the semester, as we shared more about the projects and the experience of oral history recovery, it was clear that almost every student wrote the first version of his/her paper from the third person perspective. As outsiders they had listened to these life stories, so it made sense that they captured the voice as they had heard it—from their own, third person perspective. But in nearly every case, the students found the results unsatisfying. They felt that their piece was missing something visceral and that it somehow failed to represent a reality that they could perceive but not secure. With trepidation they each, one by one, turned to a first-person model, most often as an experiment. They struggled to reproduce on the page the sound and texture and tone of the voice that they had been hearing, and they feared, perhaps more than the final grade itself, that the voice would be unfaithful to the original.

To their surprise, when it was time to share the ethnographies with their subjects, students found that the subjects were overwhelmingly delighted—even impressed—with the work. In many cases, subjects were grateful for the students' care and skillful rendition. In some cases, the subjects were sure that the students had captured the life story better than they themselves could have done. Subjects asked for copies of the narratives to give to their children, grandchildren, siblings, friends, and to save for themselves.

There were many tears of satisfaction shared in our final class discussions, but there was one noticeable exception. One student was working on the story of a very interesting friend whose immigration from Europe had taken him through a number of other countries and life paths. This subject insisted on a heroic depiction of himself as a self-made man, as one who had overcome obstacle after obstacle to reach his current successful position. The student was uneasy writing a strictly heroic narrative, knowingly selecting only the achievements and ignoring the challenges and failures. Although she admired her friend's accomplishments, she wanted also to recount some of the difficulties that led to those successes in order to create a more three-dimensional and compelling text. He threatened to pull out of the project if she didn't write things his way. Without sharing any confidential information, the student spoke to the class about her dilemma as a writer. How could she be fair to her subject and be faithful to what she believed was a larger truth? Was her job to subvert herself in the presence of his voice and write the story—as a service—that the subject wanted to hear, even if it was motivated in a way that she found offensive? How could she knowingly capitulate to a stereotype so often cast (and critiqued) in auto/biography? In the end, the student worked closely with her subject to write the most balanced paper they could produce together, a compromise that satisfied her subject and saved her from having to find a new subject late in the semester.

While this situation was disappointing to the student, I was grateful that the class had this opportunity to discuss as practitioners one of the most interesting and problematic issues in ethnography and auto/biography. This discussion fostered an awareness of the relationship among subject, text, and context in a way that thirteen weeks of reading and discussion had not done. It resulted in a new option for the assignment (which I will remember in future semesters): in difficult situations like this one, students should be allowed to write creatively or theoretically about the process of writing an oral history, a paper that would critically examine the role of writer, the development of narrative self, and the issue of authenticity. Such an exposé would be, I believe, valuable contribution to any conversation involving oral history recovery.

The most challenging aspect of the course for me was grading these oral histories. For good moral reason, I made it clear that there would be no attempt to grade the quality of a subject's life. I emphasized the fact that these narratives were being evaluated as pieces of writing where careful consideration would be given to formal concerns, such as coherence, content, unity, and development, but it was also important to take into account what the writers were trying to achieve. To this end, the students were required to turn-in a one-page abstract along with their oral histories that described what they were trying to accomplish in the piece. The abstract was designed to discuss the theme and form writers focused upon, how they came to make these decisions, and how they believed these decisions served their work. Why did they use this opening, this closing, and these stylistic or symbolic elements, for instance? In short, the abstract represented the writer's goals and, as such, it seemed to me fair to use the abstract as an informal rubric for grading. In this way, I measured the success of the paper against the author's plan rather than against my imagined construction of the story. This methodology seemed to work well.

The best papers in the class expertly captured a sensibility and not just a set of experiences. These student writers successfully suppressed their own voices and convincingly portrayed the struggles and conflicts, trials and tribulations, of another. In the papers that were not as effective, it was clear that a unique narrative persona was developing, but this persona had not yet taken on a fully realized voice. The less successful papers weren't as carefully organized or presented and the oral histories often differed markedly from their attached abstracts, as if students didn't take enough time to reflect on their writing choices or to revise.

So invested was this group of students that they asked, at the end of the class after their presentations, if we could collect their papers into a form that all could keep and read. Another student volunteered to print the materials at a family print shop. When a local publisher (who publishes journals in the field of education) heard about the project, he offered to publish our book so that the record could remain. They were published as *Nation, Language, Culture: A Collection of Oral Histories* (a title suggested by one student).

The most valuable lesson we learned from the project is that willing and appropriate subjects are seemingly omnipresent. We found that many, many people—in spite of issues of privacy—are anxious to share their tales, eager to interact with students, and happy to participate in a project that promotes community and personal understanding. Even though we had a long list of willing community participants, students most often found subjects in their families, neighborhoods, classrooms, and workplaces. And after the class, many students vowed to continue oral history recovery at home as a way to better understand their family members, their histories, and their own lives.

As for me, my father turned ninety this year, and he asked me just last week when I'll come over to hear another story. Every time I wonder whether my computer bank is full, whether I have written all the stories, Dad calls and tells me has another one he's forgotten to recover. And I gladly listen, and type, and realize how much I've grown. ■

Getting Started

The biggest initial question in writing an oral history is, of course, *Who should be the subject?* As suggested by Cassel, there are many possibilities, and candidates are perhaps more available and more willing to participate than you expect.

Family, friends, and acquaintances are possibilities. Successful service-learning oral history initiatives have also been carried out in partnership with nursing homes. (On a related note, recall the story "A Letter to Harvey Milk," in Chapter 5, the plot of which centers on Harry's life writing at a senior center.) And those are not the only options. Consider several potential sources for people before settling on one:

- Family and friends (especially those of the older generations)
- Residents in nursing homes or at senior centers
- Members of veterans' groups
- Member of church groups, civic clubs (such as the Lion's Club or the Knights of Columbus), or women's groups
- Recent immigrants (who are often reachable through community organizations that address immigrant concerns)
- Particular cultural and ethic groups (again, often best contacted via community organizations)
- Ongoing projects at local historical societies
- People in neighborhood associations
- Members of unions or your own co-workers
- People in the community from historically underrepresented groups
- Local residents who are part of an adult literacy program or an English as a Second Language program
- Those who respond to invitations to participate that are offered at homeless shelters or other social service organizations

---

WRITING TO DISCOVER

Freewrite on the following questions and then share your responses:

- What possibilities for oral history most intrigue you?
- Are there particular people or groups in the community about whom you would like to know more?
- To what potential candidates do you already have access? What candidates would you need to reach through an organization?
- At this point, what are your fears and anxieties?

Sometimes a class may opt to recruit subjects who all share some demographic characteristic, as in the example of Cassel's course, where the focus was on immigrants. In some service-learning courses, the people sharing oral histories have all been part of the same organization, making the collected individual histories a sort of history of the organization.

Interviewing

The guidelines for interviews spelled out in Chapters 4 and 7 (pp. 168–171 and 295–296) likewise apply here. Because oral histories rely so heavily on interviews, however, their interviews are usually longer and more involved than those for earlier projects. Recall Cassel's advice on interviewing:

> In preparation for the first interviews, we devoted a class to developing questions and discussing various approaches to oral history recovery, including a "scripted approach" where interviewers use a standard set of questions from which straying is not allowed; a "prompt approach" where questions are introduced to encourage interviewees to speak freely about their interests; and a "directed approach" where interviewers have in mind certain issues for which they would like responses. They develop relevant questions beforehand and then pursue leads in a more direct manner in search of in-depth knowledge about a particular topic.

Whether you adopt a scripted, prompt, or directed approach, you must prepare for interviews. They don't just "happen"; you make them happen, and your questions and prompts are necessary to move them along. If you do not prepare carefully for interviews, they can stall or run into dead ends. The question of doing interviews alone or in pairs needs to be worked out with your instructor.

Recording interviews on audiotape or videotape is a good idea, if doing so is agreeable to the teller and if doing so does not impede the storytelling. Even when you record an interview, you should be sure to take careful notes. The notes can be both descriptive—recounting what is happening—and reflective—assessing what seems to be important and why.

Before conducting your first interview, share a written plan for the session with your instructor. Include the questions and/or prompts you expect to ask as well as the themes/issues on which you hope to focus.

Because oral histories often involve vulnerable people and groups, it is particularly important to attend to ethical concerns in community-based research, which are outlined in Chapter 7 (pp. 275–277).

Drafting and Structuring an Oral History

Oral histories are based in narrative, and many of the strategies for writing effective narratives are discussed in Chapter 2. Chapter 2 focuses on the personal essay, but many of the key strategies described there also apply to oral histories. Oral histories, like personal essays, guide readers in making meaning of experience. They also work better when they focus on tensions and turns, show rather than tell, employ literary devices, and move the reader from the "known" to the "new." It might prove helpful to review Chapter 2.

As a writer of an oral history, you will do more than simply transcribe audiotapes. You might feel, out of respect, that you should have no real part in shaping the story, that your job is only to record as faithfully as possible. However, you *do* have a role in shaping the narrative, a role that you share in respectful partnership with the subject of the history. Experience is messy. A pile of interview notes will not simply present itself as a coherent narrative. As the writer, choices of wording, style, voice, and structure are very much your responsibility.

Recall the deliberations of Cassel's students on this point:

> One of the biggest challenges students faced was how, as writers, to focus and organize the information gathered from hours of discussions into a compelling and unified ten-page text. Students deliberated over what form or genre their prose would take—which style of presentation would best capture the intimacies of thought, the thrill of adventure, the profound insight of experience? Would they use the most intimate and reflective of forms, the diary, or the more deliberate and audience-focused epistle? Would they record the stories from the third person voice as a biography or attempt to speak in the first person voice of an autobiography or memoir? Given the information they had acquired, what would they gain and lose from each form, from each decision? What criteria could they use to decide?

Even though most students in Cassel's class started writing in a more objective third-person posture, all ended up writing final drafts in the first person, "I," trying to capture the voice of the teller. Indeed, it is the job of the writer of an oral history to attend to the voice, the phrasing, the resonance, the tone of the narrator. It is also the writer's responsibility to convey something of a sense of place and culture, and this might demand doing research beyond the interviews.

Selection and *structure* are other major concerns. Oral histories can't include every detail—indeed, often more is left out than is included. This means that writers need to make selections of what to include and what to omit. One way to select is to limit the span of time covered; another way is to focus on key events, turning points, or moments of revelation; another way is to organize material around one or more key themes or issues. There might, of course, be other principles of selection/omission that should guide a particular history.

Choices about structure also demand attention. A chronological narrative is one obvious option. Nonchronological narratives—with flashbacks and such— can also work. So can the letter/epistle format, as evidenced in a sample included later in this chapter, "A Land of Hope and a Future: A Memoir of a Vietnamese Immigrant," which is written in the form a letter from a mother to her children. Other options, however, are also viable.

Oral History Excerpt: Amanda Bergara, *El Mundo de los Secretos*

College student Amanda Bergara chose a diary format when structuring her oral history. Because one of the main themes of Bergara's oral history assignment was secrets, what better choice than to structure the document as a diary, which is associated with keeping secrets? This way the format complemented and reinforced the theme.

10 de julio 1952

Querido Diario,

Today is my birthday. I am fourteen years old. I didn't have a party—no cake, no piñata. But this is nothing new. Mamá only makes parties for my sisters, probably because they are light-skinned just like her. But Papá didn't forget me today. He sent me this diario, "to hold your thoughts," he wrote. I miss him.

The only special thing my family did for my birthday was take the two hour bus ride to church in Culiacán. Only this wasn't so special for me. It's not that I mind the trip. I like going to the city, even if it means going to mass. Anything is better than staying here on el rancho all the time. But I get bored with all the prayers that sound like mumbling. So I say my own versions. My favorite is:

> Santa Maria / Saint Mary
> Mata tu tia / kill your aunt
> Hecha las palos / hit her
> Hasta que ría / until she laughs

And no one even notices.

But later, after mass, when we were on our way out of the echoing church, abuelita Avodia told me to kneel at the statue of La Virgén de Guadelupe. I didn't want to. Why should I kneel and pray to a ceramic statue? Besides, every time I do I feel sick inside—I can't explain it exactly—I just feel like I'm going to vomit. Anyway, I refused to kneel—I told abuelita I had to go to the bathroom and didn't have time for any more praying, but she grabbed hold of my ear, pulled me back to La Virgén, and told me to hurry up and say my prayers. I don't even remember what I prayed for.

Happy Birthday to me.

*   *   *

11 de julio 1952

School is so boring. I have been in the third grade for three years now and I am the smartest kid in class, but that doesn't make it any better. I'm not allowed to answer any more questions out loud, the teacher says. So instead I sit quietly in the back of the stuffy classroom looking out the window.

The schoolhouse here in Sínaloa only goes up to third grade. The higher grades are taught in Culiacán, and it is too far for me to go there everyday. But I might just get my chance pretty soon. You see, Mamá had a boy and he is still alive, not like the other five who died in their cradles.

When she was pregnant, I sincerely prayed to God for the baby to be a boy and for him to live. And I made a promise, well a deal really, that if God would give me a brother that would live, I would serve Him forever. And this means I will have to become a nun.

The convent is in Culiacán. There is a school nearby. In order to become a nun, I must go to school. The nuns are educated, not ignorant like the burros here on el rancho.

In Papá's letter that came with this diario, he said he'd be coming home soon because Sabina is safe now. She wrote him a letter saying she planned to escape, and all she needed was money. He sent her money he'd made working in the strawberry fields and from digging holes for cesspools in California. Sabina and her baby girl Lydia got away and now they are home with us. Now Papá can come home. He doesn't need to stay away to keep himself from killing José Lopez, the man who dragged Sabina by the hair with one hand and had a shotgun in the other—the man who stole her from our rancho and took her to the mountains two years ago.

When Papá comes home, I will tell him about my promise, and he will understand. ∎

This oral history continues, following the same organizing principle throughout. The structure helps readers make sense of experience.

Oral History: Ross Talarico and Harry Nollsch, *Mount Rushmore*

Even poetry can work. The following example is an oral history recovery poem that poet and professor Ross Talarico composed based on a story told by Harry Nollsch, an elderly resident of Rochester, New York.

I can't begin to tell you
how strange it is
to see a face emerge, one feature
at a time, from a distance
only a young boy knows,
there in South Dakota in the Thirties,
among the stretches of cropland,
tied to the river of time
by the brown waters
of the irrigation ditch and good friends.

As an old man now
I go back, visiting George, the
other half of the graduating class
of 1933 at the little country day school
we attended in the Western plains.
He now lives in the place
my folks occupied when I left for
the service in 1942.
He takes me into the tiny room
between the ice shed and the house
where I slept as a kid, and he
points to a dusty shelf, one I remember
building over my bed more than
fifty years ago.
Still visible, the two hearts
I carved there, one with an *H*, the other with an *E*. . .

I think back to Skyline Drive
overlooking Rapid City
below me and the girl next to me
in a '36 Plymouth; the lights seem to
reach for miles. Even the glow
of Ellsworth Air Force Base offers
its promise of a country waiting.
I look up north to the darkness
surrounding Mount Rushmore, thinking
maybe the eyes of those four great men
close at night, like ours,

and maybe they too dream, like we do,
of a vast country filled with
adventure and love . . .

George tells me the young girl
in my mind is now a great-grandmother
living in a town some thirty miles away.
I wonder what we might say
to each other, what anyone says really,
after all these years.
I remind George of the irrigation ditch,
which would bring water to the fields of sugar beets, corn and
cucumbers, and where we'd go
on those September evenings for a
"Last swim" of the season, the moon
rising from behind the willow trees
as we rode our horses
out over the Dakota plains.
The moonlight would dance on the
little waves and miniature whirlpools
in the dark water of the ditch,
as we'd strip off our clothes
and jump into the ditch, incredibly happy.

I don't know, in fact,
how my father managed those days;
our farm was "dry," we had to rely on
natural rainfall, my father forced
to mortgage his livestock or farm machinery
to tide us over until another harvest.
How he ever fed us during
these times I'll never know. As a
matter of fact, gas always being
in short supply, we only made it once
to Mount Rushmore, seeing the faces
of Washington and Jefferson, and the
half-completed face of Roosevelt
slowly emerging in the midst
of such a barren and beautiful America.
Lincoln's face, his stern resolve,
was still a dream in the stone carver's
strong hands. From that day on
I took some time to stare out
across the miles at those four great men,
and to meditate on my own achievements.

I run my weathered hand, still sensitive
to the touch, over the initialed hearts
in my old room, hardly big enough,

I reflect, for a wish or two, let alone
the contemplation of a lifetime.
I know I'll never make it out to the ditch
again, and feel the cool life-giving
water under the moonlight.
But no matter where I stand, half
of me in South Dakota, half in memory,
I'm under the gaze of those
four men atop Mount Rushmore,
and I'll think about my own contribution
to a life of hard work, decency,
minor but wonderful adventures,
and of course whatever romance one can find.
And I'll stand back, the confidence
only an old man knows, feeling
that old September wind after a last swim
as we rode our tired horses back home,
that cold autumn wind, like
a sculptor's hands,
forming the expression on my face.   ∎

Whether in the form of poetry, straight-ahead narrative, letter, or something
else altogether, an oral history must have some sensible, deliberately chosen
structure in order to be successful.

Student Sample of an Oral History: Kristin Schnarr, *A Land of Hope and a Future*

The following oral history was composed as part of Cassel's course. Kristin Schnarr majored in literature and writing at California State University–San Marcos and is currently pursuing a teaching credential. When considering this work a year after finishing it, Schnarr reflected, "As I thought about the papers I wrote during college, I realized that that paper was the most meaningful one that I wrote." This is an ambitious oral history, the culminating text of a semester-long course. Your own oral history might be more limited in scope and shorter in length.

A LAND OF HOPE AND A FUTURE:
A MEMOIR OF A VIETNAMESE IMMIGRANT

November 1999

To My Darling Children,

Throughout your lives I have told you about my life, but now that you are getting older I have decided that it is time to tell you more of the specific details. I
am writing this, in part, because I want you to realize what a blessing you have

been given in that you have been raised in this country, but more importantly I want you to see what a wonderfully merciful Savior we have. I want to give you this letter so that you will be able to tell your children, and your children's children about my life, and the special way that the Lord took care of me. I know my life isn't anything very special, but it is mine, and I want you to know more about it.

As you know, I was born on September 26, 1959 in the city of Saigon, in the country of Vietnam. I don't remember my father, and when I was young I didn't know my mother, your grandma, very well, because she was always in and out of my life. I was raised by my grandparents, your great-grandparents. We lived in a small house with my aunt and her husband, my single aunt, and my cousins. It was crowded, but this was the traditional way that people lived in Vietnam. The grandparents, parents, aunts, uncles, and children all lived together in the same house. You know that this is not how we live in the United States. It is just you, Daddy, and I that live in our house, while your grandpa and grandma live back in Oklahoma. One thing I liked about how I lived in Vietnam is that the whole family is closer to each other, and is more concerned about one another. The thing I love most about how we live in the United States, however, is that you, Daddy, and I are all close together. I am so thankful to the Lord that He has given me such a close and special relationship with you both. It was a relationship that I never had with my parents while I was growing up, and I am so thankful that this is not the case with our family. If I had my life to live over again and was able to pick which manner of living I would have wanted, I am not sure that I would know which one to pick. I am not sorry that I grew up the way I did, but I am also happy living the way we do now. I am glad that the Lord already has my life laid out for me, so I don't have to make decisions like that!

Since I never knew my real father, and since your grandma really wasn't involved in my younger years, it fell to my grandparents, your great-grandparents, to raise me. Your great-grandpa was one of the best men that I have ever known. He was a good man who taught me right from wrong. He was very strict, and always made me go to school, but I know that it was because he loved me. Your great-grandma was a wonderful lady. She didn't work anywhere outside of our house, but she was busy taking care of all the grandchildren. I remember when I was younger your great-grandpa used to work as manager of a fancy hotel. All day long he worked with tourists from different countries. I remember that he knew how to speak French. When I was ten years old he retired, so he was home a lot more. When I was little, your great-grandparents really were my parents, and I knew them much better than your grandma. I am sorry that you never knew your great-grandparents; you would have loved them so much.

Whenever you complain about school, I remember doing the same thing to your great-grandpa. His continual response was that I should think of my future, and he reminded me that getting an education was important. I remember that it was hard for me to understand everything that I learned in school, but at the same time I remember how much I enjoyed it. I learned the same things that you do—math, literature, science, and history. I also was taught the English language, but I was never able to speak it very well. . . .

After I enrolled in the sixth grade I started riding my bicycle to school. In Vietnam most people didn't have cars, so they rode bicycles wherever they were going. This is one of the things that I miss most about Vietnam. Not only was it fun, it was also a source of exercise, and I miss the daily work-out. Since I am telling you about this difference between my life in Vietnam, and the life that we have here, I might as well tell you about a few more of the differences. Cars were considered a luxury, and very few people had them. This is very different than here in the United States, where the majority of people have cars, and they aren't considered a sign of wealth. Another major difference was the fact that most people didn't have telephones. Your great-grandpa didn't have one, so I didn't really experience telephones until I came to the United States. What a change that was! It seemed like every house had one! Another thing that every house seemed to have was a television, whereas in Vietnam they weren't as common. Your great-grandpa did own a television, but unlike here, it only came on at certain times of the day. There were specific times that there was something being broadcasted, and the rest of the time it was only a screen full of snow! Once I was in the United States, it was so odd to be able to turn on the television, regardless of what time it was, and be able to watch something! In fact, it was through television that I picked my American name. I always used to watch *General Hospital*, and there was a character on it who I really liked. So I started telling people to call me by her name, and when I became a United States citizen, I wrote this name on the form!

One thing that the United States and Vietnam both had was the Girl Scouts. I was a member of a troop, and I remember that we used to go camping. One time we went to Vung Tau. It was a beautiful beach, with its white sand strikingly contrasted against the beautiful blue water. The water and sand here in the United States look different than they do in Vietnam. I wish I could use better words to describe the beaches of Vietnam to you, but my words will never do justice to God's creation. I remember we would go swimming in the ocean, and had such a fun time! Our bathing suits looked very similar to the modest ones that some girls wear today. But the major difference was that we never swam with boys. In fact, girls rarely played with boys, and a girl never would have worn a bathing suit in front of a boy. Here in the United States boys and girls grow up playing together, but in Vietnam they were kept apart. Boys played with boys, and girls played with girls. This separation was also continued as they grew older. That is why public displays of affection, such as kissing, were not very common in Vietnam. In fact, public displays of affection of any kind were frowned upon, and it took me the longest time to adjust to the liberty with which girls and boys kissed here in the United States. Whenever I would see people kissing, I would get so embarrassed! As I was first getting used to the United States I thought that the children here had too much freedom, and I still think that this is a problem now. Kids grow up too fast here, and are exposed to things that they never would have been in Vietnam. In Vietnam you would never see a boy and a girl kissing, even when they were in high school. I still don't know which is the better way to grow up. I think that it is a blessing from the Lord that you both were raised here in the United States, but I am aware of how fast the children of this nation cease to be children and become adults. I think it happens too fast, and it is my prayer that this will not happen to you. Enjoy your childhood, and don't rush it. Just be grateful for the time that you have to be young and carefree. The life of a child is much more peaceful and less stressful than that of an adult. You don't have to worry about money or food, but Daddy and I do. One day you will have these worries too, but that time is not now, and I would encourage you not to try and speed up your youth. As the saying goes here in the United States, "You are only young once." I don't want my babies to grow up too fast!

Whenever I tell people about Vietnam, the difference between the two countries that they seem to automatically think of is food. Here in the United States we have such a variety of food available to us, and so we are exposed to food from many different cultures. This was not the case in Vietnam. Our main source of food was rice. We ate it for breakfast, lunch and dinner! Sometimes we would have vegetables or meat to go along with it, but rice was the main source of food that appeared with every meal. Here in the United States the only thing that appears consistently with most of our meals is some form of bread. If we choose, we can have it with every meal, but the fact that we get to choose is the major difference. I don't think that the food I ate growing up was bad, but I am glad that we have more variety in our meals here. I think it is good to be exposed to the meals of other cultures, and I think that this is one thing that many people enjoy about the United States. We can pick which country we want to eat in, just by choosing a restaurant!

Now I know that you have heard about the Vietnam War in your history classes, and are probably wondering when Mommy is going to get to the exciting part of her life! I just wanted to tell you about these seemingly insignificant aspects of my life so that you would see that my life was not as heavily influenced by the war as it was for some. I lived in Saigon, and most people think that there was a lot of fighting going on there, but this was not the case in the province where I lived. There were some areas of Saigon where people had to be evacuated because the fighting was so bad, but it wasn't that bad in the area where I grew up. I never saw fighting, but every night I could hear cannon fire. Actually, the most personal way the war affected me was that your grandma married a soldier, your grandpa. He was in charge of supplies for the American troops stationed in Saigon, and in 1972 his tour of duty was complete, so they both moved to the United States. When your grandparents moved to the United States, I just went on with my life as usual. They had never been a significant part of my life when they were in Vietnam, so it made little difference to me which country they were in. I didn't give it much thought that I probably would never see them again, because I didn't see them very often when we lived in the same city. If someone had asked me at the time if I would ever go to the United States, I probably would have laughed and said no. Going to the United States seemed like an impossible dream. So when your grandparents left, I never would have guessed that I would soon be joining them in the dream world.

On April 29, 1975 my Uncle took me and my cousin, Kiêt, for a ride on his Honda-50. He drove us down to the seaport, and then put Kiêt and me onto a commercial boat. I was confused, and didn't know why my Uncle had brought us to the boat, but then he told me that he was going back to try and bring more of the family. My Uncle never came back, and that was the last time that I ever saw him. When he left, I thought that maybe the boat was just taking us away from Saigon, so that we would be safe from the bombs, and that we would come back when the bombing had stopped. I remember that I was able to see the American Embassy from the boat. A big helicopter landed there, and the soldiers were rushing to get people from the Embassy into it. I knew that the Americans were leaving and that the North Vietnamese were going to invade South Vietnam, but at that time I didn't know that that was the *last* day that the Americans were in Vietnam. So I stayed on the boat with my cousin, assuming that we would only stay on it for a while, and that we would shortly be returning to our family in Vietnam. When we left the house that morning, I had no idea that I was leaving Vietnam, never to return. As a result I didn't get to say good-bye to anyone. Most importantly, I didn't get to say good-bye to your great-grandparents. Never again would I be able to see his loving face, or her gentle smiles. It has always made me very sad that I was never able to say good-bye, or tell them that I loved them and would miss them. Even now it still makes me sad, so I am glad that at the time I didn't know that I was leaving Vietnam forever. I think the parting would have been more unbearable. In fact, I am not sure if I would have stayed on that boat if I had known that I was not coming back. By the time I realized that we were not returning to Vietnam it was too late for me to change my mind. I was going to the United States whether I liked it or not.

I later found out that the commercial boat that we were packed into was only supposed to carry five hundred passengers, but there were somewhere between fifteen and seventeen hundred people on board. There were so many of us that my cousin and I had to sit on the edge of the boat. Since the boat had multiple levels, and we were on one of the lower levels, we weren't in direct sunlight. I do remember that there were two other boats traveling with us, but after we left the seaport we were separated, and at night we were so far apart that we couldn't see the other boats. That first night was pitch black, and there was no moon. It was an eerie feeling to be surrounded by complete darkness. The water was dark, as was the sky, and there were no visible lights. One advantage of the darkness was that I was able to see the stars. They were so beautiful! Their beauty, however, was soon interrupted by the distant sound of cannon fire. We were too far away to be in danger, but we could see that the two ships we had been traveling with were being fired upon by cannons from the shore. In the darkness we could see the flaming trails that followed the bombs and the bullets. We watched as one ship was sunk, and the other was consumed by flames. This attack was not an accident. The North Vietnamese had fired on the ships, trying to keep them from escaping. It was scary to see the fire, especially when I knew that I could have been on one of those boats with my cousin. Even then the Lord was taking care of us, and keeping us safe. . . .

We were at sea for one day before we were met by a big American battleship, and until that time I had continued to think that we were going back to Vietnam. Before I saw the American battleship I never would have dreamed that I was going to the United States, because it would have been only that, a dream. In Vietnam people dreamed about going to the United States, as if it were heaven. It seemed so impossible that it didn't even enter my mind that the United States was going to be my new home. When the realization hit me, I was overwhelmed with feelings of joy and dread all at the same time. The United States seemed like a paradise, so I was excited about going there, but even in the midst of my joy, doubts began to fill my mind. I knew that it was going to be a difficult transition, and that it would be a long time before the United States truly became my home. . . .

Despite the natural beauty that was all around us, it was a long and tiring journey, which felt even longer because the ship was so crowded. There wasn't very much room, and everyone had only a little area that was theirs. As I said, Kiêt and I sat on the edge of the boat during the trip. One night he almost rolled off the boat while he was sleeping. Thankfully, an older man caught him just in time, otherwise he would have fallen into the ocean and I would have slept right through it all. One of the benefits of the crowded conditions of the boat was that it bonded all of us together. There was one specific group that I really bonded with, and we made our own little "family" on the boat. The first person that I met, who would later become a part of our "family," was Tran Tháo. She was a year older than I was, and we became very good friends on our journey. We were both so young, and we needed the support and encouragement that the other had to offer. A little later on our voyage to the Philippines, we met Chú Ba and Chú Tháo. They were both sailors who had fought for the South Vietnamese and decided to flee the country instead of facing the North Vietnamese invasion. They were in their thirties, and each had a wife and children back in Vietnam. They were sad and lonely, so we "adopted" them into our family, and called them our "uncles." Tháo recently talked to one of the "uncles," and he told her that he never saw his wife and children again. They both left everything and tried to make new lives for themselves, all alone. So our unique "family" was composed of a six year-old, a sixteen year-old, a seventeen year-old, and two runaway sailors. Even though we were strangers, we bonded together because we needed each other. We were all embarking on a new life, and were experiencing our own fears and doubts about the new life that we were heading towards. The trip would have been so much harder if we hadn't had this family unit. The Lord knew that I needed their support in order to make the trip.

Just when it felt like the voyage would never end, someone shouted "Oh, the land!" Everyone tried to see a glimpse of the Philippines, but it was several hours before we could really see the island, let alone get off the boat. Everyone was so excited, and could hardly wait to get back on land. Yet, at the same time, everyone seemed uncertain, almost fearful. We all seemed to suddenly realize that this boat was our last connection with home, and that separations were inevitable. I was very sad at the thought of being separated from Tháo and the uncles, and the uncertain life that lay ahead of me began to fill my heart with fear. It took a long time for us to finally reach land, but we finally did, and were allowed to get off the boat. As all of us got off the ship, we each were given a number, and told that when our number was called we would be flown to the next point on our voyage to the United States. After this formality was taken care of, we were blissfully told that we could take a shower. I had not been able to take a shower for over seven days, and I felt so dirty! It felt so good to finally be clean. Kiêt and I were both so tired that we lay down to rest in the area that we had been told to wait. I woke up later only to realize that our numbers had been called, and that we had been skipped over since we had fallen asleep. Little did I know that this error would take a month to be corrected. The procedure was that if numbers were called and not responded to, then those people had to wait for a long period of time before their numbers would be called again. I panicked when I realized that we had been skipped over, but then I was glad because that meant that Kiêt and I wouldn't have to be separated from our "family" right away. You have to remember that I didn't really know anyone in the United States, except for your grandparents, and they both might as well have been strangers, considering the fact that I had spent very little time with them. So the United States sounded to me like a very lonely place, and my response to the delay went quickly from panic to joy.

For the month that Kiêt and I were in the Philippines we stayed at a base of some sort. It was very similar to a military base, with a big mess hall, and large barracks. The sleeping arrangements were actually comfortable. We each were assigned a cot, and families were allowed to remain together, unlike some places where the men and women had to be separated. So our "family" was still able to be together, and this was a blessing. Now I am sure that you are both thinking that Mommy is crazy, because I thought that a cot was comfortable. You have to remember, however, that I used to sleep on tile floor in Vietnam, so anything was more comfortable than that! Not only were the sleeping arrangements comfortable, the food was actually pretty good as well! It was served in a big mess hall, with huge tables, where families all ate together. To this day I still don't know what we ate, whether it was American or Filipino food. I just knew that it wasn't Vietnamese!

The other thing that wasn't Vietnamese was the lack of privacy. The Vietnamese, as a whole, are a very private people, and the base didn't allow for privacy. The showers were not individual stalls, and they had two or three spigots, so that more than one person could take a shower at a time. The women and men did have separate bathing facilities, but that only eased the embarrassment a little. Being completely naked and taking a shower is such a private thing, and these arrangements made it very public. It was very hard to take a shower in front of people who I didn't know, and I don't think I ever got used to it. Not only was taking a shower a public affair, going to the bathroom was as well. There was a row of toilets that were elevated off the ground, and huge containers, which needed to be cleaned out every day, were placed underneath. These toilets were divided by side walls, which formed stalls, but they did not have doors. It was so embarrassing going to the bathroom with no privacy. I think that the lack of privacy in these very private matters was one of the hardest things for me to get used to during the stay in the Philippines. There were no sinks, so we had to wash our hands and faces in the showers. The showers were also used to wash our clothes. The Red Cross had given each of us another outfit, so while we washed one, we wore the other. For most of us, the outfits that we had worn on the voyage from Vietnam to the Philippines were the traditional clothes of the Vietnamese. This traditional outfit was composed of a baggy pair of pants and a loose shirt. Actually, the closest thing we have to them here in the United States is a pair of pajamas! It was quite an experience going from this traditional style of dress to wearing the shorts, tops, and flip-flops that had been donated to the Red Cross! The one style was so modest, and the other seemed so immodest, but I was grateful for the change of clothes. I would have rather put up with getting used to a new style of clothing than having to wear the same outfit for the whole journey to the United States!

We had a lot of free time on our hands, so sometimes it was boring. One enjoyable amusement that was permitted, however, was to go swimming in the portion of the ocean that was near the base. One time Tháo and I went swimming, and I climbed up on a big rock that was in the water. Somehow I lost my balance, fell, and hurt my wrist. The medical staff at the base couldn't tell if I had broken my wrist, so they decided to send me to a hospital in Manila. I was taken to the hospital, and x-rays were taken of my wrist. Everyone was very nice to me as I waited for the results, but it was a confusing time for me because no one spoke Vietnamese, and I didn't speak English. It was decided that my wrist was not broken, but only sprained. So it was bandaged and then I was sent back to the base. That was the only time that I left the base area, and many would have considered it a treat to be able to go to Manila, but I was too scared to enjoy it!

To say the least, life was very different on that base in the Philippines than it was back in Vietnam. I wouldn't classify it as better or worse, however, it was just different. One thing that took me a while to get used to was the lack of contact with my family back in Vietnam. It was hard to go from living in the same house and talking with them every day, to not seeing them at all. It was also hard to get used to living with people who weren't my relatives. I had grown up in a house full of extended family members, and it was odd to be surrounded by strangers. Even though we were unable to have any contact with our family back in Vietnam, I was allowed to write a letter to your grandma in the United States, and the Red Cross saw to it that she received it. I had been correct in assuming that she had no idea that Kiêt and I were coming before she received the letter from the American sailor. By the time she got my letter she already knew that we were coming, but she didn't know where we were. So after she got my letter she knew where to write, in order to inform the authorities that she and your grandpa would be willing to take responsibility for Kiêt and me once we got to the United States. It was this letter that the Red Cross needed in order to send Kiêt and me to the United States, so after they received it the Red Cross began processing the paperwork for us to leave the Philippines. I was asked questions such as where was I born, who my mother and father were, and why I had left Vietnam. Once I had answered these questions, and after all the paperwork was filled out, I was told that Kiêt and I could go to the United States. Once I was officially told that we could leave I was scared about all that lay ahead of me, but I was ready to move on to the next thing, and get started with my new life.

The mode of transportation that took us on the next part of our journey was a C-141 Troop Transport. It was a huge plane that was camouflaged on the outside. I was afraid of the plane, because I had never been that close to a plane before, let alone flown in one. Since it was a troop transport, and not a passenger plane, the seats were back-to-back down the center of the plane. One drawback to this was that we couldn't see out the windows, but I was too scared to look anyway! The plane was so loud, and my ears really hurt because of the pressure and altitude changes. As scary as the flight was, Kiêt was wonderful, and he didn't complain or cry. . . .

This first portion of our flight to the United States ended at Wake Island, where we stayed for about two weeks. The first night we got there, the people in charge made sure that everyone was there, and then each family was placed in a little building, similar to a condo. This gave all of us more privacy, and it was nice to just be with our "family" in a house, instead of in a huge barracks with everyone else. This arrangement, however, was only to be for the first night. The following morning we walked to the base to have breakfast, and then we were assigned a cot in the barracks for the rest of our stay on the island.

Kiêt and I remained at Wake Island only for about two weeks, and then we were given permission to get on another C-141 Troop Transport that would take us to Honolulu. Unfortunately, it was at this point in our journey that our "family" had to be separated. Kiêt and I had been given permission to leave, because your grandparents were acting as our sponsors. Since Tháo and the "uncles" didn't have sponsors they had to wait until sponsors could be found for them. It was very hard to leave Tháo, and we both cried when it came time for Kiêt and me to leave. Tháo wished that she could come with us, and I was afraid to leave her alone. Yes, the "uncles" would still be with her, but it wasn't the same. We had always felt safe because we knew that we were watching out for each other, but no one would be able to take care of Tháo once I left. We had both gone through so much together, and she had come to be such a special friend that the thought of never seeing her again caused my heart to ache. I knew, however, that I couldn't stay in Wake Island, so I boarded the plane with a heavy heart.

After my parting with Tháo the only thought that lifted my spirits was the realization that every minute brought us that much closer to the United States, and the end of our trip. I was getting tired of traveling, and the flight to Honolulu didn't help at all! It was such a long flight, and it was so rough and turbulent that I got air sick. Thankfully Kiêt didn't get sick, or else I would have needed to take care of him while I was sick myself. Recently people have asked me if I liked Honolulu and if I thought it was pretty, but I was too sick at the time to enjoy it. For one thing we weren't allowed to look out the windows on the plane, because we would have needed to stand up in order to see out them, and this was unsafe. While we were waiting in the airport, I probably could have gotten a better view of Honolulu, but I was too scared that we would get lost or left behind. So Kiêt and I sat down in one spot and did not move until we were told to get in the plane. And this time I didn't fall asleep! I wasn't going to chance being left behind again as long as I could help it!

Our final destination was Fort Chaffee, Arkansas, and we reached this in June of 1975. We had left Vietnam in April, and it took us somewhere between two and three months to get to the United States. By the time we got to the United States I was tired of living in bases, and was ready to live in a house again. When we first arrived, however, we had to stay in a refugee camp in Fort Chaffee until your grandparents could come from Oklahoma and pick us up. I only had to stay at Fort Chaffee for one week, but several things happened during that short time. One of the most exciting things about that week was that I met Mai, a lady who used to know your great-grandma's sister. The fact that we both knew the same people made us feel like we were close friends. After being among strangers for such a long time, it was so nice to be able to talk to someone who actually knew the same people that I did. She was coming to the United States because she had married an American soldier, and she, her husband, and their son were waiting for permission to leave the refugee camp. They had left Vietnam after the Americans had officially evacuated, so they were considered refugees, even though her husband was a United States citizen. I am so grateful to the Lord that He let me meet Mai, because He knew that I needed her support during that week at Fort Chaffee.

The barracks at Fort Chaffee were very similar to those at Subic Bay in the Philippines, so we each had a cot that was set up in a large room. There were no lights inside the building, and the only light that we had at night was the light that filtered in through the windows from the outside lights. One night I woke up suddenly, unsure of what had wakened me, and then I opened my eyes again and saw a man standing by my cot. I couldn't see his face very well, because it was so dark, but I think he was about thirty years-old. He just stood there, staring down at me, and I realized that it was too dark for him to see that I was awake. I remember that I was afraid that he was going to rape me, but thankfully he finally walked away, and I never saw him again. To this day I still don't know what he wanted, but the incident scared me enough that I told Mai. After I told her, she told me to bring Kiêt and our cots to her barracks so that we could sleep there. She said that she would feel better if she knew that we were safe. So Kiêt and I moved into the other barracks for the rest of our stay at Fort Chaffee, and spent a lot of time with Mai. . . I am so grateful to the Lord for all of the special people that I met during my journey to the United States. If I had never left Vietnam, I probably never would have met them. Their friendships are just one of the many blessings that were brought about by my moving to the United States.

It wasn't until years after my immigration to the United States, however, that I was able to consider any of it a blessing. Your grandparents came to pick Kiêt and me up, and took us back to Oklahoma. That was my first ride in a car, and I was convinced that your grandparents were rich! I am sure that they would have laughed if they could have read my thoughts. This thought process was only encouraged, however, when I saw their home. It was an average house in the United States, but it seemed like a mansion to me. They had an entire house to themselves, and they didn't have to share it with other relatives. Even though I liked the way your grandparents lived that did not make my transition any easier. I didn't understand English very well, and I spoke it even less. The fact that I didn't speak English, in addition to the fact that I was the only Vietnamese girl in our town, combined to make my first years here very lonely. Your grandma was the only other person with whom I could speak Vietnamese, but she and I were like strangers. Everything was just so hard, and I was so very homesick that I didn't like anything and wanted to go back to Vietnam. I was overwhelmed by feelings of uncertainty and loneliness, and my memories of that time in my life are not very good ones. Your grandma tried to cheer me up by taking me shopping for school clothes, but I found no joy in it, especially since it was hard for me to get used to the new style of clothing.

If all of this wasn't bad enough, school made it ten times worse. I had completed the ninth grade back in Vietnam, so I was placed in the tenth grade in Oklahoma, even though I didn't speak a word of English. I hated school, and couldn't understand what was going on. It is not that people were mean to me, they just politely ignored me. I didn't understand them, and they didn't understand me, so we just left it at that. I don't want you to think, however, that everyone ignored me. There were two teachers who were very kind and really tried to help me with my English. My Home Economics teacher and my ESL teacher both made every effort to make me feel at home in the United States. There was also a lady from your grandma's church that came over to my house once a week to help me with my English. Looking back now I am grateful for their kindness to me, but at the time I wasn't interested in anything, especially not learning English.

The only thing that brought me joy was my youngest half-sister, your Aunt Jean. She was very sweet, and we got along very well. She didn't speak any Vietnamese, but this was good because it forced me to try my English. I had another half-sister, your Aunt Sandy, and half-brother, your Uncle Ken, but I wasn't as close to them as I was to Jean. Both Jean and Sandy were born in the United States, but Ken was born in Vietnam. I actually had known him before he moved to the United States with your grandparents, but I didn't know him very well because he lived with your great-grandma's sister, instead of living with your great-grandparents. I never would get to know him very well, because he was killed four months after I came to Oklahoma. On the first of October, 1975, Ken, who was only nine years-old, was hit by a car and killed. He was crossing the street in the cross-walk when a seventeen year-old boy ran a stop sign and killed him. Your grandpa and grandma were heart broken, and there was nothing that I could do about it. I didn't feel like I knew either of them well enough to know how to comfort them.

God alone knows how I made it through those first years, but I did. I worked at a fast food place, but I didn't really have any friends there. People were nice, but they tended to ignore me at work, just as the students ignored me at school. The fact that I didn't speak English made both work and school difficult. In fact, I was unable to graduate from high school, even though I had completed the remaining three years, because my English just wasn't good enough. So I dropped out of high school in 1979. In 1980, I moved to Monterey, California to go to the School of Beauty and Cosmetology. It was a lot of hard work, because there was a lot of difficult book reading that went along with it. Thankfully I graduated, and it was at that time that I finally began to appreciate the country that I had come to. There was so much freedom, and opportunity here, and I could do whatever I wanted. I actually had a future here in the United States, unlike back in Vietnam. Even as a child I never had dreams like you do about what I would do when I "grew up," because there just never seemed to be a sense of future in Vietnam. Not only did I graduate from the School of Beauty and Cosmetology in 1980, I also became an American citizen that same year. I had to take several tests in order to become a citizen, but it was worth it. At that point I began to think of the United States as my home. Unlike my first years here, I became interested in the life that was all around me. I began going to classes that would help me to speak better English, and from that year on I never was sorry that I came to the United States. I am convinced that this is the best country, and I am so fortunate to have been able to come and make a life here.

I want you to always remember, and never forget what a merciful Lord we have. He brought me to this country and gave me blessings that I never would have had in Vietnam. Each of you are one of those special blessings, and I am so thankful that the Lord has given you to me. My darlings, never forget that the Lord is watching you and taking care of you. He will always help you through difficult times, just like He helped me through my difficult journey to my new home. Always remember that I love you, but more importantly that our Lord and Savior Jesus Christ loves you.

With All My Love,

Mommy   ∎

The Companion Abstract: Reflecting on Rhetorical Choices

Part of the assignment for this chapter includes a short reflection on how and why you made key choices when writing the oral history. This document should make visible your decision-making process and convince the reader that your choices were well considered and wise.

The companion abstract should be rather brief—one or two pages. It has a dual purpose: to encourage a critical reflection and to help your instructor more accurately assess your performance.

The companion paper should at least address the following questions:

- Why did you opt to focus on particular themes or issues?
- How did you decide what to include and exclude?
- Why did you structure the oral history as you did?
- What were your most difficult writing problems and choices?
- What were your most difficult ethical quandaries?
- What did you find most rewarding about the writing process?

Also include anything that your instructor should know about the oral history.

Companion Abstract: Kristin Schnarr

Here is the abstract that Schnarr wrote to accompany her oral history:

When I first approached Carol Smith (a pseudonym) about interviewing her for this assignment, she was excited and told me that she has always wanted to have the story of her immigration to the United States written down so that she could give it to her children. With this in mind, I decided that her biography needed to be written in the first person, as a letter from Carol to her children, since they are the ones for whom this biography really is written. So as I began writing, I tried to think of the way Carol speaks to her children, and attempted to mimic her speech in this letter. I used to baby-sit her children, and I remember that she often refers to them as her babies or darlings, and so I decided to refer to them as such. Not only did this make for a more intimate letter, but it also allowed me to write this immigrant testimonial without mentioning either Carol or her children's names, as per her request.

One thing I noticed as I interviewed Carol was her constant reference to the kindness and mercy of Jesus Christ, especially in the manner in which she believes He took care of her on her immigration to the United States. When Carol spoke of her immigration to the United States, as well as her early years here, she always acknowledged the mercy and kindness of Christ, in both the happy and painful times of her life. Carol views the fact that she was able to come to the United States, as well as the opportunity she had to meet people through her immigration, as blessings from her Lord. As His name was mentioned throughout her interview, I realized that, for Carol, the kindness and mercy of Jesus Christ are the themes of her life's story.

Since Jesus Christ was constantly mentioned in the interview, I realized that this needed to be the case with the letter as well. I wanted the letter to be as realistic and "Carol-like" as possible. In order to make it as if Carol had written it, I needed to make Jesus Christ a central theme in the letter. As I wrote, I struggled with making it Carol's letter and not my own. I wanted it to be as if Carol really had written it to her children, but when I took the completed letter to her, I was anxious and feared that I had failed. As I read it aloud, however, and watched as tears of joy filled Carol's eyes, I knew that I had succeeded. ∎

Peer Review Questions for Your Oral History Draft

It can be extremely helpful to share a version of your oral history as part of a peer review workshop. This should be done after you have completed interviews and after you have made a serious attempt to structure and compose a full draft of the project. The peer review should, in turn, deliver feedback that will be helpful in the revising process.

1. Which specific parts of the draft are particularly appealing?

2. Where, in particular, do you get lost or confused?

3. What choices has the writer made about structure? Do they seem sensible? Why or why not?

4. Which themes or issues are most evident?

5. Describe the voice and style that you hear in the draft. Where does the voice seem particularly authentic and resonant? Where does it seem tinny or off?

6. Which specific parts of the draft call for more development? Which parts might be expendable?

Dissemination

The most important recipient of the oral history document is, of course, the person telling the history. These documents often serve as treasured records of family history, to be shared (as evident in Schnarr's letter) with members of younger generations.

But there is also the prospect of widening the reach of writing as social action by disseminating the oral histories to a larger audience. In Cassel's class, that meant collecting the histories into book form and publishing them. There are other possibilities: holding public readings, doing readings in or creating resources for local schools, publishing on the Web, publishing in a local or campus newspaper, and so on.

Celebrating lives through wider dissemination is premised on getting explicit permission from the tellers of the history. Their lives should be made public only if they wish to have them so. The tellers might have good reasons for keeping their oral histories private; but they might also be eager to share their life narratives with the larger community, which can benefit from hearing them.

ENDNOTE

There are many ways, in addition to composing proposals or oral histories, that you can write with the community. For example, students have launched after-school creative writing programs and organized community problem-solving dialogues. The possibilities are as open and diverse as communities themselves. Ultimately, writing-with-the-community projects depend on students and community partners thinking and working creatively to leverage the power of writing to solve problems, raise awareness, and instigate change.

10

Final Reflections

What is a capstone essay? How do you assemble a portfolio? What are the key strategies for oral reports? This chapter focuses on end-of-term activities, offering pragmatic strategies for both looking back at your work and looking ahead to your future.

Growth is the only evidence of life.

—John Henry Cardinal Newman

The final reflections encouraged by this chapter should be viewed as opportunities to synthesize your thinking, review your progress, and look to the future. Your growth as a writer and a citizen is certainly not coming to a close with the end of a semester, so whatever reflections you make now are not terminal. Still, closing reflections are "final for now," an important occasion for taking stock before moving on.

As one who has been engaged in dialogue and writing related to community action, you now have the chance to review your "collected works" as well as to think about where to go from here. If you have been engaged in service-learning, you also have a wealth of community experience on which to reflect. At this stage, you might be discontinuing your relationship with a community partner; or perhaps you have developed interests and relationships that will carry you beyond the scope of this course. Whatever the case, taking the opportunity to pause, assess, and write is time well spent.

Final reflections should involve a review of writing that you have generated, texts that you have read, and events that you have experienced. This chapter provides guidelines for three kinds of synthesizing activities: assembling a portfolio, composing a capstone essay, and giving an oral presentation. All these activities serve one of the traditional assessment functions of school writing: documenting learning. These activities can also help you contemplate how to apply what you've learned to future pursuits.

ASSIGNMENT OPTIONS
Reflective Essays and Letters

CAPSTONE ESSAY: REFLECTIONS ON SELF AS WRITER

Review all your writing from the term and compose an essay on some aspect of yourself as a writer (feel free to focus on one significant thing). Some questions that might prompt productive thinking include: What patterns are evident? How has the writing (or the writer) changed? What did you learn about yourself as a writer and thinker? What do you still need to work on in the future? Use excerpts from your own writing to support the claims you make.

CAPSTONE ESSAY: REFLECTIONS ON SELF AS CITIZEN

Consider how your thinking about social action (or one particular aspect of social action) has changed as a result of participating in community service connected to an academic course. When developing the essay, draw on your own experience as well as on course readings.

LETTER TO PORTFOLIO READERS OR FUTURE STUDENTS

Review your portfolio materials and compose a letter addressed to either portfolio readers or future students who may take this course. If the letter is addressed to portfolio readers, it will serve as a guide to, and commentary on, your collected works. If the letter is addressed to future students, you can adopt more of an advice-giving posture. Consider the same questions listed for the "Reflections on Self as Writer" assignment and make specific reference to the documents in the portfolio.

CAPSTONE ESSAY: REFLECTING ON COMMUNITY PARTNERSHIP

If you have been engaged in service-learning, think about the state of (and future of) your relationship with your community partner. Will you end it here? Will you continue some kind of connection? Do you expect to devote further energy to community action? How and why (or why not)? Given what you have learned and experienced, where do you want to go from here?

Assembling a Portfolio

A *portfolio* is a representative collection of your writing (and perhaps other artifacts) that documents your achievements over the course of time. Artists, architects, and many other professionals use portfolios because they supply a fuller sense of one's capabilities and creativity than could any single example of work. Likewise for writers, a portfolio serves as a better reflection of learning and potential than any single test or paper because it features a range of writing—formal and informal—in response to a range of assignments—major and minor—over an extended period of time. Portfolios are also in tune with the explore–draft–revise writing process, because the major pieces have developed over time and through multiple drafts. Writing portfolios are often used to demonstrate one's development as a thinker and writer; but most fundamentally, they should serve as an honest presentation of one's best self.

When deciding what to include in a portfolio, you should keep its purpose in mind. You should also consider your audience: Is it the instructor alone? instructor and classmates? an outside reader? If, for example, an outside reader will review the portfolio, you might need to explain the essay assignments that prompted the writings, but that would be unnecessary if addressing an instructor who is already familiar with the assignments. Still, most audiences require the same core content, which is outlined in the following box.

What to Include in a Portfolio

BASICS

- At least three major pieces of writing that reveal the writer's best work (usually essays and/or service-learning projects; often at least one research-based assignment must be included).
- For at least one of those major pieces, a paper trail of its chronological development—exploratory writing, notes on sources, all drafts, teacher and peer responses to drafts, and final draft. (Some instructors require this for all major writings.)
- Excerpts from a journal, if there is one (choose three or four representative entries).
- Two or three samples of informal writing (homework, in-class writing, etc.) that represents the writer's mind at work or writing to discover.
- For a writer who did a service-learning project, any comments, correspondence, or evaluations from the community partner, if available.
- For a writer who did a service-learning project, some sample of writing from the community site (such as writing done by a tutee), if appropriate. The portfolio should include such writing only if explicit permission has been granted by the community partner and, if involving a minor, from parents.
- A capstone essay or letter to portfolio readers (explained later in this chapter).

OPTIONAL

- Artifacts that reveal other dimensions of the writer's learning, thinking, and writing (photos, drawings, art, recordings, Web pages, etc.).
- An example or two of writing done outside the course (creative writing, papers from other courses, etc.)

Remember that different institutions and instructors may amend these instructions or have additional requirements. Before assembling a portfolio, you should confirm those expectations.

Beyond the content, a few other guidelines should be kept in mind when assembling a course portfolio:

- *Feature both process and product.* You want to include your very best work—as would any artist assembling a portfolio—but you also want to show your intellectual and personal growth (students are expected, after all, to engage in a process of intellectual and personal development). The need to feature process is why one should include works from all phases of the course (revealing growth over time) as well as exploratory through final drafts for a single project (making visible one's composing process).

- *Make it about your learning, not the instructor's teaching.* It is tempting to feed teachers a narrative that goes something like this: "I learned so much because you're such a wonderful teacher. Let me tell you all the things you did well." Resist this impulse. Instead, focus on your own learning, your own experience, your own writing. Be honest about how you have changed as a writer, where you have struggled, and what goals you have met or not met.

- *Organize materials purposefully.* The way your portfolio is organized can shape how readers perceive you. Are materials arranged chronologically to invite readers to track growth? Does the most significant work appear first, to signal its importance? Is work clustered by theme to highlight certain issues or connections? You should arrange materials strategically to highlight your strengths. Unless the arrangement is self-evident (or explained in the capstone essay or a letter to the portfolio reader), you should probably describe it in a short introductory note.

- *Sweat the small stuff.* Keep materials neatly organized, label documents clearly, and follow any instructions set forth by your instructor or writing program. Don't make portfolio readers fish around in disorganized materials, fuss with crumpled papers, strain to decipher opaque handwriting, or have to contact you about missing work. These kinds of things make readers frustrated and grumpy—and you don't want people assessing your work in that frame of mind!

A portfolio is incomplete without some kind of final reflection, which often takes the form of a capstone essay or a letter to the portfolio reader. Those genres are explained in the next section.

The Capstone Essay

Capstone is traditionally a builder's term that refers to the top piece that finishes a construction, that signals the close of an enterprise, that makes an enduring structure complete. Similarly, a capstone essay finishes a course or portfolio, summarizes various strands of thought, reflects on the close of a meaningful venture. Perhaps the most significant intellectual energy of writing a capstone essay is devoted to the task of *synthesis*—bringing accumulated ideas and experiences together to make sense of them for oneself and for one's readers.

Most capstone essays adopt the core rhetorical features of the personal essay, which are explained in Chapter 2. Yet capstone essays are not only about personal experience. They also involve sorting, synthesizing, and applying the various intellectual ideas and questions that emerged in response to readings, class discussions, and writing assignments.

Capstone essays involve both looking backward and looking ahead. The following section offers advice on how to gather and review the writing you have done so far in the course. This can help both to generate potential ideas for the essay and to provide specific supporting evidence for the claims you make about yourself as a writer. For example, if earlier in the semester you completed the essay assignment in Chapter 2 on writing experience and reflections, it might be worthwhile to compare how you presented yourself as a writer then with how you think about yourself as a writer now.

The letter to portfolio readers assignment is an alternative to the capstone essay, yet it is similar in purpose and content. If you choose this option, your first step is to be clear about exactly who your reader is—your instructor? your peers? outside readers? Because all writing is to a large degree shaped by audience expectations, customizing the letter to the right reader-ship is critical.

Using Your Own Writing as Evidence

According to its Latin roots, *reflect* means, literally, "to bend back" or "to turn back." A reflective essay should likewise turn back and examine your experi-ence. For a reflective essay on writing, you should look back to the texts you have produced to date. You might think of your own writings as an archive or as a data set; they invite analysis and supply much of the support for your essay's claims.

Because the documents collected in a portfolio are a rich source for the cap-stone essay (or the letter to portfolio readers), it is helpful to at least start assem-bling the portfolio before writing a capstone piece. (And even if you are not preparing a portfolio, you will need to gather as much of your own writing as possible.) When you have gathered a folder of your work—and remember, this includes both formal and informal writing—you should arrange it in chrono-logical order. As you review it, take notes in response to the guiding questions in this section. Also make notes in the margins of your own texts (or on sticky notes marking specific passages).

These guiding questions are tailored to the "Reflections on Self as Writer" capstone essay assignment or the "Letter to Portfolio Readers" assignment, but they could easily be adapted to suit the "Reflections on Self as a Citizen" essay assignment:

- What themes run through the writings? Does a particular question or is-sue surface in several of the texts?
- Are any other patterns evident?
- How has your thinking changed over time? Can you locate any turning points, moments of realization, breakthroughs? What specific texts and specific passages within those texts show evidence of such changes? What before-and-after comparisons make the changes clear?
- What readings, class discussions, encounters, or community experiences most influenced your thinking and writing? Which ones do you cite most in your writing? What authors spoke to your interests or opened new ways of thinking for you? Did you incorporate anything from their writing styles into your own prose style?
- If you have kept a journal, look it over from start to finish. What issues, questions, or anxieties recur?
- What have you learned about yourself? about your writing habits? about your shortcomings? about your strengths? about what you need to do to

produce good writing? How did you learn such things about yourself? Take note of specific documents or passages that illustrate your strengths, weaknesses, and changes.

- Describe your current writing style and select two paragraphs that exemplify it. Has your writing style changed since the beginning of the course? What rhetorical or grammatical strategies have proven most useful to you? What strategies do you use now that you didn't before? What documents from later in the course prove this?
- What are the most important things you have learned about social action? about community? about other topics? about writing itself?
- What is your favorite piece in the portfolio? Why?
- In general, what kinds of writing do you prefer, and why?
- Locate documents and passages with which you struggled the most. Why were these places tough?
- With respect to your writing, what do you most want to work on in the coming years?
- If you did a service-learning writing project, how is that community writing similar to or different from the more conventional academic pieces? Is it different only in surface features? Or was the writing process also different?
- If you were engaged in community work, what was your most powerful experience? Who or what changed your thinking? and about what, in particular?
- How does the writing in this portfolio relate to the writing you do for other courses, on the job, or in life more generally?
- How might this writing prepare you to meet future academic, career, and personal goals?

These prompts should help generate at least three pages of notes and reflections, even though they may be jumbled, unfocused, and informal at this time. At this stage, the important thing is to keep the potential ideas flowing so that you have a lot to choose from when you sit down to compose a draft.

Another powerful way to generate reflection on yourself as a writer is to share your whole portfolio with a classmate. This way, he or she gets to see your writing in a larger scope than is possible during regular peer workshop sessions with single drafts. It is generally best to do this during class (you probably don't want to let your collected works too far out of your sight) and to limit the number of questions (because the person will have so much to review).

Peer Review Questions for Evaluating Portfolios

In pairs, exchange portfolio folders. When reviewing the contents, jot notes (on a separate page) in response to a few key questions:

1. What are the strong points of this portfolio?
2. Do you see any patterns (repeated topics, similar ways of structuring pieces, etc.)?
3. Can you detect any changes in the writer over time? If so, note specific passages.
4. Describe the writer's style.

When you are done, share your notes and discuss your thoughts.

Finding a Focus

All this informal writing and peer feedback can generate several possibilities for your capstone essay. One temptation is to patch together reflections about every aspect of your writing, but that can lead to a hodgepodge of comments that are not cohesive. The purpose of a capstone essay is not to synthesize *everything* about your recent writing and service experiences. Rather, as with all essays, you need to narrow the topic to a manageable focus.

For example, building an essay around the claim "I really improved in my writing" would be problematic because this claim is much too vague and general. Rather, you should focus on one or two significant improvements, for example, and document *how* they have improved by citing textual evidence (such as passages from your past work). Or you could reflect, for example, on how one of your expectations for the semester's writing instruction or service work was confirmed, altered, or upset by particular events.

The capstone essay best fits in the personal essay genre and, as detailed in Chapter 2, personal essays usually have tension and turn. The focus of a capstone essay is often a turn from "old self" to "new self" or "old perspective" to "new perspective." Personal essays also employ literary devices such as description ("showing" rather than "telling"), scene setting, character development, and figurative language.

Consider one student's approach to the capstone essay. Audrey (whose essay is featured on pp. 340–342) opted to reflect on one aspect of her writing life: a newfound sense of flexibility. She could have reviewed each major assignment that she did during the semester, but doing so would have spread the content too thinly. By narrowing the topic to one assignment (her service-learning writing project) and one tension (an "old self" who saw writing as rigid and rule bound versus a "new self" who sees writing as flexible and context bound), she was able develop the essay effectively. She also includes details and descriptions to "show" her turn rather than just assert ("tell") it. The following capstone essay employs several of the same strategies.

Student Capstone Essay: Bill Flavell, *Trust as a Tool*

When he wrote this essay, Bill Flavell was a first-year student who had done a service-learning project earlier in the semester. That project, for the campus wellness program, was a team effort that involved researching and writing a report on social norms campaigns as they relate to changing student binge drinking habits.

TRUST AS A TOOL

Confidence, self-reliance, and capability are three words that I have long since associated with myself. I have also long since assumed that relying on others is a sign of weakness. This semester I learned that a few other words define me, especially, as a writer. These words are selfish, stubborn, and untrusting. If I have learned anything this semester, it is this: you need to have faith in others because they are often the key to unlocking your greatest potential.

This semester started off on a solitary note—and that was fine with me. The first paper I wrote was "Finding Addiction." I really enjoyed writing this piece because it gave me a chance to do what I do best, talk about myself. Everyday I worked on it, and everyday I proudly adorned my "I'm so special " grin. The paper reflected my strong sense of self-confidence because it was told in first person and is about one of my greatest triumphs in life. Even though I like the story, I have since noticed that I don't really give the other characters any credit. Lines like, "Of course this was not the end of my epiphany. No, I soon realized that my adventure into poetry had only begun," shows just how self-centered this piece was. Despite its obvious self-centeredness, "Finding Addiction" is still one of my favorite essays.

The next project was a little less interesting for me because I had to relate my ideas to the story, "A Letter to Harvey Milk." This took the spotlight away from me, so, jealously I still snuck my own opinions and beliefs into the paper. Statements like, "Knowledge and compassion are two of the greatest tools in combating problems of this kind," show how I feel, not necessarily the feelings of the piece being critiqued. My first draft was brimming with opinion and upon revision I had to omit many of my own opinions and replace them with facts. I didn't enjoy writing this paper as much as the first one and at the time I didn't understand why. I could no longer sit at my computer and chime out three or four pages in a sitting. I now had to toil under the intense heat of my 40-watt bulb lamp and I traded hours for a single paragraph.

The third project may have been my greatest challenge to date. I had to do two interviews, tons of research, and 15 hours of library time. This essay was also the longest written work I have ever created; needless to say, this was also diffi-cult to write. Even though this paper was supposed to be about the community, I again grew bored, and before long I was dowsing the paper in my ideas and beliefs, and writing for a reader who may not share them. These were just a few of my selfish writing acts that I didn't recognize until much later.

The fourth project proved to be one of the hardest things that I have ever done and a complete eye-opener. First of all, I do not work well in groups be-cause I like to believe that I am strong enough to handle everything. The second I am placed in a group setting I become James Bond at Goldfinger's restaurant. I am immediately confident and utterly suspicious of each and every person. I don't trust anyone but myself to do work that is important and that may be pertinent to my grade. Luckily, my group was very accepting and allowed me to set up schedules and be a leader. Despite this I still didn't trust my group members—no, that trust didn't come until one terrible problem and a few acts of kindness.

I remember the day quite clearly. It was the fifth of November. I remember feeling the dark and gloomy damp air as I strolled into Hale library's 24-hour room at 6:30 P.M. I waited for a few moments, disappointed that I was the first to a meeting again, and I remember thinking that I would surely put a note about this tardiness in my journal. A little while later Hunter, Steve, and Allison showed up. This was to be the night that all our sections would be pasted together for the Agency Profile Report. Our group worked steadily for about two hours. The only interruptions were the seemingly endless pauses of the archaic computers when trying to save our precious work. When we finally had everything pasted together and edited, I saved the work to my disk.

I recall closing the document and then opening it again for one final edit, the edit that would be the perfect cap to a totally productive evening. The docu-ment wouldn't open. The computer gave me some disk error message, which is really just fluffy garbage for stating that your disk has now become trash. The world stopped turning, I looked around just in time to see all my group mem-bers' jaws hit the floor. I don't think anyone moved, spoke, or even breathed for a full sixty seconds before we realized what had really happened. I was immedi-ately angry with myself for not bringing a backup and angry with my group for no reason at all. I somehow blamed the troubles on my group, as if they could have planned this unbelievable pothole in my life.

We all discussed the problem, decided we should each revise our own sections, and come back to the library to do it all again tomorrow night. All the group members wore their expressions of discontent like depressing Halloween masks as we sulked out together. I walked home quietly, angrily, and sadly in the dark. I awoke less than enthused the next morning. When we met the next night at the same place and time, I expected nothing. I didn't think anyone would have his or her section revised and I even assumed that they would all be late.

To my surprise, everyone was there and already working as I walked in. I felt stupid for misjudging my groupmates. As the evening and the work progressed, a slow feeling of melancholy began to sink into my skin that no amount of cigarette breaks were going to cure. Again surprising me, my groupmates noticed that I was feeling quite down and they all went to the work cheering me up. I remember Allyson and Steve telling me that it was okay and that we would finish everything. Hunter added to the effort by showing me a mullet website and we all had a good laugh. Now I felt even worse because I finally got a glimpse of my groupmembers as real people instead of just workers. This moment has since stuck with me and in every meeting since then I make a conscious effort to be a nicer more understanding version of myself.

This event taught me a lot about myself, my writing, and other people. I learned that you can't do everything on your own and sometimes the best things come from teamwork. Most importantly, I learned that trusting other people could be rewarding and fruitful. For example, the project that we were working on and the report we are now finishing are two of my best works. My section was good, but the paper would be nothing without each person's contribution. This semester taught me to write from other people's points of view and to be sensitive to other people's needs. I acquired a lot of new writing strategies this semester, but maybe more importantly I met some very nice people that I am now glad to call friends.   ∎

Peer Review Questions for Your Capstone Essay Draft

Sharing drafts with peers generally improves the quality of the final product. What follows are some questions to use when drafts are ready to be peer reviewed.

In groups of two or three, share drafts by either reading them aloud (in turn) or exchanging them. As you listen or read, respond to the following questions. Make your responses specific and detailed.

1. Which *specific* ideas, words, phrases, or images struck you as particularly memorable and promising?

2. Which *specific* things struck you as confusing or as needing more elaboration?

3. What is the focus? Is it either too general or too narrow?

4. Where and how does the author use evidence from his or her own writing and experience to support claims? What other kinds of evidence are used?

5. As a reader, what do you want to hear more about?

6. Offer at least two specific suggestions for revision.

After peer review, look over the response forms for your draft. Mark the bits of commentary and advice that you find compelling. Remember that just because you get advice doesn't mean you need to take it. You should consider everything; but as the writer, you are in charge.

Taking into account the peer responses as well as your own emerging ideas, write a short revision plan. This writing can be informal—a list, a few sentences—but it is important. When you revisit the draft, it will help guide your writing.

Oral Presentations

Just as the capstone essay is an opportunity for synthesis, so too is the oral presentation. Oral presentations are events at which you can both showcase the nature of your work and educate your audience. They also provide you practice in skills that are essential to public life and to many careers.

WRITING TO DISCOVER

List at least 5 characteristics that you think mark good public presentations. As a class, try to arrive at consensus on the top 10 characteristics.

Writing and speaking share roots in the ancient art of rhetoric, and they require you to master many of the same skills: understanding audience, having something original and purposeful to say, constructing logically sound arguments, marshaling appropriate evidence, anticipating audience expectations, and carrying out a polished final performance. This means that much of the advice shared so far for writing can also be applied to public speaking. Yet the following tips that are particular to oral presentations merit careful attention.

- *Prepare.* Just as it usually takes several drafts to create an effective essay, it takes time and effort to craft a good speech. Few people can just walk into an oral presentation and wing it. It is essential to prepare a script, share it with others to get feedback, revise, and practice.

- *Anticipate your audience's concerns.* Think hard about your audience's predispositions, needs, and preferences. For example, if you know that the audience will connect with one part of the presentation, it might be worth starting with that, in order to win favor and establish rapport. If you suspect that listeners might find a certain point particularly difficult, plan to slow down, use accessible terms, and include a handout or visual aid.

- *Consider visuals.* PowerPoint® presentations are standard fare with oral presentations, but you should also consider overheads or handouts (especially for detailed information or illustrations). Don't use visuals as glitzy confections—rather, be sure they are purposeful and integrated with the script. Also, if you are relying on technology, have a backup plan.

- *Forecast content and structure.* Just as forecasting statements in essays can aid reader comprehension, so too with oral presentations. Here's an example of such a forecasting statement: "Today I will speak for 15 minutes on my recent tutoring work with America Reads. The first part of the presentation will provide an overview of my experience, and the second part will detail how that experience informs my view of literacy work. At the end, I'll invite your questions."

- *Be aware of body language and voice.* Posture, gestures, facial expressions, and movement are all integral to delivery of an oral presentation. You can signal openness and engagement with your audience by leaning forward slightly, smiling, using hand movements, and (if appropriate) moving around with purpose. As for voice, you should strategically use volume, variety of tone, and pauses.

- *Rehearse, rehearse, rehearse.* There is no substitute for practice, preferably with someone offering feedback. Only by rehearsing can you finalize the timing, orchestrate the right movements, know where your tongue gets tripped up, and see where the presentation works and goes flat. You should make all your mistakes on practice runs rather than during the main event.

An Agenda for Oral Presentations

Oral presentations can be broken down into four basic steps.

PREPRESENTATION

After all the writing and preparation, rehearse in the room in which the presentation will occur, if possible. Test all equipment. Review script and visuals. Breathe deeply and relax.

INTRODUCTION

Establish rapport through eye contact, facial expressions, open gestures, and introductory remarks. Introduce yourself and the topic. Provide a brief spoken and, if possible, visual overview of the content and structure; remember that forecasting improves comprehension. Also, state the ground rules, if needed (for example, "Feel free to interrupt with questions" or "Please hold questions until the end").

BODY

Maintain eye contact with the audience (don't bury your head in notes, and don't put your back to the audience by facing a screen). Coordinate visuals strategically. Vary the delivery and insert purposeful pauses. Stay on pace but remain open to improvisation if the opportunity arises.

CONCLUSION

Signal when you are wrapping up. Close on a strong note (don't just stop or dribble to an end). Have a protocol for the question/answer session. End on time, even if it means politely cutting short discussion. Thank the audience.

The best oral presentations often look effortless—but that perception is usually the result of much hard work and rehearsal.

ENDNOTE

Composing capstone essays, assembling portfolios, and doing oral presentations should be considered occasions for reflecting on learning and celebrating accomplishments. They offer the opportunity to arrive at synthesis and—even better—to share it with others.

Credits

Index